PRAISE FOR
OF ARTHUR J. ᴅᴇɪᴋᴍᴀɴ

"Arthur Deikman is one of the pioneers of consciousness research and this collection shows the impressive breadth and depth of his many contributions." — ROGER WALSH, M.D., PhD., author of *Essential Spirituality*

"Arthur Deikman's innovative, scholarly contributions to the study of consciousness are an inspiring repository of wisdom for us all." — FRANCES VAUGHAN, Ph.D., author of *Shadows of the Sacred*

"Arthur had a remarkable ability to envision larger truths. Having known him for nearly fifty years as a superb friend, colleague and author, I view this collection of his papers as a highly valuable expression of his work and character."
— LEIGHTON WHITAKER, Ph.D., ABPP

"Arthur Deikman is a highly esteemed, much loved, and world-renowned innovator in the fielp of psychiatric research. This collection is strongly recommended for students, mental health practitioners, and philosophically and spiritually minded readers. They will find an inspiring mentor and teacher as they savor these articles from one of the foremost inquiring spirits of our times."
— IRA STEINMAN M.D., author of *Treating the 'Untreatable': Healing in the Realms of Madness*

"Arthur Deikman led the way in meditation research, helping make such study respectable. He was born with the gift of clarity, and he had an extraordinary instinct for the good. What a friend he was! What a boon to the wide world!" — MICHAEL MURPHY, co-founder of the Esalen Institute

meditations on a blue vase

meditations on a
blue vase

and the foundations of
transpersonal psychology

THE COLLECTED PAPERS OF
ARTHUR J. DEIKMAN

FEARLESS BOOKS

NAPA • CALIFORNIA

FIRST EDITION
© Copyright 2014 by Etta Deikman

FEARLESS BOOKS
PO Box 4199 • NAPA CA 94558
www.fearlessbooks. com

Permissions to reprint the papers of Arthur Deikman were acquired
as necessary by his estate. The original date and publication source are
noted at the close of each article. Any inquiries about the publication
history of papers in this volume may be
directed to the Publisher.

ISBN: 978-0-9888024-4-5

LIBRARY OF CONGRESS CONTROL No.
2014932072

COVER PHOTOGRAPHY, DESIGN & TYPOGRAPHY
D. Patrick Miller

The blue vase pictured on the cover is thesame one mentioned
in several articles in this collection. It has been preserved in
the library at Sofia University in Palo Alto, CA. Thanks to
Sofia's Library Director Katrina Rahnfor providing
photographic access to the vase.

AUTHOR PHOTO BY
Diana Peters

THE CONTENTS

FOREWORD

W HEN I finished my doctoral training in 1963, the world was
a changing and very interesting place. My research focus
through graduate school had been on hypnosis, sleep, and dreaming,
which was "far out" for the psychology and psychiatry establishments
of the time. In the general culture, psychedelic drugs were about to
have major effects, especially on young people. Eastern religions and
associated mystical practices were becoming available, promising a
spirituality based on actual, direct experience rather than a religion
based on faith. I had been an experimental subject in some psychiatric
psychedelic drug experiments while in graduate school, and had
also read widely in what were then (and still are) unusual, virtually
unknown sources for orthodox psychology and psychiatry. It was already clear to me that our "official" scientific knowledge of the human
mind, while immensely valuable in some ways, was rather narrow
and biased.

I continued my research on hypnosis and dreams for a decade
after receiving my doctorate, but as I watched the spread of psychedelic drug usage and the rapid growth of various forms of mysticism
and meditation in our culture, I realized that I needed to take a much
wider look at the unusual things that could happen to human consciousness. This resulted in my *Altered States of Consciousness* anthology, published in 1969. Two of the most important chapters in the
book were by Arthur Deikman. Indeed, discovering Deikman's ground-
breaking work was a major delight in my search for scientific literature on altered states, and his work continued to inspire me for the

next half century.

After an initial chapter dealing with the definition of altered states, the second chapter in my anthology was Deikman's "Deautomatization and the mystic experience," which he had published in the mainstream JOURNAL OF PSYCHIATRY in 1966 (volume 29, 324-338). Arthur showed that what we think of as the "normal" functionings of the mind are largely *habits* of functioning, shaped by culture in an automatized and conditioned manner. In various situations we automatically and selectively perceive *what we are supposed to perceive* — whatever our culture has defined as "normal" — and we feel and act accordingly. This generally works out well if our culture has fully understood what's important about various situations and developed adequate responses, but leads to great problems as reality changes, especially when the change is subtle.

This automatization process is almost never conscious, and can be so powerful that it amounts to blockages that make us *not* perceive certain aspects of what could be richer and more accurate experiences. Deikman's brilliant insight was that certain practices (like meditation) that reduce, even temporarily, the power of such automatization could allow us to have new perceptions and epiphanies. Whether such deautomization is then guided in a creative direction of useful insights, or toward illusion or pathology, is a separate question. I found Deikman's concept of deautomization to be of almost universal usefulness in understanding a wide variety of processes of the human mind.

Deikman's other paper reprinted in the *Altered States* anthology was "Experimental meditation," originally published in 1963 in the tigious JOURNAL OF NERVOUS AND MENTAL DISEASE (Vol. 136, pp. 329-373). Although I could find only three English-language experimental studies of meditation for my 1969 publication (there are now several thousand), Deikman's early study is still a model of intelligence and creativity. It remains one of the basic studies I have my current students read to learn more about the nature of human consciousness.

To my — and I'm sure my publisher's — astonishment, the *Altered States* anthology became a scientific and semi-popular best-seller! These kinds of major alterations of consciousness had been almost completely overlooked — or assigned to the dustbin of unimportant curiosities or even psychopathology — by orthodox science and medicine until then. Those who wanted to promote scientific research into these states had little to encourage them, since the few studies that showed such research could be done were widely scattered and unknown to most people. Now a large collection of scientific studies was readily available, showing that we could bring science, psychology, and psychiatry to bear in helping us understand these possibilities of human minds. What I consider one of the most important results of the widespread reading of *Altered States* was familiarizing people with Deikman's work on meditation and deautomization.

One of Arthur Deikman's most important qualities was his willingness to take on the Establishment when it was wrong about things, although I'm sure it made for considerable difficulties for his academic career. He was a fine scholar and writer, and I often wondered if the reason he devoted most of his professional time to private practice was prejudice in academic circles for daring to question current authorities.

To illustrate: Although interest in altered states was becoming widespread in our culture by the late 1960s, I came across a report by the Group for the Advancement of Psychiatry (GAP): *Mysticism: Spiritual Quest or Psychic Disorder?* (New York, 1976), a consideration of the kind of mystical states that might be induced by meditation or psychoactive drugs. Because of growing cultural interest, the authors, highly prestigious and senior members of the psychiatric profession, felt that their colleagues should know about the nature of meditation and psychoactive drugs.

I was very angry when I read the GAP report. It amounted to an official statement by the psychiatric profession that nothing happening in the culture was not already well understood — and that all the interest in meditation and altered states was a waste of time at best, and psychopathological at worst.

My anger wasn't useful. Psychologists were still of very low status compared to psychiatrists at that time, and I doubt that anything I could have written about errors in the GAP report would even have gotten published where psychiatrists would see it. But Deikman took on the *GAP Report* and wrote a brilliant rebuttal, exposing its short-sightedness and bias. I practically cheered out loud when I saw his response. That rebuttal is one of the things you'll read in this collection. Deikman was a brave man to go against his professional establishment like that, and also a very wise man to have a clear idea of where the truth of things lay.

Arthur Deikman's interests were very wide-ranging. His interest in the nature of consciousness, for example, not only included the mystic and altered states end of the spectrum, but the practical aspects of psychotherapy. One of his most interesting projects, reported on in several articles in this collection, is about his attempts to reform the treatment regime of a major psychiatric hospital to undertake practical psychological work with patients — which meant respecting them as people, rather than just giving them drugs and locking them away. As with the rebuttal to the GAP report, this was again going against the establishment, which was rather overly charmed with the possibilities of drug treatment or psychiatric disorders. Indeed, some people would say the psychiatric establishment is still quite overly charmed with medication. One of the frustrations of Deikman's career was that it took many years to get his reports about this daring work published in orthodox journals.

He was also quite interested in what modern science could contribute to understanding consciousness. I remember a few years ago when he devoted a year to deeply reading in the literature of modern physics, to see how quantum approaches and the new physics could cast some light on the workings of consciousness. We had a number of discussions about this, but despite some of my early initial training being in the physical sciences, he was way ahead of me in his under-standing. Not that he was a narrow-minded physical reductionist who expected that the physical sciences would eventually explain away consciousness as nothing but electrochemical actions in the brain. He grasped that there is a physical brain *involved* but not totally *identical* with consciousness, and understanding its workings is part of a full understanding of the nature of the human mind.

There are other dimensions of Deikman's understanding that you will encounter in the articles in this book, and I will let them speak for themselves. This gentle man, my friend, always impressed and stimu-lated me by the depth of his curiosity, comprehension, and clarity, and I think you will be too.

CHARLES T. TART
Sofia University, Palo Alto
University of California, Davis

Publisher's Note

THIS unusual and historic project was inaugurated at a meeting between myself, Arthur Deikman (then in an advanced stage of Parkinson's), his wife Etta, and Gari Thompson in the late summer of 2013. Although Arthur would pass away just a few weeks later, his spirit and intelligence are obviously alive on every page of this volume. This significant and profound anthology comprises not only a remarkable collection of academic papers by a pioneering psychiatrist and researcher, but also presents much of the foundational work for transpersonal psychology, often called "the fourth force" in the relatively young science of the mind (after psychoanalysis, behaviorism, and humanistic psychology).

Unlike the perspectives which preceded it, transpersonal psychology acknowledges the influence of religious thought and mystical experience in the daily life of the mind. Arthur Deikman was one of the first researchers to apply rigorous scientific principles to the study of that influence, while also acknowledging the limitations of a merely rational mode of thought in assessing the realms of the ineffable. As Charles Tart notes in his Foreword, this was hardly a safe career choice for a psychiatrist and researcher in the latter third of the 20th century. Medical professionals today who can openly discuss spirituality on popular television shows and in best-selling books certainly owe a debt of gratitude to Arthur Deikman.

The papers published here were drawn from many sources and all kinds of original media going back three or four decades, which presented a special challenge in assembling and editing them to create one comprehensive work. My thanks to Etta and Gari for their patience, persistence, and cooperation throughout the multiple rounds of organizational editing that professional publication requires. With rare and minor exceptions, the papers themselves were not copy-edited for the sake of updating, or to eliminate occasional repetitions of subject matter. The third and fourth articles, for instance, both review Dr. Deikman's notable experiment, conducted with Leighton Whitaker, in converting the previously drug-driven regimen of a psychiatric ward to a more humane and psychotherapeutic approach. But the two papers discuss this remarkable story from different perspectives, each contributing unique details and insights.

When provided, footnotes are presented in two consistent styles, although there may be some variation in the syntax of particular citations. Whenever possible, each article is followed by a notation about its original publication date and medium. While every effort was made to give this volume a coherent and accessible presentation, the content, structure, and syntax of each paper has been preserved from the original. One exception was the variant spellings "deautomization" and "deautomatization," occurring across a number of papers. For the sake of consistency and readability, only the first spelling is used in this volume. Special thanks are due to Gari Thompson for her meticulous proofreading of several manuscript and typeset drafts of this work. In a project this massive, it's entirely possible that minor errors have persisted here and there, and readers are welcome to submit corrections or queries to me at the e-mail address provided at the end of this note. Subsequent reprintings will incorporate all corrections that prove necessary.

Finally, the order of the papers is based on a loosely progressive logic rather than chronology, and in many cases the particular placement of a paper is arbitrary. Original paper titles were preserved with only occasional minor changes, whenever I felt a change would better signify the paper's content from a survey of the Table of Contents.

As an historic reference collection, the papers comprising **Blue Vase** can thus be read in the order dictated by the reader's own curiosity. But completing the whole text will provide both casual and academic readers not only with an education, but with a deep appreciation for the sharp intellect and fearless curiosity of Arthur Deikman, M.D., whose prominent place in the recent history of psychological thought, research, and clinical practice is delineated by this volume.

D. PATRICK MILLER
Publisher, Fearless Books
Contact: *info@fearlessbooks.com*

Four Questions
and Six Replies

For the Fourth Annual Conference on the Voluntary Control of Internal States,[1] I formulated a set of four questions which were discussed, one each day, by small groups of the conference participants. In order to minimize intellectual sparring and to avoid dry, impersonal speculations, I selected teaching stories from the Sufi, Hasidic, and Zen literatures to illustrate the questions in the hope that the stories would stimulate our intuitive faculties and, at the same time, provide a guide for our discussion.

The experiment was successful. The initial reading of a question and its accompanying story (or stories) was followed by silence. Then, slowly, people began to respond on a personal, questioning, and exploratory level. In some ways, the stories humbled us sufficiently to cause us to pause, think, feel, and listen. Ideas we did not know we contained came to the surface, coalesced, and recombined. We were touched more deeply than we expected.

The questions and stories beginning on the next page are presented for everyone to experience and enjoy. Perhaps they will provide a model for similar conferences where we try to discover and create truth in ourselves and with others.

QUESTION 1: *For what purpose do we wish
to control internal states?*

HOW TO CATCH MONKEYS[2]

Once upon a time there was a monkey who was very fond
of cherries. One day he saw a delicious-looking cherry, and came
down from his tree to get it. But the fruit turned out to be in a clear
glass bottle. After some experimentation, the monkey found that
he could get hold of the cherry by putting his hand into the bottle
by way of the neck. As soon as he had done so, he closed his hand
over the cherry; but then he found that he could not withdraw
his fist holding the cherry, because it was larger than the internal
dimension of the neck.

Now all this was deliberate, because the cherry in the bottle
was a trap laid by a monkey-hunter who knew how monkeys think.

The hunter, hearing the monkey's whimperings, came along
and the monkey tried to run away. But, because his hand was, as
he thought, stuck in the bottle, he could not move fast enough to
escape.

But, as he thought, he still had hold of the cherry. The hunter
picked him up. A moment later he tapped the monkey sharply on
the elbow, making him suddenly relax his hold on the fruit.

The monkey was free, but he was captured. The hunter
had used the cherry and the bottle, but he still had them.

QUESTION 2: *Do we need a new, contemporary
discipline for self-realization or enlightenment?*

THREE PIECES OF ADVICE[3]

A man once caught a bird. The bird said to him, "I am no use
to you as a captive. But let me free, and I will tell you three valuable
pieces of advice." The bird promised to give the first piece of advice

while still in the man's grasp, the second when he reached a branch, the third after he had gained the top of a mountain.

The man agreed, and asked for the first piece of advice.

The bird said: "If you lose something, even if it be valued by you as much as life itself — do not regret it."

Now the man let the bird go, and it hopped to a branch. It continued with the second piece of advice: "Never believe anything which is contrary to sense, without proof."

Then the bird flew to the mountaintop. From here it said: "O unfortunate one! Within me are two huge jewels, and if you had only killed me they would have been yours!"

The man was anguished at the thought of what he had lost, but he said: "At least now tell me the third piece of advice."

The bird replied: "What a fool you are, asking for more advice when you have not given thought to the first two pieces! I told you not to worry about what had been lost, and not to believe in something contrary to sense. Now you are doing both. You are believing something ridiculous and grieving because you have lost something! I am not big enough to have inside me huge jewels.

"You are a fool. Therefore you must stay within the usual restrictions imposed on man."

THE STORY OF THE CAPE[4]

A woman came to Rabbi Israel, the maggid of Koznitz, and told him, with many tears, that she had been married a dozen years and still had not borne a son, "What are you willing to do about it?" he asked her. She did not know what to say. "My mother," so the maggid told her, "was aging and still had no child. Then she heard that the holy Baal Shem was stopping over in Apt in the course of a journey. She hurried to his inn and begged him to pray she might bear a son. 'What are you willing to do about it?' he asked. 'My husband is a poor book-binder,' she replied, 'but I do have one fine thing that I shall give to the rabbi.' She went home as fast as she could and fetched her good cape, her Katinka, which was carefully stowed away in a chest. But when she returned to the inn with it, she heard that the Baal Shem had already left for Mezbizh. She immediately set out after him and since she had no money to ride, she walked from town to town with her Katinka until she came to Mezbizh. The Baal Shem took the cape and hung it on the wall. 'It is well,' he said, 'My mother walked all the way back, from town to town, until she reached Apt. A year later, I was born.'"

"I, too," cried the woman, "will bring you a good cape of mine so that I may get a son."

"That won't work," said the maggid, "You heard the story. My mother had no story to go by."

QUESTION 3: *If we need a new discipline, how do we construct it?*

TEACHING THE ULTIMATE[5]

In early times in Japan, bamboo-and-paper lanterns were used with candles inside. A blind man, visiting a friend one night, was offered a lantern to carry home with him.

"I do not need a lantern," he said. "Darkness or light is all the same to me."

"I know you do not need a lantern to find your way," his friend replied, "but if you don't have one, someone else may run into you. So you must take it."

The blind man started off with the lantern and before he had walked very far someone ran squarely into him. "Look out where you are going!" he exclaimed to the stranger. "Can't you see this lantern?"

"Your candle has burned out, brother," replied the stranger.

QUESTION 4: *What should the role of the scientist of this field be in our society?*

ISA AND THE DOUBTERS[6]

It is related by the Master Jalaludin Rumi and others that one day Isa, the son of Miryam, was walking in the desert near Jerusalem with a number of people, in whom covetousness was still strong.

They begged Isa to tell them the Secret Name by which Isa restored the dead to life. He said: "If I tell you, you will abuse it."

They said: "We are ready and fitted for such knowledge; besides, it will reinforce our faith."

"You do not know what you ask," he said, but he told them the Word. Soon afterwards, these people were walking in a deserted place when they saw a heap of whitened bones. "Let us make a trial of the Word," they said to one another, and they did.

No sooner had the Word been pronounced than the bones became clothed with flesh and retransformed into a ravening wild beast, which tore them to shreds.

Those endowed with reason will understand. Those with little reason can earn it through the study of this account.

THE THREE PRISONERS[7]

After the death of Rabbi Uri of Strelisk, who was called the Seraph, one of his hasidim came to Rabbi Bunam and wanted to become his disciple. Rabbi Bunam asked: "What was your teacher's way of instructing you to serve?"

"His way," said the hasid, "was to plant humility in our hearts. That was why everyone who came to him, whether he was a nobleman or a scholar, had first to fill two large buckets at the well in the market place, or to do some other hard and menial labor in the street."

Rabbi Bunam said: "I shall tell you a story. Three men, two of them wise and one foolish, were once put in a dungeon black as night, and every day food and eating utensils were lowered down to them. The darkness and the misery of imprisonment had deprived the fool of his last bit of sense, so that he no longer knew how to use the utensils he could not see. One of his companions showed him, but the next day he had forgotten again, and so his wise companion had to teach him continually.

"But the third prisoner sat in silence and did not bother about the fool. Once the second prisoner asked him why he never offered his help.

"'Look!' said the other. 'You take infinite trouble and yet you never reach the goal, because every day destroys your work. But I sit here and try to think out how I can manage to bore a hole in the wall so that light and sun can enter, and all three of us can see everything.'"

REFERENCES

1. Held at Council Grove, Kansas, April 1972.
2. Reprinted with permission from Idries Shah, *Tales of the Dervishes.* Copyrighted by E. P. Dutton & Co., 1967.
3. Reprinted with permission from Indries Shah, *Tales of the Dervishes.* Copyrighted by E. P. Dutton, 1967.
4. Reprinted with permission from Martin Buber, *Tales of Hasidim: Early Masters.* Copyrighted by Schocken Books, 1947.
5. Reprinted with permission from Martin Buber, *Tales of Hasidim: Early Masters.* Copyrighted by Schocken Books, 1947.
6. Reprinted with permission from Indries Shah, *Tales of the Dervishes.* Copyrighted by E. P. Dutton Co., 1967.
7. Reprinted with permission from Martin Buber, *Tales of the Hasidim: Late Masters.* Copyrighted by Schocken Books, 1948.

Originally published in J. HUMANISTIC PSYCHOLOGY
VOL. 14, NO. 2, SPRING 1974

A Functional Approach to Mysticism

BECAUSE MYSTICISM is associated with religion it has long been regarded as inimical to science, an enemy of the search for objective truth, not to be credited as a discipline through which knowledge of reality can be gained. At least that seems to be the official attitude that pervades scientific publications and scientific meetings, even at the present time when quantum theory has made consciousness a legitimate subject for research.

In point of fact, informal inquiry reveals that many scientists have had experiences they would describe as transcendent, as going beyond familiar sensory dimensions and providing a taste of the unified reality of which mystics speak. They don't talk about it in public but will do so in private. The greatest scientist of them all, Isaac Newton, was so haunted by the sense of the transcendent that he devoted the later part of his life to alchemical studies, expressing his yearning in a particularly poignant lament:

> I don't know what I may seem to the world, but as for myself, I seem to have been only like a boy playing on the seashore and diverting myself in now and then finding a smoother pebble or a prettier shell than ordinary, whilst the great ocean of truth lay all undiscovered before me (Newton, 1992, p.494).

Albert Einstein, another prodigious pioneer of science, echoes Newton in his belief in the reality of the mystical:

> The most beautiful and profound emotion we can experience is the sensation of the mystical. It is the source of all true science.

He to whom this emotion is a stranger, who can no longer wonder and stand rapt in awe, is as good as dead. To know that what is impenetrable to us really exists, manifesting itself as the highest wisdom and the most radiant beauty, which our dull faculties can comprehend only in their primitive forms — this knowledge, this feeling, is at the center of true religion (Einstein, 1991, p.191).

Not only is mystical experience an occurrence in the lives of most people, including scientists, but the mystical literature, which spans thousands of years and widely disparate cultures, exhibits a remarkable consistency in its description of mystical experience and its instructions for obtaining access to mystical knowledge. William James commented:

> *There is about mystical utterances an eternal unanimity which ought to make a critic stop and think* (James, p. 410).

In this paper, I will present a way of understanding the mystical experience based on the role of intention in determining consciousness. This approach may enable us to understand a variety of mystical techniques and teachings without becoming entangled in obscure doctrines or religious-sounding terminology.

Meditation and Deautomization

Before beginning medical school I had a mystical experience while camping on a lake in the Adirondacks. There were other people living in tent cabins living along the lake but, essentially, I was alone. I used the isolation to grapple with personal questions and doubts that had emerged from the college years, especially 'What did I really want? Why was I dissatisfied ?' I reflected that music and poetry had powerful appeal for me because they seemed to contain something important and satisfying. I decided that there existed a source of what the arts conveyed to me and what I needed to draw closer to that source.

Having reached that conclusion, I began a routine of sitting each day for a half hour on a boulder perched on the water's edge. With closed eyes, I would try to reach out to that unknown something that I so intensely wanted to find. I didn't know where to look — there was just the wish, the desire, and that push to contact the source.

After a week or so, my perception of my surroundings changed. I began to see the details of what was around me; the stones and leaves appeared more intricately patterned, the colors brighter. Then, I began to sense an invisible emanation coming from the sky, the trees, the surrounding natural world. It was as if I could see it, but really couldn't. I could feel it, but not with my usual senses. What was seminating to me was intrinsically positive, important, satisfying — something I knew I wanted without question. It was also clear to me that other people did not perceive it. I made note to myself not to romanticize it; what I perceived was not a guarantee of bliss — I still experienced loneliness at my lakeside camp. Yet, at the same time, the perception was felt to be of paramount value.

The experience continued through the rest of the summer, but the summer came to an end. I returned to begin medical school and the perception became weaker and gradually faded away. Later, when the opportunity to do so arose, I had begun to read the mystical literature to try and understand what had taken place years earlier. Struck by the unanimity that had so impressed James and others, I concluded that the mystics were describing a true phenomenon, that their instructions must have validity, and it might be possible to understand mysticism by employing reason, experiment, and knowledge of development and cognitive psychology. I chose to begin by investigating meditation; in particular, the concentrative meditation described in the Yoga of Pantanjali. To do this, I rounded up friends and acquaintances, sat them down opposite a blue vase, and instructed them as follows:

The purpose of the session is to learn about concentration. Your aim is to concentrate on the blue vase [located on a table in front of the subjects]. *By concentration I do not mean analyzing*

*the different parts of the vase, or thinking a series of thoughts
about the vase, or associating ideas to the vase; but rather, trying
to see the vase as it exists in itself without any connection to other
things. Exclude all other thoughts or feelings or sounds or body
sensations. Do not let them distract you, but keep them out so
you can concentrate all your attention, all your awareness on
the vase itself. Let the perception of the vase fill your entire mind*
(Deikman, 1963).

Each subject did this for half an hour, after which I questioned
them about their experiences. Most participated in about forty sessions
spread out over a few months, but striking changes in perception
were reported very soon in the experiment. The vase was seen as
becoming more vivid, more rich — 'luminous' was one description. It
seemed to acquire a life of it's own, to become animated. There was a
lessening of the sense of being separate from the vase: 'I really began
to feel... almost as though the blue and I were perhaps merging or
that the vase and I were.' Synesthetic phenomena were also reported:
'When the vase changes shape, I feel this in my body;' 'I began to feel
this light going back and forth.'[1]

Although this was not a controlled scientific study, the reports
of the subjects were consistent with those in the mystical literature.
As I thought about the changes that had been reported, it occurred
to me that they represented a reversal of the normal developmental
process whereby infants and children learn to perceive, grasp, and
categorize objects. This learning progresses and as it does it becomes
automatic; they no longer have to pay such close attention to the
nature of objects. Instead, more and more attention is free and put in
the service of thought, of abstractions. The meditation activity that
my subjects performed was reverse of the developmental process: the
precept (the vase) was invested with attention while thought was
inhibited. As a consequence, sensuousness, merging of boundaries
and sensory modalities became prominent. A *deautomization* had
occurred, permitting a different experience of the vase than would

ordinarily be the case.

Since perceptual automatization is a hierarchical developmental process it would be expected that deautomization would result in a shift toward cognitive and perceptual experience that could be characterized as more 'primitive.' There is evidence supporting this. In a statement based on studies of eidetic imaginary in children, as well as on broader studies of perceptual development, Heinz Werner concluded:

> *The image... gradually changed in functional character. It becomes essentially subject to the exigencies of abstract thought. Once the image changes in function and becomes an instrument of abstract thought. Once the image changes in function and becomes an instrument of reflective thought, its structure will also change. It is only through such structural change that the image can serve as an instrument in abstract mental activity. This is why, of necessity, the sensuousness, fullness of detail, the color and vivacity of the image must fade* (Werner, 1957, p.152).

David Shapiro offered experimental evidence supporting this conclusion by studying the response of children of different ages to Rorschach images. He found that with increasing age the children paid less and less attention to the sensual aspects of the Rorschach cards, such as texture, color, and progressively more attention to the meaning, and to formal qualities such as shape and size (Shapiro 1960).

Complementing Shapiro's findings were those of Daniel Brown who studied the Rorschach response of meditators of different levels of attainment and different meditative techniques. He found that in the case of advanced meditators, prominence was given to 'pure perceptual features of the ink blots.' As one subject put it, "...The meditation has wiped out all the interpretive stuff on top of the raw perception" (BROWN AND ENGLER, 1986). These findings are consistent with the reversal of the developmental shift from the sensory to the abstract — a deautomization (Deikman, 1996).

Although the concept of deautomization seems to explain some of the basic cognitive effects of meditation, it has been difficult to test the hypothesis neurophysiologically. Initially, it appeared to be supported by EEG studies of experienced Zen meditators. Kasamatsu and Hirai found an absence of habituation to a click stimulus (measured by alpha blocking) as compared to controls (Kasamatsu & Hirai, 1969). This, too, suggested that a sensory deautomization had taken place. However, studies of Yogi adepts, as well as Zen practitioners, showed a great variability of EGG response due to the need of control for variety of variables, such as the type of meditation being practiced, whether the eyes were open or closed, the level of advancement of the meditation subjects, their state of arousal at the time, and the meaningfulness of the stimulus (*Austin, 1998*). However, the data do suggest that a shift toward increased sensory sensitivity takes place when a concentrative meditation is practiced with an external focus, as in my initial 'blue vase' experiments.

Renunciation and Service

Renunciation and service are usually discussed in the context of morality, virtue, and saintliness. But we need not approach this as a moral issue, but as a straightforward matter of cognitive psychology. As I have described, our survival as biological organisms takes priority in development. This survival requires the development of a self that can acquire supplies, defend them against others, and take from others what might be needed or desired. This is the self-as-object, the survival self. It pervades our everyday experience. Our society keeps it activated with threats of danger, promises of pleasure, prestige and ease, and encouraging competition for wealth and power. This situation is not just a matter of runaway capitalism. After all, Buddha preached to a society existing two thousand years before our own time. The Buddhist sutras and the scriptures of Vedanta were addressed to people living well before the advent of advertising and the stock market. The fact is that self-centered consciousness has always been with us as a matter of biological necessity. The problem facing spiritual teachers was that they had to start with people who, no matter how self-consciously 'spiritual,' were devoted to the survival self. The teacher had to bring about a transition to a consciousness that was primarily other-centered, rather than self-centered. Only then could they taste of a consciousness that features a sense of the connectedness of everything, a unity, a reconciliation of the polar opposites that comprise our usual perspective. This cannot occur in the instrumental mode. Thomas Merton commented on this incompatibility in his book, *Zen and the Birds of Appetite*. He describes meat-eating birds (the survival self) looking for carrion:

> *Zen enriches no one. There is no body to be found. The birds may come and circle for a while in the place where it is thought to be. But they soon go elsewhere. When they are gone, the 'nothing,' the 'no-body' that was there, suddenly appears. That is Zen. It was there all the time but the scavengers missed it, because it was not their kind of prey* (Merton, 1968, p. ix).

Profound connection is what the word 'spiritual' properly refers to. The spiritual is not a matter of visions of angels, or of being carried away by ecstatic emotion. The mystics are clear about that. At its most basic, *the spiritual is the experience of the connectedness that underlies reality.* The depth of that experience depends on the capacity of the individual to set aside considerations of self, thereby gaining access to connection. Although people differ in the extent and frequency with which they gain that access, the genuine experience abolishes competitive comparisons. 'I am more spiritual than he' is no longer meaningful because the 'I' and the 'he' are now experienced as part of a greater whole, not separate. Comparison requires separation.

Evidence for Connection

What evidence do we have that reality is in some way connected so as to be a unified whole rather than a collection of independently existing parts? It is common to cite quantum mechanics in support of this proposition. Quantum theory, whose predictions have been repeatedly confirmed, have led many physicists to the conclusion that reality is an interconnected whole, capable of instantaneous response at a distance. In one well-known experiment involving the emission of paired photons, a change in the polarization of one photon is accompanied by a simultaneous change in the polarization of the other — no matter how far apart they are. This change is not the result of a signal passing from the first to the second (that would exceed the speed of light). Rather, there is an instantaneous correlation of events that implies a unity of which both protons are a part. The results of this experiment are often cited to support mystics' assertions. These findings may indeed be based in the same reality of which mystics speak, but they may not. Furthermore, physicists believe that the act of measurement 'collapses' the probability wave function to produce an event, others dispute the metaphor of 'collapse' and the putative role of human consciousness in that process. The fact is, the theory of physics is in continuous development and evolution. Jeremy Bernstein has warned:

> The science of the present will look as antiquated to our suc-
> cessors as much of the nineteenth-century science looks to us now.
> To hitch a religious philosophy to a contemporary science is a
> sure route to obsolescence (Bernstein, 1978).

Although the conclusions of particle physicists and the poetic utterances of mystics do invite risky comparisons, we need not rely on drawing parallels between them. Instead, we can focus on two other sources that testify to the interconnectedness and unified nature of reality: (1) the consensus of the mystical literature and (2) the reports of persons for whom service (helping others) is a major focus of their lives.

The compelling consensus of mystics is that the perception of one-self as an object — fundamentally isolated within our own conscious-ness — is an illusion, a misconception that is the source of human destructiveness and suffering. It might be argued that this consensus is due to social contagion, ideas spreading through direct contact from one mystic to another, across cultural and geographic boundaries. Against such a proposition is the fact that Buddhism, Taoism, the Upanishads and the 'wisdom' books of the Old Testament all arose in different cultures at about the same time, around 500 B.C. Something seemed to be happening during that time that resulted in a direct experience of a reality not easily comprehended and hard to imitate. Conceptual transmission by itself could not do this, especially as the mystical experience is ineffable. Techniques such as meditation could be passed along via trade routes but there must be a common reality that is thereby revealed. Something had to be there to be discovered.

Further evidence against merely social contagion is the fact that mystics from theistic religions assert a reality that is in conflict with the dogma of their church. Sometimes the conflict is open, as in the case of Hallaj, the Sufi mystic who proclaimed 'I am God' and was dismembered for his blasphemy. Christian mystics tend to be more indirect in their metaphors. They may not assert the position of Hallaj that each person is fundamentally identical with the Godhead instead of being separate, however they describe something similar that is not really compatible with Christian dogma. Here is a representative statement by St. John of the Cross:

> That inward vision is so simple, so general and so spiritual that it has not entered into the understanding enwrapped or clad in any form or image subject to sense; it follows that sense and imagination (as it has not entered through them nor has taken their form or color) cannot account for it or imagine, so as to say anything concerning it, although the soul be clearly aware that is experiencing and partaking of that rare and delectable wisdom (St. John, 1953, p. 457).

The usual theological concepts have no place in such an experience. Theistic teaching is of God the Father, of Heaven and Hell, but Christian mystics like St. John of the Cross are quite explicit in stating that the experience of the reality of God, the Ultimate, cannot be expressed in terms of the things of this world. The problem for theologians is that the concept of reward and punishment, handed out by an omnipotent, omniscient God, is a derivative of the family experience, of child and parent — definitely a conception of this world. The difference between mystics' experience and theological dogma is the reason why mystics have been a perpetual problem for traditional religion. This conflict attests to the fundamental nature of the mystics' experience. It feels ultimate, beyond the domain of the sensory and the rational, more real.

As I noted earlier, there is the additional fact that non-mystics also report experiences consistent with mystics' reports, although these moments when connection is vivid and boundaries dissolve are usually brief and of less depth. As Austin has pointed out, there is a difference between the connectedness and no-self that a lover may feel in the transports of sexual union, and the radical shift in world perspective that takes place in the much more rare event of kensho or enlightenment (Austin, 1998). Nevertheless, both experiences are along the same dimension of connection, as opposed to separation.

If connection is real, and if to experience that dimension of reality requires an appropriate mode of consciousness, then we are now in a position to understand why mystical schools in addition to prescribing meditation, stress the critical role of renunciation and service.

Since survival self aims dictate the nature of our experience, we can understand that meditation offers some relief from that tyranny by (1) shifting intention from acting to allowing, (2) from identification with emotions to identification with the observer, and (3) shifting from instrumental thinking to receptive experience. Furthermore, renunciation is not to be equated with self-denial, self-mortification, or asceticism. As one Zen master put it, 'Renunciation is not giving up the things of this world; it is accepting that they go away' (Suzuki, 1968). 'Accepting that they go away' is an orientation that opens the grasping hand and facilitates the shift away from the acquisitive aims that activate survival self consciousness. Without that letting go, renunciation could be utilized as just another way to dualism' (Trungpa, 1973). Mystics are acutely aware of the problem. Rabia, a Sufi mystic, prayed dramatically for relief from self-centered aims:

> *Oh Lord:*
> *If I worship you from fear of hell, cast me into hell,*
> *If I worship you from desire for paradise, deny me Paradise.*
> (Shah, 1968, pp. 219-20)

The Service Experience

Service is probably the most effective activity for providing access to the connectedness of reality. However, like renunciation, 'service' is loaded with moral and religion associations. It is thought to mean sacrifice, the handing over of time and money and the reward of being a 'good' person entitled to a heavenly home site. The functional dynamics of service are not appreciated. Consider the problem of motivation. If one does a good deed in the expectation that it will be noted in the Book of Heavenly Record, what is taking place is a commercial transaction. The survival self is still running the show.

To illustrate this point, imagine a businessman who becomes dissatisfied with material possessions. He then reads about the bliss of enlightenment, and wants that. So he joins a spiritual group and faxes a notice of his new intention to the computer control center in his brain. An underling reads the fax and rushes to the boss. "This guy says he's no longer interested in money; he wants enlightenment. What program should we install?" The boss glances quickly at the fax. "It's the same program: Acquisition."

It is very hard to find a way of being active that is not self-centered, that is not ultimately selfish. The cynic argues: *Doing good gives you pleasure, makes you feel good, so it is just another pleasure-seeking activity and, therefore, basically selfish.* The argument can be hard to counter, but there is a way out of the quandary: *serving-the-task.*

A carpenter may finish the underside of a chair even though he will receive no more money for doing so and his customers don't care. He does it because it feels *called for*. His motivation is not in the service of the survival self, but a response to a sense of wholeness or of need. True service, the kind that opens the doors of perception, is of this type.

Serving-the-task requires a balance of instrumental and receptive modes for optimum effectiveness. Instrumental consciousness is needed to act, but receptive consciousness allows access to subtle information derived from the unified, connected aspects of the world. This helps sense the way a particular action would fit the situation in its less obvious aspects. The experience of 'being in the zone' reported by athletes, or the 'good hour' experienced by psychotherapists, is probably based on an optimum balance of the two modes.[2]

Persons performing service in a major way are very aware of the difference between self-consciously 'doing good' versus serving-the-task, doing what is called for. The former can lead to burn-out, or self-inflation, whereas the latter energizes and connects. The difference between the two types was summarized for me by a physician who established a medical clinic in Tibet:

> *There's three kinds of people — I don't know if I can say it right — there's the one who's walking on the beach and he sees a beer can on the beach and he looks around and makes sure everybody's watching and picks up the beer can and throws it away.... The second kind of person is walking on the beach, sees the beer can thrown on the beach, but there's nobody around but he still picks it up and throws it in the garbage can because he knows God is watching. Then there's the third kind of person who's walking along the beach, sees the beer can, throws it in the garbage and doesn't care who is watching just because that's what needs to be done. I guess it's that third kind of motivation that's not ego-directed that one seeks. It's hard to get there...*

Recently, I interviewed twenty-four service providers, almost all of whom gave evidence that people who serve-the-task experience a sense of connection to something larger than themselves. Their reports are very consistent. Here is a representative statement from a man who founded an organization providing care for AIDS sufferers. He spoke of the development of capacity to serve-the-task, and the change in the experience of the self that accompanies it:

"...a self-conscious highly moralized 'doing-good' is very far from the place that I recognize as valuable... When I'm more self-consciously helping it's usually because I'm in a survival mode.... What's going through my mind is fundamentally different... [In true service] I'm not serving myself, there is not that aspect to it, or wanting to get brownie points for Heaven... 'Doing what needs to be done' is the way I used to say it to the Shanti volunteers... There's an extension of self that occurs... an extension of my self to include the other person. What's in his best interest is in my best interests.... an evolution goes on from doing things to the patient or the person you serve, to doing things with the person you serve, to doing things as the person you serve. There's an extension of myself to include the other person.... You're serving something greater and deeper than the person in front of you, knowing that person will benefit as a consequence if you can get to this place."

He concluded:

"[When serving-the-task] we've allowed our personalities, our egos, to move from the driver's seat to the backseat. And what's sitting in front is your highest self and my highest self. And that's what's connected... we allowed our higher selves to emerge... who I was serving was a lot more than just the human being in front of me."

Another service provider, a management consultant to nonprofit organizations, also commented on the experience of the connection:

"I feel that connection is real. I think it's not just the two people connection. I think it's the two people connecting to whatever this is... there's a feeling of a larger connectedness than just between two people."

Almost the same words are used by a physician who founded an organization that provides support for cancer patients. She said she knows when something is really service:

"It's a sense of connection that you have to something beyond the moment when you do that.... It's like seeing both of you as part of a much larger process that has no beginning and no end."

The experience of connection can be very helpful to the service provider. A man who heads a hospice describes his experience:

"I see in the midst of this that I am caring for myself in taking care of this other person, that I don't have such a feeling of separation in this world. When I'm standing at arm's length from this person, trying to keep their separate existence, I feel continually isolated and fragmented in a way. Whereas when I let it in, include it in my life, I don't have that feeling of fragmentation or separation so much anymore."

The testimony for connection among people who serve-the-task is striking and compelling. If we grant the possibility that the experience of connection reflects what is real, the importance of service in the mystical tradition makes perfect sense. When a server can lessen the dominance of the survival self — her 'ego needs' — she can then experience a different organization of consciousness, one that is responsive to connectedness. Through that connectedness she experiences a different, larger sense of self. What stands in the way of our accepting such testimony is the invisible nature of that connection; It is not perceptible by vision or touch. The closest some servers can come to describing the quality of the experience is to speak of 'energy':

"Some kind of current goes through the space you're in... you can really feel this flow happening. Whether it's energy or current or what it is, but I definitely know when it's happening..."

"The connection is at an energetic level... it's like food for the emotional or nervous system that really is a tangible energy exchange."

"I felt very connected to the men I was sitting next to, and in fact there was almost a literal electric charge that was passing back and forth between us..."

The nature of the connection cannot be specified, at least so far. But the testimony of the mystical literature, referred to earlier, says that the connection is real — not an illusion.

Mystical Knowledge

I do not know if energy is an accurate metaphor for the connectedness to which these people gain access, but their consensus suggests that they are experiencing something real as a consequence of the change in their motivation, in their guiding intention, a change that lessens the power of the survival self to determine consciousness. The functional understanding of mysticism that I have proposed makes this effect of serving-the-task understandable and unites these service experiences with the classical mystical literature.

This balanced interplay between modes may be what Yeats was referring to when he described Michelangelo's creative activity:

Like a spider moving upon the water

His mind moves upon silence

(Yeats, 1951, pp. 327-8)

We are now in a position to appreciate the straightforward nature of mystical knowledge. This knowledge does not require living in a monastery, wearing foreign clothing, sitting cross-legged in meditation, burning incense or chanting sutras. Exotic practices are not essential, they may even be barriers if they lead practitioners to imagine they are 'advanced,' or being 'spiritual,' thus reinforcing survival self-consciousness. What is required is a shift from a consciousness focused on the disconnected aspect of reality to a mode of consciousness responsive to its connected aspects. Although we may be intellectually persuaded that a unified world exists, the difficulty is to experience that world, not just to believe it. That experience is the goal of mysticism.

Far from being esoteric, mystics propose the most modern, and at the same time the most ancient instruction for effective functioning and a fulfilled life: 'know thyself'. But the Self of which mystics speak is often capitalized to indicate it is different from, and superordinate to, the self of which we are usually conscious. Mystics teach a way of attaining that knowledge of Self. The procedures of meditation, renunciation and service that mystics employ are not really mysterious, just radically different from our usual object-oriented, instrumental approach.

Thousands of books of philosophy line the shelves of our libraries without one book providing a satisfactory answer to the fundamental question 'What is the meaning of life?' No verbal answer has ever sufficed — thus the thousands of books. The problem is that the mode of consciousness that asks the question is not the mode of consciousness that can hear the answer. When Job questions the meaning of his life his comforters offer logic and words — to no avail. Job finally is satisfied only by seeing (experiencing) Jehovah, not just hearing about him.

Judging by the reports of those who serve-the-task, service can provide a non-verbal answer also. I say this because for people who serve in that way, the question of the meaning of life no longer arises. That non-verbal experience is what mysticism is about. With this in mind, we can now understand why the basic instruction of the mystical traditions is to 'forget the self'. To forget the self is not a matter of morality, goodness, or sainthood, but a matter of access to the connected aspects of the world and to a different, more extended experience of the self. 'Forgetting the self' is not easy, but mystics have developed ways of facilitating that process. The various techniques and activities of the mystical traditions may appear exotic, but they can be understood as a way of going beyond the limitations of instrumental, self-centered, consciousness.

Such a development is more important now than ever before. When we consider the problems that confront us — sociological, environmental, and technological — we can see that ameliorating and solving these problems will require a shift in which connected, other-centered consciousness becomes more dominant. Because of this, the further progress and survival of the human race may depend on that very shift in consciousness to which the mystical traditions are devoted. For this reason alone, as well as for achieving a more profound understanding of reality, the mystical traditions deserve our study and close attention.

1. For a detailed description of the experiment and an analysis of the data, see Tart (1990), pp. 241-65.

2. See also Csikszentmihaly (1957).

BIBLIOGRAPHY
Journal Articles

1963 *Experimental meditation.* J. NERVOUS AND MENTAL DISEASE,136: 329-343 Also in: *Altered States of Consciousness.* C. Tart (ed.), (New York: Wiley) 1969, pp. 199-218. Also in: *Psychology for Our Times.* P. Zimbarado and C. Maslach (eds.), (Glenview, Illinois: Scott, Foresman) 1973): pp. 155-164.

1966 *Implications of experimentally induced contemplative meditation.* J NERVOUS AND MENTAL DISEASE, 142: 101-116. Also in *Psychedelics.* B. Aronson and H. Oamond (eds.) (New York: Doubleday) 1970,pp. 296-320.

1966 *Deautomization and mystic experience.* PSYCHIATRY 29: pp. 324-338. Also in: *Altered States of Consciousness.* C. Tart (ed.) (New York: Wiley) 1969, pp. 23-43. Also in: *The Nature of Human Consciousness.* R. Ornstein (ed.) (New York: Viking) 1974, pp. 216-233. Also in: *Growing Edges in the Psychology of Religion.* J. Tisdale (ed.) (Chicago: Belson-Hall) 1980, pp. 201- 217. Also in: *Understanding mysticism.* R. Woods (ed.) (Garden City, New York: Doubleday) 1980, pp. 240-260.

1971 *Bimodal consciousness.* ARCH. GENERAL PSYCHIATRY 25: 481-489. Also in: *Biofeedback and Self-Control.* J. Stoyva et al (eds.) (Chicago: Aldine and Atherton) 1972: 58-73. Also in: *The Nature of Human Consciousness.* R. Ornstein (ed.) (New York: Viking) 1974, pp. 67-86. Also in: *Understanding mysticism.* R. Woods (ed.) (Garden City, New York: Doubleday) 1980, pp. 261-279.

1971 *Phenothiazines and therapist's fear of identification.* J. HUMANISTIC PSYCHOLOGY 9: 196-200.

1977 *Comments on the GAP report on mysticism.* J. NERVOUS AND MENTAL DISEASE 165:318-329. Also in: *Consciousness: Brain, States of Awareness and Mysticism.* D. Goleman and R. Davidson (eds.) (New York: Harper and Row) 1979:191-194.

1977 *Sufism and psychiatry.* J. NERVOUS AND MENTAL DISEASE 165: 318-329. Also
in *Transpersonal Psychotherapy.* S. Boorstein (ed.) (Palo Alto: Science and
Behavior Books) 1980: 200-216. Also in: *Beyond Health and Normality* R.
Walsh and D. Shapiro (eds.) (New York: Van Nostrand and Rheinhold)

1983 *The evaluation of spiritual and utopian groups.* J. HUMANISTIC PSYCHOLOGY
23: 8-19

1979 with L.C. Whitaker. *Humanizing a psychiatric ward: changing from drugs to
psychotherapy.* PSYCHOTHERAPY: THEORY, RESEARCH AND PRACTICE, 17: 85-93.

1980 with L.C. Whitaker. *Psychotherapy of severe depression.* PSYCHOTHERAPY.
THEORY, RESEARCH AND PRACTICE,17: 85-93.

1983 *The evaluation of spiritual and utopian groups.* J. HUMANISTIC PSYCHOLOGY 23:
8-19.

1991 with Charles T. Tart. *Mindfulness, spiritual seeking and psychotherapy.* J.
TRANSPERSONAL PSYCHOLOGY, 23: 29-52.

1996 "I" = Awareness. J. CONSCIOUSNESS STUDIES, 3:4.

1997 *The Spiritual heart of service.* NOETIC SCIENCES REVIEW, Winter

2000 A functional approach to mysticism. J. CONSCIOUSNESS STUDIES, 7: 11/12

2001 *Mental health, aging, and role of service.* Harvard Mental Health Letter. [Date
unknown].

Articles in Books

1974 *The meaning of everything.* In *The Nature of Human Consciousness.* R.
Ornstein (ed.) (New York: Viking) pp. 317-326. Also in: *The Meeting of the
Ways: Explorations in East/West Psychology.* J. Welwood (ed.) (New York:
Schocken Books) pp. 45-55.

1977 *The missing center.* In *Alternate States of Consciousness.* N. Zinberg (ed.)
(New York: The Free Press) pp. 230-241.

1984 *The state-of-the-art of meditation.* In *Meditation: Classical and Contemporary
Perspectives.* D. Shapiro and R. Walsh (eds.) (New York: Aldine) pp. 679-
680.

1996 *Intention, self, and spiritual experience: a functional model of consciousness.* In
Toward a Scientific Basis for Consciousness, eds. SR Hameroff, AW Kaszniak,
AC Scott (Boston: MIT Press) pp.695-706.

1996 *Treating former members of cults.* In *Textbook of Transpersonal Psychiatry
and Psychology,* eds. BW Scotton, AB Chinen, JR Battista (New York: Basic
Books) pp. 316-326.

2000 *Service as a way of knowing.* In *Transpersonal Knowing,* Hart et al. (eds)
SUNY Press.

Books

1976 with P. R. Lee, R. E. Ornstein, D. Galin, and C. Tart. *Symposium on Consciousness.* (New York: Viking) 182 pp.

1976 *Personal Freedom: On Finding Your Way to the Real World* (New York: Viking) 163 pp.

1982 *The Observing Self: Mysticism and Psychotherapy.* (Boston: Beacon Press) 194 pp.

1990 *The Wrong Way Home: Uncovering the Patterns of Cult Behavior in American Society* (Boston: Beacon Press)

Monographs

1988 *Evaluating Spiritual and Utopian Groups.* (Tunbridge Wells, England: Institute for Cultural Research) pp. 5-16.

Teaching Materials

1976 *The Receptive Mode* (videotape). Division of Interpretation, National Park Service, U.S. Department of the Interior.

1976 *A Guide to Implementing the Receptive Mode.* Division of Interpretation, National Park Service, U.S. Department of the Interior.

Reviews

1965 *Semantic restraints and the psychedelics.* H. Jenkins. ETC, 22: 484.

1966 *Technique of Relaxation: Self-Relaxation.* H. Kleinsorge. Int. J. CLINICAL AND EXPERIMENTAL HYPNOSIS, 14: 82.

1967 *Dialogue with Erik Erikson.* R. I. Evans. The Berkshire Eagle, December 2.

1972 *Biochemical orthodoxy.* VOICES, 8: 7-8.

1975 *Sufi Studies: East and West.* L. F. Williams (ed.) J. TRANSPERSONAL PSYCHOLOGY, Spring.

1977 *Freedom in Meditation.* P. Carrington. J. NERVOUS AND MENTAL DISEASE, 171: 264-265.

1978 *Psychiatry and Mysticism.* S. R. Dean (ed.) J. NERVOUS AND MENTAL DISEASE, 166: 825-826.

1979 *The ESP Experience.* J. Ehrenwald. J. NERVOUS AND MENTAL DISEASE, 167: 769.

1983 *Studies in Non-Deterministic Psychology.* G. Epstein. J. NERVOUS AND MENTAL DISEASE, 171: 264-265.

1984 *The Amazing Brain.* R. Ornstein and R. Thompson. San Francisco Chronicle, December 10.

1986 *Freedom from the Self.* M. Shafii. J. NERVOUS AND MENTAL DISEASE, 174: 503-504.

1986 *Kara Kush.* I. Shah. San Francisco Chronicle, June 22.

1990 *Combating Cult Mind Control.* S. Hassan. J. NERVOUS AND MENTAL DISEASE.

1991 *Cults and New Religious Movements.* M. Galanter (ed.) J. NERVOUS AND MENTAL DISEASE, 197:115.

1991 *Our Wish to Kill: The Murder in All Our Hearts.* H. Stearn and L. Freeman. San Francisco Chronicle, July 9.

1991 *The Spirit of Shamanism.* Roger N. Walsh, M.D. J. NERVOUS AND MENTAL DISEASE.

1992 *Beyond Countertransference: The Therapist's Subjectivity in the Therapeutic Process,* J. Natterson. J. NERVOUS AND MENTAL DISEASE.

1994 *Therapeutic Conversations,* S. Gilligan and R. Price, eds. J. NERVOUS AND MENTAL DISEASE.

1994 *The Commanding Self,* I. Shah. J. TRANSPERSONAL PSYCHOLOGY.

1996 *Thoughts Without a Thinker: Psychotherapy from a Buddhist Perspective.* M. Epstein. J. NERVOUS AND MENTAL DISEASE.

1999 *Zen and the Brain,* Austen, J. *Times Literary Supplement.*

Originally published in JOURNAL OF CONSCIOUSNESS STUDIES: *Controversies in science & the humanities* Vol. 7, No. 11-12, November/December 2000. Special Issue 'Cognitive Models and Spiritual Maps'

Humanizing A Psychiatric Ward:
Changing From Drugs To Psychotherapy

WITH LEIGHTON C. WHITAKER, PhD, ABPP

Abstract

During the course of a year the authors changed a psychiatric ward from primary reliance on drugs to an intensive psychological approach. There were both strong institutional supports and resistance reflecting the ambivalence attending efforts to develop more personal, humanized ways of relating to mental patients. An open ward community setting evolved in which staff became highly accessible and caring, patients shared major caring and treatment responsibilities, and certain special psychological treatment techniques were developed. Many previously "untreatable" patients were involved and the improvement criteria were ambitious; the results suggest that such an approach is superior in long-term cost/benefit effectiveness to the prevalent "revolving door" programs which emphasize drugs and "dischargeability."

Introduction

During the course of a year the authors and their colleagues changed a psychiatric ward from primary reliance on drugs to primary reliance on an intensive psychological approach. The evolution of the psychological treatment approach, revealing many of the resistances and hazards in the way of such programs, is presented in this article, an approach to psychological treatment of severe depression is presented. It is hoped that our accounts will encourage and stimulate further work with intensive psychological treatment of severely disturbed patients within hospital settings.

The Setting

The setting for our efforts was in many respects typical of psychiatric teaching hospitals. The hospital was physically old and decrepit. There was no air conditioning, though it was greatly needed, and the noise level was high because of the lack of carpets, drapes, or soundproofing. Psychiatric residents and clinical psychology interns or fellows rotated through the ward every six months. Medical students and nurses in training rotated every four to six weeks. The permanent staff of each ward consisted of a psychiatrist who was ward chief, a clinical psychologist, a psychiatric social worker, an occupational therapist, and several psychiatric nurses and aides.

Prior to our beginning the new ward program treatment throughout the hospital was characterized by heavy reliance on drugs, much more so, it was later revealed, than most staff realized. Nearly all patients were admitted through a psychiatric emergency room in the nearby general hospital. An independent researcher found that all of the many patients diagnosed schizophrenic were placed immediately on phenothiazines before they could be observed in the psychiatric hospital. Such established prescription regimens would then be carried on routinely by the resident on the ward. Virtually all patients regardless of diagnosis were quickly placed on some kind of medication to reduce symptoms, thus obliterating the opportunity to observe individuals in their natural condition. Further, the habit of placing patients on drugs was so ingrained that non-drug alternatives for the hastily diagnosed "schizophrenic" patients were considered "malpractice" by some residents.

In accord with the reliance on drugs, the main focus of staff concern seemed to be reduction of the patient's symptoms and early discharge, hopefully before thirty days when most insurance coverage ceased. Not surprisingly, the average length of stay turned out to be slightly less than thirty days. A nurse's performance tended to be judged by her superiors on the basis of whether or not the ward was quiet: thus, patients who were noisy often had their tranquilizing medications increased. Post-discharge psychotherapy was difficult to obtain. Patients were not transferred to the department of psychiatry's large outpatient clinic but were sent to a facility originally set up to provide group psychotherapy but which really was used only to dispense medications.

Psychological approaches were not impressive. Individual therapy was usually supervised by the resident's off-ward psychiatrist supervisor who had little knowledge of the ward and was likely to concentrate, as did the resident, on the resident's outpatients. Some residents conducted "group therapy," usually without supervision. The hospital also provided occupational therapy and the social worker was utilized primarily for disposition and "after care" planning. Almost all staff and patients were involved in daily "patient-personnel meetings" which like the group therapy often seemed without clear conceptual guidelines and goals. As in many psychiatric hospitals, "milieu therapy" was more a vague notion than a practical reality. However, on balance, the hospital would have compared quite favorably with the average, in Rosenhan's (1973) sample.

Beginning the New Ward Program

The new ward program began when the senior author of this article, Dr. D., became ward chief just prior to the annual July changeover of psychiatric residents. He informed the staff that he intended to establish a new policy. Whereas previously, the goal had been to reduce symptoms so patients could leave the hospital, now the treatment goal for most patients would be for them to become psychologically stronger than they were before they had decompensated. In other words, the patients' own psychological abilities were to be increased to the point that they were before they were hospitalized.

An important feature of this policy was that drug treatment with new patients would not be instituted until the ward had attempted to treat them psychologically, and such efforts had failed. It was emphasized that all behavior, that of the staff as well as the patients, was expressive of motives and meanings that influenced the clinical course of the patients on the ward. Ward staff initially reacted to the new ward chief's announcement with considerable apprehension. They expressed their doubts that a program that did not rely on drugs could be effective and they were anxious in their uncertainty as to how to proceed.

Specific Therapeutic Methods

An important feature of the ward was a special form of group psychotherapy. Each group met four times a week and each was composed of five to eight patients, the supervising psychologist (the co-author, Dr. W.), a psychiatric resident, and a psychology intern or postdoctoral fellow. The therapists-in-training and the supervisor met by themselves on the fifth day for a supervisory hour. An important aim of group therapy was to clarify and bring about a change in the negativism of psychotic patients. This negativism was expressed directly and indirectly in three typical forms:

"I am a hopeless case, therefore it makes no sense for me to participate or care about what happens, so leave me alone"

or, *"My problem is that the world is rotten"*

or, *"I need something, but you can't provide it"*

Until such negativism could be reduced, a therapeutic alliance could not be established, and individual psychotherapy could hardly be effective. To cope with this problem we made much use of irony, role playing and satire to demonstrate the absurdity of self-defeating assumptions. The following is an example of how the "I am a hopeless case" defense was sometimes dealt with in group therapy. Each patient would be asked his or her opinion as to whether or not the other patients were hopeless. The patient being questioned would invariably say that none of the patients were hopeless. Then when asked about himself or herself, the patient would affirm vigorously that he or she, however, was hopeless.

The same procedure would be repeated with each patient in the group until each patient had maintained that he or she was hopeless while the others were not, and the absurdity of the situation became too evident to be ignored. After a while, the most resolutely hopeless patient would begin smiling despite the grimmest of intentions.

In a similar fashion, other typical defensive responses or inappropriate behaviors were focused upon and dramatized so that their invalidity and illogic would be made clear to the point of blatant absurdity. Many supportive, empathic and sympathetic communications were offered also, as patients developed more positive orientations which naturally drew such positive reactions. As a result of this process which was directed to the basic beginning dilemma of many psychotic individuals, patients tended to make constructive use of the individual therapy offered them.

Sometimes the entire group's attention would be focused by the therapists on a single individual for entire sessions at a time, often in conjunction with psychodrama-like playing out of important vignettes in a patient's life which we felt were central to the patient's core conflicts. Role playing of both the maladaptive original situation and a hypothetical adaptive situation was done regularly in sequence, occasionally over the span of as many as three sessions. This kind of concentration on an individual in the group is a major subject of Part II of this article and is detailed therein.

Individual psychotherapy was conducted by the residents three to four times a week with most patients, and was supervised by the ward chief, generally. The theoretical orientation was that of Artiss (1959) and Knight (1962). Residents were encouraged to work actively with their patients, challenging behavioral defenses verbally as well as offering emotional support and encouragement. They were taught to regard the patient's overt symptoms as communications

and to use their own emotional response as their guide to understanding the dynamics of the therapy situation, as well as the content of the
patient's message. For example, a resident might be helped to become
aware of his rage at a patient who regularly used muteness to express
anger and defiance. The resident's anger resulted from the threat
to his or her self-esteem at being unable to exercise his "doctor"
skills around which his esteem was based. The resident's resulting
helplessness and suppressed fury was a reenactment of the patient's
feelings in dealing with controlling parental figures. Once the resident
could acknowledge and understand his rage, he no longer felt trapped
but could use this understanding to communicate with the patient. In
the course of this work, the residents had many opportunities to gain
insight about their own conflicts, as well as those of their patients. It
was not until the ward milieu had developed fully into a psychological
treatment unit that the roles and responsibilities of staff and patients
could be clearly defined, however.

Development of the Milieu

The ward's development seemed to stem from our insistence that
a psychological treatment approach be attempted prior to considering
the use of tranquilizing drugs. In the past, when the staff had to deal
with an acute disturbance on the ward they would often resort to
drugs or to discharging the patient. Now they were instructed that a
ward disturbance involved everyone and should be dealt with by the
entire ward. A policy was established that the nursing staff could and
should call a meeting of the entire ward any time they felt they needed
help in dealing with a disturbance. As basic and routine as this procedure might seem to be, however, in practice the nursing staff needed
repeated encouragement to follow it, for reasons discussed below.

Staff learned about themselves, as well as the patients, at such
meetings. For example, at one point most of the staff had expressed
strong feelings that a particular patient should be discharged, although
there was no evidence of improved functioning, because it was feared

that the patient would remain in the hospital "forever." As a full discussion ensued, it became clear that the staff thought the patient (and others, as well) would become totally "dependent." When confronted with the physical reality of the ward, which was overcrowded, noisy, and bleak, the staff began to see that their own wishes to be taken care of and treated as patients were playing dominant roles in their response. It also became possible to see that if, indeed, a patient preferred the hospital ward to the outside world then the outside world must appear to be a very frightening place and that was the very problem we sought to treat.

Once the patients and staff, as a group, began considering the circumstances surrounding a specific incident, they could see that whether or not a particular patient's behavior got "out of hand" depended on whether the ward group wished it to get out of hand and, consequently, whether the group members were spectators, instigators, or moderators of the behavior. Often it was possible to point out a pattern of covert reinforcement of the "sick" behavior of a particular patient while his or her healthier behavior was ignored. It became apparent that subtle choices were being exercised by patients and staff alike.

It was very sobering to discover that the nurses and attendants had been insufficiently trained for a primarily psychological therapeutic role, such as our ward program required. Their training had been for the usual medical role and they were implicitly, if not explicitly, instructed to hide their feelings and maintain a "professional," i.e. distant attitude toward the patient. When deprived of the pill-dispensing function, they seemed to feel that they had no other resources at their display; they did not trust their emotional responses and therefore could not make use of them to understand a given situation. Despite specific encouragement at staff "feelings meetings" it was only with great difficulty that nurses and attendants acknowledged the anger that they experienced toward patients. They felt quite guilty about these feelings and thought that meant that they were bad therapists.

As we discussed this problem, everyone saw how hard it was to tolerate screaming and rage and, conversely, how much easier to tolerate apathy and depression. It became clear that in the past, staff anger had often been covertly expressed in recommendations that certain patients be put on drugs or given electric shock or transferred elsewhere. Recognition of their own anger, frustration, anxiety, and dependency wishes was an important step for the entire staff. It enabled them to begin using their own feelings as a guide to what the patients were communicating and what was taking place in a given situation on the ward.

From the beginning of the new ward program, the nursing staff expressed a wish for more responsibility and decision-making power than they had in the old program, but when explicitly given that power and urged to call ward meetings on their own initiative, they were slow to do so. This slowness was directly related to their feeling a lack of competence to conduct meetings and their fear of the emotional flux of an expressive ward meeting. As the nursing staff's confidence increased, however, and they became more experienced in the use of their emotions as guides, it became a regular procedure for the nurses and attendants on duty to call ward meetings rather frequently, as they sensed the need for them.

Medical students and nursing students have been allowed in the past to form a treatment relationship with a particular patient for a relatively brief but significant period of time and then leave abruptly at the end of their six-week rotation. Clinical experience suggests that the loss of a needed person is often the trauma precipitating a psychotic episode. Unwittingly, these students had been reinstituting prior traumas without the skill or opportunity to help resolve them. Their abortive encounters reinforced a patient's tendency to withdraw and made future therapeutic relationships more difficult. Consequently, the practice of assigning patients to students of extremely limited stay was discontinued. Instead, the students were offered the role of functioning as part of the nursing team and working with the patient group as a whole in the various activities of the milieu program.

For the medical students there was also the option of participating in the group therapy sessions. For the same reasons, psychiatric residents were assigned to the ward for an entire year and encouraged to continue with some of their patients on an outpatient basis the following year.

Having begun to change the roles of staff from relatively passive onlookers and drug dispensers to active, concerned, and personally caring roles, it was then possible to help patients become active, concerned, and personally caring instead of passive, drug-dependent, and powerless objects.

Our daily, one-hour patient-personnel meetings were increasingly influenced by the initiative patients began to take. Prior to the new program, patients' questions in these meetings were often simply turned back on them in a way that paralyzed thought and action and kept staff aloof. For example, a patient might ask, "What is this meeting supposed to be about?" The patient might be brave enough to venture an answer despite the implication that everyone else knows the right answer. He or she might say, "I think it's to try to help us but I'm not sure how," whereupon staff would ask other patients what they thought until the topic was changed. Patients were thus given to understand that there was no point in asking questions because you never got an answer. The defensive and destructive nature of such interchanges was pointed out to the staff who then were encouraged to tell the patients what they thought the meeting should be about and set an example by active participation. In response, gradually, the patients began to venture forth with ideas they had for improving the usefulness of the meetings and they were given the latitude to try almost any idea they recommended if the patient group as a whole seemed to be in favor of it. In October the ward milieu took a decisive turn in the direction of greatly increased patient responsibility and self-determination.

Opening the Door

During the first three months of its development, the ward had operated as a locked unit. Some of the sixteen patients had full ground privileges, others could go off the ward only with an attendant, and some were restricted to the ward. The nurses' jobs involved a great deal of time scurrying to and from the door to let people in or out and checking to see who was on the ward. Patients broke out and "eloped" regardless of closed door regulation, and it became apparent that the closed door was exceedingly irksome to all staff. Other wards that made use of phenothiazines had their doors open much of the time. Our staff became increasingly insistent that they cease to be "jailors" and spend more time with the patients.

The ward chief felt strongly that establishing an open ward would sacrifice treatment possibilities for a significant number of patients who could not be held in the hospital long enough to get treatment underway. However, when faced with the intensity and unanimity of staff feelings against his position, he capitulated. A general ward meeting was then called, and the patients were asked if they wanted the door to be open. There was an overwhelming affirmative response, with the exception of two patients who were constantly escaping — they wanted it closed! The patients were told that we did not have the personnel to conduct an open-door ward without the patients themselves being involved; we needed their help in watching and accompanying whatever patients were acutely disturbed at the time. The patients readily agreed to this plan, and at the conclusion of the meeting the doors of the ward were unlocked and left unlocked from that time forward.

Not only was the open-door policy greeted with much relief by the patients and the staff, but it led to a further development in participation. If the patients were to be assigned responsibilities in watching other patients and alerting the staff to other patients who became suicidal, they had to be included in the treatment planning and given knowledge of particular patients. The regular ward meetings with patients thus began to include more and more discussions of the status of individual patients until the time came when a therapist, if he or she became concerned about a patient, would bring that concern to the ward meeting to ask for suggestions and help.

By this time, there was a gradual but noticeable increase in the "family feeling" of the ward. There developed a sense that the ward was a unit where everyone belonged and where everyone was the object of care. Viewed in retrospect, this "caring" feeling may have been a more potent therapeutic force than any of the formal therapeutic activities. At times when the group focused on an individual patient, it seemed almost a palpable force. It arose, in part, out of the specific ethos of the small therapy groups: the role of each patient was to talk about his or her problems, to listen to others when they spoke of theirs, and to try to help one another. At the time of the open-door meeting, this ethos was extended and made explicit for the entire ward. The patients readily accepted this principle and referred to it frequently, confronting one another on matters that arose on the ward. As patients became more involved in the treatment process, they would spontaneously carry on small group activities on their own. In one instance, group therapy work was carried on late at night with a particularly withdrawn, psychotically depressed woman, by the patients belonging to her regular therapy group. The morning at the ward meeting another patient complained: "Why didn't anybody wake me up so I could be in on it?"

Patients were often encouraged to share their feelings and were told essentially that it was good to do so. Yet in the initial phase of development of the ward program, staff did not share their own feelings, thereby conveying the opposite message to patients. It soon became apparent that getting staff to share their feelings with other staff, much less the patients, was our most difficult task. The staff, especially the nursing staff, had been accustomed not to show disagreement with one another publicly, or even to share irritation: they had been trained not to reveal their own feelings, attitudes, or beliefs in the presence of patients. Only gradually, and with much reluctance, did the staff begin to speak up, and it was with some help from the patients that they did so.

By the end of October, the patients had become quite outspoken and took considerable initiative in ward functions. They had begun to run some of the patient-personnel meetings that were held routinely each morning. On some occasions patients determined the topics to be discussed, the specific purposes of the meetings and even whether staff would play the roles of patients and patients would play staff roles during a particular meeting. We found that both staff and patients welcomed these temporary role reversals and that they gave a sense of perspective that simply could not be obtained any other way.

Opposition from Other Wards

The new ward program was supported by the hospital director. Furthermore, there was considerable positive feedback and encouragement from other service divisions in the department of psychiatry. Despite this, there was strong opposition from other wards in the hospital and from the nursing administration. News of our "no drug" policy had spread immediately throughout the other wards and brought forth an anxious and angry response from other personnel, not dissimilar from the anxiety that our own staff had experienced at first at the idea of managing psychotic patients without relying on drugs. The other wards feared the possibility that they would be required to do the same and they resented the implication that the new procedures being instituted were superior to what they had been doing. Consequently, the ward found itself vehemently criticized and had to devote considerable energy to fending off attacks from the rest of the hospital. Staffing vacancies were not filled by the hospital's nursing administration because prospective nurses and attendants were told that our ward was "experimental" and that the personnel there were "unhappy." The ward's acting head nurse found herself eating alone in the hospital dining room and other staff continually received messages of anger and criticism, often directed at the ward chief. Nurses on our ward found that they were being harshly criticized by the hospital's nursing administration office, harassed in a variety of ways and threatened with bad nursing evaluation reports. At the same time there were some staff on other wards who became positively interested in our approach.

Residents on the emergency psychiatric service supplied virtually all admissions to the hospital. These residents plus those who had been on the old ward attempted to shunt all "schizophrenic" patients away from our ward, declaring that withholding drugs from these patients constituted "malpractice." The "war" did have one benefit: under the constant outside attack, the feeling of group loyalty and cohesion on the new ward increased out of necessity. It was not until later, when the ward's position was more secure, that intragroup conflicts came to the fore.

The staff's hopes that the ward would "get into shape" and become "stable" was finally seen to be unrealistic. Involvement with patients meant allowing oneself to be vulnerable to the emotional onslaught that is often the medium of communication of these patients. Eventually, we realized that the emotional level of the ward would always fluctuate, and that lows and highs would tend to be the rule. The lows occurred out of frustration with particularly difficult pa-tients and in situations in which the staff's own dependency wishes had become intensified. A sign of the latter was readily apparent in the eagerness staff often exhibited to do the patient-staff role reversals described earlier. The highs came about in situations in which staff and patients felt a real identity, a oneness as people, a oneness based on the fact that the foundation of their being turned out to be love and not hate and that they could all function best as collaborators rather than adversaries. Such highs occurred quite often enough to balance the lows and at this stage the ward began attracting staff who wanted a meaningful psychological treatment role. The acquisition of a very capable and strong head nurse in the latter phase of the ward's development gave the nursing staff some of the leadership that they had been missing.

The easing of the struggle with the other wards made it more possible for the staff to express some of their own discomforts in staff meetings. It became clear that the staff needed a great deal of support and understanding just as the patients did. There had to be a place where the staff could clarify their feelings and receive encouragement and support from their colleagues. "Feelings meetings," usually called in the evening, became the means for such activity. These meetings helped resolve personal and interpersonal conflicts among the staff that had been interfering with their effectiveness.

Staff fatigue is a constant problem in working psychologically with psychotic patients and the staff often experienced the feeling of an overwhelming burden and of endless demand. However, when the ward developed to the point where the staff members could bring the treatment problems to the staff group or to the entire ward, we discovered that patients and staff could provide help, support, and creative solutions to treatment problems that the therapist was not able to solve alone. Staff, as well as patients, felt themselves to be part of a family and could draw on the group's resources and strengths as needed.

An unexpected result of the program was its marked influence on a number of the ward staff. Some experienced personal crises stemming from the necessity to confront their own feelings and goals. Those who chose to stay on the ward and face themselves experienced considerable personal growth. Most of the residents matured as professionals, a number of ward attendants decided to go on for further schooling, some excellent personal relationships developed, and we were led to conclude that the ward experience could be "therapeutic" for staff as well as patients. In the long run many staff experienced a strong desire to continue to have the kinds of involvement and personal satisfaction in their future occupational lives that they had experienced in the ward program.

The year of the new or "experimental" ward ended in mid-summer with the turnover in residents, new and increased responsibilities assigned to one of us (Dr. W.), and a decision by the ward chief (Dr. D.) not to continue because of his obligation to complete a long-term research project contract before the ward program began. Finally, there were important financial considerations for the hospital which began to impose sharp limits on length of stay because of decreasing outside funding. Other wards had begun to emulate the "experimental ward" in some respects but without its full implications. We did, however, begin then to follow up many of our ward patients and did intensive follow-up studies on a few of the most severely disturbed.

Therapeutic Outcomes

The "new ward program" was fully operative for ten months. During this period there were a total of 51 patients treated: 20 patients were discharged in 30 days or less; another 31 were on the ward more than 30 days. The latter group averaged 4.7 months of hospital stay. The first 20 patients represented mostly milder disturbances, most often neurotic depressive reactions with rapid symptomatic improvement. The other 31 patients represented much more severe disturbances, usually some of the kind that would have been transferred from other wards to a state hospital for "longer-term care."

We did not start our program with a research effort that would have permitted us to make rigorous statistical statements about the overall results. There was no control group with which to compare our experimental group and we did not gather independently-arrived-at evaluations of outcome. We were as much interested in the methods and dynamics of developing such a program as we were in the results. Furthermore, we had not anticipated much of the professional resistance which often preoccupied us in the early months and which we feel helped to develop an understanding of why such programs are seldom developed. We did, however, attempt to follow up those patients who were in the program more than 30 days and whose disturbance had been relatively severe. While not suggesting that this data is in any way definitive, we regard it as more adequate than the usual criterion of "dischargeability" with no follow-up.

TABLE 1. DIAGNOSES AND IMPROVEMENT OF PATIENTS ON THE WARD MORE THAN 30 DAYS								
Diagnosis	N	Degree of Improvement						
		0	1	2	3	4	5	
Neurotic	9	1		2	4	1	1	
Acute Schizophrenic	3				1	1	1	
Chronic Schizophrenic	7	2		2	1	2		
Psychotic Depression	5					4	1	
Manic Depressive	2			1	1			
Character Disorder	5	1	1	1	2			
Total N	31	4	1	6	9	8	3	

Table I shows the diagnoses of the 31 "long-term" patients together with ratings of degree of improvement by the authors. Each rating on our six-point scale was based on ward observation, plus follow-up observations after discharge. In several cases the authors interviewed former patients several months after discharge and, in a few cases, there was extensive follow-up including psychological testing and interviews as long as two years afterward. We emphasized follow-up observation in cases we regarded as especially severe. Each evaluation of improvement was based on a comparison of the patient's adaptation level before the crisis leading to hospitalization to his or her adaptation level several months to two or more years after discharge. Thus, a patient might have a good clinical course on the ward but be rated low due to poor adaptation after discharge, unless we felt that life circumstances after discharge were much more adverse than before hospitalization. One such exception was a chronic schizophrenic man we rated 2, rather than 0 or 1, despite a rehospitalization within a year after discharge, which was precipitated by his especially destructive alcoholic mother. He was nevertheless much improved on second admission to his condition on first admission.

The 0 rating position representing no improvement is illustrated by the case of a man who eloped from the ward after a week's stay and, as far as we could tell, simply resumed his sociopathic behavior. Likewise, no improvement was shown by two chronic schizophrenic patients: both patients were young but had long-insidious psychotic disintegrations featuring considerable drug abuse (LSD) and had entered the hospital before the new ward program began; their treatment got off to very poor starts with several changes of therapists. Each subsequently required long-term treatment at another hospital before they could be safely discharged to outpatient treatment.

At the other extreme, illustrating the 5 position, is a woman whose psychotic depression had progressively worsened during the year before she entered the new ward program. At the time she entered the ward, she was almost mute, never expressed positive affect, and was delusional. The patient progressed on the ward to a distinctly nonpsychotic level. Six months after discharge, psychological testing (Rorschach, TAT, WAIS) and clinical interview revealed excellent reality testing, very creative use of her superior intellectual resources, and strongly adaptive social behavior.

An example of the 4 position is a 19-year-old girl who appeared to be psychotically depressed. The entire staff of the ward had predicted her future to be one of suicide or becoming an extremely long-term state hospital patient. She was treated intensively, especially in group and individual outpatient psychotherapy, and married. Almost two years after discharge it was reported by reliable sources close to her that she was doing fairly well, in marked contrast to the original prognosis, and she was interviewed by one of the authors who had similar impressions.

The two character disorder cases rated 3 were treated painstakingly over a long period. They showed a definitely improved level of functioning several months after discharge but still needed considerable attention as outpatients to sustain further improvement from what were still fairly vulnerable positions. However, we felt that each of these patients would have gone on to chronic state hospital status or penal institutions had there been less ambitious treatment.

Showing less, but still appreciable, improvement were two chronic schizophrenic patients, rated 2, who showed less vulnerability to major disablement months after discharge but were not impressive in their improvement overall. The only patient we rated 1 was an older chronic alcoholic man who was severely suicidal with frequent previous hospitalizations. He made definite progress on the ward and did not commit suicide in the year following discharge, and did not require hospitalization. There was, however, no marked change in his precarious lifestyle.

There are two further indices of treatment outcome. The rehospitalization rate for patients in our program was somewhat less than the going rate for the rest of the hospital, despite our choosing to treat extremely difficult patients on our ward instead of sending them to the state hospitals. During the initial summer one patient eloped and committed suicide. After that, for the ten months that the ward was in full operation, there were no suicides, no serious suicide attempts and only one permanent elopement. In contrast, another ward experienced three suicides during the same ten-months period. Also, as far as we have been able to tell, there have been no suicides of any of our patients since they were discharged several years ago.

Discussion

We do not regard the program described as the solution to the problem of psychosis or of other severe emotional disturbances. We do believe, however, that our experience suggests that much more is possible in the psychological treatment of severely disturbed patients than is usually believed. After less than a year of this program, we felt we had just begun to tap the therapeutic power that can be developed in the ward situation.

While our theoretical orientation was in our minds, that of ego psychology, a psychologist trained in gestalt therapy felt strongly that we were doing gestalt therapy; another psychologist, an acknowledged "expert" in behavior therapy, insisted that we were doing behavior therapy. One of us, Dr. W., often practiced psychodrama approaches. What finally appeared to be of overwhelming importance theoretically was an evolving philosophy of power building and power sharing. It began to dawn on staff and patients alike that we had either to win together or to lose together and that we needed each person to be as powerful and competent as possible in order to maximize the effectiveness of our collective efforts. Thus, we would emphasize a theory of organizational development more than any specific "school" of psychotherapy.

The question remains, "Why are drugs the dominant treatment mode in most hospital settings?" In answering this question we would point to certain economic considerations on the one hand and to certain psychological factors on the other. In the short run, it would appear economic to hospitalize patients for less than thirty days: many insurance plans will not pay for more than this length of stay. Thus, rapid reduction of symptoms becomes the criterion for a successful treatment outcome. Adequate outpatient psychotherapy afterward is usually lacking. Once these goals are set, there is a premium placed on any measures which will "restore" the patient to his prehospitalization level with minimum involvement of expensive hospital and staff time. The treatment which is still considered to be most useful in such efforts is drug treatment. Certain other goals of treatment, such as were established in our program, tend to be set aside in these efforts. The prevalent goals are strongly reinforced by the usual basis of reimbursement: bed occupancy, *per se*, for up to thirty days, rather than evidence of treatment effectiveness.

Among the appeals of drug treatment, there are some which are peculiar to the doctor-patient relationship. Kartus and Schlesinger (1957) have discussed how the counter-transference potential of the physician can be activated so that sedatives will be prescribed for nontherapeutic or antitherapeutic reasons. They advise that physicians be aware of the possible meanings of patients asking for sedatives and their own wishes to prescribe them. Deikman (1971) observes that remarkably little attention is paid to the unconscious motives of staff in prescribing phenothiazines and similar drugs and discusses the wish of staff to "disidentify" with such patients to avoid the communication of the psychotic's perspective; to avoid the intensity of psychotic affect and dependency wishes; and to express the unconscious rage that is provoked in them when the patient frustrates their wish to "help."

The question may still be raised as to whether drugs should not be the treatment of choice for severely disturbed psychiatric hospital patients if they promote quick discharge, for more rapid discharge would seem to be economically advantageous. Quick discharge, however, really begs the question of treatment effectiveness since it does not say whether an individual will be able to function productively. In New York State, for example, it has been found that patients do not function productively when merely discharged, that enormous community problems ensue, and that patients often return to the hospital, thereby creating a "revolving door" effect which in the long run is more expensive. The "miracle" of drug treatment is then rather like the fable of the emperor's new clothes. Recently three excellent studies have been reported demonstrating that drug treatment may well be inferior to psychological approaches.

Bockhoven and Solomon (1975) reported the results of comparing two five-year follow-up studies on hospitalized persons, one on patients receiving modern psychotropic medication and the other on patients treated in the absence of psychotropic drugs. They state:

> The finding of no substantial change in the outcome of schizophrenic patients was not expected in view of the absence of psychotropic drugs during the entire five years of the Boston Psychopathic Hospital follow-up period, compared with the extensive use of

psychotropic drugs at Solomon Center for both initial treatment on admission and the entire period of aftercare. This finding suggests that the attitudes of personnel toward patients, the socio-environmental setting, and community helpfulness guided by citizen organizations may be more important in tipping the balance in favor of social recovery than are psychotropic drugs.... Their extended use in aftercare may prolong the social dependency of many discharged patients.

Carpenter *et al* (1977) showed a significantly superior outcome for acutely schizophrenic patients given psychosocial treatment and only sharply limited medication versus similar patients receiving the usual treatment emphasizing drugs. These authors remark that "the treatment of schizophrenia has become so extensively drug-oriented that a significant impediment has arisen to the exploration of alternative therapeutic approaches." Evidence of the potentially greater economy offered by the psychological treatment of severely disturbed persons is found in the work of Karon and Vanderbos (1975). They have shown in their studies of treatment costs of psychotherapy versus medication for schizophrenic patients "that despite the expense of psychotherapy, there were savings of 22% to 36% in total treatment costs because of the shorter hospitalization of patients." We would not be surprised if similar studies with psychotically depressed individuals would also show savings for the psychotherapy approach. Arieri (1974) has stated, "In my experience psychotic depressions tend to recur unless adequately treated with psychotherapy." And that "Drug therapy... in my experience is not sufficient in most cases to cure affective psychoses even from the manifest symptomatology."

Psychological approaches in hospitals have long had the advantages of considerable thought. For example, the work of Cumming and Cumming (1970) presented excellent theoretical and practical approaches to psychiatric hospitalization. It becomes difficult then to fathom why it is that psychological approaches are so neglected in practice, except that drugs represent the wish for a cheaper, easier way of dealing with difficult patients. In our opinion, the extreme reliance on drugs is wishful self-deception on the part of the psychiatric profession. In the long run, a practical approach to psychological treatment of severe emotional disturbance will have to be based on revised concepts of what constitutes good treatment and an implementation of these concepts in treatment plans. Such concepts would emphasize outcome measures of ability to function productively, not merely decreases in disturbing symptomatology and quick discharge. Diagnostic assessment, which now is so limited to superficial observation of behavioral proclivities, should emphasize meaningful predictive measures of an individual's ability to think and to behave adaptively, both before and after treatment (Whitaker, 1973; Whitaker, 1978; Whitaker, in preparation).

Reimbursement plans would emphasize out-patient services both as preventive and after-hospital treatment. We believe that adequate reimbursement for follow-up psychotherapy would make it possible to shorten hospital stays compared to our program.

For the present, treatment of severely disturbed individuals will have to be accomplished in special settings where appropriate administrative support, financial backing, and suitable personnel are available.

References

Arieti, S. *Affective disorders: manic-depressive psychosis and psychotic depression.* In AMERICAN HANDBOOK OF PSYCHIATRY Vol. 3, Ch. 21, pp. 450-490. New York: Basic Books, 1974.

Artiss, K. *The symptom as communication in schizophrenia.* New York: Grime and Stratton, 1959.

Bockhoven, J. S. & Solomon, H. C. Comparison of two five-year follow-up studies, 1947 to 1952 and 1967 to 1972. AMERICAN JOURNAL OF PSYCHIATRY, August 1975, 132:8.

Carpenter, W. T., McGlashan, T.H. & Strauss, J. S. *The treatment of acute schizophrenia without drugs, an investigation of some current assumptions.* AMERICAN JOURNAL OF PSYCHIATRY, January, 1977, 134:1.

Cumming, J. & Cumming, E. *Ego and milieu.* New York: Atherton Press, 1970.

Deikman, A. J. *Phenothiazines and the therapist's fear of identification.* HUMANISTIC PSYCHOLOGY, 1971, 11, 196- 200.

Edelson, J. *Sociotherapy and psychotherapy.* Chicago: University of Chicago Press, 1970.

Karon, B. P. & Vanderbos, G. R. *Treatment costs of psychotherapy versus medication for schizophrenics.* PROFESSIONAL PSYCHOLOGY, 1975, 6, 293-298.

Kartus, I. & Schlesinger, H. J. The psychiatric hospital-physician and his patient. In *The patient and the mental hospital.* Glencoe, Illinois: Free Press, 1957.

Knight, R. I. *Management and psychotherapy of the borderline schizophrenic patient.* In PSYCHOANALYTIC PSYCHIATRY AND PSYCHOLOGY. New York: International Universities Press, 1962.

Schlesinger, H. J. & Holzman, P. *The therapeutic aspects of the hospital milieu.* BILL MENNINGER CLINIC, 1970, 34(1), 1-11.

Whitaker, L.C. *Whitaker index of schizophrenic thinking (WIST): Manual*; Forms A and B; Scoring keys. Los Angeles: Western Psychological Services, 1973.

Whitaker, L.C. *Validity and usefulness in four WIST studies recently reported in the Journal.* JOURNAL OF CLINICAL PSYCHOLOGY, July 1978, 34:1.

Whitaker, L.C. *The measurement of schizophrenic thinking.* Los Angeles: Western Psychological Services.

Woodbury, M. Milieu. *Symptoms and Schizophrenia: The seven-year history and evolution of a psychiatric ward*; Psychiatric research report 19. AMERICAN PSYCHIATRIC ASSOCIATION, 1964, 20-36.

Originally appeared in PSYCHOTHERAPY: THEORY, RESEARCH AND PRACTICE, **Vol. 16 #2, Summer 1979.**

The Empathic Ward:
Reality and Resistance in Mental Health Reform

WITH LEIGHTON C. WHITAKER, PhD, ABPP

This article provides perspective on our experiment to change a psychiatric hospital ward from reliance on drug therapy to psychological treatment. Resistances to the change took many forms, including delaying publication of the results for nearly a decade. Although successful, the treatment program itself was never adopted. The work did have a major impact on the "right to refuse treatment" case originally titled Rogers v. Okin (1979), which barred forced medication and involuntary seclusion except in certain emergencies if an outside consultant agreed. Two publications (Deikman & Whitaker, 1979; Whitaker & Deikman, 1980) described much of the program and its vicissitudes but did not include some of the more resisted features reported in this article.

T HE PURPOSE of this article is to provide perspective on our previous successful experiment to change a psychiatric hospital ward from the practice of relying on drug therapy to relying on psychological treatment. Although achieving our goal of improving treatment outcomes for severe mentally disturbed persons, we encountered severe resistance to accepting our reports as valid. The resistance took many forms, but one result was that we were not able to publish our observations and results for nearly a decade (Deikman & Whitaker, 1979; Whitaker & Deikman, 1980).

Our findings aroused an antagonism for which we were not prepared. For example, when we submitted the first article to a major psychiatric journal, two of six reviewers refused even to read our manuscript. The reviewers believed that not using drug treatment for such patients was unacceptable, perhaps even malpractice. Eventually, we circulated our unpublished manuscripts to a few colleagues, one of whom, Michigan State University professor Bertram Karon, suggested submitting the manuscript to a psychology journal, which we did. The result was that the articles were finally published in PSYCHOTHERAPY: THEORY, RESEARCH AND PRACTICE, an American Psychological Association Journal.

However, the manuscripts did strike a chord with some professionals. As a result, even before publication, Dr. Whitaker was asked to be a consultant to a VA hospital, to be an expert witness in the "right to refuse treatment case" in Boston's U.S. District Court, to propose a new Massachusetts state mental health plan, and to become superintendent of a state hospital. Publication of our two articles brought about 400 reprint requests, including many from foreign countries.

But the treatment program itself has never been adopted. Nor did it appear to have any effect on the tidal wave of drug treatment that has taken place in the United States and throughout the industrialized world, despite evidence of drug-induced damage on the one hand and superior results for interpersonal forms of caring on the other. There has been one hopeful development: The right to refuse treatment case, originally titled Rogers v. Okin (1979) set a precedent to disallow forced medication or involuntary seclusion except in certain emergencies and then only if an independent outside consultant agreed.

In the present article, besides reviewing our ward program efforts, the nature of the helping processes, and how staff and patients alike were challenged, we try to explain how the more serious personal and institutional resistances can be understood. Along the way, we shall disclose material we felt unable to publish earlier, including more of the evolution of power- and responsibility-sharing with the patients. We start by relating how we came to think of operating such a program. We anticipated resistance, but we did not know just what kind of resistance would emerge.

Before The Ward

Dr. Whitaker had been serving one of the several psychiatric wards and supervising other psychologists working in the hospital and in the outpatient clinic. Dr. Deikman had been pursuing his career-long, grant-funded research on meditation and states of consciousness. They were both aware that, in sharp contrast to the outpatient clinic's psychoanalytic orientation and ample provision of psychotherapy, the psychiatric hospital relied heavily on drug treatment, with little attention to developing individual or group therapy or the psychosocial aspects of the milieu. Whitaker had written a critique of the psychiatric hospital's treatment program for the sake of his own understanding, assuming it would be of no serious interest to others. But a new hospital director was appointed and he did show interest; he responded by having Whitaker join him in teaching a seminar for the hospital's psychiatric residents, as well as co-lead a group therapy seminar with a staff psychiatrist. Meanwhile, Deikman was planning to take a year off from his research to serve as a psychiatric ward chief. In discussing their professional interests, Whitaker talked particularly of how effective certain forms of group therapy could be, and Deikman talked of how the ideas of psychiatrist K. Artiss (1959) could be applied to milieu therapy. Whitaker and Deikman began to visualize creating a model of treatment integrating group, milieu, and individual therapy, with the goal of making the patients stronger than they were before they became hospitalized.

Whitaker had also been doing research to develop a test of schizophrenic thinking, seeking to determine specifically how people's thinking broke down into the looseness, slowness, and lack of reflective awareness that seemed to define their disabilities, eventually resulting in the Whitaker Index of Schizophrenic Thinking (WIST; 1973,1980,1985) and a book (Whitaker, 1992) that rejected the standard but unproven, fatalistic claim of "once a schizophrenic, always a schizophrenic." Whitaker regarded the term "schizophrenia" as a useful working construct only, and not some sort of entity, an "it" or object needing somatic eradication or at least dampening. Such reification of the construct into a presumed entity, a kind of sacred icon, leads to pseudoscience rather than genuine science.

We felt that inadequate and harmful interpersonal environments were the principal causes of the disabilities called "schizophrenic disorders" and "psychotic depressions," and that positive interpersonal influences could be powerfully therapeutic. But the question remained: might psychotropic medication be helpful also, perhaps adjunctively, in combination with the psychological help? And would we be subject to malpractice charges if we did not employ the recommended standard treatment, that is drugs, especially if either self-inflicted or other-directed violence occurred?

Deikman asked Whitaker, who had already been looking into the effects of drug treatment in his own research project, to do a review and critique of the neuroleptic medication research literature, since antipsychotic drugs such as Thorazine were assumed to be helpful, even if not curative. Whitaker's research using the WIST was already suggesting that the neuroleptics, while making most schizophrenics subdued and unresponsive emotionally, had little or no positive effect on the kind of adaptive thinking ability that is essential to functioning well and productively in the world. Whitaker had not yet realized that while the research literature showed little evidence of drug-produced positive effects on thinking disturbance, there was already ample evidence of damage to bodily systems, not only to the central nervous system, as was especially apparent, for example, in Parkinson-like symptoms such as tremor and shuffling gait, but also a host of other adverse somatic effects. He concluded that while the neuroleptic drug research was severely flawed in terms of substantiating the nearly universal claims of therapeutic benefit, it did clearly substantiate widespread damaging effects.

In further pursuit of assessing the effects of the neuroleptics, Deikman decided to experience the effects of Thorazine first-hand; Deikman actually gave himself a dose one morning and later observed that it was like going around all day covered over by a heavy shag rug. The effect was more dysfunctional and unpleasant than was suggested by the pleasant sounding major tranquilizer label put on the neuroleptics. It did not seem unreasonable that psychological treatment could be superior to forcing a rug over human beings' natural liveliness. In fact, Deikman considered the widespread use of neuroleptic drugs, such as Thorazine, to reflect therapists' unconscious fears keeping them from empathizing and identifying with their emotionally disturbed patients. If nothing else, prescribing pills carried the message: "You're sick — unlike me who doesn't need to take them" (Deikman, 1971). In view of the apparent dearth of truly helpful effects of the phenothiazines, they seemed to be a case of the "emperor's new clothes."

With these factors in mind, Deikman established a policy that neither neuroleptic nor other psychiatric drugs would be prescribed for patients on the ward unless psychological approaches had been tried and found to be insufficient; patients already taking prescribed drugs would be weaned off of them. This new policy clashed with the hospital's standard practice in the psychiatric emergency room. There, psychiatric patients were automatically given powerful neuroleptic drugs at the time of admission. Because of this policy there was seldom opportunity for observation of drug-free behavior.

Thus, we rejected the assumption that schizophrenia and psychotic depression were biochemically-based disease entities requiring medical treatment in the form of drugs. We chose not to regard our patients as needing to be patient, passive, and compliant to the staff. Rather, we endeavored to get them emotionally engaged. The degree of quietness on the ward ceased to be a measure of staff competence; instead, successful treatment was expected to result in noise, upsets of various kinds, and challenges to the staff. Our activity was focused on helping patients develop the interpersonal abilities and strengths needed to live adaptively — meaning actively and constructively — outside of the hospital. Becoming able to negotiate the social dynamics of the ward — including both patients and staff — was crucial to that goal. Yet the nurses and aides were traditionally taught and graded on the absence of trouble or conflict.

Initially, we had considerable turnover at the head-nurse position before we found someone suitable to the milieu and treatment philosophy we were developing. Staff on the other hospital wards were frightened by the news of the no-drug policy of our ward. They interpreted that to mean that they might have drugs taken away from them and they had not been taught any other strategies except the use of the seclusion room or restraints. This fear of being left helpless to deal with their patients led them to shun our nurses, to ostracize them, and to refuse to eat with them in the dining hall.

Ward Trust Building and Power Sharing

In our previous articles (Deikman & Whitaker, 1979; Whitaker and Deikman, 1980), we described many of the challenges to staff and patients alike during the eleven months of full operation of the ward. Now, we will relate some examples of trust building and power sharing that, for political reasons, we felt unable to publish previously because they seemed too radical. As described in our previous articles, patient-personnel meetings of the entire ward were characterized increasingly by active patient initiatives to the point that patients began to run some of the meetings. Occasionally, they chose to reverse patient and staff roles and a kind of ironic humor emerged when patients mimicked staff with consequent laughter all around; the patients came to sober realizations as they came to appreciate the difficult challenges of being staff. They concluded that they preferred their easier roles as patients. These temporary role reversals engendered considerable empathy, staff for patients and patients for staff, with a consequent sense of mutual responsibility for one another. What we did not report in our previous articles were the more extreme instances of this growing dynamic.

In October, about eleven weeks into the full operation of the ward, the patients decided to hold a Halloween party for patients and staff, but did not reveal the particulars until the party was underway. It turned out that what the patients had planned was a Salem witch trial during which each staff member was accused of a therapeutic crime and sentenced to have a hand or foot immersed in ice water for a length of time appropriate to the gravity of their misdeed. Every staff member was accused, convicted, and sentenced for their crimes. For example, with suitable irony, Deikman was accused and convicted of prescribing too many drugs.

Next came a more radical request: the patients wanted the keys to the padded, soundproofed isolation room, into which they would herd and seclude all of the staff, and then retain the keys for an unspecified period of time. There was remarkably little hesitation by staff or patients, although patients were nervous about the implicit responsibility, and staff knew it would have been impossible for them to be heard crying out to other hospital personnel for help; some staff were concerned they might become the laughing stock if the patients did not unlock the door and release us. After about 20 minutes of being crowded together in the isolation room, the patients let the staff out for good behavior. (The isolation room, literally a padded cell, was never used, before or after Halloween, for involuntary patient isolation; any patient who wished to use it for the sake of peace and quiet was allowed to, but none ever did.)

After the Halloween party, the sense of being a family became much stronger and there was a request by the nurses — voiced at a joint meeting of patients and staff — that the ward be unlocked. Deikman at first turned down the proposal fearing that new patients might elope before they had a chance to respond to the family atmosphere. The nurses told him that he could keep the doors locked, but he could then run the ward by himself because they would leave — they were tired of running back and forth to open and lock the door. Deikman yielded to this very persuasive argument. It was interesting that the patients, as well as the staff, wanted the door unlocked — except for a few patients who had previously wanted to run away! So the door to the ward was unlocked permanently.

However, since the open door would require more staff time than was available it was necessary to discuss how the patient group might help out. It was decided that when new patients, deemed elopement risks, arrived on the ward, some of the patients would monitor them and encourage their participation. This initial involvement in the treatment process became even more prominent when psychodrama sessions were instituted to help patients confront early trauma. For example, the patient group might learn that a particular patient had great trouble becoming conscious of anger and would retreat into delusion. The patient would be confronted by other patients when the issue seemed to manifest itself, for example, "You are really very angry now, aren't you? Let it out!" Delusions were seen as defenses, rather than dismissed as craziness. Such confrontations by other patients were very frequent and regarded as a responsibility. One patient even complained that the group did not wake her up at night when they worked with another patient,

The feeling of being a family had been growing on the ward and there was much humor evident. In December the patients wanted an evening party featuring Santa Claus. Again, they insisted upon particulars that deprived staff of any remaining professional distance. They chose to have Whitaker made up as Santa Claus; he would thus sit in a chair costumed for his role, ready to hear the wishes of patients and staff. An otherwise psychotically depressed, hallucinating young woman who had been severely suicidal appointed herself to apply his makeup, which she did with cheerful enthusiasm and skill. Then every staff member and patient each took a turn on Santa's lap, telling him what they wanted for the coming holidays.

Staff Feelings

In the process of changing over from reliance on drugs to reliance on psychological treatment, strong staff feelings were aroused. In patient-staff meetings, group psychotherapy, and the overall culture of the ward milieu, staff were challenged to consider their own feelings, as well as the patients' feelings. Instead of restricting themselves to the kind of distancing that is typically considered integral to professionalism, staff were emotionally interactive with patients in ways that tested staff's sensibilities. It became clear that staff emotions could neither be avoided nor dismissed as entirely due to patients' behavior. Individual staff had idiosyncratic emotional reactions that had to be taken into account. In psychoanalytic terminology, staff not only experienced patient transferences to them, but their own countertransference reactions. The latter were considered not to be unfortunate feelings about patients, but potentially valuable resources for understanding treatment dynamics, just as in psychodynamic psychotherapy. As Stanton and Schwartz (1954) pointed out in their study of mental hospitals, patient "acting out" is often an expression of staff conflict.

Staff "feelings meetings" were held during some evenings; any staff person could call one at any time it was judged necessary. At such meetings, everyone was encouraged to talk about their own feelings, with the understanding that they were not being judged. One result was that staff, the present writers included, could express their otherwise pent-up frustrations, for example over the fact that there were and would continue to be disruptions to whatever treatment goal or harmony on the ward we were pursuing. We could then sense the commonality of such frustration and the unrealistic wish that we could overcome conflict once and for all, mirroring the inevitable, never-fully-resolved quality of life itself. Thus, we did not have to conclude individually or collectively that we were not providing good treatment.

The Question of Violence Against Others or Oneself

Patients' other-directed and self-directed violence aroused the greatest concern. Standard practice was to limit the patient by means of drug treatment or isolation. A patient who was already acting out by assaulting others would have to be physically restrained. In one instance on another ward, six male staff tried to contain a young man who appeared out of control; in the process, a psychiatric resident was kicked in the groin and had to be hospitalized. Our challenge was how to provide adequate restraint of such a person when even drugs, isolation, and several staff could not avoid injury. In general, the ward culture's therapeutic effect was powerful enough in preventing violence; the ward culture disapproved of violence.

We assumed, throughout the eleven months of our ward program, that malpractice charges might be brought against us if we had even one serious suicide attempt, let alone an actual suicide or any homicidal behavior. In contrast, if we were engaging in standard practice by using drugs, the isolation room, and the forceful management techniques that were considered acceptable, malpractice would probably not be an issue. For example, during the same year as the experimental ward, another ward that was fully staffed, had a psychiatric expert in pharmacology, and sent its most severely disturbed patients to longer-term hospitals, incurred three actual suicides. We felt our ward culture acted as a significant safeguard against both inner- and outer-directed violent behavior.

We turn now to some specific challenges to our program, starting with the example of a woman who swallowed sharp objects. We found that a psychiatric resident had been covertly administering drugs to her without that stopping her behavior. After learning of the covert medicating, stopping that, and not knowing how to stop her from harming herself, the solution came from patients who, knowing of our concern, decided to intervene. They gathered at her bedside one evening and directly expressed their wish to help her, asking how they could do so. She responded by suggesting that they simply tell her to stop, which they did; she stopped and did not resume self-destructive behavior, even after discharge when she was evaluated more than a year later. Aside from her potentially suicidal behavior and that of many others, during the eleven months of the ward program, there were no suicides or suicide attempts.

Staff attitudes and cohesion integral to the ward milieu also had a strong immediate influence on even newly admitted patients' self-destructive behavior. For example, Whitaker did an intake interview one morning with a severely anorexic woman with whom forced feeding would have been considered. The ward staff sat on both sides of the room and the patient and Whitaker faced one another in the middle. Whitaker told the patient that he understood she was not eating and then said that he appreciated that because the hospital had severe budgetary problems and that she could help reduce food costs. Furthermore, he added, the hospital food was of poor quality anyway so she would not be missing anything. She then looked on each side of the room at staff and asked "Is this man crazy?" Staff replied soberly that they had wondered about that but did not know and that she would have to decide for herself. The ward lunch hour followed the interview; subsequently, staff informed Whitaker that she had not only eaten the main course but also three desserts. She also continued to eat during her ward stay, was discharged, and about two years later greeted Whitaker on the street, appearing slim but not anorexic, and thanked him.

In the second of our previous articles (Whitaker & Deikman, 1980), we gave examples of how group therapy, done in psychodrama-like fashion, was apparently adequate to stop suicidal behavior, such as with a patient who, having been revived after being declared medically deceased, was admitted to our ward. We followed up on this and other cases of severe suicidal behavior and inclination for up to two years and found no further suicide risk. In the case just cited, the follow-up was informal; after discharge, she stopped by Whitaker's office periodically, expressed thanks and told him how pleased she was with her new life.

Elopements from a psychiatric hospital can be quite worrisome.

While we had no actual elopements, we were of course concerned about the possibilities. Seemingly, the possibilities could have increased given both the open-door policy and sometimes, in good weather, having group therapy outdoors on the hospital grounds, especially given depressed patients with suicidal inclinations. Although the physical environment of the hospital was rather bleak, the tone of the program became emotionally rewarding enough to forestall elopements during the eleven months the program was fully functioning. During one outdoor sessions, a patient suddenly got up and said she was going to run away. All that was necessary was for Whitaker to say, "You won't leave. You like it too much here." The group members agreed; she smiled and sat down.

At least of equal concern was the threat of violence toward others, such as when particularly challenging male patients were admitted to our ward. Knowing that we were treating even the most disturbed and out of control patients with only psychological means, one morning the psychiatric hospital director asked Whitaker to do a one-way mirror demonstration interview with a young man admitted the night before. The director and psychiatric residents would be observing "Sam," a young man who had been brought to the hospital by police, following a fist fight with his father; he had kept the ward awake all night, pacing the floor, claiming he was Superman, keeping his arms raised, flexing his biceps and threatening to hit people. Sam had not been medicated, as would have happened ordinarily, although he had given the impression of being delusional and having a schizophrenic breakdown as well as dangerously prone to violence.

The interview room was small and had no furniture except two chairs arranged opposite one another; thus, the patient and interviewer would sit facing one another with little space in between. Apparently, Sam had not been told of the one-way mirror or that the hospital director and psychiatric residents would see him during the interview. He was already seated farthest from the interview room door when Whitaker walked in and sat down in the other chair, with the door immediately behind him. This arrangement could have connoted threat and violent confrontation to both patient and interviewer. Whitaker took a relaxed position in his chair and slowly arrived at a question, simply asking "do you have any hobbies?" Sam said he liked to fix up old cars. Whitaker remarked, truthfully, that he himself was a mechanical idiot and would appreciate Sam telling him how he fixed up old cars. For about ten minutes, Sam described what he did to restore cars and Whitaker listened attentively. Then, Sam leaned forward in his chair and told the interviewer "I like you." The interviewer responded by leaning forward also and told Sam "I like you." Sam then asked "Would you like to know how I got in here?" Whitaker said he would.

For the next 30 minutes Sam related, in a completely coherent manner, how he and his father had gotten into a fistfight, and that police had been called and brought Sam to the hospital. Whitaker then said that he thought Sam liked feeling strong, like Superman, and that he too liked feeling strong and suggested that anytime Sam and he would see each other on the ward and Sam flexed his biceps, Whitaker would do likewise and they would smile at one another. This agreement served to further the empathy, rapport, and trust Whitaker and Sam had begun to establish. Both henceforth enjoyed their occasional, quite casual confrontations that were marked by a witting awareness on both sides, and Sam was no longer even a minor management problem on the ward.

Another particularly memorable, severely dangerous patient soon began to be an arson and outright homicide threat. He had managed to secrete matches on his person and throw lit matches onto the carpeting in the group therapy room. When staff and patients objected, he would stop for some days but then resume. Nothing short of searching his person, frisking him daily — which we did not want to do — would keep him from obtaining matches as we had an open-door policy. His taunting manner made it clear that he was trying to upset everyone, especially as it was known that the antiquated hospital was quite vulnerable to fire. It became evident that neither the influence of the ward milieu nor the group therapy sessions had been adequate to stop his dangerous behavior.

One day Mike upped the ante; he spoke of his intent to murder a nurse on another ward. Whitaker encountered him in the hallway just outside his office where Mike was due to be in a group therapy session. But instead of entering the room, he told Whitaker he was going upstairs to the floor of the ward above and would murder the nurse. Whitaker asked him why. Mike, who was black, said he hated her because she was black. Whitaker told Mike he had a choice; if he tried to go up the stairs Whitaker would certainly physically stop him, or he could join the session and they would figure out the problem. Mike immediately chose to join.

The next 90 minutes was focused on Mike, with patients and Whitaker alike purling over why a black person would want to kill a person for no apparent reason except that the other person was also black. Mike said he hated himself because he was black. The discussion evolved into an empathic understanding of how bigotry got to the core of its victims, by their identifying with the bigots. The other patients in the group, who were White, expressed their feelings about Mike's would-be tragic disrespect for himself and other black people. They felt that imitating the bigoted behavior of white people was itself totally opposite of what they wanted and, together now with him, saw through the hoax of racial prejudice. The group consensus, heartfelt support, and the insight seemed to cohere into a new orientation for everyone. During and after that session, Mike got positive attention and respect. There were no further threats of homicide or arson.

Patients' Roles as Therapists

The structure of group therapy sessions set a framework for treatment and for the ward as a whole. As elaborated in our earlier articles, patients were told they were expected to be helpful to other patients as well as themselves. For the four times per week group sessions, new members were told clearly what their responsibilities were: they could not be more than five minutes late for a session, and they were expected to try to talk, with intention to help themselves and others in the group. This structuring of therapeutic aims set the stage dynamically. Patients accustomed to being passive, even chronically mute or dismissive of others, were immediately faced with responsibility, and challenged to develop at least the rudiments of constructive interpersonal behavior. Peer pressure of a positive kind evolved, helping to counter the typical negativism of many patients considered by themselves and others to be untreatable, at least psychologically. Staff clearly presented themselves as active empathizing listeners as well as structuring expectations and the purposes of the sessions.

One of the influences on our cultivating patients' roles as active participants, including as therapists, was a book alluded to earlier in this article, *The Mental Hospital* by Stanton and Schwartz (1954). Those authors emphasized the relation of social interaction and mental functioning and how hospital practice negated therapeutic efficacy:

> *Built solidly into the procedures, techniques and even the language of the mental hospital is the assumption that patients are mere passive objects of treatment: they are to be "cared for," "protected," "treated," "respected," "handled," "controlled." Psychiatric administrative language consistently speaks of the patient as if he were not actively a participant, as if he were an unconscious or half-conscious body upon an operating table* (p. 408).

As will be addressed in the next section, one of the major resistances to implementing the orientation is the assumption that it is not financially feasible.

Cost and Value Considerations

The question of whether a hospital treatment program makes

sense economically has usually been answered simplistically by limiting inquiry to the expediency of short-term considerations. Customarily, patients were treated with drugs and discharged short of their 30-day insurance coverage limit. The treatment criterion was dischargeability, tied to the goal of restoring patients to their prehospitalization level of functioning.

Typically, the treatment process was geared to getting the patients adjusted to the hospital ward, such as measured by a ward adjustment scale. In the process, patients were managed to ensure patient compliance especially as related to medication prescribed to make them more passive and, therefore, more manageable. A favorable rating of the patient's adjustment to the ward — meaning compliance and manageability — would promote discharge from the hospital, most importantly before the 30-day limit on insurance reimbursement.

Our ward program operated against the grain of this custom. We thought that the criteria of improvement based on compliance and passivity and return of the patients to their prehospital vulnerability to breakdown begged the question of substantial improvement. We asked ourselves how we could help patients attain a higher level of psychological strength and well being than they had before their breakdown, so as to favor better adaptive functioning in the real world outside of the ward, and thereby make another breakdown less likely.

While many of our patients were hospitalized within the 30-day insurance reimbursement limit, many stayed longer. Our ward discharged 20 of our 51 patients before the 30-days' limit; the other 31 patients, who were far more severely disturbed, averaged 4.7 months' stay. The latter were almost always patients that other wards would have transferred to a state hospital for longer-term care. Thus, our treatment standard was immediately problematic if one considered only the nonreimbursable expense for our particular hospital of running over the 30-days' limit on insurance coverage, whereas discharged patients who needed to be rehospitalized could be handled with budgetary expediency even for our hospital because readmission could start a new 30 days of insurance coverage. And if such patients were admitted to other hospitals in the state system, or even outside of the state system, their stays could be reimbursed by new 30-day provisions. Therefore, the proverbial revolving door of readmissions to the same or different hospitals was not problematic in terms of the original hospital's budget because the same kind of 30-days' insurance provision could be reinstituted at the same or another hospital. The rate of readmission of patients from our ward to our hospital was 20% less than the average for the other wards.

Expanding the question of treatment cost to include the over-all system of hospitals leads to an altogether different evaluation of treatment effectiveness from both monetary and patient well-being points of view. We were aware that failure to treat effectively, in terms of strengthening patients' ability to live adaptively outside in the real world, actually meant severe costs to the mental health system and to society at large. If patients in our short-term hospital were sent directly to either of the longer-term state psychiatric hospitals (Fort Logan or Pueblo), as was the custom with more difficult cases, then those hospitals had more expense, albeit often chargeable to insurance companies, than if the patients were treated successfully by our hospital (Colorado Psychiatric Hospital). In general, other mental health facilities, hospitals included, would have expense due to repeated admissions following premature discharges from our hospital.

Ultimately, society as a whole pays both directly for care costs and, quite importantly, in lost income tax revenues since dysfunctional people earn little or no money that can be taxed, they become a financial burden on others, and are less equipped to be good parents.

Calculating the expenses of persons diagnosed as schizophrenic, Strauss and Carpenter (1981) noted that the direct treatment cost was perhaps $17 billion a year while the indirect or hidden costs, such as years of unemployment, food, and housing probably raised the burden to nearly $40 billion per year (p. 71). According to Talbott,

Goldman, and Ross (1987), schizophrenic persons were occupying 25 % of all hospital beds and accounted for 40 % of all long-term care days though they comprised only 1 % of the population, and they calculated that 85 % of the total cost of "chronic mental illness" of severely disturbed people results in the extreme expense of chronic disability. In essence, not greatly helping severely disturbed people results in the extreme expense of chronic disability.

Now, considering the question of the cost of hospital psychiatric treatment *per se*, we note that, overall, psychiatric hospital treatment has been shown to be a poor choice compared to alternative forms of treatment, for example, doing family therapy instead of admitting would-be hospital patients (Langsley, 1985). As Charles Kiesler (1982) showed, all ten studies of alternatives to hospitalization for mental patients in the recent years prior to his study indicated superior results for nonhospital treatment, and all nine alternative treatment programs that provided economic cost data were definitely less expensive. Genuinely effective treatment would mean less expensive treatment in the overall, longer-term picture. Clearly, our program had to be more effective than ordinary psychiatric hospital treatment to be economically justified.

Furthermore, we questioned whether treatment of severe mental illness was merely ineffective overall, or was the prevailing customary treatment of mental illness harmful overall? Recently, Robert Whitaker (2007) has provided an important answer based on both epidemiologic evidence and an understanding of the perturbation effects of psychiatric drugs. His comprehensive review of the outcomes literature shows that since 1955 — when neuroleptic or antipsychotic drugs began to be standard treatment for schizophrenia — the percentage of Americans disabled by mental illness has increased nearly sixfold. The rapid decline in the nation's mental health continued at a rapid rate through the 1980s, when the serotonin reuptake inhibitors (SSRIs) were introduced. The nation's downward trend in functioning ability continues to correlate with the increasing reliance on psychiatric drugs that are now well understood to perturb neurotransmitter systems. In contrast to the common claim that psychiatric drugs "correct chemical imbalances," R. Whitaker (2007) states that the drugs can best be described as chemical imbalances. The notion of pre-existing biochemical imbalances — prior to drug administration — is unsupported by evidence. Thus, the bottom line conclusion is that the ever-increasing use of psychiatric drugs is producing evidence of actual physical and mental illness and record amounts of disability.

Given the evidence of harm caused by the standard treatments of drugs, electroshock, and psychosurgery (lobotomy and related procedures), the question of cost effectiveness requires a whole new kind of equation. Instead of assuming treatment benefit, we have to consider not only the cost of administering treatment but also the costs resulting from the treatment, whereas typically it is assumed that the treatment is of benefit including economically for society. If we add the cost of the harm done by the treatment to the cost of its administration, one sees the absurdity of the usual way of reckoning cost: assuming the treatment is of positive value to patients and taking into account only a short period of time. Clearly, then, the standard treatments are not only costly in the short-term but the cost is compounded over the long-term.

For those of us biased in favor of predominantly psychosocial treatment, we should ask how costly it is when both administration and longer-term outcomes are considered. One can argue that interpersonal modes of treatment can result in morbid forms of dependency. We believe that we obviated that danger with our requirement that patients had to take on responsibility for themselves and others, both in group therapy and on the ward generally. Our aim was to help patients develop interpersonally. In this way, we could afford not to be fully staffed, such as when we lacked a head nurse for the first few months of the program. We challenged the usual role of the patient, which was to be passive. Instead, our patients were helped to become helpful so that they could become more functional and be less helpless after discharge.

After the Ward

As became clearer after the actual operation of the ward, our discontinuing the standard reliance on the neuroleptics obviated the common adverse side effects, such as tardive dyskinesia and akathesia, and there were other health benefits as well. For example, since patients would not be neuroleptically deprived of their natural dopamine, a neurotransmitter that facilitates normal stimulation and pleasure, they would not have the ravenous medication-induced compensatory penchants for nicotine, caffeine, and overeating consequent to neuroleptically induced dopamine reduction. Disallowing smoking on the ward was readily tolerated by patients, fortunately so because the decrepit old hospital building was oon to be condemned for patient care due to fire hazard. Nor did patients complain about not being prescribed drugs. In short, the ward program obviated the production of actual disease.

Would we now do things differently? The newer antipsychotic and antidepressant drugs are supposed to be both more effective and safer, though evidence to date does little to support such claims. The newer drugs appear to offer no greater benefit to patients than placebos and to have their own damaging effects. The claim that schizophrenia is a disease like diabetes is ironic in that the new antipsychotics are now linked to helping produce actual diabetes. But why not at least try to use those medications, at least as adjuncts to a program using psychosocial treatment primarily?

Bertram Karon (2006) has put this question into temporal perspective by documenting long-term studies of outcome for psychotic patients. The clear conclusion is that psychotherapy is superior to medication; the latter actually diminishes chances for recovery. Thus, not only does psychotherapy work when properly done, but when brain-damaging treatment is avoided, long-term outcome can be enhanced rather than worsened. In conclusion, Karon states, "If the patient or therapist want medication, it can be used, but it should be withdrawn as rapidly as the patient can tolerate" (p. 227). In this light, we feel that our psychological approach was warranted and that programs of treatment today should take heed from history rather than simply trying to quell disturbing symptoms at the cost of patients' and society's well-being.

Looking back on the ward program, Dr. Deikman concluded:

> *Empathic connection is the key factor in psychological treatment; it is much more powerful than drugs. The more our ward developed a family feeling, the more effective it became as a therapeutic agent. How can we understand this? How can we understand that someone with psychosis can be brought out of their acute psychotic phase in a few days without the use of drugs? How can we understand that severely depressed patients, who had received antidepressants as well as electroconvulsive treatment (ECT) without improvement, would experience recovery from depression through the use of psychological means alone? We used psychodrama, humor in group therapy meetings, one-on-one psychotherapy, and, especially, unscheduled, constant, individually prescribed confrontation of patients by other patients.*

What we would like to suggest is that through these means, patients and staff began to feel connected to the ward group as if they were members of a family. This connection was palpable and proved critically effective because their illnesses had arisen through feeling alone, isolated, unprotected. The family feeling permitted and fostered the experience of empathic connection, countering the isolation underlying the patient's presenting symptoms and providing support for further maturation. This was true of the staff experience as well. As a result, for most of the staff as well as the patients, participation in the ward not only decreased dysfunction; it included a gain in maturation and strength beyond that which had been the case even before the breakdowns that resulted in their hospitalization. From

that perspective, the basic therapeutic task is to lessen the barriers
to the experience of connection.

References

Artiss, K. (1959). *The symptom as communication in schizophrenia*. New York:
Grune and Stratton.

Deikman, A, J. (1971). *Phenothiazines and the therapist's fear of identification.*
HUMANISTIC PSYCHOLOGY, 11,196-200.

Deikman, A.]., & Whitaker, L. G (1979). *Humanizing a psychiatric ward:
Changing from drugs to psychotherapy.* PSYCHOTHERAPY: THEORY, RESEARCH,
AND PRACTICE, 16(2), 204-214.

Karon, B. P. (2006). *Can biological and psychological intervention be integrated into
the treatment of psychosis? Probably not.* ETHICAL HUMAN PSYCHOLOGY AND
PSYCHIATRY, 8(3), 225-228.

Kiesler, G A. (1982), *Public and professional myths about mental hospitalization:
An empirical reassessment of policy-related beliefs.* AMERICAN PSYCHOLOGIST,
27, 1323-1339.

Langsley, D. G. (1985). *Prevention in psychiatry: Primary, secondary, and tertiary.*
In H. I. Kaplan & B. J. Saddock (Eds.), *Comprehensive textbook of psychiatry*
(4th ed., pp. 1885-1888). Baltimore: Williams &. Wilkins.

Rogers v. Okin, 478F. Supp. 1342 (D. Mass. 1979).

Stanton, A. H., & Schwartz, M. S, (1954). *The mental hospital; A study of
institutional participation in psychiatric illness and treatment.* New York:
Basic Books, Inc.

Strauss,]. S., & Carpenter, W. T. (1981). *Schizophrenia.* New York: Plenum Press.

Talbott, J. A., Goldman, H. H., & Ross, L L (1987). *Schizophrenia: An economic
perspective.* PSYCHIATRIC ANNALS, 17(9), 577-579.

Whitaker, L. C. (1985). *Objective measurement of schizophrenic thinking: A
practical and theoretical guide to the Whitaker index of schizophrenic thinking
(WIST)* Forms A and B; scoring keys. Los Angeles: Western Psychological
Services.

Whitaker, L. C, (1992). *Schizophrenic disorders; Sense and nonsense in
conceptualization, assessment, and treatment.* New York: Plenum Press.

Whitaker, L. C., & Deikman, A. J. (1980), *Psychotherapy of severe depression.*
PSYCHOTHERAPY: THEORY, RESEARCH AND PRACTICE, 27(1), 85-93.

Whitaker, R. B. (2007). *Reality check: What science has to tell us about psychiatric
drugs and their long-term effects.* In L. G Whitaker & S. E. Cooper (Eds.),

Pharmacological treatment of college students with psychological problems (pp. 97-123). New York: Haworth Press.

Psychotherapy of Severe Depression

Abstract

In the ward program described in a previous article (Deikman & Whitaker, 1979) there were many opportunities to try psychological treatment approaches with severely depressed, suicidal and "untreatable" patients. Three case illustrations are presented here, showing particularly the collaborative efforts of patients and staff in group psychotherapy. In these cases, many assumptions about "untreatable" patients were critically examined and rejected. Psychological approaches were designed which successfully reached the bases of conflict by re-instituting traumatic situations and providing ways of developing corrective emotional experiences. Psychological theories helpful in such basic psychotherapeutic work are discussed.

The authors do not identify their approach with one particular theoretical school or type of psychotherapy. They feel that the problem with most current approaches to treatment of severe depression is that our understanding of the psychodynamics of depression is not really put to use in designing treatment programs.

In this article certain approaches to the psychological treatment of severe incapacitating depression and psychosis are described. Illustrative cases are discussed particularly in relation to group psychotherapy within the ward milieu, and with reference to treatment outcomes. Severe, incapacitating depression is usually treated by electroshock or anti-depressant drugs. Both of these treatments have certain advantages in terms of economics and expediency. Neither costs much money initially or takes much time to administer and each may alleviate depressive symptomatology, at least in the short run. Furthermore, it is thought there exists no viable treatment alternative.

During the course of a year during which the authors were developing an experimental psychiatric ward at a university teaching hospital, there were many opportunities to try psychological treatment approaches with severely depressed patients. Ordinarily these patients would have received somatic treatment and/or have been sent to a state hospital for long-term institutionalization. Most had been treated unsuccessfully for months or even years with antidepressants, and, in some cases, electroshock before we made our psychological treatment attempts. Each of our illustrative cases was declared "untreatable" by consensus of the staff before we made our treatment attempts.

It seemed to us that there were some important disadvantages to the somatic treatment methods and that a psychological approach would promote better understanding of severe depression. Somatic treatments do not by themselves aid in the patient's learning what his or her depression is all about nor in developing different emotional, cognitive, and behavioral responses which would avert future depressions and lead to a more satisfying productive life. Furthermore, we were struck by the impersonality and avoidance of interpersonal closeness between patient and staff in these cases particularly. The patients' characteristic withdrawal seemed reinforced by staff, who were threatened and made anxious by the patients, as if the patients' despair and self-destructiveness might be catching. Prescribing drugs often seemed motivated by the need to disidentify with patients.

Most importantly, we felt that there was evidence that psychological treatment would be effective and that there existed adequate theoretical rationales for its effectiveness. We wondered whether the suicidal crises couldn't become psychologically creative events in the lives of our patients, our thinking had some similarity to Tabachnich's (1973) concept of "Creative Suicidal Crises." The case to be presented first will illustrate some of these points.

The Case of Mrs. H.

Prior to starting the new, experimental ward, one of the authors (Dr. W.) had opportunity to work with a fifty-year-old woman who had thoroughly convinced ward staff that she would commit suicide upon release from the hospital despite several weeks of treatment. The circumstances of admission and chief complaint are quoted here as reported by her psychiatric resident but with names deleted: "Patient was transferred to Psychiatric Hospital from General Hospital follow-ing a serious suicidal attempt in which she almost died. This included a cardiac arrest in the ambulance between an outlying hospital and General. She required a tracheostomy and maintenance on a respira-tor for a four-day period, but was saved essentially without noticeable brain damage through heroic medical efforts."

Her psychological history was replete with evidence that she would be a most difficult treatment case. The resident reported "...a long-standing history of fairly severe hysterical character disorder in which the patient had been extremely narcissistic, used to having her own way at a very early age. It was said, her... characteristic way of han-dling painful situations is massive denial and depression until the reality becomes overwhelming, unable to avoid any long (*sic*), at which point she feels overwhelmed, betrayed, and helpless. This has occurred repeatedly in her life, the most recent time being when she felt betrayed and overwhelmed by her friend criticizing her as well as her husband divorcing her, and attempted suicide."

In addition to her severe characterological problems and her highly stressful life situation, the patient had suffered diabetes mel-litus for two years, for which she was taking forty insulin units per day. Both her parents had diabetes and her mother committed suicide by overdosing with sleeping pills when the patient was age nineteen. The dire implications of this history were not relieved by any evi-dence that the patient would cooperate with treatment efforts. Her clinical course in both the general and psychiatric hospitals was de-scribed as "stormy." Having spent several days in the general hospital she was then placed on a ward of the psychiatric hospital where her psychiatric resident reported that "...the patient was a rather haughty, imperious lady who tended to alienate, at times, both patients and staff from her, and seemed to be extremely narcissistic and demanding during much of her stay here." Nevertheless, this patient's treatment outcome was quite favorable following a psychological treatment approach of about one week toward the end of her six-week stay on the psychiatric ward.

At a ward conference on her case, about four weeks after her psychiatric admission, it was predicted by ward staff that, unless carefully guarded, the patient would take every opportunity to escape the hospital and follow through on her suicide plans. Staff were unanimous in their opinion that further treatment attempts, including her ongoing individual and group therapy, would be ineffective. Dr. W. then obtained permission to try a short-term approach that he thought might work. The primary setting for this approach was group therapy where Dr. W. and a psychology postdoctoral fellow (Dr. P.), who had been trained in psychodrama, were co-therapists.

The treatment was based on the premise that the patient had denied her rage at her husband and was directing it at herself. We enacted the original rage-producing situation. Dr. P. played the husband while Dr. W. and the other group members encouraged the patient to express her rage at her surrogate husband, Dr. P. It was anticipated that her initial response to our provocations would be to try to avoid the group therapy sessions and when forced to attend, would try to escape the room by the window or the door. Accordingly, precautions were taken to ensure her attendance and one of the co-therapists stood ready by the window while another blocked the door. Other patients in the group were fully informed of the treatment plan and gave their support.

The enactment was based as faithfully as possible on the actual circumstance in which her husband had informed her of his leaving. Instead of actually leaving, however, the "husband" was to stay in the room. It was hoped that the patient, finding her exits blocked, would find no other outlet for her feelings than to attack him. The "husband," a strong young man, was prepared to encourage and accept her attack, using a sofa cushion to protect himself from the full force of her blows. The other patients were prepared to tell the patient at the right time that her "husband" was a cruel deserter and to encourage her to attack him.

This treatment procedure required three consecutive daily sessions. Arriving at the first session, not knowing what was planned, the patient appeared to be withdrawn, depressed, sullen, and prepared, as usual, to avoid listening, talking, or in any way participating constructively in the session. She was then told that Dr. P. had something to tell her and that he was her husband. Dr. P. then enacted the actual leave-taking scene that preceded her suicide attempt. The patient quickly got up from her seat and tried to leave by the door. Blocked at the door, she then tried the window, she next tried to avoid the enactment by closing her eyes and covering her ears with her hands. Dr. P. then held her hands, preventing her from covering her ears and told her that what he had to say was important, and that he was leaving her for a very attractive woman he had met. He said he would be going to Sweden with this woman and he wouldn't have his job or any income there so he had no money to leave for her (his wife). The scene was reenacted several times during the first two sessions. Gradually Mrs. H. began to make sporadic attacks on her "cruel husband," and with each attack was supported vocally by everyone else in the room. By the end of the second session the patient was attacking her "husband" with unrestrained murderous intensity, and Dr. P. had to rely on his protective cushion as she tried to beat him with her fists.

In the third session, Mrs. H. announced that she was feeling much better and she appeared interested in talking. The group then discussed how it is that so many people, including this patient and other patients in the group, got to thinking of suicide because "they've been angry" and couldn't or wouldn't express it to the person they felt the anger toward. Mrs. H., both in this session and on the ward, condemned her own "stupid," self-destructive behavior and talked about the things she yet wanted to do in life and about her pride in her children and her desire to visit them in their out-of-state homes. After the session, she continued in the daily group therapy sessions for a few more days but was no longer the group's major focus of concern. During this time, the patient stated spontaneously and convincingly that she would never attempt suicide again because she now experienced her life as worthwhile. She was discharged from the hospital shortly thereafter and obtained the kind of office secretarial work she had done successfully many years before. No formal follow-up was planned except that she would come in occasionally for sessions with her individual therapist, a psychiatric resident. Two weeks after discharge she stopped by Dr. W.'s office for a few minutes, telling him about a book she had enjoyed reading and how it might interest him. She also said enthusiastically that she was feeling good and liked her job. Two months after discharge, she stopped by again, cheerfully relating how she had made friends and was enjoying personal relations with people at the office where she was working.

The experience with Mrs. H. suggested that other severely suicidal and depressed patients, who did not respond to the usual somatic treatments, might be helped by intensive, though not necessarily lengthy, psychological treatment. During the year in which the authors were developing the experimental ward, it was possible both to work with several such patients and to plan more systematic outcome evaluations for some who lived in the metropolitan area. Only one of these cases will be presented in detail in this paper because of space limitations. However, the next case to be described does represent the type of work done with fairly chronic cases and the average outcome for this treatment. The chronic case which had the least favorable outcome will be discussed briefly later.

The Case of Elizabeth

The patient was a seventeen-year-old girl admitted to our ward a couple of months before the change in ward policy and leadership. Chronically and severely depressed, Elizabeth had made repeated suicide attempts, had many hypochondriacal complaints and hallucinated on several occasions. She was from a family of several children, most of whom were older than she and who had left home in their early teens. All attempts to work with the parents had failed and the consulting psychiatrist said the family presented the worst prospects for family therapy of any he had ever seen. Consequently, the treatment plan had consisted of phenothiazines and attempts to place the patient in a foster home, but foster placement was strongly opposed by her family as well as the patient. At the time of the changeover in ward leadership, Elizabeth was about to be discharged to a state hospital because the treatment had been unsuccessful.

The staff was unanimous in predicting that she would become a chronic state hospital patient if she did not kill herself first. The authors decided not to discharge Elizabeth but, instead, to initiate a program of intensive psychological treatment. Six months after the new treatment began, an interview was held which we present here to indicate how the experimental program was experienced by the patient. The interview is quoted verbatim:

DR. D: "...when you came into the hospital... Describe how things were then."

ELIZABETH: "Very confused."

DR. D: "What was confused?"

ELIZABETH: "My mind. I really couldn't think through anything. The only thing in my mind was this. I thought I had to die... the only way out."

DR. D: "You had to die? Why?"

ELIZABETH: "Yes, I felt like I didn't have anything to live for, nobody wanted me to live, nobody loved me, so why should I live.

I was just destined to die. My thoughts all went to the negative side of things. I felt as though everything I had to do led up to kind of my dying. I couldn't look at myself because I was a terrible person... I had evil thoughts about people."

DR. D: "What kind of thoughts seemed so evil?"

ELIZABETH: "I can remember thinking one certain thought about a person I had been in contact with that was a good friend of mine. I can remember thinking that 'Why is she — I can't stand that. She must be bad.' I remember that silly thought that I should die for that thought right there. I hated people. I had this thing, I had to strive to love everybody and before that excluded anger. There was no anger at all, I couldn't feel it, I didn't want the feeling."

At the beginning of her new treatment Elizabeth was restricted to the ward, and her parents agreed not to see her for two to three months. No phone calls or visits from friends were allowed. In this way we hoped that the patient would depend on her parents less and the ward community more. A particular feature of the ward was the assignment of all patients to a special form of group psychotherapy in addition to individual psychotherapy three or four times per week. Each of the groups met four times a week; they were composed of about six patients plus the supervising psychologist, a psychiatric resident, and a psychology fellow. The trainees and supervisor met by themselves on the fifth day of each week for an hour of supervision. In Elizabeth's case, it was decided to act on the hypothesis that the psychotic and suicidal behavior were a way of dealing with intense, denied anger originally felt toward her parents. As in the case of Mrs. H., psychodrama vignettes were employed in the group therapy sessions. A psychodrama scene was enacted by either Dr. P. or Dr. W., faithfully modeled after a detailed account the patient had given of some typical antagonistic and frightening interactions with her father, who was played by one of the two therapists in any given session. In addition, the ward nursing staff was assigned the job of repeatedly confronting the patient with her anger in any ward situation in which they felt sure that anger was present.

ELIZABETH: "People drove at me all the time, saying 'You appear to be a little angry. You're angry you're angry, please admit it. You're angry at your father, you're angry at you mother,' and I wouldn't admit these things. Then after they threw them at me, I can remember two doctors here, acting out the psychodrama, and this is when it all started. Dr. P. played my father, and I played myself. And I can remember the feeling just escaping inside me and coming out and running over and just trying to strangle Dr. P.... just had my hands around him, trying to squeeze his neck... I was so angry I could kill him, and that is when it really got bad, when I felt angry that day."

DR. D: "What made it so bad?"

ELIZABETH: "Well it was hard. I had never experienced anything so hard. It's like I had shut myself off from all these kinds of emotions, and I can actually say that they may have been there, but I didn't feel them."

DR. D: "You didn't feel the anger at all?"

ELIZABETH: "Yeah, I didn't feel anything. I mean that day, just these overwhelming feelings came upon me. I felt hot, and I felt rushed; I felt like I could just scream at him, and I could just choke him and 15,000 things at once. I didn't know what to do, and I was scared... I thought I was going crazy for sure."

In the case of Elizabeth, the intensive group focus on her was carried on for about a week, but then the attention of the group shifted to another patient, and Elizabeth managed to suppress the anger toward her father that had surfaced. The ward confrontation continued, however, and about a month later her feelings erupted once more.

ELIZABETH: "About two days after that, I succeeded to suppress all those feelings, and a month later I got very ill. I couldn't figure out why I was ill. I was suffering a loss, you know, I had lost somebody who had really meant a lot to me, and I couldn't — and I went through this shaking and screaming at the top of my lungs, and I couldn't control any of it. And then I just decided, 'I'm angry because I'm screaming,' and I'm saying things I've never said in my whole life, and I couldn't stop it, and this went on for three solid days, just screaming at the top of my lungs. Just all kinds of things like, 'I hate you,' talking about my father and saying, 'I didn't do this, you're a bastard because you did this to me' and admitting feelings that people didn't know I had in me."

Under the old ward policy, the screaming would not have been tolerated. Elizabeth would have been "medicated" with sufficient phenothiazines to render her quiet. In this case, however, the ward staff behaved differently.

ELIZABETH: "...At that time I thought they were driving me crazy."

DR. D: "Pressure on you?"

ELIZABETH: "Yes, you know. 'Go ahead Elizabeth, scream Elizabeth, it's okay, go ahead.' And this was how they are coming across to me. I can remember one of the nurses say, 'Scream, go ahead, it's all right. Don't be ashamed.' And I can remember saying, 'You're trying to drive me crazy,' but yet I can remember saying, 'Don't leave me alone, please.' I remember wanting the staff to be with me at all times during those few days because I was so scared, but I really was very close to them, but yet in another way it's really bad because I felt 'Well, maybe they're trying to drive me crazy.' I remember a one-to-one basis with the attendant, and I can remember not liking him at all. But I really believe he taught me how to express my feelings, and he kept talking to me every single night that I was here for six months. We had sessions that lasted from an hour to two hours, and I really began to trust him. That was one of my most important experiences here."

The patient screamed, and she was encouraged to do so, for the treatment plan was to try to make her anger conscious, to get her to express her feelings instead of suppressing them. At the same time, she was provided with personal support by the nursing staff. One attendant, as she indicated, spent a great deal of time with her. During this period she became "worse" in that she was hallucinating.

ELIZABETH: "I remember when I became kind of psychotic that night, hallucinating really bad. The third night just before it was over with I remember an attendant on the ward with me, and I started screaming. I said, 'Get away from me!' and as he kept saying, 'Well, what's going on?' to me his face had become completely different. He was my father. I had lost touch with everybody."

Elizabeth had also hallucinated her grandfather.

ELIZABETH: "it was strange because I went to bed the third day that night, and I'm lying there thinking, 'Well, it will be better tomorrow. I won't be feeling...my grandfather will come and take me away. I won't have to stay here any longer. He promised he'd come in the morning. And I can remember waking up and the shaking was gone. I wasn't shaking anymore. And I can remember looking out the window and saying to myself, 'It's 10:30, and he's not here.' And this was the first time in my whole life that I could actually say, 'You know, I am angry.' It was hard. I guess I threw it out of my thoughts so I couldn't think about it anymore. It was strange because no more shaking: I could very calmly talk about things compared to the way I was with the shaking and screaming. It was just strange the way it happened. I just kept admitting to myself that I was angry, to get it over with and to talk about everything I was angry about. And then when it was all over, there was no more to talk about..."

For the next month, from time to time, she would see her father's face in different objects or pictures, and she would hear voices saying: "You'll never get away with it. You'll pay for everything you've done, you'll never get away with it."

ELIZABETH: "I was feeling guilty about being angry, and I can actually say I felt worse afterwards about a few things, but they weren't as intensified as they had been. When I decided to finally look at it and work on it, my doctor said, 'Well, these voices mean something to you,' and it scared me. I didn't want to hear them any more. And after that I didn't hear them any longer."

The patient's reports of hearing voices helped us and the patient to understand why she had the need to punish herself. Ordinarily, such reports would have led to medicating a patient, thereby obliterating an opportunity for insight. Elizabeth began, at this point, to make much better use of her individual psychotherapy sessions. Her suicidal preoccupation decreased markedly, she had no further hallucinations or delusions, and the individual psychotherapy focused on working out problems of dependence and independence in her relationship with family. At this point the patient began attending high school classes outside the hospital and participated in family conferences.

Three months later there were no signs of psychotic functioning or suicidal threat and she was doing well in school. Consequently she was discharged from the hospital to outpatient psychotherapy. The following interview was conducted shortly before discharge.

DR.D: "What kind of things have you come to understand about how things got so bad... What kind of a jam did you get into?"

ELIZABETH: "I think the whole story is that making my family all I wanted and all I have and also with whatever they said was true, no matter what it was. This was the whole thing because it was like they'd say, 'Little doll, you do this, do it, and then jump on your shelf.'"

DR. D: "Why did you try to do that?"

ELIZABETH: "Because I didn't want them to reject me in any way because I felt they were my whole world, and I had nobody else."

DR. D: "So it was to hang on to them?"

ELIZABETH: "Oh yeah, not knowing how I felt about anything and not getting angry at them to their faces so they would never get angry at me."

DR. D: "Do you have any problems now?"

ELIZABETH "Oh yeah."

DR. D: "What kind?"

ELIZABETH: "I think they're typical teenage problems, you know, but are so much milder, just like — with my parents over things I want to do and they don't want me to do."

DR. D: "Like what?"

ELIZABETH: "My parents aren't very liberal, and I find myself to be very liberal now, and maybe it concerns going to this person's house and my parents don't like them because they are hippies. This thing with whom my friends should be, and I don't want them to pick my friends. I think picking my friends is my job."

DR. D: "Do you think about the future? How does it look to you for yourself?"

ELIZABETH: "I like to look at the future. I think the most important thing... I'm going to be myself and not what anybody else wants me to do, whatever that means. I also feel as though whatever it takes to make Elizabeth happy, for once I'm going to do it. If it means yelling at people, then if that makes me happy, I'm going to do it. I look at the future as being very bright, leaving home and having a life of my own, never ending up in a psychiatric hospital."

The treatment program produced far more than merely banishing Elizabeth's overt psychotic symptoms. Her view of herself and her family became more appropriate and realistic. Prior to treatment, her thoughts had been turned backward, clinging and holding onto her parents. After this period of treatment, she was actively thinking and planning in terms of her life ahead. Elizabeth made successful social adjustments at school where there had been none previously, and she dealt with subsequent problems of loss and transition with appropriate affect and without recourse to suicidal thoughts or activities. She left the hospital with significantly increased ego strength, including better ability to think, to plan ahead, and to control her own behavior. Elizabeth was in general more mature than before her decompensation. The risk of recurrence had been reduced and the scope and quality of her life experience had changed to something more open, alive, and forward-looking.

Following her discharge from the hospital Elizabeth stayed with her family for a short time. She then took an apartment, got a job, and for four months following discharge was in outpatient psychotherapy with the same woman psychiatric resident who had been her inpatient individual therapist.

Two and a half years after her discharge, the patient and her husband of two years contacted Dr. W. because they were interested in further outpatient psychotherapy for her. Both described their marriage as "pretty successful" though it had been somewhat "downhill" for the past five months. Her husband, also a former hospital patient, had done well in his follow-up outpatient psychotherapy and had started college while Elizabeth worked as an order clerk for a hardware company. Though claiming that she didn't resent supporting her husband, she said she wanted a college education for herself also, and she wanted to finish what she had started in psychotherapy but didn't want a woman therapist again. Elizabeth also expressed fear of her husband's abandoning her, but said that she realized she was irrational in always interpreting his anger as rejection. The second issue, which one can confront only to the degree that the first is resolved, is that of treatment effectiveness. There can be no meaningful measures of treatment effectiveness unless various approaches to treatment exist and can be compared. Unfortunately, studies of primarily psychological treatment approaches to extreme depression are rare. There is a body of literature, however, that strongly suggests the workability of psychological approaches with such patients and which helps to explain the results we achieved.

As Fenichel (1945) has stated succinctly, "Freud explained the depressive self-reproaches as accusations directed against the introjected object... Abraham added that often complaints appear to come counterwise from the introjected object actually made against the patient" (p. 398). While this classic dynamic explanation of depression may not fit all cases, it certainly seemed to fit the cases we treated. It would help to explain the patient's withdrawal and avoidance, which may be furthered by others' complicity in avoidance. Confirming Freud's ideas, Scholz (1973) found that suicidal patients showed more turning against the self as a defensive procedure than nonsuicidal patients. Scholz concluded "critical to the management and therapy of the suicidal individuals, then, is not merely the easing over of a particular crisis, but furthering the development of new means of coping with similar stress in the future" (p.2). Whereas Tabachnick (1973) says that some suicidal patients may have "creative suicidal crises" we believed that many suicidal crises could be made creative if "new means of coping with similar stress" could be developed during an "in vivo" experience in which powerful group influence could play a major reconstructive role.

The specific psychotherapeutic approach we took in these cases may be thought of as reinstitution of the original (basic) genetic event or transaction and then providing a corrective process. Since group influence, originally in the family group, is important in the development of severe depressive and suicidal behavior, it makes sense to marshal group corrective emotional experiences and thus we emphasized group therapy and the ward milieu.

Some authors, such as Bemporad (1970) question the classical psychoanalytic theory of depression. Bemporad emphasizes "dependency on a dominant other" but his concept does not necessarily conflict with Freud's. Rather it seems to point up, correctly, one of the major outcomes of the depressive's training, i.e., continuing to yield to the irrational authority of another person in ways that are self-destructive and depressing. Our enactments of harsh authoritarian oppression served not only to simulate the original kinds of "training" situations but reflected current situations for the patient also. Bemporad adds that the depressive's inability to express anger is related possibly to not being able to achieve autonomy and independence. The solution, then, would seem to be in eliciting a daringly independent, angry assertiveness on the part of the patient, in an objectively safe environment which encourages this appropriate assertiveness. This method would restore, as it were, the individual's instinctive response to oppression and relieve him or her of having to introject the anger.

The psychological treatment we employed can be reduced essentially to these steps:

1. Formulation of the conflict situation to which the patient originally responded with depression and suicidal inclinations.
2. Reenactment of the conflict situation.
3. Provision of corrective group influence, i.e., encouragement of assertiveness against the oppressive "authority."
4. Group approval (social reinforcement) of the new coping response.

5. Repeated sequences like the above, with repeated reenactment and later, verbal review of the process and further social reinforcement of the new response. This process is consistent with what Yalom (1975) had delineated as critical incidents in psychotherapy (pp. 25-29) providing corrective emotional experiences in group psychotherapy.

We do not identify our approach with any one school of psychology or psychotherapy. Psychodrama, psychoanalysis, and behavior modification were certainly in our minds at the time, though we were not "choosing a theory" so much as using what ideas were available. The problem is that, in general, none of these valuable theoretical models seem to get much use in determining the actual treatment of severe, incapacitating depression.

Our treatment results suggest that this approach can be quite effective. Our standard of effectiveness was "greatly increased ability to function productively in the real world," not just symptomatic relief. We do not endorse a standard such as "dischargeability" or "symptom relief" by themselves, because these criteria beg the question of real improvement and can mislead professionals and the public into emphasizing suppression instead of improvement.

The varieties of treatment outcomes suggested to us that the factor of acute vs. chronic was important but that even quite chronically depressed persons could benefit, in terms of our improvement criteria. The fact that none of our several depressed patients, who were deemed hopeless cases when we started, have committed suicide or required rehospitalization has been encouraging. We emphasize, however, that hospital treatment of this type needs to be followed by good quality outpatient psychotherapy. Effective hospital treatment can give the patient a real developmental opportunity.

References

Bemporad, J.R. New views on the psychodynamics of the depressive character. In S. Arieti (Ed.), *The world biennial of psychiatry and psychotherapy,* Vol. 1. New York: Basic Books, pp. 219-243, 1970.

Deikman, A. & Whitaker, L. *Humanizing a Psychiatric Ward: Changing from Drugs to Psychotherapy.* PSYCHOTHERAPY: THEORY, RESEARCH & PRACTICE, 16(2), 204-214, 1979.

Fenichel, O. *the psychoanalytic theory of neurosis.* New York: Norton, 1945.

Scholz, J.A. *Defense styles in suicide attempters.* J. CONSULT. PSYCHOL. 41, 70-73, 1973.

Tabachnick, N. *Creative suicidal crises,* ARCH. GEN. PSYCHIATRY, 29, 258-263, 1973.

Yalom, I.D. *The Theory and Practice of Group Psychotherapy,* 2nd Ed. New York: Basic Books, 1975.

Originally appearing in PSYCHOTHERAPY: THEORY, RESEARCH AND PRACTICE, Vol. 17 #1, Spring 1980

Phenothiazines and the
Therapist's Fear of Identification

IN THE current enthusiasm for phenothiazines in the treatment of psychosis, relatively little attention is given to the unconscious motives of the therapist for prescribing such medications. However, if we are to understand the prominent role of drug treatment we need to pay more attention to the need of staff members for phenothiazines. This article discusses several categories of staff anxiety and indicates the way in which the dispensing of medication to patients helps reduce that anxiety.

Identification

A primary source of anxiety for the staff lies in the unpleasantness of empathizing and identifying with the psychotic patient. In this respect, it is much more comfortable to work with neurotic patients. The staff tends to see neurotic patients as like themselves except for "hang-ups," and it is easy to identify with such patients and later "return" to one's own self with equanimity. The hallmark of psychotic behavior, however, is that it is not of this world: it is alien, bizarre, strange — the psychotic patient is "not in contact with reality" and "lives in a world of his own."

For example, it is one thing for a staff member to identify with a woman who is moderately depressed because her husband has left her. It is quite another matter for the staff member to identify with a patient who is screaming, who is smearing feces, who is psychotically suicidal and assaultive, who mutilates herself and tears off her clothes. Although the impulses represented by these psychotic behaviors are present in every staff member, they constitute precisely those impulses most strenuously suppressed and rigidly controlled. The deepest infantile wishes are represented in the overt and seemingly guilt-free regression of the psychotic patient who abandons the status of the adult for the humiliations and gratifications of the infant. Such passive, infantile wishes may be even more taboo than neurotic sexual behavior. To be labeled homosexual, impotent, or frigid can engender shame, but often less shame than to be labeled infantile. The penalty for giving way to such impulses is demonstrated in the fate of the psychotic patient: he is socially ostracized, imprisoned, assaulted by "treatment," and designated, perhaps for life, as inferior, dangerous and untrustworthy. To communicate with a psychotic patient by means of empathic identification is to recognize and experience the possibility that the psychotic form of experience could be one's own. It is understandable that staff may unconsciously struggle to achieve the opposite — disidentification.

Disidentification is accomplished whenever the staff member gives phenothiazines to a patient because it increases the psychological distance between that staff person and his patient: "Here is my psychotic patient, he is suffering from a disease for which he must have medicine, unlike myself who does not take such medicine. (I hope I do not catch his disease)." Giving the medicine implies that the problem is biochemical, possibly genetic, and reduces the possibility that the staff member might be vulnerable to psychosis.

Communication

The fear of identification and "contagion" on the part of the staff member is central to the problem of communicating with the psychotic patient. Communication means that two people come into psychological contact, and the boundary between them temporarily dissolves. It is not that communication is so difficult, but rather, that communication is so feared by the staff. Ordinarily, one assumes that the difficulty in teaching people to listen to what the psychotic patient is saying has to do with the obtuse symbolic form in which the patient's message is often communicated. But it becomes clear to a supervisor that the difficulty does not lie there, but in the staff member's *wish* not to hear, the wish not to be in contact, the wish to be able to continue regarding psychosis as something ego-alien; a foreign, other-world disease (Laing, 1967). It is precisely such an I-It relationship that is reinforced by the giving of phenothiazines, while the I-Thou relationship that is feared is correspondingly diminished (Buber, 1958). The staff member often seems even more intent on establishing a protective barrier than is the patient.

Intensity

Beyond the problem posed for the staff member by the primitive nature of psychotic impulses and their affective components, is the problem posed by the very *intensity* of psychotic affect. It is one thing to be angry; it is another thing to be murderous. In the range of unmodulated affect, the nightmare enters reality. If one works psychologically with psychotic patients, it is impossible not to be involved in that same intense, emotional flux. For many people, intense affect of any kind is anxiety-provoking and something alien to their ordinary lives. It often seems that among the helping professions this fear of intense affect tends to maintain the fantasy that because they are in the business of understanding patients' problems, the staff should not have "bad" feelings. Thus, the most difficult problem for nursing staff and resident psychiatrists and staff psychiatrists to deal with is their own intense anger, depression, erotic arousal, and frustrations in relation to their patients. They may assume that such intense feelings in themselves indicate that they, the staff, are bad helpers, that they should not have such feelings or that if they do, intellectual understanding should be able to take care of them; that is, to dispose of them. Only over a long period of time does a staff person develop the confidence that he can enter into such experiences knowing that he will "come back" undamaged, wiser, and with benefits for the patient and for himself.

If one studies the exact sequence of events that precede a decision to medicate a particular patient, one often discerns that the patient has shifted from a position of inactivity, depression, apathy, or indifference to one of noisy, "crazy," threatening, or messy activity. The staff person advising the use of or increase of phenothiazines in such a case often has not attempted to think of the change in behavior as potentially meaningful and possibly a sign of "progress." The staff member tends to react with alarm and feel the need to suppress the behavior, to lower the intensity of the patient's new affect and activity. In its worst form, the staff action constitutes a double message to the patient. On the one hand, the patient is told to talk about or otherwise communicate his feelings, and on the other hand, the actual communication by the patient is repudiated by the staff member. The giving of medication says, "Stop what you are doing, stop talking those crazy things — it makes me anxious. I prefer quiet symptoms (apathy is okay), your screaming and noisiness are intolerable." One gets the impression that, frequently, the actual expression or communication of the patient's feelings and thoughts is negatively reinforced or even punished.

Anger

As if this problem were not enough, the psychotic patient's negative attitude towards being "helped" puts a further strain on the would-be therapist. Psychotic patients do not readily grant the staff member the status of an actual helper, but indeed, equate him with the exploiter or the manipulator and are quite skillful in perceiving the need of the therapist for gratification, as their own parents wished for gratification from the success of their child (Hoover, 1971). The game of leading the therapist to his own position of impotence, frustration, and helplessness is embarked on with great energy and usually with complete success (Farber, 1966). To have one's self-esteem tied up in being a helping person and then to have that help rejected, to have one's sadism exposed and stimulated, all pose an experience not likely to be attractive to staff, particularly inexperienced staff, hoping to demonstrate that they are worthwhile by virtue of their ability to "save" their patients. The less sophistication the staff has as to what "help" is for psychotic patients, the more vulnerable they are to being reduced to tears, or rage, and finally, initiating a series of "therapeutic" decisions that run the gamut from transferring the patient to another hospital, to administering higher levels of drug dosage, or electric shock, or even lobotomy.

Thus, decisions to institute or increase drug programs can be the expression of suppressed anger or despair on the part of the staff at the frustrations the patient imposes upon them. They can maintain the image that they are being kindly and helpful, since drugs are "treatment," while at the same time they serve notice to the patient that the staff member is not defenseless and can reject as well as being rejected.

Dependency

Even if the therapist is successful in involving himself with the patient, the gratification he obtains from this development is soon modified by a horrified awareness of the intensity of the patient's dependency wishes. The therapist may have fantasies of being swallowed alive, of being drained to death, of having the patient's frantic fingers wrapped around his throat for life. In the intensity of that therapeutic embrace, nuclear, shared human anxieties are inescapably aroused, and staff members often become highly anxious by virtue of the equality therein revealed.

Giving the patient medication offers a way out, "I cannot stand the demands you make on me or the vision into myself you reveal. Go away, here's a pill instead. Take this instead of me."

Conclusion

Identification as a Reward

After such a list of horrors, the question may be asked, "Why would anyone want to work with psychotic patients?" And for many people the answer is a firm, "I don't," expressed either directly and consciously, or indirectly by their actions. In point of fact, however, the identification that the staff member unknowingly tries to defeat with medication is the road to growth and deep satisfaction for himself and his patient. Working psychologically with psychotic patients can be enriching, liberating and productive of that wisdom which seems to be hard won in any discipline; it is the wisdom that you are at one with other people, psychotic or not. This experience can be reassuring if we persist, because the effect of authentically encountering a psychotic patient is to see the costume of a monster dissolve and in its place find an engaging, understandable, and quite worthwhile human being (Green, 1964). In the process of exorcising the patient's demons — his self-condemnation, his fear of his impulses, his underestimation of his love and courage, his compressed hate and imprisoned grief — the therapist frees himself, for his own demons are not fundamentally different, just less strong or better contained. When the "I-Thou" of empathic identification is achieved, it effectively combats the sense of alienation that afflicts therapists as well as patients. Through this process, the identification that was feared becomes an affirmation.

Ultimately, psychological engagement with psychotic patients is an engagement with life in its full depth. If terror, despair, and rage are initial states of that process, love, nobility, and hope are not far away.

References

Buber, M. *I and thou.* New York: Charles Scribner's Sons, 1958.

Farber, L. *The therapeutic despair.* In *The Ways of the will,* New York: Basic Books, 1966, 158-183.

Green, H. *I never promised you a rose garden.* New York: The New American Library, 1964.

Hoover, C. *Prolonged schizophrenia and the will.* JOURNAL OF HUMANISTIC
   PSYCHOLOGY, 1971, 11, 2.
Laing, R. D. *The politics of experience.* New York: Pantheon Books, 1967.

Originally appearing in THE JOURNAL OF HUMANISTIC
PSYCHOLOGY, Fall 1971, Vol. 11 No. 2

Sufism and Psychiatry

T HE QUESTIONS "What is the purpose of living?" and "Why do I exist?" haunt modern Western civilization and the absence of an adequate answer to them has given rise to the "illness" of meaninglessness or anomie. Psychiatrists, themselves, are afflicted with this same illness, partly because the problem of the meaning of life is solved by a special type of perception rather than by logic — psychiatry is trapped by its commitment to rationalism.

Sufism, on the other hand, is a tradition devoted to the development of the higher intuitive capacity needed to deal with this issue. By taking advantage of the special science of the Sufis, Western civilization may be able to extricate itself from its dilemma and contribute to the development of man's full capacities.

"I think it not improbable that man, like the grub that prepares a chamber for the winged thing it never has seen but is to be — that man may have cosmic destinies that he does not understand." — Justice Oliver Wendell Holmes[3]

Psychiatry can be defined as the science of reducing mental suffering and enhancing mental health. To date, the field has been primarily concerned with the first part of the definition. For example, in the Index to the *Standard Edition of the Complete Psychological Works of Sigmund Freud,*[19] the word "neurosis" has over 400 references. In contrast, "health" is not even listed. The imbalance tends to be true of contemporary texts, as well. This situation is understandable because psychiatry originated to deal with disordered function. The question, "What is the function of a healthy person?" which requires the further question, "What is the purpose of human life?" is not usually asked because it is assumed to be answered by simple observation of the everyday activities of the general population.[18]

Underlying all of our activities are purposes that give meaning and direction to our efforts. One might go to college to become a lawyer, or save money to buy a car, or vote to elect an official; all of these actions are vitalized by purpose and if the purpose is removed, the activities may cease. That being the case, what is the purpose of human life, itself? What answer do we have to the question, "Why am I?" A direct answer is not usually attempted in our culture but an indirect answer is there, implicit in scientific publication and in the world view that permeates from scientific authority to the public at large. We are told either that the question lies outside the scope of science or that the question is false because the human race has developed by chance in a random universe. Erwin Schrodinger, the physicist, commented on this problem:

> "Most painful is the absolute silence of all our scientific investigations towards our questions concerning the meaning and scope of the whole display. The more attentively we watch it, the more aimless and foolish it appears to be. The show that is going on obviously acquires a meaning only with regard to the mind that contemplates it. But what science tells us about this relationship is patently absurd: as if the mind had only been produced by that very display that it is now watching and would pass away with it when the sun finally cools down and the earth has been turned into a desert of fire and snow." [9]

We pay a price for the nonanswer of science. Psychiatry has recognized the existence of "anomie" — an "illness" of meaninglessness, of alienation or estrangement from one's fellow men. Anomie stems from the absence of a deeply felt purpose. Our contemporary scientific culture also has had little to say about meaning, itself, except to suggest and assume that man imposes meaning; he does not discover it. That this assumption may be incorrect and productive of pathology is a possibility that needs to be considered. It may be that the greatest problem confronting psychiatry is that it lacks a theoretical framework adequate to provide meaning for its patients, many of whom are badly handicapped in their struggle to overcome neurotic problems because the conceptual context within which they view themselves provides neither meaning, direction, nor hope. That context derives from the modern, scientific world view of an orderly, mechanical, indifferent universe in which human beings exist as an interesting biochemical phenomenon—barren of purpose. Survival is a purpose, but not enough. Working for the survival of others and to alleviate suffering is a purpose but it loses its meaning against a picture of the human race with no place to go, endlessly repeating the same patterns, or worse.

The issue of meaning increases in importance as one's own death becomes less theoretical and more probable. Life goals of acquisition become utterly futile, for no achievements of money, fame, sex, power, and security are able to stop the relentless slide toward extinction. Our bodies age and our minds grow increasingly restless seeking a solution to death. As former goals lose their significance, life can easily appear to be a random cycle of trivial events and the search may end in the most profound despair or a dull resignation. The widespread use of sedatives, alcohol, and narcotics is related to the wish to suppress despair and substitute sensation for meaning.

Such "existential" despair is so culturally accepted that it is often defined as healthy. Consider the following extract from *The American Handbook of Psychiatry*:

> "To those who have obtained some wisdom in the process of reaching old age, death often assumes meaning as the proper outcome of life. It is nature's way of assuring much life and constant renewal. Time and customs change but the elderly tire of changing; it is time for others to take over, and the elderly person is willing to pass quietly from the scene."[5]

So we should end, according to the voice of reason, neither with a bang nor a whimper, but in a coma of increasing psychological fatigue.

The problem is illustrated concretely and poignantly by the dilemma of many psychiatrists, themselves. A recent article in the AMERICAN JOURNAL OF PSYCHIATRY concerned a number of professional therapists, ages 35 to 45, mostly of a psychoanalytic background, who formed a group which at first provided peer supervision and later attempted to function as a leaderless therapy group for its members who, as it turned out, were in a crisis:

> "The original members of the group we have described were remarkably homogeneous in their purposes in joining. The conscious reason was to obtain help in mastering a phase in their own development, the mid-life crisis. We refer to that stage of life in which the individual is aware that half of his time has been used up and the general pattern or trajectory of his work and personal life is clear. At this time, one must give up the normal manic defenses of early life — infinite faith in one's abilities and the belief that anything is possible. The future becomes finite, childhood fantasies have been fulfilled or unrealized, and there is no longer a sense of having enough time for anything. One becomes aware that one's energy and physical and mental abilities will be declining. The individual must think of prolonging and conserving rather than expanding. The reality of one's limited life span comes into sharp focus, and the work of mourning the passing of life begins in earnest."[4]

The "healthy" attitude recommended here would seem to be a stoical and courageous facing of a reality defined by certain assumptions prevalent in our culture: limited human capacity and limited meaning to life. From this point of view, it can be maintained that the second half of life should be used to adjust oneself to the final termination of individual consciousness. The grimness of such a goal may have resonated in the authors' minds for they go on to brighten up the picture.

> "In Erikson's terms, the individual must at this time struggle to achieve intimacy and creativity and avoid isolation and

stagnation. If the work of mourning one's lost youth is carried through and the realities of the human situation are fully accepted, the ensuing years can be a period of increased productivity and gratification."[4]

"Increased productivity" and "gratification" are invoked to suggest that something good is still possible after 40, but the possibilities still would seem to call more for resignation than for vitality and continued growth. This ultimately circumscribed view of human life is widely held by psychiatrists. Even in the relatively affirmative writings of Erikson, the Eight Stages of Man have some of the flavor of a survival manual.[1]

In contrast to our scientific culture and its psychology, Eastern introspective (mystical) disciplines have focused on meaning and purpose but have employed a strategy in which the use of intellect and reason is neither central nor basic to the process of investigation. Procedures such as meditation, fasting, chanting, and other unusual practices have been employed as part of an integrated strata whose exact pattern and content depended on the nature and circumstances of the individual and of the culture in which the teaching was taking place.

Unfortunately, the literature of Eastern psychological disciplines has not been much practical use for contemporary Western readers. Academic study of such texts does not seem to develop wisdom or improve personality functioning, and exotic practices themselves have proven to be elusive and tricky instruments. For example, procedures such as meditation that were once part of a unique and individually prescribed pattern of development are now extracted from their original context and offered for consumption as if they were a kind of vitamin that was good for everyone, ridiculously cheap, and devoid of side effects. Those who use these components of a specialized technology may obtain increased calmness, enjoyment, and improvement of efficiency — but without noticeable gain in wisdom. They answer the question, "Who am I?" by reciting dogma, not by realization, and for all of the "bliss" that may be displayed, the person's essential knowledge appears unchanged. For those who fare less well with meditation, schizoid withdrawal, grandiosity, vanity, and dependency flourish under the disguise of spiritual practice. Perhaps the worst effect of indiscriminate and unintegrated use of these techniques is that people come to believe that the effects they experience are the measure of Eastern esoteric science. The end result is that they confirm and strengthen their customary conceptual prison from which they desperately need to escape.

The crux of the problem is that modern Westerners need technical means specific to their time and culture. Although such a statement makes perfect sense to most people when the subject concerns the training of physicians or physicists, training in the "spiritual" is believed to be a different matter. Programs and techniques 2000 years old are assumed to be adequate to the task: indeed, it seems that that the older and more alien they are, the better they are received.

Fortunately, some traditional materials have recently been made available in a form suitable for contemporary needs; they offer practical benefits of interest to psychiatry as well as the general public. These materials address themselves to the question, "Who am I?" but they do so in a unique manner:

Why We Are Here

Walking one evening along a deserted road, Mulla Nasrudin saw a troop of horsemen coming towards him. His imagination started to work; he saw himself captured and sold as a slave, or impressed into the army. Nasrudin bolted, climbed a wall into a graveyard, and lay down in an open tomb.

Puzzled at this strange behavior, the men — honest travelers — followed him. They found him stretched out, tense and quivering.

"What are you doing in that grave? We saw you run away. Can we help you?"

"Just because you can ask a question does not mean there is a straightforward answer to it," said the Mulla, who now realized

what had happened. "It all depends upon your viewpoint. If you
must know, however: I am here because of you, and you are here
because of me."[11]

"Why We Are Here" is a teaching story adapted from the classical
literature of Sufism. Teaching stories, in a form appropriate to the
modern reader, are the means now being made available to prepare
Western intellects for learning what they need to know. The stories,
such as "Why We Are Here," are built of patterns, depth upon depth,
offering resonance at the reader's level, whatever that may be. Teaching
stories have more than one function. They provide the means for
people to become aware of their patterns of behavior and thinking so
as to accomplish a refinement of their perception and the development
of an attitude conducive to learning. Some stories are also designed
to communicate with what is conceived to be the innermost part of
the human being.

Speaking metaphorically, Sufis say the stories make contact with
a nascent "organ" of superior perception, supplying a type of "nutrition" that assists its development. It is this latter function that is of
particular importance to understand; it is the key to the possible role
of Sufism in helping to diagnose and cure, eventually, the basic illness
that afflicts psychiatrists as well as their patients.

Sufism is usually thought of as a Middle Eastern mystical religion.
According to Idries Shah,[3] that description is misleading. Referring
to copious Sufi classics, he states that Sufism is the method of developing the higher perceptual capacity inherent in human beings and
vital to their happiness.

This method is referred to by classical Sufi authorities as a "science" in the sense that it is a specific body of knowledge, applied according to the principles known by a Teacher, to achieve a specific
and predictable result. That result is the capacity to know, directly
(not through the senses or the usual intellectual functions) the meaning of human life and the inner significance of ordinary events. The

change in consciousness that results is regarded as the next step in the evolution of the human race, a step that we must take or perish.

Ordinarily, we do not consider that the zone of normal perception may be so limited as to preclude the experience of a significant dimension of reality, the one with which mystical disciplines were ordinarily concerned. According to the Sufis, meaning is just such a perceptual problem.

An illustration of this issue at the level of biology has been described by C. F. Pantin, former Chairman of Trustees of the British Museum:

> "A danger in this sort of behavior analysis — one which I fell into myself —is that it looks so complete that if you are not careful, you may start to imagine that you can explain the whole behavior of the sea anemone by very simple reflexes — like the effect of a coin in a slot machine. But quite by accident, I discovered that apart from reflexes, there was a whole mass of purposive behavior connected with the spontaneous activity of the anemone about which we simply know nothing. (Actually, this behavior was too slow to be noticed; it was outside our sensory spectrum for the time being)." [2]

Similarly, the purpose of human life may be outside the perceptual spectrum of the ordinary person. To widen that spectrum, to provide "sight," is the goal of Sufism.

The Sufis claim that mankind is psychologically "ill" because people do not perceive who they really are and what their situation is. Thus, they are "blind" or "asleep" because their latent, higher capacity is underdeveloped — partly because they are too caught up in the exercise of their lesser capacities for purposes of vanity, greed, and fear. The development of the necessary perception is called "awakening" and the perception, itself, is called "Knowledge." It is often said that the science of awakening mankind has been present for many thousands of years but, because of the special nature of the process and of the Knowledge that it brings, the dissemination of the science has fluctuated throughout history and has never taken place on a large scale, partly because of the resistance this idea provokes. [14]

Radios

"I was once in a certain country where the local people had never heard the sounds emitted from a radio receiver. A transistorized set was being brought to me; and while waiting for it to arrive I tried to describe it to them. The general effect was that the description fascinated some and infuriated others. A minority became irrationally hostile about radios.

"When I finally demonstrated the set, the people could not tell the difference between the voice from the loudspeaker and someone nearby. Finally, like us, they managed to develop the necessary discrimination of each, such as we have.

"And, when I questioned them afterwards, all swore that what they had imagined from descriptions of radios, however painstaking, did not correspond with the reality."[12]

If, instead of talking of a radio receiver, the term "intuition" is used, the meaning of the analogy might be more clear. Ordinary intuition, however, is considered by the Sufis to be a lower level imitation of the superior form of intuition with which Sufism is concerned. For the moment, however, some consideration of the place of ordinary intuition in the activity of the scientist may be helpful in illustrating the practical reality of the Sufic position.

Although the scientific method is taught as if data plus logic equal discovery, those who have studied how discoveries are actually made come to quite different conclusions. Wigner, a Nobel prize-winning physicist comments:

"The discovery of the laws of nature requires first and foremost intuition, conceiving of pictures and a great many subconscious processes. The use and also the confirmation of these laws is another matter... logic comes after intuition."[2]

An extensive, detailed study of the process of scientific discovery was made by Polanyi, formerly Professor of Physical Chemistry at the University of Manchester and then Senior Research Fellow at Merton College, Oxford.[7] Polanyi studied scientists' descriptions of how they arrived at their "breakthroughs" to a new view of reality. He found, like Wilmer, that logic, data, and reasoning came last — another channel of knowing was in use. There was no word for that channel in ordinary vocabulary so he used an analogy to convey its nature:

"And we know that the scientist produces problems, has hunches, and elated by these anticipations, pursues the quest that should fulfill these anticipations. This quest is guided throughout by feelings of a deepening coherence and these feelings have a fair chance of proving right. We may recognize here the powers of a dynamic intuition. The mechanism of this power can be illuminated by an analogy. Physicists speak of potential energy that is released when a weight slides down a slope. Our search for deeper coherence is guided by a potentiality. We feel the slope toward deeper insight as we feel the direction in which a heavy weight is pulled along a steep incline. It is this dynamic intuition which guides the pursuit of discovery."[2]

Not only do the Sufis contend that man needs more than intellect and emotion to guide him, but that those two "servants," in the absence of the "master;" have taken over the house and forgotten their proper function:

The Servants And The House

At one time there was a wise and kindly man, who owned a large house. In the course of his life he often had to go away for long periods. When he did this, he left his servants in charge of the house.

One of the characteristics of these people was that they were very forgetful. They forgot, from time to time, why they were in the house; so they carried out their tasks repetitiously.

At other times they thought that they should be doing things in a different way from the way in which their duties had been assigned to them. This was because they had lost track of their functions.

Once, when the master was away for a long time, a new generation of servants arose, who thought that they actually owned the house. Since they were limited by their immediate world, however, they thought that they were in a paradoxical situation. For instance, sometimes they wanted to sell the house, and could find no buyers, because they did not know how to go about it. At other times, people came inquiring about buying the house and asking to see the title-deeds, but since they did not know anything about deeds the servants thought that these people were mad and not genuine buyers at all.

Paradox was also evidenced by the fact that supplies for the house kept mysteriously appearing, and this provision did not fit in with the assumption that the inmates were responsible for the whole house.

Instructions for running the house had been left, for purposes of refreshing the memory, in the master's apartments. But after the first generation, so sacrosanct had these apartments become that nobody was allowed to enter them, and they became considered to be an impenetrable mystery. Some, indeed, held that there was no such apartment at all, although they could see its doors. These doors, however, they explained as something else: a part of the decoration of the walls.

Such was the condition of the staff of a house, which neither took over the house nor stayed faithful to their original commitment."[15]

The Sufis specify that the development of man's superior capacity has its own rigorous requirements: adequate preparation of suitable students, the correct learning situation, and the activity of a Teacher — one who has reached the goal and by means of that special knowledge is equipped to teach according to the needs of the particular culture, the particular time, historical period, and the particular person. Because of these requirements, there is no set dogma or technique that is utilized in a standard fashion: the form is only a vehicle and is constantly changing.

"All religious presentations are varieties of one truth, more or less distorted. This truth manifests itself in various peoples, who become jealous of it, not realizing that its manifestation accords with their needs. It cannot be passed on in the same form because of the difference in the minds of different communities. It cannot be reinterpreted, because it must grow afresh."[17]

Thus, Sufis differentiate their science from traditional religions, whether Christian, Judaic, Buddhist, Moslem, or Hindu, because such religions have solidified around set rituals, forms, exercises, and dogmas that tend to be handed out to everyone regardless of the context and individual differences. According to Idries Shah, *"even organizations designated as Sufi Orders may undergo this... crystallization into priesthood and traditionalism. In the originally Sufic groupings where this fossilization has indeed taken place, their fixation upon a repetitious usage of Sufi materials provides a warning for the would-be Sufi that such an organization has 'joined the world.'"*[17]

We have examples of this problem within the field of psychiatry, itself. In Freud's time, for example, the Vienna Circle was open to all who had sufficient interest and capacity to participate, regardless of what formal degrees or titles they possessed. Today, the American Psychoanalytic Institute will not accord full membership to anyone not possessing an M.D., even though the functional relevance of a medical degree for the theory and practice of psychoanalysis can scarcely be discerned. A similar stiffening, sclerosing process seems to invade every human organization.

With this in mind, we can understand the Sufic contention that religions were initially based on the development of a higher form of perception but, inevitably, they became ossified, lost their capacity to function in that way, and now persist as archaic structures, hollow shells good only for fulfilling social and emotional needs. Furthermore, most "mystical experiences" are regarded by the Sufis as being primarily emotional and have little practical importance — except for the deleterious effect of causing people to believe they are being "spiritual" when they are not. Self-deception is at work in such cases and blocks progress toward the development of higher perceptions.

Strange Agitation

Sahl Abdullah once went into a state of violent agitation, with physical manifestations, during a religious meeting.

Ibn Salim said: "What is this state?"

Sahl said: "This was not, as you imagine, power entering me. It was, on the contrary, due to my own weakness."

Others present remarked: "If that was weakness, what is power?"

"Power," said Sahl, "is when something like this enters, and the mind and body manifest nothing at all."[17]

The ordinary man is said to suffer from confusion or "sleep" because of his tendency to use his customary thought patterns and perception to try to understand the meaning of his life and reach fulfillment. Consequently, his experience of reality is constricted, and dangerously so, because he tends to be unaware of it. Sufis assert that the awakening of man's latent perceptual capacity is not only crucial for his happiness but is the principal goal of his current phase of existence, it is man's evolutionary task. Rumi, the great Sufi poet, stated this explicitly:

This Task

"You have a duty to perform. Do anything else, do any number of things, occupy your time fully, and yet, if you do not do this task, all your time will have been wasted."[17]

How Far You Have Come!

*"Originally, you were clay. From being mineral, you
became vegetable. From vegetable, you became animal, and from
animal, man. During these periods man did not know where he
was going, but he was being taken on a long journey nonetheless.
And you have to go through a hundred different worlds yet."* [17]

According to the Sufis, only with the knowledge that perceptual
development brings can human beings know the meaning of human
life, both in terms of the particular events of a person's life and the
destiny of the human race.

*Once upon a time there was a city. It was very much like
any other city, except it was almost permanently enveloped in
storms.*

*The people who lived in it loved their city. They had, of
course, adjusted to its climate. Living amid storms meant that
they did not notice thunder, lightning and rain most of the time.*

*If anyone pointed out the climate they thought he was being
rude or boring. After all, having storms was what life was like,
wasn't it? Life went on like this for many centuries.*

*This would have been all very well, but for one thing: The
people had not made a complete adaptation to a storm-climate.
The result was that they were afraid, unsettled and frequently
agitated.*

*Since they had never seen any other kind of place in living
memory, cities or countries without some storms belonged to
folklore and the babbling of lunatics.*

*There were two tried recipes which caused them to forget,
for a time, their tensions: to make changes and to obsess
themselves with what they had. At any given moment in
their history, some sections of the population would have their
attention fixed on change, and others on possessions of some
kind. The unhappy ones would only then be those who were*

doing neither.

Rain poured down, but nobody did anything about it because it was not a recognized problem. Wetness was a problem, but nobody connected it with rain. Lightning started fires, which were a problem, but these were regarded as individual events without a consistent cause.

You may think it remarkable that so many people knew so little for so long.

But then we tend to forget that, compared to present-day information, most people in history have known almost nothing about anything and even contemporary knowledge is daily being modified — and even proved wrong.[12]

Most psychotherapy focuses on uncovering the fantasies that shape neurotic action and on clarifying and resolving the conflicts of wishes and fears that lead an individual to the repetitive, self-defeating behaviors for which they usually seek therapy. These functions of psychotherapy are necessary and important. However, the resolution of neurotic problems, while it may be a necessary first step for an individual, is neither the measure of health nor of human potentiality. Freud's model of man as an organism seeking relief from tension, forced to negotiate a compromise among instinct, reason, and society, leaves even the most successful negotiator in a position of impoverishment as pathological, in its own way, as any illness listed in the diagnostic manual. This is because the usual psychiatric concept of health is both barren and narrow. Even the most "humanistic" of current psychologies that offer, in principle, equal attention to such dimensions of human experience as the playful, the creative, and "the spiritual," have no clear concept of the nature of the problem and little to suggest for its solution. "Self-realization" is advocated, but just what the self is that is to be realized and what that realization might be are not made explicit.

All of these therapies and theories are in the same boat because they share the fundamental limiting assumptions about man that are basic to our culture. Unwittingly, they help maintain the lack of perception that is the basic dysfunction of the human race and hinders the development of the higher capacities that are needed. In this sense, psychiatry, whether of the neurochemical or psychoanalytic variety or a combination of both, perpetuates the endemic illness of meaninglessness and arrested human development — it has no remedy for the cultural affliction that cripples normal people.

Thus, we arrive at the dilemma of the group of psychiatrists in "mid-life" crisis described above. They illustrate the point. Their science is caught within the same closed room in which they find themselves; indeed, it helps to bar the door. Psychoanalytic theory, the masterpiece of a genius, is so powerful and encompassing a schema that all phenomena seem to be contained within its walls; its proponents have come to love their city — storms notwithstanding — and they are almost never forced to reappraise their world.

However, existentialism has helped some psychiatrists look to the underpinnings of their profession. Rychlak, writing in *The American Handbook of Psychiatry*, summarizes:

> "Building on the theme of alienation first introduced by Hegel, and then popularized in the writings of Kierkegaard, the existentialists argue that man has been alienated from his true (phenomenal) nature by science's penchant for objective measurement, control, and stilted, non-teleological description." [8]

Through existentialism, purpose and meaning have come to have advocates such as the psychoanalyst, Avery Weisman:

> "The existential core of psychoanalysis is whatever nucleus of meaning and being there is that can confront both life and death. Unless he accepts this as his indispensable reality, the psychoanalyst is like a man wandering at night in a strange city." [21]

How can the psychoanalyst find that nucleus of meaning, let alone accept it? The group of psychiatrists in mid-life crisis are missing that center because it is missing from the very discipline they practice and teach. Psychiatry cannot address the issue of meaning because of the limited nature of its concept of man and because of its ignorance of the means needed to develop the capacity to perceive it.

In contrast, Sufism regards its task as the development of the higher perceptual capacity of man, his conscious evolution. According to Sufi authorities, the knowledge of how to do this has always existed. It had a flowering in Islam during the Middle Ages, during which the term "Sufis" came into use, but it had other names, centuries before. The Sufis regard Moses, Christ, and Mohammed as Teachers of the same basic process — their external forms and the means they employed were different, but the inner activity was the same. The traditional forms that we see around us in current times are said to be the residue of a science whose origins extend back to the beginnings of man's history. The problem is that our thinking has been conditioned to associate "awakening" to vegetarian diets, chanting, chastity, whirling dances, meditation on "chakras," koans and mantras, beards, robes, and solemn faces — because all of these features of once vital systems have been preserved and venerated as if they were still useful for achieving the same goal. The parts, or a collection of them, are mistaken for the whole. It is as if a car door, lying on the ground, were labeled "automobile" and hopeful travelers diligently opened and closed its window, waiting expectantly for it to transport them to a distant city.

Meditation, asceticism, special diets, and the like, should be regarded as technical devices that sometimes had a specific place in a coherent system prescribed for the individual. When used properly by a Teacher, they formed a time-limited container for a content that was timeless. Now, many old and empty containers labeled "spiritual" litter the landscape. The importation and wide use of these unintegrated forms attest to the immortality of institutions and customs, rather than the present usefulness of the activities.

The Sufis maintain that, nevertheless, amid all this confusion, the science of "conscious evolution" continues in a contemporary form, invisible to those expecting the traditional. *"Speak to everyone in accordance with his degree of understanding"* was a saying of Mohammed.[10] Idries Shah states that he is one of those speaking now to contemporary man, Eastern as well as Western, in a way appropriate to the task of educating people who do not realize how much they have to learn. R. L. Thomson, writing in *The Brook Postgraduate Gazette*, agrees:

> *"The problems of approaching the Salle work are such that Idries Shah's basic efforts do seem necessary. Little help is to be found in the academic approach based on linguistics and history."*[20]

Most of Idries Shah's writings consist of carefully selected and translated groups of teaching stories, including the ones I have quoted. His translations are exceptionally clear and digestible to a modern reader. The stories provide templates to which we can match our own behavior. We accept them because they are so deceptively impersonal — the situations are preserved as the history of someone else. The story slides past our vigilant defenses and is stored in our minds until the moment when our own thinking or situation matches the template — then it suddenly arises in awareness and we "see" as in a mirror, the shape and meaning of what we are actually doing. The analogical form can evade the categorizing of our rational thought and reach other sectors of the mind.

The Design

> *A Sufi on the Order of the Naqshbandi was asked:*
>
> *"Your Order's name means, literally, 'The Designers.' What do you design, and what use it is?"*
>
> *He said: "We do a great deal of designing, and it is most useful. Here is a parable of one such form":*
>
> *Unjustly imprisoned, a tinsmith was allowed to receive a rug woven by his wife. He prostrated himself upon the rug day after day to say his prayers, and after some time he said to his jailers:*

"I am poor and without hope, and you are wretchedly paid. But I am a tinsmith. Bring my tin and tools and I shall make small artifacts which you can sell in the market, and we will both benefit."

The guards agreed to this, and presently the tinsmith and they were both making a profit, from which they bought food and comfort for themselves.

Then, one day, when the guards went to the cell, the door was open, and he was gone.

Many years later, when this man's innocence had been established, the man who had imprisoned him asked him how he had escaped, what magic he had used. He said:

"It is a matter of design, and design within design. My wife is a weaver. She found the man who had made the locks of the cell door, and got the design from him. This she wove into the carpet, at the spot where my head touched in prayer five times a day. I am a metal-worker, and this design looked to me like the inside of a lock. I designed the plan of the artifacts to obtain the materials to make the key — and I escaped."

"That," said the Naqshbandi Sufi, "is one of the ways man may make his escape from the tyranny of his captivity."[16]

Teaching stories, such as the above, are tools that depend on the motivation of the user and his or her capacity or level of skill. As understanding increases, the tools can be used for finer and deeper work. The more one experiences and uses them, the more remarkable they seem to be: they lend credence to Idries Shah's claim that Sufism is a science whose boundaries contain modern psychology but go beyond it. He states:

"... Sufism is itself a far more advanced psychological system than any which is yet developed in the West. Neither is this psychology Eastern in essence, but human."[14]

According to Shah, the initial step needed to be taken by most human beings is to become aware of automatic pattern-thinking, the conditioned associations and indoctrinated values that limit human perception and receptivity. The teaching story is used for this purpose, illustrating at one step removed, the egocentric thinking of which we are usually oblivious:

That's Why They Bunged It Up

Nasrudin was very thirsty and was happy when he saw by the roadside a water-pipe whose outlet was bunged with a piece of wood.

Putting his open mouth near the stopper, he pulled. There was such a rush of water that he was knocked over.

"Oho!" roared the Mulla. "That's why they blocked you up, is it? And you have not yet learned any sense!"[13]

Personal Wisdom

"I don't want to be a man," said a snake.

"If I were a man, who would hoard nuts for me?" asked the squirrel.

"People," said the rat, "have such weak teeth that they can hardly do any gnawing."

"And as for speed..." said a donkey, "they can't run at all, in comparison to me."[12]

Teaching stories such as these have clarified patterns of my own thought, permitting me to notice similar patterns in my patients and to make appropriate interventions. One such story whose content is explicit, is the following:

Vanity

A Sufi sage once asked his disciples to tell him what their vanities had been before they began to study with him.

The first said: "I imagined that I was the most handsome

man in the world."
    The second said: "I believed that, since I was religious,
I was one of the elect."
    The third said: "I believed I could teach."
    And the fourth said: "My vanity was greater than all
these; for I believed that I could learn."
    The sage remarked:
    "And the fourth disciple's vanity remains the greatest, for
his vanity is to show that he once had the greatest vanity." [12]

Having read this story, I later observed myself using the same
strategy as the fourth disciple; specifically, I was berating myself for
a personal failing. The context differed from the specific situation
of the story but the pattern was the same. The story flashed in my
mind like a mirror and I understood the role of vanity in my self-
reproach. The "illumination" provoked a wry smile and ended my
self-flagellation. Sometime later, I listened to a patient present a
simi-lar pattern, recognized it, and, using humor, was able to point
out the concealed intent.

The point of view and the learning principles presented in the
teaching stories are tough-minded and emphasize the responsibility
of each person for his or her own conduct and fulfillment. Such an
attitude is not unfamiliar to psychiatry. However, developing a correct
attitude is only the first step in Sufic science, a step called "learning how to learn." Responsibility, sincerity, humility, patience,
generosity — these are not ends in themselves but are tools that
must be acquired before a person can proceed further. It is what comes
after this first step that sharply distinguished Sufism from all of
the psychotherapeutic and "growth-oriented" disciplines with
which we are familiar. The Sufis regard their system as being far in
advance of ours because it extends beyond conceptual and technical
limits of our psychology and embodies a method for assisting man

to develop the special perception upon which his welfare, and that of the human race, depends. When asked to prove their assertion, Sufis insist that we should pay attention to the necessity for undertaking preparatory training and then experiencing the domain in question. Such claims and requirements often provoke a haughty dismissal:

Three Epochs

1. Conversation in the 5th century:

"It is said that silk is spun by insects, and does not grow on trees."

"And diamonds are hatched from eggs, I suppose? Pay no attention to such an obvious lie."

"But there are surely many wonders in remote islands?"

"It is this very craving for the abnormal which produces fantastic invention."

"Yes, I suppose it is obvious when you think about it — that such things are all very well for the East, but could never take root in our logical and civilized society."

2. In the 6th century:

"A man has come from the East, bringing some small live grubs."

"Undoubtedly a charlatan of some kind, I suppose he says that they can cure toothache?"

"No, rather more amusing. He says that they can 'spin silk.' He has brought them with terrible sufferings, from one Court to another, having obtained them at the risk of his very life."

"This fellow has merely decided to exploit a superstition which was old in my great grandfather's time."

"What shall we do with him, my Lord?"

"Throw his infernal grubs into the fire, and beat him for his pains until he recants. These fellows are wondrously bold. They need showing that we're not all ignorant peasants here, willing

to listen to any wanderer from the East."

3. In the 20th century:
"You say that there is something in the East which we have not yet discovered here in the West? Everyone has been saying that for thousands of years. But in this century we'll try anything: our minds are not closed. Now give me a demonstration. You have fifteen minutes before my next appointment. If you prefer to write it down, here's a half-sheet of paper." [12]

If history has any value as a guide, it indicates that we should pay attention to the information now being provided to us by contemporary Sufism and not pass this opportunity without investigating it. Robert E. Ornstein, in his textbook, *The Psychology of Consciousness*, concludes:

"A new synthesis is in process within modern psychology. This synthesis combines the concerns of the esoteric traditions with the research methods and technology of modern science. In complement to this process, and feeding it, a truly contemporary approach to the problems of consciousness is arising from the esoteric traditions themselves." [6]

Psychiatrists need to recognize that their patients' psychological distress stems from three levels:

a) from conflicts of wishes, fears, and fantasies;

b) from an absence of perceived meaning; and

c) from a frustration of the need to progress in an evolutionary sense, as individuals and as a race.

The first level is the domain in which psychiatry functions. The second and third levels require a science appropriate to the task. The special knowledge of the Sufis may enable us to put together materials already at hand: our present knowledge of psychodynamics, our system of universal education, our technology, our resources, and our free society, to create the conditions that will permit the development of man's full capacities, as yet unrealized.

References

1. Erickson E. *Childhood and Society*. W. W. Norton, New York, 1950.
2. Greene, M., Ed. *Toward a Unity of Knowledge*. PSYCHOL. ISSUES, 6: (2). International Universities Press, New York, 1969.
3. Holmes, O. W. Cited in Murphy, G., *Human Potentialities*. Basic Books, New York, 1958.
4. Hunt. W., and Issacharoff, A. *History and Analysis of a leaderless group of professional therapists*. AM. J. PSYCHIATRY, 132: 11, 1166, 1975.
5. Lidz, T. *On the life cycle*. In Artieti, S., Ed., *The American Handbook of Psychiatry*. Basic Books, New York, 1974.
6. Ornstein, R. E. *The Psychology of Consciousness*. W. H. Freeman & Co., San Francisco, 1972.
7. Polanyi, M. *Personal Knowledge*. University of Chicago Press, Chicago, 1956.
8. Rychiak, J. F. *The personality*. In Artieti, S., Ed., *The American Handbook of Psychiatry*, Basic Books New York, 1974.
9. Schrodinger, E. *What Is Life? Mind and Matter*. Cambridge University Press, London, 1969.
10. Shah, I. *Caravan of Dreams*. Octagon Press, London, 1966.
11. Shah, I. *The Exploits of the Incomparable Mulla Nasrudin*. E. P. Dutton, New York. 1972. ©1966 by Mulla Nasrudin Enterprises, Ltd.
12. Shah, I. *The Magic Monastery*. E. P. Dutton, New York, 1972, ©1972 by Idries Shah.
13. Shah, I. *The Pleasantries of the Incredible Mulla Nasrudin*. E. P. Dutton, New York, 1971. ©1968 by Mulla Nasrudin Enterprises, Ltd.
14. Shah, I. *The Sufis*. Doubleday, Anchor Books. Garden City, N. Y., 1971.
15. Shah, I. *Tales of the Dervishes*. E. P. Dutton, New York, 1970.
16. Shah, I. *Thinkers of the East*. Penguin Books, Baltimore, 1972. ©1971 by Idries Shah.
17. Shah, I. *The Way of the Sufi*. E. P. Dutton, New York, 1970.
18. Strachey, J., Ed. *The Standard Edition of the Complete Psychological Works of Sigmund Freud*, XXI. Hogarth Press, London, 1961.
19. Strachey, J,, Ed. *The Standard Edition of the Complete Psychological Works of Sigmund Freud*, XXIV. Hogarth Press, London, 1974.
20. Thomson, A. L. *Psychology end science from the ancient east*. BROOK POSTGRAD. GAZ., 2: 1, 1973.
21. Weisman, A., *The Existential Care of Psychoanalysis*. Little, Brown, and Co., Boston, 1965.

22. Williams, L. F., Ed. *Sufi Studies: East and West*. E. P. Dutton. New York, 1974.

Originally published in *The World of the Sufi*
by Idries Shah, Ishk Book Service, 1979

Bimodal Consciousness

The human organism has two basic modes of function: (1) the receptive mode oriented toward the intake of the environment, and (2) the action mode oriented toward manipulation of the environment. Both physiological and psychological dimensions are integrated in these modes. By utilizing this model we can understand a number of puzzling phenomena in the fields of attention, mystical perception, hallucinogenic drugs, and psychosis. Although states of consciousness associated with the receptive mode are often pejoratively labeled as "regressive" or "unreal," there is evidence for considering such modes of consciousness to be mature organismic options appropriate to particular dimensions of reality.

WHEN WE consider the psychological and physiological variations that occur from day to day and from minute to minute as we work, eat, play, or respond to emergencies or drugs, or to radical shifts in our environment or goals, we are presented with a confusing mass of observations that are difficult to organize. Changes occur in body boundaries, in muscle tension, in sensory vividness, in electroencephalograms, in imagery, in logic, and in self-awareness. Some of these changes are slight, others can be extreme. Discussions of states of consciousness usually do not integrate these many physiological and psychological variables and, in addition, it is usually assumed that unusual states of consciousness are pathological or unreal. This paper will present a model in which psychological and physiological variations are viewed as manifestations of two basic organismic states or modes that are coordinated to a particular function. The model will be used to clarify phenomena in the fields of attention, mystical perception, hallucinogenic drugs, and psychosis.

Action Mode and Receptive Mode

Let us begin by considering the human being to be an organization of components having biological and psychological dimensions. These components are coordinated in two primary modes of organization: an "action" mode and a "receptive" mode.

The action mode is a state organized to manipulate the environment. The striate muscle system and the sympathetic nervous system are the dominant physiological agencies. The EEG shows beta waves and baseline muscle tension is increased. The principal psychological manifestations of this state are focal attention, object-based logic, heightened boundary perception, and the dominance of formal characteristics over the sensory; shapes and meanings have a preference over colors and textures. The action mode is a state of striving, oriented toward achieving personal goals that range from nutrition to defense to obtaining social rewards, plus a variety of symbolic and sensual pleasures, as well as the avoidance of a comparable variety of pain.

The attributes of the action mode develop as the human organism interacts with its environment. For example, very early in life focusing attention is associated not only with the use of the intrinsic muscles of the eyes, but also becomes associated with muscle movements of the neck, head, and body, whereby visual interest is directed toward objects. Likewise, thinking develops in conjunction with the perception and manipulation of objects and, because of this, object-oriented thought becomes intimately associated with the striate muscle effort of voluntary activity, particularly eye muscle activity.[1] Specific qualities of perception, such as sharp boundaries, become key features of the mode because sharp boundaries are important for the perception and manipulation of objects and for acquiring knowledge of the mechanical properties of objects. Sharp perceptual boundaries are matched by sharp conceptual boundaries, for success in acting on the world requires a clear sense of self-object difference. Thus, a variety of physiological and psychological processes develop together to form an organismic mode, a multidimensional unity adapted to the requirements of manipulating the environment.

In contrast, the receptive mode is a state organized around intake of the environment rather than manipulation. The sensory-perceptual system is the dominant agency rather than the muscle system, and parasympathetic functions tend to be most prominent. The EEG tends toward alpha waves and baseline muscle tension is decreased. Other attributes of the receptive mode are diffuse attending, paralogical thought processes, decreased boundary perception, and the dominance of the sensory over the formal. The receptive mode is aimed at maximizing the intake of the environment and this mode would appear to originate and function maximally in the infant state. The receptive mode is gradually dominated, if not submerged, however, by the progressive development of striving activity and the action mode.

In the course of development the action mode has priority to insure biological survival. The receptive mode develops also — but it occurs as an interlude between increasingly longer periods of action mode functioning. This developmental preference for the action mode has led us to regard the action mode as the proper one for adult life, while we have tended to think of the more unusual receptive states as pathological or "regressive."

Within each mode the attributes or components are interrelated to form a system, so that a shift in any one component can affect any of the others. For example, a decrease in muscle tension can decrease anxiety because of a shift in mode. Depending on the relative strength of competing motives and functional orientation, a change in one component of a mode may or may not bring about a noticeable shift to the other mode and with that shift change in other components. The components are not independent of each other or caused by each other (e.g., lowering muscle tension lowers anxiety; muscle tension, therefore, equals anxiety), but are related through the pattern or mode of organization in which they participate. If the balance of motivational force is very strong in favor of a particular mode, that mode will be quite resistant to change, even if a component is changed.

A very commonplace instance can be given of these two different modes in daily experience. Try thinking about a problem while lying flat on your back and then contrast that with thinking about the same problem while sitting upright. You will notice that maintaining a directed, logical stream of thought is much easier in the upright position. This can be understood as a function of two different organismic states, initiated by postural changes, but not determined by postural changes alone. It is possible to think logically while supine but it is more difficult. Our action mode activities develop in conjunction with an upright posture while receptivity originated in the reclining, infant state.

Language, it should be noted, is the very essence of the action mode; through it we discriminate, analyze, and divide up the world into pieces or objects which can then be grasped (psychologically and biologically) and acted upon. The richness of our vocabulary reflects the extent to which we apply the action mode to a particular sector of our environment. For example, the average person has only one word for snow, the skier has several, and the Eskimo many. It is not just a matter of how much we detect differences between varieties of snow or any other dimension. Consider the experience of "love." Here again, the average person has only one word for love, yet he has probably experienced a variety of love states. We have not developed words for these states because love is experienced in the receptive mode; indeed, it requires the receptive mode for its occurrence. Color experience (rather than color as a sign) requires the receptive mode; colors have only a few names compared to the vast variety of hues to which we are sensitive. In the case of the artist, however, who works with, manipulates, and makes color objects, the case is different. An artist's vocabulary is much expanded. The Whorfian hypothesis, that we are unable to think outside of our language structures, has relevance only for the action mode. We manipulate our environment through language-directed strategies.

To illustrate the modes more concretely, consider a cab driver in heavy traffic, struggling to get a passenger to the airport in time. He is in the action mode, contending maximally with his environment, trying to direct and control what happens, and focusing intensely on a goal located in future time. His conscious experience features sharp boundary perception, high field articulation, and verbal, logical thought patterns. His EEG is desynchronized and his baseline muscle tension is high. At the opposite pole is the monk in meditation who is in a receptive mode with a corresponding state of consciousness that may feature merging of the self with the environment or an ineffable (nonverbal) perception of unity, or both. Muscle relaxation, cortical synchrony, and sensory dominance are principal features of his state. The monk endeavors to adopt an attitude of selflessness and abandonment of personal striving. To this end, he gives up personal choice and material gain. Language and thinking are given low priority and a vow of silence may be taken.

These two modes are not to be equated with activity and passivity. The functional orientation that determines the mode has to do with the goal of the organism's activity: whether or not the environment is to be acted upon, or whether stimuli or nutriment are to be taken in. "Letting it" is an activity, but a different activity than "making it." Likewise, it is not the presence or absence of physical activity *per se* that is the mode determinant. In the pure state of the receptive mode the organism does seem helpless to act on the environment, as in states of ecstasy or drug intoxication. In most receptive mode conditions, however, an active relationship with the environment takes place, as in the case of the monk working in the garden or lovers in sexual intercourse. Characteristically, the relationship to the environment in the receptive mode is what Buber describes as the "I-Thou," in contrast to the "I-It" of the action mode.[2] For example, the monk at work in the garden could have two quite different experiences depending on which mode is dominant. Likewise, the lovers may be "screwing" rather than "making love." In most cases, we are talking about a modal balance or mixture, whose characteristics depend on the extent of dominance of a particular mode. The enlightened monk, working in the garden, operates in the action mode only to the extent needed to conduct his work activity, and the receptive mode can thereby still play a prominent role in his conscious experience.

Just as the action mode and the receptive mode are not the equivalents of activity and passivity, they are also not to be equated with the secondary and primary process of psychoanalytic theory. There is some similarity between aspects of the receptive mode and the cognitive style associated with the primary process. The bimodal model, however, addresses itself to a functional orientation — that of taking in versus acting on the environment. The receptive mode is not a "regressive" ignoring of the world or a retreat from it — although it can be employed for that purpose — but is a different strategy for engaging the world, in pursuit of a different goal.

The choice of mode is determined by the motives of the individual organism. Motivations exist, however, at different levels and with different time scales. It is hard to say much about the specific hierarchy of motives that affect the choice of mode. It is my impression, however, that the baseline of mode choice is set by the general orientation of the individual's culture. In Western civilization, that orientation is toward the individual's exerting direct, voluntary control over all phases of his life. This orientation of control is enhanced by the ideal of the self-made man and by the pursuit of material and social goals — all of which call for manipulation of the environment and of the self. The action mode dominates our consciousness. Men, however, have been concerned for many years with ways to shift to what I have described as the receptive mode. Later on I will discuss an example of a system that was developed to make the receptive mode the dominant orientation.

Although this bimodal analysis of organismic states at first may seem to be quite arbitrary and make little theoretical difference, I will now show how this model is very useful in clarifying a number of problems that otherwise would remain obscure.

Poetzel Effect

Poetzel observed a difference in what happens to stimuli that are perceived in the periphery of awareness as compared to those in the center.[3] A stimulus that is incidental, on the margin of the field of awareness, is "processed" differently than stimuli in the center. In the former case, dream processes dominate, in the latter case, rational logic holds sway. This phenomenon can be understood in terms of the two organizational modes. Stimuli at the center of awareness are subject to the organizational mode associated with object manipulation — the action mode. In terms of thought processes, this means object-based logical thought. Stimuli in the periphery are processed according to the more indirect, sensually oriented, intake goal of the receptive mode. This mode of thought uses paralogical strategies.

Silverman's Chronicity Study

Silverman and his colleagues have described changes in the cognitive style of schizophrenic patients as their stay in the hospital increases.[4-5] They report that with confinement of three years or more the attentional style of schizophrenic patients changes toward diminished field articulation and diminished scanning. Similar results were found in prison inmates.[6] These findings are not easy to explain on the basis of chemical deficits or "deterioration." The mode model does, however, suggest a way of understanding the shift. Diminished field articulation means that an object is less sharply differentiated from its surroundings, and diminished scanning means that fewer objects in the visual field have awareness centered on them. On the other hand, where field articulation is sharp and scanning is wide, the subject is in the best position to encounter and manipulate, to actively engage the object environment. This active striving style, however, is specifically defeated by the hospital environment if the patient must stay in it over several years. Such long-term frustration of active striving would be expected to result in diminished striving and a shift to the receptive mode.

Gaffron Phenomenon

Gaffron has described different modalities of conscious experience according to where on the object attention is focused.[7] For example, if visual awareness is centered on the near side of an object, ("grasping") the object is perceived "exteriorly" and the dominant qualities of the experience are form, surface, distance, and separateness from the observer. Awareness centered on the far side of an object ("mere looking") features "proprioceptive" qualities of volume, weight, and "interior" feelings of tension and inner movement. The object seems to intrude or extend into the boundaries of the self. The reader can observe this for himself if he stops for a moment and looks at a nearby object in these two ways.

It is most instructive to observe this shift of mode in situations such as eating a pear. In reaching for the pear, the focus is on the near side, in preparation for grasping it. As the pear is brought to the mouth, the focus shifts to the far side and beyond. In the act of eating, the pear is inside the zone of focus and, literally, being incorporated into the organism. The grasping of the pear is associated with the action mode and the intake of the pear with the receptive. The accompanying visual shifts are integral parts of the change in mode so that a shift of visual activity is accompanied by a shift in other components of the mode involved, for example, muscle relaxation and parasympathetic stimulation. The developmental coordination of the visual focus and body activity persist even though the objects involved may not be ones that can be eaten.

Neurotic Styles

Shapiro has presented evidence that the characteristic way an individual attends to stimuli, his attentive style, has important effects on his conscious experience.[8] Shapiro distinguishes between two main groups — sharply focused attention (obsessive-compulsive and paranoid styles) and diffuseness of attention with absence of sharp focus (hysterical styles). His conclusions are as follows: "the most conspicuous characteristic of the obsessive-compulsive's attention is its intense, sharp focus. These people are not vague in their attention, they concentrate and particularly do they concentrate on detail... (they) seem unable to allow their attention simply to wander or passively permit it to be captured. Thus, they rarely seem to get hunches, they are rarely struck or surprised by anything." The consequence of such a pervasive style of attention is that "he will often miss those aspects of a situation that give it its flavor or its impact; thus, these people often seem quite insensitive to the 'tone' of social situations." "Certain kinds of subjective experiences, affect experiences, particularly require, by their nature, an abandonment or at least a relaxation of the attitude of deliberateness and where such relaxation is impossible, as in the obsessive-compulsive style, those areas of psychological life tend to shrink."

Shapiro's conclusions support the concept of different organizational modes. In the case of the obsessive-compulsive, his thought and style is focused on object manipulation, an activity at which he is usually quite successful. Hunches or moments of inspiration that come about involuntarily in creative states or moments of mystical revelation are, however, quite absent from the experience of persons rigidly committed to the object-manipulative mode of cognition and perception. Likewise, rich affective experience is not found with that mode because "abandonment" and "relaxation of the attitude of deliberateness" is not compatible with the action mode. In the diffuse, hysterical style, however, we see the counterpart to the receptive-sensory mode. Here, sensory details, inspiration, and affect dominate the experience.

Body Boundaries, Muscle Relaxation, and Perception

Reports of subjects undergoing autogenic training, a European treatment technique of self-suggested relaxation, and reports of subjects undergoing relaxation training by means of feedback devices, indicate the frequent occurrence of body boundary changes correlated with deep levels of muscle relaxation [9,10] (and J. Stoyva and Budzynski, personal communication). Similar phenomena are noted under conditions of sensory isolation and in the induction phase of hypnosis. These correlations become understandable when we identify fluid boundaries and muscle relaxation as components of the receptive mode, components that tend to vary as a group when a shift in mode takes place. The conditions of autogenic training, sensory isolation, and hypnosis all predispose to a taking in of the environment rather than an orientation towards acting on the environment. Although the direct influence on muscle tension or sensory input is important, the shift in mode may be due as much to the accompanying shift in the orientation of the subject.

This line of reasoning also suggests an explanation for instances of reduction of anxiety as a consequence of muscle relaxation. Insofar as anxiety is an affect linked to future action (e.g., "If I perform this destructive or forbidden act, I will be destroyed"), the shift to the receptive mode could be expected to decrease anxiety because the state of receptivity is not organized around action to be directed at the environment. In the time dimension, the action mode is the Future and the receptive mode is the Now.

Experimental Studies of Meditation

For many centuries contemplative meditation has been prescribed as a technique for bringing about an altered perception of the world and of the self. This different mode of perception is characterized by a sense of unity of the person with his environment. In some cases, heightened sensory vividness is part of the description as well as timelessness, exultation, strong affect, and a sense that the horizon of awareness has been greatly expanded. In an attempt to study the possible connection between contemplative meditation and mystical experiences, I instructed a group of normal subjects in a basic procedure adapted from the Yoga of Pantanjali:

The purpose of the sessions is to learn about concentration. Your aim is to concentrate on the blue vase. By concentration I do not mean analyzing the different parts of the vase, or thinking a series of thoughts about the vase, or associating ideas to the vase; but rather, trying to see the vase as it exists in itself, without any connections to other things. Exclude all other thoughts or feelings or sounds or body sensations. Do not let them distract you, but keep them out so that you can concentrate all your attention, all your awareness on the vase itself. Let the perception of the vase fill your entire mind.

Each subject performed this exercise for one-half hour at a time, for 40 or more sessions spread over several months. The subjects' perceptions of the vase changed in the following directions: (1) an increase in the vividness and richness of the vase percept (for example, they described it as "luminous," "more vivid"); (2) the vase seemed to acquire a kind of life of its own, to be animated; (3) there was a decrease in the sense of being separate from the vase, occurring in those subjects who continued longest in the experiment (e.g., "I really began to feel, you know, almost as though the blue and I were perhaps merging or that the vase and I were. It was as though everything were sort of merging"); and (4) a fusing and alteration of normal perceptual modes (e.g., "when the vase changes shape, I feel this in my body," "I began to feel this light going back and forth").

As I have discussed in an earlier paper, these data are not easily explained by the usual concepts of suggestion, projection, auto-hypnosis, or sensory isolation.[11] I interpreted these changes as being a "deautomization," an undoing of the usual ways of perceiving and thinking due to the special way that attention was being used. The meditation exercise could be seen as withdrawing attention from thinking and reinvesting it in percepts — a reverse of the normal learning sequence. However, the concept of modes serving a particular function clarifies the phenomenon even further. It was required that the subjects adopt a particular attitude, that of a passive abandonment. This attitude represented an important shift for the subject away from the action mode and towards the receptive mode. Instead of grasping, manipulating, or analyzing the object in front of him, he was oriented to a different function. Instead of isolating and manipulating the object, he becomes one with it or takes it into his own space. Then sensuous attributes of the object, which are ordinarily of little importance, became enhanced and tend to dominate.

It is of interest that after the experiments subjects tended to report that they had learned something important in that experirience but could not specify what it was, "I've experienced... new experiences, and I have no vehicle to communicate them to you. I expect that this is probably the way a baby feels when he is full of something to say about an experience or an awareness and he has not learned to use the words yet." The experience was ineffable in the sense of not being suited for verbal communication, not fitting the customary categories of language of the action mode.

Physiological studies of Yogis, Zen masters, and students of transcendental meditation indicate that proficiency in meditation is characterized by a predominance of alpha waves plus such changes as a lowered respiratory rate.[13,15] Beginning students, intermediate students, and masters could be separated on the basis of their EEG during the meditation state — the further advanced the student, the greater the dominance of alpha waves. These data can be understood if we regard meditation training as developing the receptive mode.

Zen Consciousness

Zen Buddhism aims at changing the experience of a person to that particular view of himself and the world which is called "enlightenment." If one looks closely at the psychosocial system of a Zen monastery, it becomes clear that different aspects of that system are coordinated towards changing the individual's usual orientation of striving for personal goals. The monastery aims at producing a state of acceptance and "nondiscrimination." The principal means by which this is accomplished are meditation, communal living, and an ascetic way of life.

The highest form of Zen meditation is shikan-taza or in "just sitting." At first it is hard to grasp the literalness of the instruction to "just sit." But it means exactly what it says. A person meditating is "not supposed to do" anything except to be sitting. He is not to strive for enlightenment because if he is truly "just sitting," he is enlightened. That state of beingness is enlightenment itself. During meditation, thinking and fantasy are treated as intruders or distracting influences, to be patient with until they go away. Pain from the cross-legged sitting posture is regarded as part of the sitting and not to be avoided or categorized or even fought. "Be the pain" might be the instruction given to a student. The "being" that is referred to is essentially a sensory-perceptive experience. The teaching is aimed specifically at doing away with categorizing and classifying, an activity that is felt to intervene between the subject and his experience.

In meditation, the sense of time can change to what might be called timelessness. Again, the urgency to accomplish things is undermined by this timeless orientation. Furthermore, during meditation the subject may experience a sense of total satisfaction with his moment-to-moment experience so that the need to strive for a distant satisfaction is diminished once again.

The sessions of sitting meditation take place three or more times daily within the setting of a communal society. No one accrues profits in that society. There are some status rewards but these tend to be minimized. The students share in whatever work needs to be done, share the same daily routine, the same daily food, and the same discipline. Every activity is represented as being equally important as any other. Thus, washing dishes is held to be as "good" an activity as walking in the woods. Once again, such an attitude and structure militates against an orientation towards the future, because the future contains nothing intrinsically more satisfying than what is contained in the present.

I stress the matter of the shift in functional orientation because the concept of an organizational mode is based on the idea that psychological and biological activities are integrated in the service of the total organism and the functional attitude of that organism is the crucial determinant of which mode is adopted. To take another example, the wish for perpetual survival is perhaps the most powerful desire motivating the ordinary person's life. It is very interesting to see how this problem is handled in the Zen system. To begin with, the idea of being dead versus being alive is labeled a fallacious concept based on dualism. The Buddhist cosmology of constant change, of a basic Nothing that takes an endless variety of forms, says that the student is part of a process that does not end but simply changes or flows. Most important of all, the student is taught that his notion of a soul, of an enduring self, is erroneous. Indeed, the concept of a self is held to be the cause of all suffering. During meditation the student may have the concrete experience that his sense of separateness is arbitrary and an illusion.

The principal purpose or goal held out for the students as legitimate and worthwhile is that of the Buddhist vow "to save all sentient beings" from the suffering of delusion. It should be noticed that this is a selfless goal. The student will not be rewarded by having a special place in heaven if he accomplishes this, but rather that purpose is the purpose of the universe of which he is a part. Such an ethic of action directed toward the good of others (the basic ethic of almost all religions) provides a dimension for participation in the world in an active and energetic way but one that attempts to minimize the mode of consciousness associated with striving for one's own personal goals.

The asceticism of the Zen community is not that of the anchorite who despises sensual pleasure as an enemy, but an asceticism that forms a backdrop against which the student can see clearly the role that his desires play in his suffering. In this connection it should be noted that a contemporary Zen master described renunciation as, "We do not give them up, but accept that they go away."[16] This open-handed approach to life means that any sensual pleasure that comes along is to be enjoyed for its own sake, but there is to be no attempt to hang on, to grasp, to strive for, to reach for. If we look at the goals around which we organize many of our activities, we see that they are often oriented towards prolonging or bringing back a particular pleasure that we have had, often at the detriment of the pleasure available at the moment. This lesson of nongrasping is brought home to the student over and over again in the different situations that arise at the monastery.

Thus, the emphasis on experiencing, or enduring, and on being — rather than on avoiding pain or seeking pleasure — provides the groundwork for a mode of consciousness that Zen texts describe as nondualistic, timeless, and nonverbal. It is part of the mode of organismic being that I have categorized as the receptive mode.

Mystical Psychosis

One of the puzzling phenomena of psychosis is that of the mystical state preceding or marking the onset of many cases of acute schizophrenia. As Bowers and Freedman have described,[17] the specific configurations of these states vary from case to case but they share basic features: marked heightening of sense perception; a feeling of communion with people, the world, God; intense affective response; and blurring of perceptual and conceptual boundaries. First-person accounts of this type of psychotic experience are strikingly similar to reports of sensate mystical experience and suggest a similar process. In terms of the bimodal model, the experience is one of a sudden, sharp, and extreme shift to the receptive mode: decreased self-object differentiation, heightened sensory intake, and nonverbal, nonlogical thought process.

Both mystical and psychotic states appear to have arisen out of a situation in which the individual has struggled with a desperate problem, has come to a complete impasse, and given up hope, abandoned the struggle in despair.[18] For the mystic, what emerges from the "cloud of unknowing" or the "dark night of the soul" is an ecstatic union with God or Reality. For the psychotic person, the world rushes in but does not become integrated in the harmony of *mystico unio* or *satori*. Instead, he creates a delusion to achieve a partial ordering and control.

As I have discussed earlier, mystical practice can be viewed as a cultivation of the receptive mode by means of a particular functional orientation and control of thought and environment. No such training program precedes the many examples of mystical psychotic episodes cited above. How are we to understand them then? Maternal deprivation in the case of children and loss or rejection by a loved person in the case of adults are frequently reported as precursors or precipitants of psychosis.[19] In my own experience and in that of others, therapeutic investigation reveals intense hatred and destructive fantasies directed towards the loved person but not acknowledged by the patient. The emergence into consciousness of the anger directed towards the appropriate person is usually accompanied by a dramatic improvement in the patient's condition and marks the demise of the psychotic defense. This suggests the possibility that the psychotic alteration in consciousness is a defensive shift to a mode that will preclude destructive action on the other person. If someone is ecstatic, Christlike, overcome with the significance of a thousand details, buffeted by alternate winds of fear, exultation, grief, and rapture, he is in a state that maximizes what comes in and minimizes the possibility of aggressive action on someone else. Not incidentally, maximum sensory intake can be viewed as dealing with the painful emptiness following deprivation of love.

Although such a person may pass to a phase of tightly ordered paranoid delusion in which he can be dangerous, in the mystical, flooded stage he is helpless, like an infant. The shift to the mystical state is a functional shift on the part of an organism desperately concerned over final loss of nutriment. The control gates are thrown down and the world floods in through the senses and through the inner stores of affect and memory. The action mode is abandoned. When the person begins to drown in the overload, he asserts control in a delusional compromise that to some extent restores order and effectiveness while providing a substitute object.

The mystics' success in achieving a harmonious integration of self and world may be explained by a consideration of the many factors that differentiate the life and practice of the mystic from that of the psychotic. But the similarity of the initial experience that occurs when striving towards the world is abandoned suggests a similar basic organismic shift — the giving up of the action mode in favor of the receptive. In the case of acute mystical psychosis, a crucial rejection or life impasse triggers a collapse of the action mode and a sudden rush of receptive mode cognition and perception ensues for which the person is unprepared and unsupported. Delusional reordering then takes place to solve the affective impasse.

Lysergic Acid Diethylamide (LSD)

Accounts of LSD experiences reveal a cluster of characteristics identifying it with the receptive mode: a marked decrease in self-object distinction; a loss of control over attention; the dominance of paralogical thought forms; intense affect and vivid sensory experience; decreased field articulation and increased parasympathetic stimulation; plus a reification of thought and feeling with a corresponding decrease in "reality testing."

As in the case of meditation, I hypothesized that the general effects of LSD and related drugs were those of "deautomization," an undoing of the automatic psychological structures that organize, limit, select, and interpret perceptual stimuli.[20] In considering the problem of explaining the perceptual and cognitive phenomena of mystic experience as a regression, I stated, "One might call the direction

regressive in a developmental sense, but the actual experience is probably not within the psychological scope of any child. It is a deautomatization occurring in an adult mind, and the experience gains its
richness from adult memories and functions now subject to a different mode of consciousness." That mode of consciousness I would
now designate as the receptive mode and consider it to be a mature
cognitive and perceptual state, one that is not ordinarily dominant,
but is an option that has developed in richness and subtlety in parallel
with the development of the action mode that is our customary state
of consciousness. Reports of the LSD experience show the complex
possibilities of thought and perception that can occur in the receptive
mode.[21-22]

It is noteworthy that one of the effects of widespread use of LSD
and other psychedelics has been to stimulate a revival of interest in
Eastern religions. This orientation towards Eastern mysticism can
be understood if Yoga and Zen are viewed as developments of the receptive mode: a perception and cognition that features the blurring
of boundaries; the merging of self and environment, coupled with
affective and sensory richness and marked by a detachment from the
object-oriented goals of the action mode.

Physiological Dimensions in Psychosis and LSD

The physiological data pertaining to meditating Yogis and Zen
monks are clear and support the mode hypothesis. In the case of acute
and chronic schizophrenia, however, the data are ambiguous or contradictory. Chronic schizophrenic patients tend to have EEGs suggesting cortical activation and high anxiety levels.[23,25] A study of hospitalized schizophrenic patients undergoing acute decompensation
shows an increase and wide variability of muscle tension, rather
than the decreased muscle tension predicted on the basis of the
receptive mode model.[26] On the other hand, Salamon and Post,[27] using
a special method of measuring alpha waves, found increased alpha-
wave production in schizophrenic patients as compared to controls.

Studies of autonomic function are likewise variable and unclear. Issues of diagnosis, chronicity, and drug effects undoubtedly confound the data. In the case of LSD states, there is not much data to work with, but the clinical variability of the states and the frequent occurrence of anxiety suggest a situation similar to the psychoses. Although a more detailed and systematic physiological investigation needs to be done to solve this problem, in these instances we are probably dealing with an unintegrated mixture of modes. One way of understanding this is to consider the fact that, in the case of schizophrenia, the shift to the receptive mode may arouse great anxiety and a compensatory attempt to control the receptive mode experience, an attempt that is an action mode response. That such a response creates a problem is suggested by the lore of LSD users whose standard advice for those about to take LSD is not to fight the experience, but to "go with it," to "float downstream," and abandon oneself to what feels like "ego death." It is said that if one can do this, chances are good that the experience will be beatific. On the other hand, if the subject attempts to control or fight the experience, a "bad trip" is the likely result. Giving oneself up to an unusual experience, abandoning oneself to "ego death," is precisely what Yogis and Zen monks are trained to do, but what schizophrenic persons find most difficult. Perhaps this difference underlies the different physiological portraits accompanying these different situations.

Implications

Control of Psychological and Physiological Dimensions

The concept that dimensions of a state of consciousness are components of organismic modes suggests the possibility of indirect control over specific aspects of each mode. For example, it becomes reasonable to affect the sharpness of perceptual boundaries by increasing muscle tension or to decrease anxiety by lowering it. Similarly, by restricting analytic thinking and attending to a sensory mode, alterations in muscle tension, EEG, and galvanic skin response can be obtained. By delineating other dimensions of the modes we may be able to widen our repertoire of techniques for change along a variety of organismic dimensions.

Strategic Options

The receptive mode seems to be one in which certain *activities* are facilitated. The examples below are assumed to involve instances of the receptive mode by virtue of their emphasis on relinquishing conscious striving and intellectual control:

Subjects who learn to control functions of the autonomic nervous system, such as alpha-wave production or finger temperature, learn that they must let it happen rather than make it happen. In the case of temperature control, Green et al[28] have termed this activity "passive volition."

Accounts of the process of creative synthesis show several distinct stages: first a stage of directed intellectual attack on the problem leading to a feeling of impasse, then the stage of "giving up," in which the person stops struggling with the problem and turns his attention to other things. During this unfocused rest period the solution to the problem manifests itself as an "Aha!" or "Eureka!" experience — the answer is suddenly there of itself. The final stage sees a return of directed intellectual activity as the "answer" is worked over to assess its validity or fit with the object world. In terms of the mode model, the first stage is one in which the action mode is used, followed by the receptive mode in which the creative leap is made, followed by a return to the action mode to integrate the discovery with the object world.

It may be that paranormal phenomena require the development of the receptive mode. Such a possibility fits well with assertions of classical Yogic literature and with contemporary dream research.[29]

A prosaic example of the need to switch to the receptive mode to achieve a particular aim is the attempt to recover a forgotten name. Typically, the person struggles with it and then gives up, saying, "It will come to me in a minute"— and it does. What could not be gained by a direct effort was accomplished by relinquishing effort and becoming relatively receptive.

In ordinary life circumstances, the receptive mode probably plays its most important role in sexual intercourse. Erikson describes the psychological importance of the healthy sexual act as "...a supreme experience of the mutual regulation of two beings (that) in some way breaks the point off the hostilities and potential rages caused by the oppositeness of male and female, of fact and fancy, of love and hate. Satisfactory sex relations thus make sex less obsessive, overcompensation less necessary, sadistic controls superfluous."[30] Psychotherapeutic investigation shows that an individual's capacity for such a satisfying sexual experience is in proportion to his or her capacity to relinquish control, to allow the other person to "enter in," to adopt what I have termed the receptive mode orientation. It is of interest to this discussion that sexual climax in persons with such a capacity is associated not only with intensely heightened sensation and diffuse attention, but with a decrease in self-other boundaries that in some cases results in experiences properly classified as mystical.[31] An inability to shift to the receptive mode, however, results in a serious impairment of the sexual act. Sensation, release, and feelings of closeness become attenuated or absent.

Knowledge

Although this discussion of modes began with a simple dichotomy of action — namely, manipulating the environment versus taking it in — the study of mystical consciousness suggests that the receptive mode may provide a way of "knowing" certain aspects of reality not accessible to the action mode. The "knowing" that takes place is usually a nonverbal experience, although it may later be translated into words in order to be shared with others. Thus, what is taken in is not only those aspects of the environment with which we are familiar but other aspects as well.

Contemporary psychological models, such as primary process

theory, view the object world as the standard by which to judge the realism of perception and cognition. The receptive mode and other modes yet to be discerned or utilized can, however, be conceptualized as modes by which the organism addresses itself to reality dimensions other than those of the object world associated with the action mode and logical thinking. The "thinking" of the receptive mode may be organized in terms of a different logic in pursuit of aims located along different dimensions of reality than those to which we ordinarily address ourselves.

It may be felt that to talk of other dimensions of reality is to indulge in romantic thinking, but however it may be judged the idea of other dimensions is not illogical. Considerations of developmental psychology provide the basis for the possibility that the organism has exercised a considerable selection over what features of the world it gives the priority of its attention and the structuralization of its language. That the view of the world thus obtained is relative, rather than absolute, and incorrect in certain applications is held by many theoretical physicists. Furthermore, it has been noted that the correspondence between the cosmology of mystics and that of contemporary physicists is striking.[32] Such a correspondence suggests that the receptive mode of mystic consciousness may have validity in terms of the "external world" if the sector of reality being considered is different from that of the biological with which we are familiar and in which we developed.

Values

The crises now facing the human race are technically solvable. Controlling population, reducing pollution, and eliminating racism and war do not require new inventions. Yet these problems may prove fatally insolvable because what is required is a shift in values, in self-definition, and in worldview on the part of each person — for it is the individual consciousness that is the problem. Our survival is threatened now because of our great success in manipulating our environment and acting on others. The action mode has ruled our individual lives and our national politics, and the I-It relationship that has provided the base for technical mastery is now the primary obstacle to saving our race. If, however, each person were able to feel an identity with other persons and with his environment, to see himself as part of a larger unity, he would have that sense of oneness that supports the selfless actions necessary to regulate population growth, minimize pollution, and end war. The receptive mode we have been discussing is the mode in which this identification—the I-Thou relationship — exists and it may be needed to provide the experiential base for the values and world view now needed so desperately by our society as a whole.

Conclusion

I believe it is important that we recognize the relativity of different modes of consciousness rather than assign an absolute primacy and validity to that mode with which we are familiar. The simple dichotomy of receptive and action modes is undoubtedly not a complete inventory of the options available to the human organism. Whether or not we are successful in adopting a variety of appropriate modes of consciousness may well depend on factors with which psychoanalysis is very familiar: defenses against the unknown, against relinquishing conscious control, against the blurring or loss of self boundaries. Perhaps the first step in awarding ourselves new options is to make them legitimate. The limits of what is thinkable tend to be prescribed by the assumptions that permeate a culture. In our own culture mystical means unreal or "kooky," altered states of consciousness are considered "regressive" or pathological, "spiritual" wishes and intuitions are labeled "omnipotent." There are instances where these cultural assumptions are justified but the area encompassed by unusual experiences is much larger than that allotted by such pejorative categories. I hope I have been able to indicate how different states of consciousness can be viewed as organismic modes that may have an important reality-based function necessary for our growth, our vitality, and our survival as a species. Instead of "regression" or "unrealistic" or "autistic," we might better term our organismic options "alternate modes" and be receptive to what they have to teach us.

This study was supported by research grant MH 16793-02 from the Public Health Service and by the Department of Psychiatry, University of Colorado Medical Center. Drs. I. Charles Kaufman, David Metcalf, and Robert Emde advised in the preparation of this manuscript.

References

1. Piaget J: *The Construction of Reality in the Child*. New York, Basic Books Inc Publishers, 1954.
2. Buber M: *I and Thou*. New York, Charles Scribner's Sons, 1958.
3. Poetzl O, et al: *Preconscious stimulation in dreams, associations, and images*. PSYCHOL ISSUES 2:1-18, 1960.
4. Silverman J: *Variations in cognitive control and psychophysiological defense in the schizophrenias*. PSYCHOSOM MED 29:225-251, 1967.
5. Silverman J: *A paradigm for the study of altered states of consciousness*. BRIT J PSYCHIAT 114:1201-1218, 1968.
6. Silverman J, Berg P, Kantor R: *Some perceptual correlates of institutionalization*. NERV MENT DIS 141:656- 657, 1965.
7. Gaffron M: *Some new dimensions in the phenomenal analysis of visual experience.* J PERSONALITY 24:285-307, 1956.
8. Shapiro D: *Neurotic Styles*. New York, Basic Book Inc Publishers, 1965.
9. Schultz J, Luthe W: *Autogenic Training—A Psychophysiologic Approach in Psychotherapy*. New York, Grune & Stratton Inc, 1959.
10. Kleinsorge H, Klumbies G: *Technique of Relaxation*. Bristol, England, John Wright & Sons Ltd, 1964.
11. Deikman AJ: *Experimental meditation.* J NERV MENT DIS 136:329- 343, 1963.
12. Deikman AJ: *Implications of experimentally induced contemplative meditation.* J NERV MENT DIS 142:101- 116, 1966.
13. Bagchi B, Wenger M: *Electro-physiological correlates of some Yogi exercises.* ELECTROENCEPH CLIN NEUROPHYSIOL 7:132-149, 1957.
14. Akishige Y (ed): *Psychological studies on Zen.* KYUSHU PSYCHOLOGICAL STUDIES 5:1-280, 1968.

15. Wallace RK: *The physiological effects of transcendental meditation.* Science 167:1751-1754, 1970.

16. Suzuki S: *Lecture given at Zen Mountain Center,* July 1968. Wind Bell 7:28, 1968.

17. Bowers MB, Freedman DX: *Psychedelic experiences in acute psychoses.* Arch Gen Psychiat 15:240-248,1966.

18. Bowers MB: *Pathogenesis of acute schizophrenic psychosis.* Arch Gen Psychiat 19:348-355, 1968.

19. Mednick SA, Schulsinger F: *Factors related to breakdown in children at high risk for schizophrenia,* in Roff M, Ricks DF (eds): *Life History Research in Psychopathology.* Minneapolis, University of Minnesota Press, 1970, pp. 87-88.

20. Deikman AJ: *Deautomization and the mystic experience.* Psychiatry 29:324-338, 1966.

21. Masters REL, Houston J: *The Varieties of Psychedelic Experience.* New York, Dell Publishing Co Inc, 1967.

22. Harman W, et al: *Psychedelic agents in creative problem solving: A pilot study,* in Tart C (ed): *Altered States of Consciousness.* New York, John Wiley & Sons Inc, 1969, pp. 445- 461.

23. Lindsley D: *Electroencephalography,* in Hunt J McV (ed): *Personality and the Behavior Disorders.* New York, Ronald Press Co, 1944, pp. 1081-1083.

24. Venables PH: *Input dysfunction in schizophrenia,* in Maher B (ed): *Progress in Experimental Personality Research.* New York, Academic Press Inc, 1964, p 41.

25. Kennard M: *The EEG in schizophrenia,* in Wilson W (ed): *Applications of Electroencephalography in Psychiatry.* Durham, NC, Duke University Press, 1965, pp. 168-184.

26. Whatmore G: *Tension factors in schizophrenia and depression,* in Jacobson E (ed): *Tension in Medicine.* Springfield, 111, Charles C Thomas Publisher, 1967.

27. Salamon I, Post J: *Alpha blocking and schizophrenia.* Arch Gen Psychiat 13:367-374, 1965.

28. Green EE, Green AM, Walters ED: *Voluntary control of internal states: Psychological and physiological.* Psychologic 12:107, 1970.

29. Ullman M, Krippner S: *A laboratory approach to the nocturnal dimension of paranormal experience: Report of a confirmatory study using the REM monitoring technique.* Biol Psychiat 1:259-270, 1969.

30. Erikson E: *Childhood and Society.* New York, WW Norton & Co Inc. Publishers, 1950, p 230.

31. Laski M: *Ecstasy.* London, Cresset Press Ltd, 1961, pp. 145-153.

32. LeShan L: *Physicists and mystics: Similarities in world view.* J Transpersonal Psychology, fall, pp. 1- 20, 1969.

Originally published in Arch Gen Psychiat
Vol. 25, Dec. 1971

The Relation Between Electroencephalographic Activity and Meditation

Abstract

Other investigators, using experienced meditators, have shown striking changes in the electroencephalogram (EEG) and the electromyogram (EMG) during meditation.

Data on associated subjective experiences has been minimal. In this study, naive subjects were trained in a Yoga meditation for fifty sessions. EEG and EMG were recorded for each session and extensive post-session interviews provided information about the subjects' experience during their meditation. A non-meditating control group was utilized. The meditation practice produced profound changes in consciousness which were not reflected in the EEG or EMG. These results suggest that the shifts in EEG and EMG reported by other investigators may be due to changes in attitude and self-experience brought about by long meditation practice, rather than by changes in consciousness, *per se.*

Introduction

During the past decade, scientists have begun to investigate the phenomena of meditation. Although there are many forms of meditation, almost all forms involve a decrease in ordinary thinking activity and a focus on a repetitive, monotonous or undifferentiated target such as repeated words, the sensations of breathing, watching a candle flame, etc. — or just the maintenance of a diffuse alertness. The practitioner does not strain to accomplish the meditation task but calmly returns to the desired focus if he finds he has drifted off into thoughts. Basic to meditation is a particular attitude: the giving up of conscious striving.

Typically, meditation requires years of practice to realize its potential. Since meditation is said to produce very important benefits, such as peace of mind, improved mental functioning, increased enjoyment of life and, ultimately, insight into the basic nature of one's self, there has been hope that ways might be found to produce such effects more quickly and more reliably. These hopes have been encouraged by reports that Yogis and Zen masters show distinct physiologic changes and by recent discoveries that physiological feedback can be used to train subjects to control functions previously thought to be involuntary, such as alpha waves, finger temperature, and heart rate. It has been proposed that every mental event has its appropriate physiological correlates (Green, 1970) and that the discovery of the physiological correlates of an unusual state of consciousness would permit that state to be produced at will, using biofeedback techniques.

Research into the physiology of meditation has appeared to support the first assumption. Eletroectroencephalographic (EEG) studies by Bagchi and Wenger (1957), and by Anand, et al (1961), and by Kasamatsu and Hirai (1969), had indicated that Yogis and Zen masters entered into states characterized by more or less continuous alpha production. In addition, studies by Banquet (1973), by Wallace (1971), and by Das and Gastaut (1955), showed changes in frequency and amplitude of the EEG. Using the electromyograph (EMG) Ikegami (1968) showed that during meditation there was a decrease in muscle tension in meditating Zen monks. Wallace (1971) investigating metabolism, found evidence that Transcendental Meditation (repeating a series of syllables to oneself, silently) produces changes in the basal metabolic rate (BMR) and in respiration.

Research in biofeedback has demonstrated the feasibility of controlling both EEG and EMG. Kamiya (1969) showed that subjects who had had no formal instruction in meditation could be trained with EEG feedback to increase their production of alpha waves. Furthermore, some of his subjects reported experiences suggestive of states described in the classical literature on meditation and the mystical experience. Budzynski and Stoyva (1970) have demonstrated that non-meditating subjects could be trained to reduce muscle tension by means of EMG feedback.

These findings have supported the hope that the effects of meditation could be duplicated by the use of biofeedback. However, studies of the physiologic changes associated with meditation have not simultaneously assessed the psychological state of their subjects during the meditation period. Reports tend to be anecdotal with no indication of the type of questioning which elicited them. Banquet (1973) did have his subjects press buttons to signal five categories of events, but such categories are limited as descriptions of states of consciousness, even if the subjects were accurate in their use.

In addition, these meditation studies used subjects already indoctrinated into a particular system of meditation, with its attendant philosophy and practitioner's lore. For example, Wallace and Benson (1971) used subjects who had practiced Transcendental Meditation for a mean length of 29.4 months. The problem of subject bias may be significant.

With these considerations in mind, the following experiment was designed to investigate the correlation between EEG and EMG, on the one hand, and the psychological events of meditation practice, on the other.

Procedure

General Design

Naive subjects were trained in meditation for fifty sessions.

EEG and EMG were recorded for each session, and extensive post-session interviews provided information about the subjects' experiences during meditation. A non-meditating control group was utilized. Each subject served as his own control for changes occurring over the course of the meditation training. As much as possible, the setting, instructions, and interviews were kept free of religious, spiritual, or other ideological contexts.

Subject Selection

Nine subjects, aged 21 to 35, were recruited through a newspaper ad and a notice placed on a local college bulletin board. The advertisement asked for persons interested in paid participation in research on concentration. They were offered $3.50 per hour with a $50 bonus for finishing a series of fifty experimental sessions. Respondents were screened to exclude those using drugs of any kind, practicing meditation or a spiritual discipline, under psychiatric care, or having a history of heavy drug use, epilepsy, or "nervous breakdown."

The remainder were given an MMPI and then interviewed by the author. Those judged to have evidence of a thought disorder or to be borderline were excluded.

Of the subjects selected, eight were graduate students, none of whom were majoring in psychology. One subject was a housewife. Eight subjects were right-handed; one was left-handed.

The nine subjects were assigned at random to Experimental Groups A and B and to Control Group C (one male and two females in each group).

Midway in the experiment, one subject (from Group B) dropped out at the 25th session.

Experimental Conditions

Group A: Subjects focused attention upon a continuous tone of 400 cycles/second delivered through headphones. The volume was adjusted at each session so that it was just loud enough to be heard without straining.

Group B: Subjects focused attention upon their awareness of being aware.

Group C (Control Group): Sat quietly.

All subjects were instructed to keep their eyes open.

Instructions

Instructions were read to the subjects at the beginning of the first three or four experimental sessions, until they felt that they knew what was required. Every fifth session they were asked to state what they were trying to do. For the initial baseline sessions, all subjects were told to just sit in the chair while we made EEG measurements. The apparatus was explained to them and their questions about the machines were answered. After the three baseline sessions were completed, the following instructions were read to the appropriate group:

Groups A and B: Introduction

"This is an experiment in how we perceive and experience things. Ordinarily we look at the world around us with only part of our attention; the rest is taken up with *thinking* about what we are seeing or with unrelated thoughts. This experiment will explore what you experience when you *cease thinking* altogether and concentrate your attention on only *one* thing."

Group A — Focus on Reflexive Awareness

"In this experiment we will explore what you experience when you shift your attention away from things and become aware of your own mind, itself. Take a step back, as it were, and become aware of the sensation of being aware. Try it now. Let the surrounding world go out of focus and, instead, focus your attention inside your own mind — not to the thoughts themselves, but to the feeling of awareness. Have your entire mind concentrated on that awareness. At the same time, remain open to the experience. Let whatever happens happen."

OR

Group B — Focus on Sound

"Listen to the sound intently. Focus all your interest on it. Try to hear it as directly as possible without studying or analyzing it. Have your entire mind concentrated on the sound. At the same time, remain open to the experience — let whatever happens happen."

Groups A & B: Conclusion

"All thinking must come to a stop so that your mind becomes quiet. Do not let yourself be distracted by incidental thoughts, sounds, or body sensations — *keep them out* so that you can concentrate all your attention on the awareness/sound.

"If you find that you have drifted into a stream of thought — stop — and bring your attention back to the awareness/sound. I will tell you when 30 minutes are up. Any questions? Your eyes should be open. Begin now."

Instructions for Group C (Control Group)

"This is an experiment to obtain information about brain waves. Your job is to sit quietly with your eyes open. You'll need to stay awake and let whatever happens happen. I'll tell you when 30 minutes are up."

Physiologic Measurements

EEGs were obtained using an eight-channel Type T Offner Electroencephalograph. Beckman biopotential electrodes were employed and fixed to the scalp with wax. Recordings were taken from P3-01, P4-02, 01-02, F3-C3, F4-C4, and C3-C4. The signal from P3-01, for the eight right-handed subjects, and from P4-02 for the one left-handed subject, was led through an 8-12 Hz band pass filter and an alpha-time counting circuit: trains of alpha waves larger than a pre-set threshold and lasting longer than 0.2 seconds actuated a digital clock. The amplitude threshold was 15 microvolts for most subjects. In the case of subjects who produced large amounts of alpha, the threshold was adjusted so that their alpha count did not exceed 30 % in the baseline condition.

In addition to the cumulative alpha-time totals for each session, there were minute-by-minute subtotals so that the first half of a session could be compared with the last half for each subject and with each group. Any event located during a session could be correlated with the alpha output at that time by referring to the EEG record and to the digital clock record.

Each subject had at least three baseline EEG sessions (sitting quietly) before beginning the meditation series.

EOG

For the first three subjects, (one in each experimental group), EOG recordings were obtained.

Initially, it was felt advisable to have a record of eye movements in the event that (1) the production of alpha waves was being influenced by upward-directed gazing, (2) subjects showed REM phenomena during the sessions and (3) as a check to be sure the subjects kept their eyes open as instructed. Experience with the first three subjects indicated that eye position remained steady, the eyes stayed open (on the few occasions when they did close, it was apparent to the experimenter in the room who was observing the subject), and no REM activity was observed. For these reasons, EOG recordings were eliminated from the procedure.

EMG

For the last six subjects, muscle tension was recorded from supra-orbital leads on the frontalis muscle, using a Grass pre-amplifier and an EMG scoring device, "BIFS" (Budzynski & Stoyva, 1970, 1973) that gave a readout representing cumulative muscle unit firings over the course of the 30-minute sessions.

Muscle tension measurements were taken at one-minute intervals for the first five minutes and then at five-minute intervals, with a final cumulative total.

Immediately following the meditation session, the subject was given an open-ended interview of about half an hour. Certain questions were asked, as indicated below, to make sure that key areas were described. If the subject covered them spontaneously, they were not mentioned. From time to time, the experimenter might be called on to give reassurance to a subject who had been frightened by events of that session. The experimenter responded in a non-directive style to elicit the feelings involved and then might reassure the subject by pointing out that the procedure was completely under the subject's control; he or she could stop at any time. The subject would then be encouraged to keep exploring the experience at whatever pace he or she felt able to do.

The interview questions were as follows:

1. How did it go?
2. How long did it seem?
3. Describe the course of the session.
4. How much of the time were you able to concentrate so that you were aware only of the awareness/sound and nothing else?
5. How did you go about concentrating? What did you do?
6. What thoughts did you have during the session?
7. What emotions or feelings did you have?
8. What was your experience of the awareness/sound?
9. What was your perception or experience of yourself?
10. (After every fifth session) ... You mention that _____ occurred during the ___ session. Has that continued, changed, or stopped?
11. (About every fifth session) ... What is your intent as you (Groups A & B) focus on the awareness/sound? (Group C) sit in the chair.

In the case of the control subjects, Questions 4, 5, and 8 were omitted.

Experimental Procedure

A subject, after having electrodes applied, would be taken to a comfortably furnished, softly-lit room where they were seated in an armchair six feet away from a blank wall. The experimenter was seated at a desk to one side and slightly behind the subject with the EEG and other equipment.

All subjects wore headphones, although only Group B heard a sound signal.

At the conclusion of the meditation session, the half-hour interview was conducted. The subject was then taken to another room where the electrodes were removed.

Each subject came to the lab two or three times a week. Because of problems of scheduling, vacations and illness, it took about six months to complete the series for each subject.

Scoring of Physiologic Data

The EEG records were scanned for obvious changes in patterns, and hand measurements were done to ascertain differences in amplitude of the alpha waves, differences in frequency, and comparisons between the alpha amplitudes of the left and right hemispheres.

The alpha-time and EMG daily totals were subjected to computer analysis of variance to detect (1) changes over time for individual subjects, (2) differences between the two experimental groups, and (3) changes between the combined experimental groups and the control subjects. In addition, a runs test was performed to detect trends. The individual protocols were examined to detect EEG and EMG changes specifically associated with any intense psychological events that were reported.

Three of the subjects were able to say a word or two during some of the experimental sessions without interrupting their concentrated state. In those cases, there are a number of points on the EEG records that can be correlated precisely with the concurrent psychological events as they were reported immediately following the meditation session. In the case of the other subjects, a more indirect correlation had to be made, utilizing their estimates of the time of occurrence of different phenomena. In some cases, those time estimates could be checked against certain distracting noises or movements of the experimenter that had been noticed by the subject.

Since most of the phenomena that will be discussed seemed to have a duration of three to ten minutes, greater precision of timing did not seem to be essential.

Scoring of Interview Protocols

In evaluating data as complex as subjective descriptions of unusual states of consciousness, it is very hard to determine unambiguous
scoring dimensions for measuring the intensity and profundity of
changes of consciousness. I felt it would be best to rely on the intuitive judgment of a single experienced scorer who would compare
one report with another. For this reason the following procedure was
employed:

The interviews were scored independently by a scorer who had
considerable research experience in altered states of consciousness.
The scorer worked from typed transcripts that were identified only by a code number so that the name of the subject, the serial
position of the particular session, and the nature of the experimental
condition were unknown to him. (However, in some subjects, the
type of target could be inferred from the content of the responses.)
All the protocols of each subject were scored at one time, separately
from those of other subjects. The scorer followed these instructions:
"The subjects of this experiment have performed different kinds of
meditation exercises in the laboratory. Your task is to grade their
reports according to the intensity and profundity of the change in
their state of consciousness that occurred during each session. Score
the most intense as ten and the least as one. I suggest that you begin by sorting the reports into high, middle and low groups and
then subdividing further according to the character of the sessions.
You need not arrive at an even distribution or have all grade levels
represented. For example, level number six might have many sessions
clustered in it, while level three might have none. Allow yourself to
respond intuitively to the material with this exception: in assessing
the reports, you should not give major weight to the experience of
anxiety as an indicator, in and of itself."

Results

EEG and Subjective Experiences:

The interview material indicated that the meditation subjects tended to develop vivid experiences during the course of the experiment. All reported one or more of the following: a decreased awareness of outside stimuli, a sense of alienation from normal reality, the blurring and disappearance of body boundaries and the occurrence of dreamlike imagery, hallucinatory perception, and ineffable, mystic-like states. However, the vivid mental events and altered states of consciousness experienced by these subjects were not correlated with changes in alpha waves or in general EEG patterns.

Several illustrative examples appear on the following pages. Breaks in the graph line or absent graph bars represent data missing due to equipment malfunction:

DISAPPEARANCE OF EGO BOUNDARY

Subject 2, session 33, focus on awareness:

"In the first half of the period of awareness I had a kind of feeling of complete openness, almost as if I were free-floating, spread-eagle; (then it became)... a non-existence kind of openness. It's really hard to explain it. Kind of being and non-being. It was just a feeling of openness that I just kind of disappeared into it — and I had no awareness of concentrating on awareness. It wasn't the feeling of the two separate things. I didn't feel like I was part of it; I just was. It was more of a verb than a noun and a verb."

EXPERIMENTER: "Do you recall what was happening when you said 'just now' toward the end?"

SUBJECT: "When I said it, it was over with ... or it was... it was never really over with any of those times, but the concentration was broken, so the awareness feeling sort of stayed throughout the whole 20 minutes, or whatever, but I know each time I said it ('just now'), it was because concentration was broken at that time — but I think I must have gone almost straight back into it..."

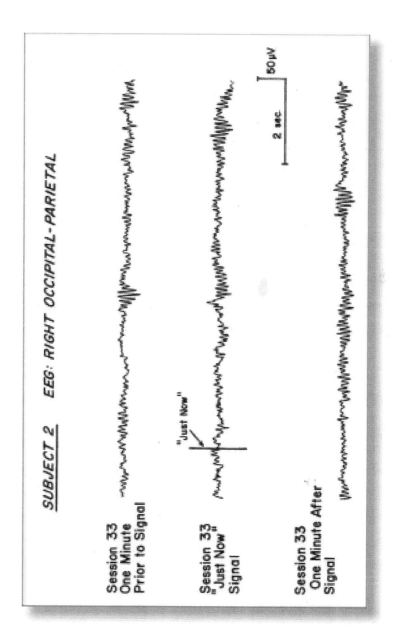

No difference is evident before the signal (state of "openness"),
after the signal (concentration "broken"), and a short time later
when subject presumably went "straight back into it."

DISAPPEARANCE OF EGO BOUNDARY

Subject 2, session 28: focus on awareness (Fig. 2)

"...This (the signal 'just now') was towards the end of the session. Before I went into full concentration, which was maybe the last four minutes of the session, it was just kind of like the outline of my body sitting in the chair and was just kind of dimming and going off into vapor... When I went into full concentration, I wasn't aware of completely vaporizing; I was just completely, not anywhere... It wasn't a matter of going into my mind and into awareness; I just kind of became... there was no I... The awareness was kind of a very gentle type of a vapor sort of feeling — I guess very open and very gentle, but still energy. I'm quite shaken by it; I can still feel it. It's over the top of my head right now."

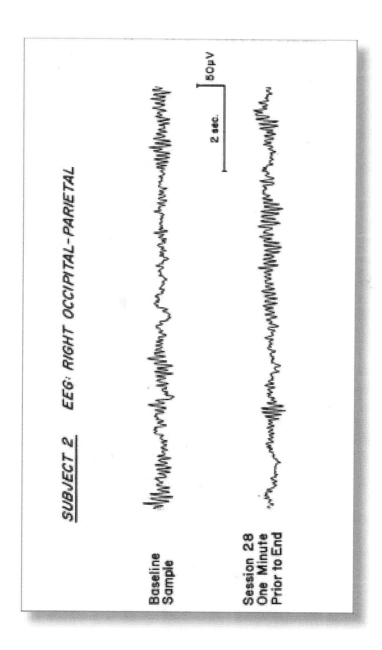

*Comparison shows no difference between baseline sample and
that taken during complete loss of ego boundaries.*

HALLUCINATORY PERCEPTION

Subject 4, session 44, focus on sound:

"The sound would go from right to left around, counter-clock-wise ... It wasn't a steady, even speed, but it would do what I wanted it to; I could stop breathing, hold my breath, and it would stay right wherever it was... It wasn't a solid thing that went around, it was like a steady stream... then it went from that to where it seemed to broaden or get wider... and again the speed was not a steady thing, but I noticed I could hold my breath and it didn't stop. It would slow down but it didn't stop like it had before, which I think is where the first... it wasn't panic, but this is where it seemed to pick up speed, and by then it was not only going fast, but it was coming closer. By then I was starting to panic and I stopped for just a minute, and my heart was pounding, only it didn't stop... It seems like more of a dream or something... oh, this sounds so dumb. And here you were up here, only it wasn't really you, it was a head or an image, and you were just laughing and I was getting so mad because you weren't going to help me, you weren't going to pull me up. And, if I didn't stop this myself, then nobody would..."

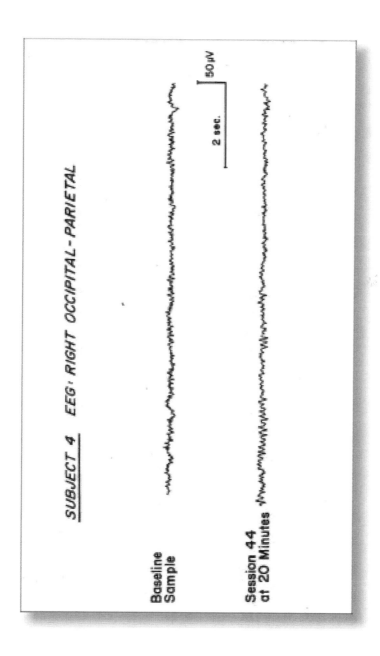

Comparison with baseline shows only a slight increase in alpha,
in this particular portion of the record.

VIVID, AUTONOMOUS FANTASY

Subject 5, session 20, focus on sound (Fig. 4)

"It kind of seems as if there was a person this time out on this beach or this sandy place, and I couldn't figure out who it was... When the sound would be all around and it seems as if it was me; yet, on the other hand, it didn't seem as if it really was me. I was wondering who it was, and it sounds dumb. Then, a little butterfly came along and the butterfly was humming along like the sound does. This butterfly was going to help somehow decide who it was... it was a yellow butterfly, like a monarch butterfly. It was all the vivid colors. So then the butterfly was going to help me look for a name, and so then the butterfly... this sound became a motorboat... the butterfly and I went out in the motorboat to look for a name for the person, and we'd go all around. Some of the places would be pleasant, and some would be unpleasant. Some of the... like you'd be sitting along an open lake, and then we'd go into the dark trees up a river, and it would be sort of frightening because there would be lots of motion in the water."

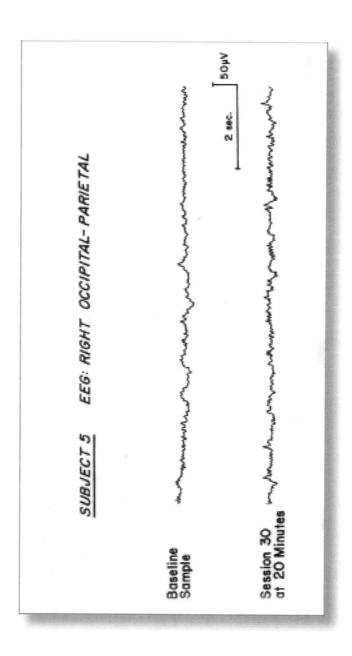

Comparison with baseline shows no striking change.

Thus, there was a remarkable absence of EEG changes during periods of profound changes in the subjects' state of consciousness.

Similarly, the longitudinal changes in EEG (total alpha, session-by-session, for each subject) did not reach significance.

Analysis of variances of Groups A, B, C, yielded results well below significance. However, a runs test did indicate that in Group A alpha-time increased in amount over sessions as compared to the controls.

The variability of individual subjects from one session to the next was so large as to render the differences statistically insignificant. Figure 5, shown on the next page, is a typical graph:

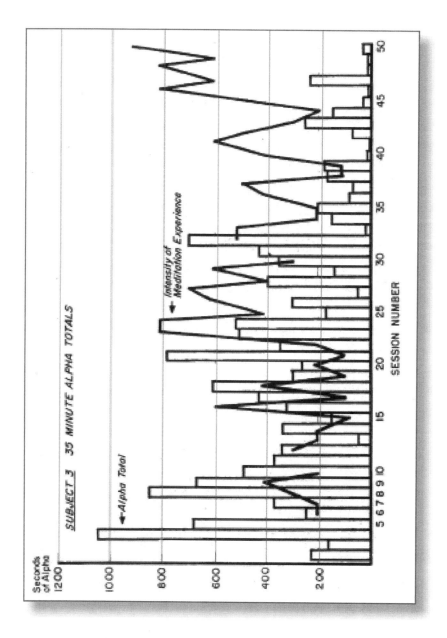

Note the lack of correlation between intense experiences
and amount of alpha.

EMG

No significant difference was apparent between experimental groups or between the experimental and control subjects. A runs test failed to show a significant change in EMG over time.

Figure 6 is a typical graph:

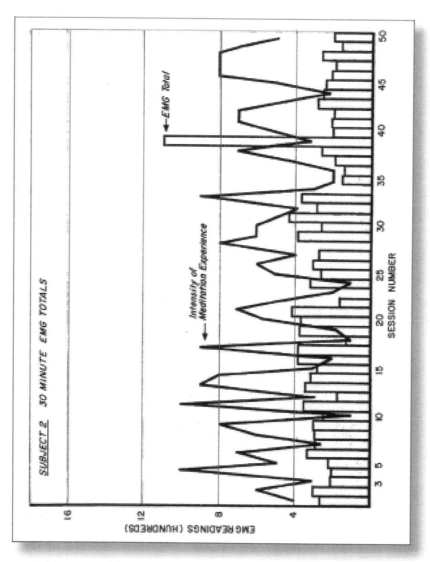

Subjects 1 and k showed a trend of increasing muscle tension as the sessions progressed but the considerable variability from session to session rendered this trend insignificant. All other subjects showed no trends and no subjects showed any correlation of EMG level with the intensity of individual sessions.

Control Group

The control subjects (Group C) spent an equal amount of time sitting in the experimental room while the same type of data was collected. Their retrospective accounts revealed that they had experiences within the limits of ordinary daydreaming. They planned future activities, mulled over personal problems and engaged in fantasies. Judging by their subjective reports, the experiences of the control group subjects were ordinary and clearly different from those of the experimental groups whose experiences ranged from the curiously unusual to the frightening, exhilarating, or bizarre. The EEG and EMG records for individual control subjects were unremarkable and without significant trends.

Subjective Intensity

In order to compare subjects with each other in terms of intensity of their experiences, the scorer was asked to select the highest scoring session of each subject and rank-order the resulting group of protocols.

The results show a clear differentiation between control and meditation subjects. One control subject scored high on a session in which she had a vivid fantasy, but otherwise her sessions were unremarkable.

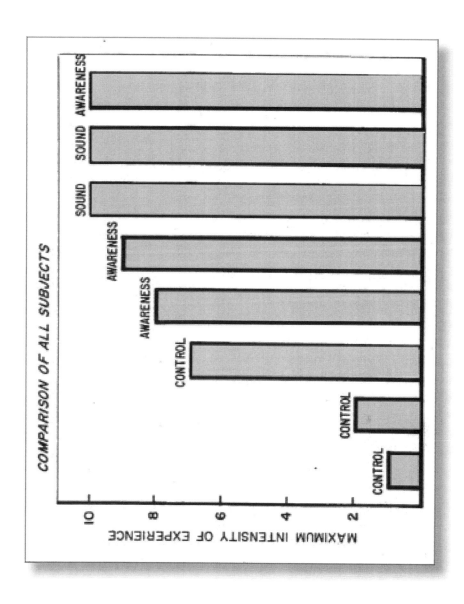

Sensory Versus Non-sensory Targets

Those subjects focusing on the non-sensory target (the awareness of being aware), seemed to undergo changes in consciousness
affecting body boundaries and the experience of self. These experiences were often positively valued and enjoyed. Descriptively,
they approached classical accounts of the mystical experience.

Those subjects focusing on the sensory target (the steady-tone signal), experienced changes in consciousness in the direction of vivid,
dream-like fantasies often accompanied by anxiety. In the case of
one subject, a catharsis occurred of traumatic childhood experiences associated with fears of death and dying. The subject seemed
to have benefited from the meditation experience as if she had been
in psychotherapy. This may have been due to the fact that the subjects talked about their experiences with the experimenter immediately following each session. The experimenter would respond non-
directively, but with encouragement.

On the whole, the sensory target sessions were less enjoyable and
less valued as compared to those with the non-sensory target. The
one subject who dropped out was in the sensory target group and he
seemed to find the procedure increasingly stressful. However, there
was no correlation between subjects' reports of stress for a given
session and decrease (or increase) of alpha-time or EMG totals.

Discussion

These results show that meditation practice produced profound
changes in consciousness which were not reflected in the EEG and
EMG. However, a number of factors must be considered in evaluating these results: experimenter bias, type of meditation, subject factors,
computer analysis of the EEG, and target differences.

Experimenter Bias

Orne introduced the term "demand characteristics" to describe
the powerful effect on subjects of the expectations implicit in the
experimental situation (1962). This influence can never be completely

eliminated but there are indications that it was not a major factor in determining these negative results.

To begin with, I expected that there would be a correlation between alpha production and meditation training. I even hoped to discover an interrelationship between EEG and EMG that would permit a potent biofeedback design. When the analysis of the data was completed, I found the results disappointing. Furthermore, the surprise and anxiety that a number of subjects experienced during the meditation sessions, the autonomous character of the process they reported, and the difficulty they experienced in putting their experiences into words all suggest that the subjects' reports reflected meditation effects rather than subject compliance. Assuming this is so, it is very unlikely that demand expectations affected the EEG and EMG tracing, since the subjects had no feedback available to them and were not informed of their "score." I and my research assistants did not keep track of what was happening to the scores from one session to the next and did not know what neurophysiological results we were obtaining.

Type of Meditation

The particular meditation instructions used in this experiment were based initially on a specific text, the Yoga of Pantanjali (Woods, 1914), classified as Raja Yoga; the text instructions were modified slightly to accommodate the experimental method and to communicate to contemporary Westerners. The subjects were instructed to keep their eyes open during the concentration exercise, as in earlier experiments by the author (Deikman, 1963, 1966).

This conforms to Zen meditation practice as well as to certain types of Patanjali Yoga. (However, Transcendental Meditation, a form of Yoga, requires that eyes be closed.)

Although there are important differences between Zen and Yoga meditations, possibly reflected in such laboratory phenomena as the reported absence of alpha blocking in Yogis (Anand, 1961) — these research reports indicate that sustained alpha rhythms and theta rhythms, as well, are characteristic end-products of meditation training. Indeed, Kasamatsu and Hirai (1969) claimed to be able to differentiate the stage of attainment of Zen monks on the basis of the EEG. On the basis of these studies, it was expected that the subjects of this experiment would develop large amounts of alpha whether or not they were performing a specific Yoga or Zen meditation, provided that what they were doing conformed to basic meditation practice, as described earlier.

Subjects' Tension

It might be argued that the absence of a strong alpha effect is due to the subjects' tension over succeeding at the task or making an effort to concentrate; something more experienced meditators have learned to surmount. However, the subjects' EEG and EMG data are not significantly different from baseline measures where subjects had no task other than sitting quietly in the chair. By the experimental subjects' third baseline session, there was no indication by observation or interview that any appreciable tension was present. A comparison of the baseline tracing with records taken during intense experiences shows no significant differences. The EMG data likewise does not suggest that tension is the explanation. Furthermore, the retrospective reports of some subjects indicated a marked loss of body and ego boundaries. At such times, the subjects' experience of striving is likely to have changed (Deikman, 1971).* Yet the EEG records, as well as the EMG, do not appear different immediately before, during, and after those experiences.

Lack of Proficiency

Because the subjects practiced this form of meditation for only fifty sessions, it might be said that they had not become sufficiently proficient to show an alpha effect. This may be true but, if it is, becoming proficient in meditation is not to be measured by change in the state of consciousness, *per se*. As the above quotations indicate, these novice subjects apparently experienced radical alterations in their customary state of consciousness. Even in this relatively brief series of sessions, profound changes occurred.

Computer Analysis

Computer analysis of frequency and amplitude of the EEG was not done in this experiment. Some investigators using such analysis have reported changes associated with meditation. Wallace and Benson (1970) reported an increase in mean square amplitude of alpha in the central and frontal regions for their subjects as a group, and the appearance of 5-7 Hz in five of their thirty-six subjects. Banquet (1973) reported an extension of alpha from the occipital-parietal to the central and frontal regions, as well as an increase in amplitude of alpha at the end of meditation.

However, the sample EEG tracings that Wallace and Benson and Banquet included in their published reports show clear and obvious changes by visual inspection alone. No such differences could be seen in the records of my subjects, despite very careful reading. This same point holds true for other EEG studies of experienced meditators reported by Anand et al, Bagchi and Wenger, Das and Gastaut and others. Their EEG records show large and clear changes correlated with meditation activity, the changes being immediately evident by gross inspection.

Sensory Versus Non-sensory Target

The explanation for the different subjective effects of focusing on a non-sensory versus a sensory target may be that the focus on awareness itself expands the subjective sense of self or the "I," which is closely linked to basic awareness and, consequently, affects the related experience of time and space. There is some evidence that the characteristics of time, space, and self are related so that changing one dimension can affect the others (Deikman, 1971).

Implications

These results raise the questions:

1) Why were there no clear changes in EEG accompanying the marked changes in consciousness reported by the subjects of

this experiment?

2) What is responsible for the EEG changes described by other investigators?

The data of this experiment suggests that there is a significant difference between naive subjects practicing a laboratory form of meditation and experienced meditators who have been trained in a meditation discipline within the context of a particular ideology. This difference is probably not a function of change in state of consciousness, as usually conceived. Contrary to popular belief, the occurrence of hallucinations, loss of body and ego boundaries, and oblivion to ordinary stimuli, etc., apparently are not criteria denoting "advancement" in meditation since they occurred in my subjects and were not accompanied by the EEG changes found in other studies.

Our tendency is to think of meditation in terms of the unusual experiences it can produce: mystical states with dramatic changes in self/object differentiation, in time and space, in sensory vividness and in the very quality of realness, itself. These phenomena are reported in classical accounts of widely differing cultures and have also been demonstrated in the laboratory (Deikman, 1963,1966).

Furthermore, Satori or Enlightenment is sometimes described in dramatic perceptual and cognitive terms. Such phenomena can be understood as by-products of a deautomization, or undoing, of the automatic perceptual and cognitive processes that organize, limit, select, and interpret perceptual stimuli (Deikman, 1963). However, it is my hypothesis that the basic purpose and effect of meditation may be something quite different: the reorientation of a person's fundamental attitude toward the world and with it a change in the experience of the self.

Traditionally, meditation has been developed and taught as part of an inclusive spiritual practice whose major activity is training in selflessness — the giving up of personal striving and the concomitant development of detachment, of "letting-go."

For example, in Zen meditation, called zazen, one may be instructed to "just sit," rather than to do something. The spiritual community, the philosophy and the daily life of the monastery or ashram in which intensive meditation training is conducted are all integrated to accomplish a change in the participant's basic approach to life — a change from striving to acceptance. The striking changes in the EEG of monks and yogis may reflect this change in fundamental attitude — what might be termed a person's basic organismic strategy — rather than the occurrence of changes in perception and cognition, *per se*.

There is reason to believe that such a shift in a person's basic attitude will be reflected in many psychological and physiological dimensions. A variety of clinical and laboratory phenomena suggest that mental and physical processes may be coordinated in basic modes to serve the underlying purpose of the organism (Deikman, 1970). Our usual mode, which I have termed the Action Mode, is organized to act on the environment. It features sharp perceptual and cognitive boundaries, focal attention, logical (object-based) thinking, and increased striate muscle activity. Language develops as a tool of the Action Mode. In that mode, the formal characteristic of objects (shape, size, meaning) predominate in consciousness. In contrast, the Receptive Mode is organized to take in the environment. Attention becomes diffuse, boundaries become indistinct, and thinking tends towards the paralogical, linear time fades away. Smooth muscle activity is increased, while sensuous dimensions of perception are enhanced, such as color and texture. The sense of self, which in the Action Mode is usually experienced in the head and behind the eyes, becomes less vivid in the Receptive Mode and may be experienced more diffusely throughout the body or even fade away completely.

It is my hypothesis that a change in basic strategy or attitude is brought about by meditation and this change results in a shift to the Receptive Mode and a corresponding change in the EEG. The subjects of this experiment had not had sufficient time, support, or indoctrination to bring about a change in their basic attitude, although the meditation procedure was sufficient to affect their state of consciousness,

per se. In contrast, the subjects of other investigators had been participating in an organized meditation discipline for many months or years,
bringing about a change in their underlying goal-strategy or attitude
that was then reflected in the EEG.

Conclusion

Meditation is a practice in letting go of thought processes, of self-
concerns, of the need to control. This leads to the development of an
attitude of acceptance, of detachment from personal concerns, of openness to immediate experience. It is also a practice of shifting one's
self, one's center of awareness, from thinking processes "in" the head
to sensations "in" the body, or to "exterior" percepts. Difficult as it
may be to measure or even to precisely define these dimensions, they
are important psychological realities, brought into sharp focus by the
practice of meditation.

In contrast to the absence of changes in EEG and EMG found in
the subjects of this experiment, the marked changes reported in studies of experienced meditators may reflect the effect of meditation
on basic attitudes and self-experience, rather than on the more
spectacular phenomena of consciousness. The dimensions of attitude and self-experience are basic to the spiritual disciplines from
which various meditation practices developed and in which they are
practiced. It would not be surprising if we have been neglecting these
essentials because they are more difficult to measure and are foreign
to the framework of our science.

References

1. Anand, B., Chhina G., Singh, B., *Some Aspects of Electroencephalographic
   Studies in Yogis.* ELECTROENCEPH. CLIN. NEUROPHYSIOLOGY,1961, 13, A52-A56.
2. Bagchi, B., and Wenger, M., *Electrophysiological correlates of some Yogi
   exercises.* EEG CLIN. NEUROPHYSIOLOGY, 1957, 7: 132-49.
3. Banquet, J. P., *Spectral analysis of the EEG in meditation.* ELECTROENCHEPH,
   CLIN. NEUROPHYSIOL., 1973, 35: 143-151.
4. Budzynski, T. H., Stoyva, J. M., Adler, C.S., *Feedback-induced muscle*

relaxation: Application to tension headache. J. BEHAV. THER. EXP. PSYCHIATRY, 1: 1970, 205-211.

5. Budzynski, T. H., et al.: *EMG biofeedback and tension headache: A controlled-outcome study.* PSYCHOSM. MED., 35: 1973, 484-496.

6. Das, N., Gastaut, H., *Variations in the Electrical Activity of the Brain, Heart, and Skeletal Muscles During Yogic Meditation and Trance.* ELECTROENCEPH. CLIN. NEUROPHSIOL., 1955, Suppl. No. 6, 211-219.

7. Deikman, Arthur J., *Experimental meditation.* J. NERV. MENT. DIS., 1963, 136, No.4, 329-343.

8. Deikman, Arthur J., *Implications of experimentally induced contemplative meditation.* J. NERV. MENT. DIS., 1966, 142, No. 2, 101-116.

9. Deikman, Arthur J., *Bimodal consciousness.* ARCH. GEN. PSYCHIAT., 1971, 45, 481-489.

10. Deikman, Arthur J., *Deautomization and the mystical experience,* PSYCHIATRY, 1963, 29:4, 324-338.

11. Green, E., Green A., Walters E.D., *Voluntary Control of Internal States Psychological and Physiological.* J. TRANS. PSYCHOL., 1970, 1: 1-26.

12. Ikegami, R., *Psychological Study of Zen Posture.* KYUSHU PSYCHOL STUDIES, V. Bull, Fac, Lit. Kyushu Univ., 1968, No. 5, 105-135.

13. Kamiya, J., *Operant control of the EEG Alpha Rhythm and Some of its Reported Effects on Consciousness* In *Altered States of Consciousness,* Charles Tart, ed., John Wiley & Sons, Inc., New York, 1969, 507-518.

14. Kasamatsu, A., Hirai, T., *An Electroencephalographic Study of the Zen Meditation* In *Altered States of Consciousness,* Charles Tart, ed., John Wiley & Sons, Inc., New York, 1969, 489-502.

15. Orne., M., *On the social psychology of the psychological experiment: with particular reference to demand characteristics and their implications.* AMER. PSYCHOL., 1962, 17, 776-783.

16. Wallace, R. K., Benson, H., Wilson, A. F., *A wakeful hypometabolic physiologic state.* AMER. J. PHYS., 1971, 221: 3, 795-799.

17. Woods, J. H., *The Yogi System of Pantanjali.* Harvard Univ. Press Cambridge, 1914 (Harvard Oriental Series, Vol. 17).

This study was supported by the National Institute of Mental Health, Grants MH16800 and MH1 6793 and by the University of Colorado Medical Center. David Galin gave valuable assistance in the preparation of the manuscript.

*Presented at the Conference on Altered States of Consciousness and Suggestology, Pepperdine University, Los Angeles, May 1975.

Implications of Experimentally Induced Contemplative Mysticism

Introduction

Unusual perceptions have always been the subject of intense interest, desire, and speculation. In early history it was customary to interpret and seek such occurrences within a religious context. Even the gross disorders of epilepsy and psychosis were thought to be cases of supernatural possession, blessed or otherwise. Strange experiences were valued, and the use of fasting drugs, ceremony, and dancing to induce a strange experience was common in cultures ranging from the Amazon Indians to ascetic European monks. Only with the rise of Western science did man become dissatisfied with theological inquiry and seek to understand strange experiences as a type of natural phenomena, to be explained by the same powerful mechanical and mathematical models that were conquering the planets and the chemical elements. Psychological science began studying conscious experience and the advent of psychoanalysis ushered in the exploration of unconscious functioning. The problem of unusual perceptions, however, is still a puzzle, a challenge, and a matter of philosophical dispute.

The classical mystic experience is the prime example of an unusual perception still subject to conflicting interpretations. Both Eastern and Western mystic literature describe an experience that goes beyond ordinary sensory impressions and yet is a perception, a perception of something so profound, uplifting, and intense as to lie beyond communication by language and to constitute the highest human experience. It would appear that contemplative meditation is one instrument for achieving such a state, although not necessarily sufficient in itself.

This paper reports some results of a phenomenological investigation of meditation phenomena and attempts to explain the data and relate it to a broader context.

Procedure

In order to investigate the mystic experience, an experimental procedure was devised based on classical descriptions of contemplative meditation. This procedure can be described as one of perceptual concentration. An initial short-term experiment study showed that very striking changes in the perception of the self and of objects were possible through the use of this procedure, and there were also indications that analogues to the classical mystic experience could be achieved as well. The rationale, procedure, results, and conclusions of this experiment have been reported elsewhere.[3]

The same procedure, somewhat simplified, was then employed to study the effects of perceptual concentration over a longer period of time. Although much of the phenomena that resulted seemed readily explainable on the basis of after-images, auto-kinetic movement, phosphenes and the like, certain data did not seem adequately accounted for by reference to familiar perceptual phenomena or by the use of such theoretical explanatory concepts as are currently available, e.g., suggestion or projection. Additional hypotheses seem necessary, and it is the purpose of this paper to present these data and the postulates derived from them.

The original experiment involved a total of twelve "concentration" sessions. It was hoped that four to six subjects could next be studied over a total of 70 or more sessions. One of the subjects of the original experiment did continue for a total of 78 sessions, at which point she changed jobs, moving to a distant area. Six subjects who began the experiment did not proceed beyond ten sessions for a variety of reasons ranging from job conflict (the procedure calls for three experimental sessions per week, during the day) to an inability to adopt the way of psychological functioning required. Four subjects continued for 30 to 40 sessions. One additional subject completed 106 sessions and is currently involved in a different experiment.

The data with which this paper is concerned came primarily from the two subjects, A and G, who completed the longest series of sessions. These subjects had the most intense and unusual experiences of the group, approximately in direct relationship to the number of sessions. In this connection, it should be noted that vivid experiences seemed, on the one hand, to indicate a tolerance and compatibility with the procedure and, on the other hand, to motivate the subject to continue over a long period of time. Subjects C, D, and L (30 to 40 sessions) appeared to have gone partway along the some paths as A and G in that they experienced the beginnings of breakdown in the self-object distinction, had some experience of light, strange imagery, and the like. However, they appeared less able to relinquish control and "accept whatever happens."

Subject A was a 38-year-old psychiatric nurse who was undergoing psychoanalysis at the time of the experiment.[A] Subject G was a 40-year-old housewife. Both subjects were personally known to the experimenter and were asked to participate in the experiment on the basis of their apparent intelligence, interest, and available time. Subject G was paid, Subject A was not. It seemed clear that money was not a crucial factor in their participation. There was evidence of neurotic conflicts (by history and MMPI), but both subjects were functioning relatively normally in their environment.

The experiment was conducted in a comfortable, carpeted office — the lighting, colors, and atmosphere of which were subdued. The subject sat in an armchair about ten feet from a medium blue vase which rested on a simple brown end table; the experimenter sat to one side and behind the subject at a desk on which there were two tape recorders. It was necessary to move to a different experimental room twice during the course of the experiment but the general atmosphere was maintained and the change did not seem to affect the phenomena reported by the subjects.

Contemplative meditation requires that the subject relinquish his customary mode of thinking and perceiving. Thoughts must be stopped, sounds and peripheral sensations put out of one's mind, and the contemplation of the meditative object be conducted in a nonanalytic, nonintellectual manner. This aim determined the composition of the instructions that were read by the experimenter to the subject immediately preceding the first few sessions. Subject A, who had begun the first experiment, received the following directions: "The purpose of these sessions is to learn about concentration. Your aim is to concentrate on the blue vase. By concentration I do not mean analyzing the different parts of the vase, or thinking series of thoughts about the vase, or associating ideas to the vase, but rather, trying to see the vase as it exists in itself, without any connections to other things. Exclude all other thoughts or feelings or sounds or body sensations. Do not let them distract you but keep them out so that you can concentrate all your attention, all your awareness on the vase itself. Let the perception of the vase fill your entire mind."

Subject G received a differently worded set of instructions as an attempt had been made to present the required concept more clearly for the second experiment and thus decrease the need for additional explanations: "This is an experiment in how we see and experience things. Ordinarily we look at the world around us with only part of our attention; the rest is taken up with thinking about what we are seeing or with unrelated thoughts. This experiment will explore the possibilities of seeing and experiencing when you cease thinking altogether and concentrate your attention on only one thing: the blue vase on the table in front of you.

"Look at the vase intently, focus all your interest on it, try to perceive the vase as directly as possible but without studying or analyzing it. Have your entire mind concentrated on the vase, at the same time remain open to the experience — let whatever happens happen.

"All thinking must came to a stop so that your mind becomes quiet. Do not let yourself be distracted by thoughts, sounds or body sensations — keep them out so that you can concentrate all your attention on the vase."

The intent of both sets of instructions was the same and the different wording did not seem to be significant; the same type of questions was raised by both subjects and the experimenter was required to amplify and explain the instructions in the early sessions in approximately the same way. The principal difficulty encountered by subjects was grasping the concept of *not thinking:* to cease actively examining or thinking about the vase. The main problem that required additional explanation was the confusion about whether to try to block out all sensations arising during the session. They were told that insofar as the sensations were part of the experience of concentration rather than distraction or interference, they should accept them.

Both sets of instructions concluded with the directions: "While you concentrate I am going to play music on the tape machine. Do not let the sounds occupy your attention or disturb your concentration. If you find you have drifted into a stream of thought, stop and bring your attention back to the vase. At the end of ____ minutes I will tell you that the session is over but take as much time as you like to stop."

After a few initial sessions of ten and 15 minutes of concentration, with cello music played as a background on the tape recorder, the concentration period was extended to 30 minutes and performed in silence. At the end of the designated time the experimenter gave the signal "30 minutes" and the subject could stop or continue longer if desired. All subjects were able to complete 30 minutes, but they seldom continued much longer.

After the subjects had finished concentrating, the experimenter conducted an inquiry based on the following questions:

1) "How did it go?"
2) "Describe the course of the session."
3) "How much of the time were you able to concentrate so that

you were aware only of the vase and nothing else?"

4) "What means did you use to maintain concentration?"

5) "What thoughts did you have during the session?"

6) "What feelings did you have?"

7) "What was your experience of the vase?"

8) (Optional; introduced as sessions progressed.) "What is your intent as you look at the vase?"

9) (Subject is asked to go to the window.) "Look out the window and describe what you see and the way it looks."

As the experiment progressed, the subjects tended to cover the main question areas spontaneously so that the experimenter asked questions mainly to clarify statements of the subject. The interview was flexible, designed to elicit whatever phenomena the subject had experienced and to follow up anything of interest to the experimenter. During the inquiry the experimenter endeavored to be as neutral as possible but from time to time it was necessary to re-instruct subjects in the procedure and to deal with the subject's anxiety when startling phenomena occurred. In the latter case this was done by stressing that the experience was under the subject's control, the phenomenon was very interesting and, apart from its newness, need not be frightening. The inquiry lasted about 20 minutes and was tape recorded in its entirety.

Results and Discussion

In trying to understand the data that resulted from the experiment, a basic question was asked: "What was the subject perceiving?" The bulk of the percepts resulting from the experiment seemed readily explained in terms of such familiar concepts as after-images, phosphenes, stabilized retinal images, projection, and distortion. The data selected for discussion below consists of perceptual phenomena whose explanation may require the construction of additional hypotheses. For the purpose of clarity the data will be presented in three groups, each followed by discussion. It should be noted that these phenomena did not occur in every session, but once the subject experienced a percept it tended to recur in later sessions, usually with greater intensity.

Light

G; 28th session: "...the vase changes in concept for me, then short-ly after that, suddenly, I begin to feel this light going back and forth. It's circular. I can't follow it all the way to my forehead but I can certainly follow it about as far as my hand... and I can feel it go the rest of the way."

G; 67th session: "... somewhere between the matter that is the wall and myself, somewhere in between the matter is this moving, this vibrating light and motion and power and very real substance... it's so real and so vital that I feel as though I could reach out and take a chunk of it and hand it to you."

C; 41st session: "It seems as if you were turning a light down, that you were turning the intensity of the light down and yet I still had this kind of shimmering sensation of very bright light simultaneously with the idea that everything is getting dark."

G; 87th session: "This circle of light, this area that goes in and then out to encompass me... it's not like sunlight... it isn't even like moonlight, it's kind of cold light in a way... it's jagged in a way around the outside... it's a kind of compaction or compression and suddenly out of this compression comes a light. It's not like a searchlight, it isn't like a beacon, it's very irregular in its outline."

G; 104th session: "You can't discern a shimmering in the room can you, a color or bright shimmering in this whole area."

(Experimenter): "No."

G: "Well, it's very real to me, it's so real that I feel you ought to be able to see it."

A; 54th session: "It was also as though we were together, you know, instead of being a table and a vase and me, my body and the chair, it all dissolved into a bundle of something which had... a great deal of energy to it but which doesn't form into anything but it only feels like a force."

G; 55th session: "...like a magnetic attraction as though I had iron in me and there was a magnet pulling, but you would have to imagine that I had iron in every one of my cells...."

A; 53rd session: "...at the point when I felt as though everything was coming from there directed against me... some kind of force, I can't say what it was as though a force were enveloping me."

G; 93rd session: "...I felt this strong, strong pull in my thoughts. I could feel it as I have never felt anything before ... one instant there was this tranquil sort of thing and the next minute there was this vital, pulling, pushing force ... it felt as though somebody had hooked up or made a connection with a vital thing that was real that was pulling my thoughts. Not only pulling them, but compressing thoughts too."

Motion

A; 17th session: "...the table and tile vase were rocking. Now I was both conscious that they were not in any sense moving, but the sensation of rocking, their rocking or rocking inside of me back and forth, was quite prominent for quite some time."

C; 21st session: "I had the distinct impression... that what I could see of the vase was drifting... it was in motion just very slightly... it just seemed to be wavering somehow... the whole thing seemed to be moving."

(Experimenter): "You saw it move or you had the impression it was moving?"

C: "I had the impression that it was moving."

G; 5th session: "It's almost us though within that cone, movement is taking place back and forth. I'm still not sure though whether it's the motion in the rings or if it's the rings. But in a certain way it is real... it's not real in the sense that you can see it, touch it, taste it, smell it or anything but it certainly is real in the sense that you can experience it happening."

G; 8th session: "It's the feeling of something pulling your whole being together to a point and you can feel it in an actual sensation of motion." These perceptual experiences were characterized by: 1) an unusual way of perceiving (e.g., light is *felt*; motion of the vase is *felt* but not seen; force envelops) although the usual perceptual routes are also employed; 2) the percepts are primitive and basic (i.e., force, light, and motion); and 3) the percepts are intensely real.

To answer the question, "What was perceived?," we must consider both the possibility that the relevant stimuli were of internal origin and the possibility that the stimuli originated external to the subject. In the discussion that follows, the assumption of internal stimuli and the possible explanations of suggestion, projection, dreaming and hypnagogic state will be taken up first, followed by a consideration of the hypotheses of sensory translation and reality transfer. Then, assuming external stimuli, the hypothesis of perceptual expansion will be presented.

Internal Stimuli
Suggestion

"Suggestion" refers to a subject's reporting a perception corresponding to some previous overt statement by the experimenter pertaining to what the subject would perceive. This concept is often extended to include cues, given unconsciously by the experimenter, that indicate to the subject what phenomena are expected. The subject may make suggestions to himself producing "auto-suggestion." In the perceptual concentration experiment, the experimenter's verbalizations were recorded, transcribed and compiled under the category "Experimenter's Role." These records indicate that no direct verbal suggestion pertaining to expected phenomena was made by the experimenter, with the exception of such statements as "most people have found this (concentration) to be interesting and rewarding." In no case was a statement made indicating the actual phenomena reported by other subjects or reported in the classical meditation literature. None of the subjects had read about meditation phenomena and all were instructed not to discuss the phenomena with anyone else. (One subject began reading mystic literature toward the end of the experiment and was excited to note the similarity between her experiences and those described by various authors. None of the subjects were close friends and the identity of the experimental subjects was unknown to each other. In one instance during the first experiment, when an exchange of information did take place between subject A and another subject, the phenomena reported were quite different and, indeed, subject A felt very disappointed that both prior to the conversation and afterwards, she was not able to have the experiences reported to her by the other subject. In addition, this subject and most of the others demonstrated on many occasions their resistance to statements made by the experimenter that did not seem accurate to them when he attempted to paraphrase their own reports.

There were some indications of the experimenter supplying covert cues. From time to time subjects remarked that they felt he expected them to report new phenomena as the experiment progressed. In one case, subject A felt aware, correctly, of the experimenter's interest in a particular phenomenon (disappearance of the vase) and remarked that she therefore thought that he wanted such phenomena to occur. She stated in this connection that this was the only cue she had detected in the course of the experiment. There was also some opportunity for extra-experimental covert influence since all of the long-term subjects were personally known to the experimenter and G, C and D were social acquaintances and friends of his. The possibility for covert suggestion cannot be eliminated and, to some extent, was always present. If the experimenter gave covert cues to the subjects as to what phenomena delighted and fascinated him, this would undoubtedly result, at the least, in a biased selection by the subject of the phenomena reported. In a broad sense this may well have taken place since the interview did not consist of systematic questioning of all arena of perceptual phenomena but was largely a following up of the subject's report plus questions directed at main subject categories. As sessions progressed fewer of such questions were asked of the subjects as they reported striking phenomena that spontaneously covered the areas of questioning themselves. There was no evidence of successful auto-suggestion. On different occasions subjects would try to repeat an experience they had had and usually found this very difficult, if not impossible. Indeed such attempts were found to be an interference in the concentration process.

Perhaps the most important argument against suggestion being no important determinant is the fact that, on the one hand, the very striking phenomena reported were quite unexpected and surprising to the experimenter who had not believed that classical phenomena such as "merging" or unity experiences could occur without years of practice but, rather, had expected the phenomena to be mostly that of image breakdown. Further evidence against suggestion or auto-suggestion is the fact that phenomena such as animation of the vase or currents of force are not part of classical meditation ventures. (It should also be mentioned that there are almost no published accounts of the day-by-day phenomena of long-term "meditation" practice, and none that I know of dealing with long-term concentration upon an object such as a vase.) Also very significant in this connection was the subject's experience of anxiety and disbelief at the initial appearance of a phenomenon. The subjects often stopped the process quickly the first time it occurred. Only as they became more familiar with it were they able to let the phenomena develop further. It would seem reasonable that suggested phenomena would not elicit such a response of anxiety unless the experimenter had also suggested an anxious response — but there is no evidence that he did so. For all these reasons, suggestion does not seem to be an adequate explanation of the subjects' experiences.

Projection

In terms of psychoanalytic theory such perceptions as have been quoted could be regarded as "projections" of internal stimuli. The usual explanation of mystic experiences, and of unusual experiences in general, is to regard them as a "projection" and reinterpretation of repressed infantile memories[18] or in the case of psychotic hallucinations, as a synthetic product reestablishing object relations.[6] In his

paper on Schreber, Freud defined projection: "The most striking
characteristic of symptom formation is the process which deserves the
name of *projection*. As internal perception is suppressed and, instead,
its content, after undergoing a certain kind of distortion, enters consciousness in the form of an external perception."[6] In *Beyond the
Pleasure Principle* Freud discussed the genesis of this mechanism:
"...a particular way is adopted of dealing with any internal excitations
which produce too great an increase of unpleasure: There is a tendency
to treat them as though they were acting, not from the inside but from
the outside, so that it may be possible to bring the shield against stimuli into operation as a means of defense against them. This is the
origin of projection, which is destined to play such a large part in
the causation of pathological processes."[8] The basic phenomenon to
which Freud applied the concept of projection consisted of paranoid
hallucinations and delusions. In this view, the function of projection
is to defend the person against awareness of his own internal psychological contents and, consequently, it is these contents that are "pro-
jected" and perceived as external to the subject. Although later workers
have attempted to broaden the concept of projection,[13,14,19,20] nothing
further seems to have been hypothesized about how projection takes
place, and the broadened definitions gain wider scope at the expense
of explanatory potency.[B]

For the purpose of this discussion, "projection" shall refer to Freud's
definition emphasizing its function of defense against the awareness
of anxiety-provoking internal content. If we apply this concept to
to the subjects' experience already quoted we see that the content of
their perception did not consist of affect, motives, or ego-alien ideation
but, rather was composed of sensations referable to such qualities as
force, light and motion. Such sensory qualities do not lend themselves
readily to explanations centered on defense against drives (or even
the effect of style or stimulus interpretation). Although a "need" may
be ascribed to the subjects (e.g., to have unusual experiences), it is
not at all clear what the mechanism would be that would give them

the experiences they had. Neither do the experiences seem to be reconstructions of lost objects. The classical concept of "projection' does not seem to explain these data.

Dreaming

Were the subjects asleep and were their experiences actually dreams? When occasionally questioned specifically by the experimenter, A and B felt sure they had not been asleep when the reported phenomena occurred. They referred to the continuity of the vase and the table percept throughout most of the experiences in question. The vivid phenomena seemed to be superimposed on that continuity. On some occasions, the subjects specifically mentioned that they had fallen asleep for a brief time as they had become "suddenly" aware that their heads had fallen forward and that there had been a break in the continuity of the concentration. Nevertheless, the subjects could have had brief periods of sleep of which they were not aware. The perceptual continuity they experienced would argue against a dream state, as does the fact that their experiences did not have the complex structures normally associated with dreaming.

Hypnagogic State

However, there are important similarities to be noted between the subject's experience and the hypnagogic state described by Silberer.[22]

Sensory Translation Hypothesis

To account more adequately for the experimental data cited, I would like to postulate the process of *sensory translation*. Sensory translation is defined as the perception of psychic action (conflict repression, problem-solving, attentiveness, etc.) through the relatively unstructured sensations of light, color, movement, force, sound, smell or taste.[B] This hypothesis is related to Silberer's concept but differs in its referents and genesis. In the hypnagogic state and in dreaming a *symbolic* translation of psychic activity and ideas occurs but, although light, force, and movement may play a part in hypnagogic and dream construction, the predominant percepts are complex visual, verbal, conceptual, and activity images. "Sensory translation" refers to the experience of nonverbal, simple, concrete perceptual equivalents of psychic action. It comes into operation as a consequence of the altered cognitive mode brought about by the experimental instructions which focus on perceiving instead of thinking. The altered cognitive mode does not appear to be one of sleep or drowsiness.

This postulate lends itself well not only to the data quoted above but to the analysis of other, more detailed, reports that suggest a possible retranslation back to the stimuli themselves:

A; 63rd session: "...when the vase changes shape... I feel this in my body and particularly in my eyes... there is an actual kind of physical sensation as though something is moving there which recreates the shape of the vase." Here, this subject may be experiencing the perception of a re-synthesis taking place following the deautomization of the normal percept; that is, the percept of the vase is being reconstructed outside of the normal awareness and the process of reconstruction is perceived as a physical sensation.

G; 60th session: "...shortly I began to sense motion and shifting of light and dark as this became stronger and stronger. Now when this happens it's happening not only in my vision but it's happening or it feels like a physical kind of thing. It's connected with feelings of attraction, expansion, absorption and suddenly my vision pinpointed on a particular place and this became the center for a very powerful... I was in the grip of a very powerful sensation and this became the center." The perception of motion and shifting light and darkness may be the perception of the movement of attention among various psychic contents. "Attraction," "expansion," "absorption," would thus reflect the dynamics of the efforts to focus attention — successful focusing is then experienced as being "in the grip of" a powerful force.

G; 78th session: "...that feeling of pulling on the top of my head and then this awareness all of a sudden that I wasn't occupying my body, at least not completely as I usually do." Here the pulling may be the splitting of the normal synthesis, of body-self and mental-self leading to a feeling of being "suspended" or levitation.

G; 93rd session: "...I felt this strong, strong pull in my thoughts. I could feel it as I have never felt anything before — just really making contact and it was a glorious kind of feeling because it was such a powerful way of thinking, using the mind. It's almost as though something has opened up a whole batch of doors in my mind that haven't been opened before and that all this power had come rushing to and fro, that it was a connecting link between something out of the natural laws of the universe and me, my thoughts..." Perhaps this experience was a relatively direct perception of the release of psychic energy, presumably though a lifting of defensive barriers occurring as a consequence of the experimental program.

Realness and the Reality Function

Not only were these percepts unusual, they were often vividly real, seemingly palpable. Both A and B stated on some occasions that they were sure the experimenter must be able to see what they saw, even photograph it. It is necessary to account for the realness of these perceptions. There is clinical data demonstrating the great variability in the *realness* of our sensory percepts: 1) In states of de-personalization or de-realization perception is intact but the percepts "feel" unreal or lack the "feeling" of reality. 2) Persons who have had mystic experiences or who have taken LSD report states of consciousness that they feel are "more real" than normal. 3) In the case of some dreams, their "realism" may persist into the waking state. *Thus, realness and sensation are not a unity but the concurrent operation of two separate functions.* Realness (the quality of reality) and reality testing (the judgment of what is external versus what is imaginary) likewise appear to be two different functions although they usually operate in synchrony.

Freud discussed reality testing as a learned judgment: "A perception which is made to disappear by all action is recognized as external, as reality: where such an action makes no difference, the perception originates within the subject's own body."

A; 63rd session: "...when the vase changes shape... I feel this in my body and particularly in my eyes ... there is an actual kind of physical sensation as though something is moving there which recreates the shape of the vase." Here, this subject may be experiencing the perception of a re-synthesis taking place following the deautomization of the normal percept; that is, the percept of the vase is being reconstructed outside of the normal awareness and the process of reconstruction is perceived as a physical sensation.

G; 60th session: "... shortly I began to sense motion and shifting of light and dark as this became stronger and stronger. Now when this happens it's happening not only in my vision but it's happening or it feels like a physical kind of thing. It's connected with feelings of attraction, expansion, absorption and suddenly my vision pinpointed on a particular place and this became the center for a very powerful... I was in the grip of a very powerful sensation and this became the center." The perception of motion and shifting light and darkness may be the perception of the movement of attention among various psychic contents. "Attraction," "expansion," "absorption," would thus reflect the dynamics of the efforts to focus attention — successful focusing is then experienced as being "in the grip of" a powerful force.

G; 78th session: "... that feeling of pulling on the top of my head and then this awareness all of a sudden that I wasn't occupying my body, at least not completely as I usually do." Here the pulling may be the splitting of the normal synthesis, of body self and mental self leading to a feeling of being "suspended" or levitation.

G; 93rd session: "... I felt this strong, strong pull in my thoughts. I could feel it as I have never felt anything before – just really making contact and it was a glorious kind of feeling because it was such a powerful way of thinking, using the mind. It's almost as though something has opened up a whole batch of doors in my mind that haven't been opened before and that all this power had come rushing to and fro, that it was a connecting link between something out of the natural laws of the universe and me, my thoughts..." Perhaps this experience was a relatively direct perception of the release of psychic energy, presumably through a lifting of defensive barriers occurring as a consequence of the experimental program.

Reality Transfer Hypothesis

The experimental data and clinical examples cited above warrant the hypothesis that there is a specific ego function that bestows the quality of reality on the contents of experience. I would like to hypothesize that this function can be influenced and that the quality of reality can be displaced, intensified or attenuated — a process of *reality transfer.* In the meditation experiment, the sensory percepts are invested with this quality resulting in the vivid, intensely real experiences reported. Why does this take place? An initial speculation is that since, in the meditation experience, the object world as a perceptual experience is broken down or de-differentiated[3], the cognitive organization based on that world is disrupted in a parallel fashion. An ego function capable of appropriately bestowing reality quality must be linked developmentally with the organization of logical, object-based thought. It seems plausible that an alteration in that organization would affect the reality function. In the meditation experiment the subject is instructed to banish analytical, logical thought and to allow perception to dominate the field. In a formal sense these instructions constitute a regression to the primitive cognitive state postulated for the infant and young child, a state in which the distinction between thoughts, actions, and object is blurred as compared to the adult. Such a regression is likely to be enhanced by the passive dependent relationship with the experimenter. The body immobility, reduction in sensory input, and the relatively stabilized retinal image are additional factors capable of producing perceptual and cognitive disorganization. If we add all these forces together we see that the experimental meditation procedure is potentially a very powerful technique for undoing of the normal cognitive and perceptual modes. Such

an undoing might be expected to result in a mobility of "reality quality" permitting its displacement to internal stimuli, a displacement
congruent with the regressive push of the specific experimental
situation.

Deautomization

At this point it would be appropriate to discuss the concept of "de-
automatization," as it is relevant to the understanding of meditation
as well as other altered states of consciousness. Hartmann explicates
the concept of automatization as follows: "In well established achievements they (motor apparatuses) function automatically: the integration
of the somatic systems involved in the action is automatized, and so
is the integration of the individual mental acts involved in it. With
increasing exercise of the action its intermediate steps disappear from
consciousness ... not only motor behavior but perception and thinking
too show automatization." "It is obvious hat automatization may have
economic advantages in saving attention cathexis in particular and
simple cathexis of consciousness in general... Here as in most adaptation processes we have a purpose of provision of the average expect-
able range of tasks."[12] Thus, automatization performs the function
of eliminating details and intermediate steps of awareness so that attention is freed for other purpose. Gill and Brennan developed further
the concept of de-automatization: "Deautomization is an undoing of
the automatizations of apparatuses — both means and goal structures
— directed toward the environment. Deautomization is, as it were, a
shakeup that can be followed by an advance or a retreat in the level of
organization.... Some manipulation of the attention directed toward
the functioning of an apparatus is necessary if it is to be deauto-
matized."[22] Thus, deautomization is the undoing of automatization, presumably by *reinvesting actions and precepts with attention.*

The experimental procedure produces a deautomization of normal perceptual modes permitting the operation of sensory translation. At the same time a deautomization of the reality function

occurs such that the sense of reality normally bestowed on objects is now "transferred" to abstract psychical entities. As stated earlier, the experimental pressure away from abstract thought and towards pure perception fits this explanation.

External Stimuli

Perceptual Expansion Hypothesis

A further possibility remains. Some of the visual phenomena of the meditation experience (reported in the first experiment[3] and present throughout the long-term project) such as loss of the third dimension of the vase, diffusion of its formal properties and a tendency toward a homogenous color field, appear to be a result of a deautomization leading to a breakdown of the percepts in the direction of a primitive visual experience. However, the area: striking perceptions of force, movement and light — as well as other entities to be described below — may possibly be the product of a deautomization that permits the awareness of new dimensions of the total stimulus array. These experiences are not necessarily in the direction of a less organized de-differentiation as such, but of a real sensation that apparently is at variance with everyday perception. Such a concept of deautomatization as a liberating process leads to a third explanatory hypothesis for the meditation phenomena: *perceptual expansion* — the widening of perceptual intake to encompass "new" external stimuli, with a new perceptual route strongly implied. Perceptual expansion is made possible by deautomization of the selective gating and filtering processes that normally are in constant operation.

There is a developmental concept implicit in such an hypothesis; namely, that our earliest experience is probably one of being in more direct contact with numerous, vivid, primitively organized stimuli. As we mature, a learning process takes place in which stimuli and percepts are organized towards a high level of differentiation based on formal characteristics. This learning process not only takes place at the expense of the vividness and variability of sensory stimuli but possibly involves a loss of special perceptual functions other than those to which we are accustomed. There is evidence to support this concept.

Werner, in a statement based on studies of eidetic imagery in children as well as on broader studies of perceptual development, states that the image "... gradually changes in functional character. It becomes essentially subject to the exigencies of abstract thought. Once the image changes in function and becomes an instrument in reflective thought its structure also changes. It is only through such structural change that the image can serve as an instrument of abstract mental activity. This is why of necessity the sensuousness and fullness of detail, color and vividness of the image must fade."[25] The experimental work of Kohler illustrates this concept. In reviewing his experiments on the effects of treating distorting lenses for days at a time, Kohler concludes, "We are confronted here with the peculiar relationship between optical and physical facts. We always find that it is the physical dimension of things which have a tendency to become visually correct. This is due to the fact that physical dimensions are among the most frequent and symmetrically distributed stimuli. Consequently, it is with these stimulus qualities that unique perceptual experiences of straightness, right angularity, and good form tend to become associated. It is always the physically unique stimuli which gradually become the reference standards for our percepts. This is the reason why in the process of adaptation it is always the world which we are familiar with that wins out in the end. It does so in the interest of simplicity and economy."[17]

From another field of inquiry Shapiro has summarized evidence for the primacy of color responses in children with particular emphasis on Rorschach data. He writes "... although the Rorschach data did not indicate that color responsiveness *per se* diminishes with development, they do indicate unmistakably that the relative significance of the color as an essential and overriding aspect of the percept diminishes." Shapiro concluded "...color perception as such is a more immediate and passive experience than form perception, requiring less in the way of perceptual tools for organizing capacity. It is associated with a passive perceptual mode and it becomes more dominant, more compelling in quality and perhaps antagonistic to form articulation in conditions in which active perceptual organizing capacity is impaired or only rudimentary."[21] Further support for the concept of selective automatization is found in the report by Von Senden of the visual experiences of congenitally blind persons who began using the visual function for the first time following surgery for removal of lens cataracts.[24] His accounts support the idea that as perceptual learning takes place the vivid qualities of stimuli decrease in proportion as formal organization is imposed upon them through perceptual learning. The gain in economy and utility through automatization is paid for by a foreclosure of possibilities, a dulling or "jading" of sensory experience that is an all-too-common occurrence. The extent of this loss of vividness and detail resulting from automatization can be appreciated when one undergoes the experience of deautomatization through such techniques as meditation, use of LSD-25, sensory isolation or spontaneous mystic experience: colors may appear to have gained (temporarily) a new richness and vividness so that the natural world is seen in a "fresh" state. Again, this makes good sense developmentally, for intensity and sensory richness are usually not important stimulus properties for the accurate manipulation of objects.

If, as evidence indicates, our passage from infancy to adulthood is accompanied by an organization of the perceptual and cognitive world that has as its price the selection of some stimuli to the exclusion of others, it is quite possible that a technique could be found to reverse or undo temporarily the automatization that has restricted our communication with reality to the active perception of only a small segment of it. Such a process of deautomization might then be followed by an awareness of aspects of reality that were formerly unavailable to us.

To return to the data from the meditation experiment, it may be that the simpler perceptions of color, light, energy, force and movement represent a shift of the *normal* perceptual processes to aspects of the stimulus array previously screened out — or it may be that these percepts are registered through the operation of *new* perceptual processes. In the course of the experiment certain reports of A and G were very suggestive of this latter possibility. They seemed to be struggling to convey their perception of unfamiliar reality dimensions, difficult to verbalize exactly, requiring metaphors, and seemingly encountered in another realm so that they spoke of "coming back," "elsewhere," "the other place." The following data are very striking in their implication of a type of new perception:

G; 14th session: (While looking out the window after the meditation period.) "I am looking differently than I have ever looked before. I mean it's almost as though I have a different way of seeing. It's like something to do with dimensions. It's as though I am feeling what I am looking at. It's as though I have an extension of myself reaching out and seeing something by feeling it. It's as though somebody added something, another factor to my seeing.

G; 62nd session: "... things seem to sharpen and time, and there is a different nature to the substance of things. It's as though I'm seeing between the molecules... the usual mass of solidity loses its density or mass and becomes separate."

A; 58th session: "The only way I can think of to describe it is being suspended between something and something, because the world all but disappears, you know, the usual world, while some sounds intrude very little so that I'm in a world of converging with that, whatever it is, and that's all there is.

G; 64th session: "...I've experienced... new experiences and I have no vehicle to communicate them to you. I expect that this is probably the way a baby feels when he is full of something to say about an experience or an awareness and he has not learned to use the words yet."

A; 60th session: "...it's so completely and totally outside of anything else I've experienced."

G; 66th session: "It was like a parallel world or parallel time..."

A; 26th session: "...it's the only way I can describe it... walking through the looking glass... in walking through the looking glass I would become ethereal and, you know, filmy and somehow don't have the same kind of substance to me that I do otherwise and then when it begins to come back... it was like having walked back out of the clouds somehow and becoming solid as I did so.

G; 74th session: "...solid material such as myself and the vase and the table... seems to be attributed then with this extra property of flexibility such as in its natural, fluid state. It's almost as though we are, myself and the vase and the door, a form which has lost its fluidity the way water loses its property of fluidity when it is frozen... we're without the ability to exercise one of the properties that we have when we think of ourselves in the conditioned state of solid matter but if you can remove that impediment... of a way of thinking (and this is what this condition seems to do) this new element gives the ability to recognize this validity that otherwise I'm not aware of."

The postulated new perceptual route is possibly that referred to by the subjects when they use the term "feeling." By this they do not mean feeling in the usual sense of touch nor the sense of feeling an emotion, but rather perception that cannot be located in the trusted perceptual routes of sight, hearing, and the like. In summary, it may be that the unusual experiences here cited are perceptions of unusual stimulus dimensions, modified in some way by the subject, but nevertheless constituting a new perceptual experience made possible by the deautomization of the ordinary perceptual route, that normally dominate consciousness.

Some support for this hypothesis is present in the evidence that there exists in us psychological capacities different from those we usually employ or with which we are familiar. Von Neumann has observed: "Just as languages like Greek or Sanskrit are historical facts and not absolute logical necessities, it is only reasonable to assume that logics and mathematics are similarly historical, accidental forms of expression. They may have essential i.e., they may exist in other forms than the ones to which we are accustomed. Indeed the nature of the central nervous system and of the message systems that it transmits indicates positively that this is so. We have now accumulated sufficient evidence to see that whatever language the central nervous system is using is characterized by less logical and arithmetical depth than what we are used to." In his discussion of the brain as computer, he advanced the idea that the human brain programs itself to think logically with the implication that other superordinate thought functions are inherent in our brain. The creative, preconscious solution of problems is a common experience of another mode of functioning.

Specifically in the perceptual sphere, it is relevant to cite observations on synesthesia, especially the association of colors with sounds. This function is found more commonly in children and tends to disappear as the child grows older. From the point of view of adaptation it seems plausible that synesthesia is biologically superfluous and therefore would lose out to other perceptual and cognitive processes that provide a more direct biological reward. Evidence for parasensory modes in telepathy experiments is difficult to evaluate, perhaps because such possibilities are discordant with our present scientific cosmology. If there is any validity to the work that has been done in such investigations, it would seem reasonable to conclude that telepathic phenomena represent the operation of perceptual channels ordinarily not utilized or available. The subjective data of the classical mystic experience, of drug states and of acute psychosis can also be cited in support of the hypothesis of perceptual expansion. In these diverse accounts from varied cultures and epochs we read the claim that new dimensions are perceived, physical, spiritual or unclassifiable. These widely disparate authors report certain basic, *similar* perceptions: the unity of existence, timeless properties of the self, and multiple worlds of existence beyond the familiar. The similarity of their perceptions may simply reflect their similar basic psychological structure. Because they are perceiving their own internal psychological structure and modes of activity, their experiences are basically similar despite cultural differences. Logically, however, we must grant the possibility that these unusual experiences contain the percepts of actual characteristics of reality, normally not perceived.

Inside or Outside?

In trying to decide between the two major possibilities for interpreting unusual experiences — the perception of something that is actually internal versus the perception of something that is actually external — and allowing for the presence of both possibilities in one situation, we come quickly to the basic epistemological problem that we have no way of knowing, with certainty, whether or not a percept refers to an extended source.[26] Why not test the "knowledge" claimed by the subject of an unusual experience and see if it results in greater success in dealing with the world? Even in the most precise area of physics we find contradictory worlds; the world of quantum mechanics and the world of special relativity: "... any theory which tries to fulfill the requirements of both special relativity and quantum theory will lead to mathematical inconsistencies, to divergencies in the region of very high energies and momenta."[15] If such incongruencies exist there, we can expect even greater difficulty in matching a set of data of the order of mystic revelation with the incredibly complex field of psychological and biological dimensions where a "test" would take place. Unless such a test of new knowledge were in the same dimensional plane as the knowledge itself, the results would not be relevant.

The evidence of scientific experience, thus far, is solidly behind the psychological theories that assume an internal origin of the "knowledge" or stimuli of unusual experiences. However, we cannot exclude the possibility that the classical mystic experience, LSD reactions, certain phases of acute psychosis, and other unusual experiences represent conditions of special receptivity to external stimuli ordinarily excluded or ignored in the normal state.

A. When questioned (at the end of the experiment) as to any interaction between her psychoanalysis and the meditation, A replied: "...my guess would be that, had I not been in analysis, I would have not had the same kind of experience that I did in this. I think I would have been less prone to or I would have been far more restricted... they were two very special experiences going on at the same time and that there was interaction between them but they both remained separate in their own ways and were special in their own ways." She replied in the negative when the experimenter asked if any of the things she had found out about herself in the analysis had explained any of the experiences she had had in the experiment.

B. There is an indication in the *New Introductory Lectures* that Freud had an idea tending in the same direction: "It is easy to imagine, too, that certain mystical practices may succeed in upsetting the normal relations between the different regions of the mind, so that, for instance, perception may be able to grasp happenings in the depths of the ego and the id which were otherwise inaccessible to it."[10]

References

1. Bagchi B. K. and Wenger, M. A. *Electrophysiological correlates of some yogi exercises.* INTERNATIONAL CONGRESS OF NEUROLOGICAL SCIENCES, FIRST, vol. 3, pp. 141-176. Brussels, 1967.
2. Chase, Philip, H. *A note on projection.* PSYCHOL. BULL., 57: 289-290, 1960.
3. Deikman, Arthur J. *Experimental meditation.* J. NERV. MENT. DIS., 136: 329-343, 1963.
4. Federn, Paul. *Ego Psychology and the Psychoses,* pp. 241-260. Basic Books, New York, 1955.
5. Freud, S. *The Standard Edition of the Complete Psychological Works of Sigmund Freud,* vol. V, p. 542. Hogarth, London, 1958.
6. Freud, S. *The Standard Edition of the Complete Psychological Works of Sigmund Freud,* vol. XII, pp. 66, 77. Hogarth, London, 1958.
7. Freud, S. *The Standard Edition of the Complete Psychological Works of Sigmund Freud,* vol. XIV, p. 232. Hogarth, London, 1957.
8. Freud, S. *The Standard Edition of the Complete Psychological Works of Sigmund Freud,* vol. XVII, p. 29. Hogarth, London, 1955.
9. Freud, S. *The Standard Edition of the Complete Psychological Works of Sigmund Freud,* vol. XIX, p. 237. Hogarth, London, 1961.
10. Freud, S. *The Standard Edition of the Complete Psychological Works of Sigmund Freud,* vol. XXII, pp. 79-80. Hogarth, London, 1963.
11. Gill, Merton and Brenman, Margaret. *Hypnosis and Related States,* p. 178. Int. Universities Press, New York, 1959.
12. Hartmann, H. Ego *Psychology and the Problem of Adaptation,* pp. 88-91. Int

Universities Press, New York, 1958.
13. Havens, Leston L. *The placement and movement of hallucinations in space: Phenomenology and theory.* INT. J. PSYCHOANAL., 43: 426-435, 1962.
14. Heimann, Paula. *Notes on the Theory of the Life and Death Instincts, Developments in Psycho-Analysis*, pp. 321-342. Hogarth, London, 1952.
15. Heisenberg, Werner. *Physics and Philosophy*, p. 162. Harper, New York, 1958.
16. Kasamatsu, Akira and Hirai, Tomio. *Science of zazen.* PSYCHOLOGIA, 6: 86-91, 1963.
17. Kohler, Ivo (Fiss, Harry, trans.) *The Formation and Transformation of the Perceptual World.* PSYCHOL. ISSUES, vol. 3, No. 12, p.128, 1964.
18. Lewin, Bertram D. *The Psychoanalysis of Elation*, pp. 144-150. Norton, New York, 1950.
19. Murstein, Bernard I. And Pryer, Ronald S. *The concept of projection: A review.* PSYCHOL. BULL., 56: 353-374, 1959.
20. Schachtel, Ernest G. *Projection and its relation to character attitudes and creativity in the kinesthetic responses.* PSYCHIATRY, 13: 69-100, 1950.
21. Shapiro, David. *A perceptual understanding of color response.* In Rickers-Ovsiankina, Maria A., ed. *Rorschach Psychology*, pp. 154-201. Wiley, New York, 1960.
22. Silberer, Herbert. *Report on a method of eliciting and observing certain symbolic hallucination-phenomena.* In Rapaport, David, ed. And trans. *Organization and Pathology of Thought*, p. 16,. Columbia Univ. Press, New York, 1951.
23. von Neumann, John. *The Computer and the Brain*, p. 82. Yale Univ. Press, New Haven, 1958.
24. Von Senden, M. *Space and Sight.* Free Press, Glencoe, Illinois, 1960.
25. Werner, Heinz. *Comparative Psychology of Mental Development*, p. 152. Int. Universities Press, New York, 1957.
26. Wyburn, G. M., Pickford, N. W. and Hirst, R. J. *Human Senses and Perception*, pp. 242-335. Univ. of Toronto Press, Toronto, 1964.

Deautomization and the
Mystic Experience

T o STUDY the mystic experience one must turn initially to material that appears unscientific, is couched in religious terms, and
seems completely subjective. Yet these religious writings are data and
not to be dismissed as something divorced from the reality with which
psychological science is concerned. The following passage from
"The Cloud of Unknowing," a fourteenth-century religious treatise, describes a procedure to be followed in order to attain an intuitive knowledge of God. Such an intuitive experience is called mystical because
it is considered beyond the scope of language to convey. However,
a careful reading will show that these instructions contain within
their religious idiom psychological ideas pertinent to the study
and understanding of a wide range of phenomena not necessarily
connected with theological issues:

> ... forget all the creatures that ever God made and the works
> of them, so that thy thought or thy desire be not directed or
> stretched to any of them, neither in general nor in special... At
> the first time when thou dost it, thou findst but a darkness and as
> it were a kind of unknowing, thou knowest not what, saving that
> thou feelest in thy will a naked intent unto God... thou mayest
> neither see him clearly by light of understanding in thy reason,
> nor feel him in sweetness of love in thy affection... if ever thou
> shalt see him or feel him as it may be here, it must always be in
> this cloud and in this darkness .... Smite upon that thick cloud of
> unknowing with a sharp dart of longing love.[1]

Specific questions are raised by this subjective account: What constitutes a state of consciousness whose content is not rational thought
("understanding in thy reason"), affective ("sweetness of love"), or sensate ("darkness," "cloud of unknowing")? By what means do both an
active "forgetting" and an objectless "longing" bring about such a
state? A comparison of this passage with others in the classical mystic
iterature indicates that the author is referring to the activities of renunciation and contemplative meditation. This paper will present a
psychological model of the mystic experience based on the assumptions
that meditation and renunciation are primary techniques for producing
it, and that the process can be conceptualized as one of deautomization.

Phenomena of the Mystic Experience

Accounts of mystic experiences can be categorized as (1) untrained-
sensate, (2) trained-sensate, and (3) trained-transcendent. "Untrained-
sensate" refers to phenomena occurring in persons not regularly engaged in meditation, prayer, or other exercises aimed at achieving a
religious experience. These persons come from all occupations and
classes. The mystic state they report is one of intense affective,
perceptual, and cognitive phenomena that appear to be extensions
of familiar psychological processes. Nature and drugs are the most
frequent precipitating factors. James cites the account of Trevor to
illustrate a nature experience:

> For nearly an hour I walked along the road to the "Cat and
> Fiddle," and then returned. On the way back, suddenly, without
> warning, I felt that I was in heaven — an inward state of peace
> and joy and assurance indescribably intense, accompanied with
> a sense of being bathed in a warm glow of light, as though the
> external condition had brought about the internal effect — a
> feeling of having passed beyond the body, though the scene around
> me stood out more clearly and as if nearer to me than before, by
> reason of the illumination in the midst of which I seemed to
> be placed. This deep emotion lasted, though with decreasing

strength, until I reached home, and for some time after, only gradually passing away.[2]

For an example of a drug experience James cites Symonds's description of undergoing chloroform anesthesia:

> *... I thought that I was near death; when suddenly, my soul became aware of God, who was manifestly dealing with me, handling me, so to speak, in an intense, personal present reality. I felt him streaming in like light upon me... I cannot describe the ecstasy I felt. Then, as I gradually awoke from the influence of the anaesthetics, the old sense of my relation to the world began to return, the new sense of my relation to God began to fade.*[3]

More recent accounts of experiences with LSD-25 and related drugs fall into the same group.[4]

The "trained-sensate" category refers to essentially the same phenomena occurring in religious persons in the West and in the East who have deliberately sought "grace," "enlightenment," or "union" by means of long practice in concentration and renunciation (contemplative meditation, Yoga, and so forth). One example of this group is Richard Rolle, who wrote:

> *... I was sitting in a certain chapel, and while I was taking pleasure in the delight of some prayer or meditation, I suddenly felt within me an unwanted and pleasant fire. When I had for long doubted from whence it came, I learned by experience that it came from the Creator and not from creature, since I found it ever more pleasing and full of heat...*[5]

A more elaborate experience is recorded by Julian of Norwich:

> *In this [moment] suddenly I saw the red blood trickle down from under the garland hot and freshly and right plenteously.... And in the same showing suddenly the Trinity fulfilled my heart most of joy. And so I understood it shall be in heaven without end to all that shall come there.*[6]

Visions, feelings of "fire," "sweetness," "song," and joy are various accompaniments of this type of experience.

The untrained-sensate and the trained-sensate states are phenomenologically indistinguishable, with the qualification that the trained mystics report experiences conforming more closely to the specific religious cosmology to which they are acccustomed. As one might expect, an experience occurring as the result of training, with the support of a formal social structure, and capable of being repeated, tends to have a more significant and persisting psychological effect. However, spontaneous conversion experiences are also noteworthy for their influence on a person's life. Typical of all mystic experience is a more or less gradual fading away of the state, leaving only a memory and a longing for that which was experienced.

Mystics such as St. John of the Cross and St. Teresa of Avila, commentators such as Poulain, and Eastern mystic literature in general, divide the effects and stages through which mystics progress into a lesser experience of strong emotion and ideation (sensate) and a higher, ultimate experience that goes beyond affect or ideation. It is the latter experience, occurring almost always in association with long training, that characterizes the "trained-transcendent" group. The trans-sensate aspect is stated specifically by a number of authors, such as Walter Hilton and St. John of the Cross:

> From what I have said you may understand that visions of revelations by spirits, whether seen in bodily form or in the imagination, and whether in sleeping or waking, do not constitute true contemplation. This applies equally to any other sensible experiences of seemingly spiritual origin, whether of sound, taste, smell or of warmth felt like a glowing fire in the breast or in other parts of the body, any thing, indeed, that can be experienced by the physical senses.[7]

> ... that inward wisdom is so simple, so general and so spiritual that it has not entered into the understanding enwrapped or clad in any form or image subject to sense, it follows that sense and

imagination (as it has not entered through them nor has taken their form and color) cannot account for it or imagine it, so as to say anything concerning it, although the soul be clearly aware that it is experiencing and partaking of that rare and delectable wisdom.[8]

A similar distinction between lower (sensate) and higher (transcendent) contemplative states may be found in Yoga texts. "Conscious concentration" is a preliminary step to "concentration which is not conscious (of objects)."

For practice when directed towards any supporting-object is not capable of serving as an instrument to this [concentration not conscious of an object]... Mind-stuff, when engaged in the practice of this [imperceptible object], seems as if it were itself non-existent and without any supporting-object. Thus [arises] that concentration [called] seedless, [without sensational stimulus], which is not conscious of objects.[9]

In the transcendent state, multiplicity disappears and a sense of union with the One or with All occurs, "When all lesser things and ideas are transcended and forgotten, and there remains only a perfect state of imagelessness where Tathagata and Tathata are merged into perfect Oneness...."[10]

Then the spirit is transported high above all the faculties into a void of immense solitude whereof no mortal can adequately speak. It is the mysterious darkness wherein is concealed the limitless Good. To such an extent are we admitted and absorbed into something that is one, simple, divine, and illimitable, that we seem no longer distinguishable from it... In this unity, the feeling of multiplicity disappears. When, afterwards, these persons mine to themselves again, they find themselves possessed of a distinct knowledge of things, more luminous and more perfect than that of others... This state is called the ineffable obscurity... This obscurity is a light to which no created intelligence can arrive by its own nature.[11]

This state is described in all the literatures as one in which the mystic is passive in that he has abandoned striving. He sees *"grace"* to be the action of God on himself and *feels himself* to be receptive. In addition, some descriptions indicate that the senses and faculties of thought *feel suspended,* a state described in Catholic literature *as* the "ligature."

Human variety is *reflected in* the superficial differences between the various mystic records. However, perusal of these accounts leads one to agree with Marechal when he writes,

> *A very delicate psychological problem is thus raised: the consensus of the testimonies we have educed is too unanimous to be rejected. It compels us to recognize the existence in certain subjects of a special psychological state, which generally results from a very close interior concentration, sustained by an intense affective movement, but which, on the other hand, no longer presents any trace of "discursiveness," spatial imagination, or reflex consciousness. And the disconcerting question arises: after images and concepts and the conscious Ego have been abolished, what subsists of the intellectual life? Multiplicity will have disappeared, true, but to the advantage of what kind of unity?*[12]

In summary, mystic literature suggests that various kinds of people have attained what they considered to be exalted states of mind and feeling, states that may be grouped in three divisions: untrained-sensate, trained-sensate, and trained-transcendent. The most important distinction would appear to be between an experience grounded in customary affect, sensations, and ideations, and an experience that is said to transcend such modalities.

Basic Mystic Techniques

How is the mystic experience produced? To answer this question I will examine the two basic techniques involved in mystical exercises: contemplation and renunciation.

Contemplation is, ideally, a nonanalytic apprehension of an object or idea — nonanalytic because discursive thought is banished and the attempt is made to empty the mind of everything except the percept of the object in question. Thought is conceived of as an interference with the direct contact that yields essential knowledge through perception alone. The renunciation of worldly goals and pleasures, both physical and psychological, is an extension of the same principle of freeing oneself from distractions that interfere with the perception of higher realms or more beautiful aspects of existence. The renunciation prescribed is most thorough and quite explicit in all texts. The passage that begins this paper instructs, "Forget all the creatures that ever God made... so that thy thought... be not directed... to any of them..." In the Lankavatra Scripture one reads... he must seek to annihilate all vagrant thoughts and notions belonging to the externality of things, and all ideas of individuality and generality, of suffering and impermanence, and cultivate the noblest ideas of egolessness and emptiness and imagelessness..."[13] Meister Eckhart promises: "If we keep ourselves free from the things that are outside us, God will give us in exchange everything that is in heaven.... itself with all its powers...."[14] In Hilton one reads, "Therefore if you desire to discover your soul, withdraw your thoughts from outward and material things, forgetting if possible your own body and its five senses..."[15] St. John calls for the explicit banishment of memory:

> Of all these forms and manners of knowledge the soul must strip and void itself, and it must strive to lose the imaginary apprehension of them, so that there may be left in it no kind of impression of knowledge, nor trace of aught soever, but rather the soul must remain barren and bare, as if these forms had never passed through it and in total oblivion and suspension. And this cannot happen unless the memory be annihilated as to all its forms, if it is to be united with God.[16]

In most Western and Eastern mystic practice, renunciation also extends to the actual life situation of the mystic. Poverty, chastity, and the solitary way are regarded as essential to the attainment of mystic union. Zen Buddhism, however, sees the ordinary life as a proper vehicle for "satori" as long as the "worldly" passions and desires are given up, and with them the intellectual approach to experience, "When I am in my isness, thoroughly purged of all intellectual sediments, I have my freedom in its primary sense... free from intellectual complexities and moralistic attachments...."[17]

Instructions for performing contemplative meditation indicate that a very active effort is made to exclude outer and inner stimuli, to devalue and banish them, and at the same time to focus attention on the meditative object. In this active phase of contemplation the concentration of attention upon particular objects, ideas, physical movements, or breathing exercises is advised as an aid to diverting attention from its usual channels and restricting it to a monotonous focus.[18] Patanjali comments,

> Binding the mind-stuff to a place is fixed-attention... Focusedness of the presented idea on that place is contemplation.... This same [contemplation] shining form [in consciousness] as the intended object and nothing more, and, as it were, emptied of itself, is concentration... The three in one are constraint.... Even these [three] are indirect aids to seedless [concentration].[19]

Elaborate instructions are found in Yoga for the selection of objects for contemplation and for the proper utilization of posture and breathing to create optimal conditions for concentration. Such techniques are not usually found in the Western religious literature except in the form of the injunction to keep the self oriented toward God and to fight the distractions which are seen as coming from the devil, (The Spiritual Exercises of St. Ignatius is a possible exception).[20]

The active phase of contemplative meditation is a preliminary to the stage of full contemplation, in which the subject is caught up and absorbed in a process he initiated but which now seems autonomous, requiring no effort. Instead, passivity — self-surrender — is called for, an open receptivity amidst the "darkness" resulting from the banishment of thoughts and sensations and the renunciation of goals and desires directed toward the world.

When this active effort of mental concentration is successful, it is followed by a more passive, receptive state of samadhi in which the earnest disciple will enter into the blissful abode of noble wisdom...[21]

For if such a soul should desire to make any effort of its own with its interior faculties, this means that it will hinder and lose the blessings which... God is instilling into it and impressing upon it.[22]

It should not be forgotten that the techniques of contemplation and renunciation are exercised within the structure of some sort of theological schema. This schema is used to interpret and organize the experiences that occur. However, mere doctrine is usually not enough. The Eastern texts insist on the necessity for being guided by a guru (an experienced teacher), for safety's sake as well as in order to attain the spiritual goal. In Western religion, a "spiritual advisor" serves as guide and teacher. The presence of a motivating and organizing conceptual structure and the support and encouragement of a teacher are undoubtedly important in helping a person to persist in the meditation exercises and to achieve the marked personality changes that can occur through success in this endeavor. Enduring personality change is made more likely by the emphasis on adapting behavior to the values and insights associated both with the doctrinal structure and with the stages of mystical experience.

How can one explain the phenomena and their relation to these techniques? Most explanations in the psychological and psychoanalytic literature have been general statements emphasizing a regression to the early infant-mother symbiotic relationship. These statements range from an extreme position, such as Alexander's, where Buddhist training is described as a withdrawal of libido from the world to be reinvested in the ego until an intrauterine narcissism is achieved — "the pure narcissism of the sperm" — to the basic statement of Freud's that "oceanic feeling" is a memory of a relatively undifferentiated infantile ego state.[23] Lewin in particular has developed this concept.[24] In recent years hypotheses have been advanced uniting the concepts of regression and of active adaptation. The works of Kris, Fingarette, and Prince and Savage illustrate this approach to the mystic experience.[25] This paper will attempt an explanation of mystic phenomena from a different point of view, that of attentional mechanisms in perception and cognition.

Deautomization

In earlier studies of experimental meditation, I hypothesized that mystic phenomena were a consequence of a de-automatization of the psychological structures that organize, limit, select, and interpret perceptual stimuli. I suggested the hypotheses of sensory translation, reality transfer, and perceptual expansion to explain certain unusual perceptions of the meditation subjects.[26] At this point I will try to present an integrated formulation that relates these concepts to the classical mystic techniques of renunciation and contemplation.

Deautomization is a concept stemming from Hartmann's discussion of the automatization of motor behavior:

> In well-established achievements they [motor apparatuses] function automatically: the integration of the somatic systems involved in the action is automatized, and so is the integration of the individual mental acts involved in it. With increasing exercise of the action its intermediate steps disappear from consciousness... not only motor behavior but perception and thinking, too, show automatization....
>
> It is obvious that automatization may have economic advantages, in saving attention cathexis in particular and simple cathexis of consciousness in general.... Here, as in most adaptation processes, we have a purposive provision for the average expectable range of tasks.[27]

Gilland Brennan developed the concept of deautomization:

Deautomization is an undoing of the solid automizations of apparatuses — both means and goal structures — directed toward the environment. Deautomization is, as it were, a shake-up which can be followed by an advance or a retreat in the level of organization.... Some manipulation of the attention directed toward the functioning of an apparatus is necessary if it is to be de-automatized.[28]

Thus, deautomization may be conceptualized as the undoing of automatization, presumably by *reinvesting actions and percepts with attention.*

The concept of psychological structures follows the definition by Rapaport and Gill:

Structures are configurations of a slow rate of change... within which, between which, and by means of which mental processes take place.... Structures are hierarchically ordered.... This assumption... is significant because it is the foundation for the psychoanalytic propositions concerning differentiation (whether resulting in discrete structures which are then coordinated, or in the increased internal articulation of structures), and because it implies that the quality of a process depends upon the level of the structural hierarchy on which it takes place.[29]

The deautomization of a structure may result in a shift to a structure lower in the hierarchy, rather than a complete cessation of the particular function involved.

Contemplative Meditation

In reflecting on the technique of contemplative meditation, one can see that it seems to constitute just such a manipulation of attention as is required to produce deautomization. The percept receives intense attention while the use of attention for abstract categorization and thought is explicitly prohibited. Since automatization normally accomplishes the transfer of attention from a percept or action to abstract thought activity, the meditation procedure exerts a force in the reverse direction. Cognition is inhibited in favor of perception; the active intellectual style is replaced by a receptive perceptual mode.

Automatization is a hierarchically organized developmental process, so one would expect deautomization to remit in a shift toward a perceptual and cognitive organization characterized as "primitive," that is, an organization preceding the analytic, abstract, intellectual mode typical of present-day adult thought. The perceptual and cognitive functioning of children and of people of primitive cultures have been studied by Werner, who described primitive imagery and thought as (1) relatively more vivid and sensuous, (2) syncretic, (3) physiognomic and animated, (4) de-differentiated with respect to the distinctions between self and object and between objects, and (5) characterized by a dedifferentiation and fusion of sense modalities. In a statement based on studies of eidetic imagery in children as well as on broader studies of perceptual development, Werner states:

> The image... gradually changed in functional character, it becomes essentially subject to the exigencies of abstract thought. Once the image changes in function and becomes an instrument in reflective thought, its structure will also change. It is only through such structural change that the image can serve as an instrument of expression in abstract mental activity. This is why, of necessity, the sensuousness, fullness of detail, the color and vivacity of the image must fade.[30]

Theoretically, deautomization should reverse this development in the direction of primitive thought, and it is striking to note that classical accounts of mystic experience emphasize the phenomenon of Unity. Unity can be viewed as a dedifferentiation that merges all boundaries until the self is no longer experienced as a separate object and customary perceptual and cognitive distinctions are no longer applicable. In this respect, the mystic literature is consistent with the deautomization hypothesis. If one searches for evidence of changes in the mystic's experience of the external world, the classical literature is of less help, because the mystic's orientation is inward rather than outward and he tends to write about God rather than nature. However, in certain accounts of untrained-sensate experience there is evidence of a gain in sensory richness and vividness. James, in describing the conversion experience, states: "A third peculiarity of the assurance state is the objective change which the world often appears to undergo, 'An appearance of newness beautifies every object'..." He quotes Billy Bray: "... I shouted for joy. I praised God with my whole heart.... I remember this, that everything looked new to me, the people, the fields, the cattle, the trees. I was like a new man in a new world." Another example, this one from a woman, "I pled for mercy and had a vivid realization of forgiveness and renewal of my nature. When rising from my knees I exclaimed, 'Old things have passed away, all things have become new.' It was like entering another world, a new state of existence. Natural objects were glorified. My spiritual vision was so clarified that I saw beauty in every material object in the universe..." Again, "The appearance of everything was altered, there seemed to be as it were a calm, sweet cast or appearance of divine glory in almost everything."[31]

Such a change in a person's perception of the world has been called by Underhill "clarity of vision, a heightening of physical perception," and she quotes Blake's phrase, "cleanse the doors of perception."[32] It is hard to document this perceptual alteration because the autobiographical accounts that Underhill, James, and others cite are a blend of the mystic's spiritual feeling and his actual perception, with the result that the spiritual content dominates the description the mystic gives of the physical world. However, these accounts do suggest that a "new vision" takes place, colored by an inner exaltation. Their authors report perceiving a new brilliance to the world, of seeing everything as if for the first time, of noticing beauty which for the most part they may have previously passed by without seeing. Although such descriptions do not prove a change in sensory perception, they strongly imply it. These particular phenomena appear quite variable and are not mentioned in many mystic accounts. However, direct evidence was obtained on this point in the meditation experiments already cited.[33] There, it was possible to ask questions and to analyze the subjects' reports to obtain information on their perceptual experiences. The phenomena the subjects reported fulfilled Werner's criteria completely, although the extent of change varied from one subject to the next. They described their reactions to the percept, a blue vase, as follows: (1) an increased vividness and richness of the percept — "more vivid," "luminous"; (2) animation in the vase, which seemed to move with a life of its own; (3) a marked decrease in self-object distinction, occurring in those subjects who continued longest in the experiments: "... I really began to feel, you know, almost as though the blue and I were perhaps merging, or that vase and I were.... It was as though everything was sort of merging...."; (4) syncretic thought and a fusing and alteration of normal perceptual modes: "I began to feel this light going back and forth," "When the vase changes shape I feel this in my body," "I'm still not sure, though, whether it's the motion in the rings or if it's the rings [concentric rings of light between the subject and the vase]. But in a certain way it is real... it's not real in the sense that you can see it, touch it, taste it, smell it or anything but it certainly is real in the sense that you can experience it happening." The perceptual and cognitive changes that did occur in the subjects were consistently in the direction of a more "primitive" organization.[34]

Thus, the available evidence supports the hypothesis that a de-automization is produced by contemplative meditation. One might be tempted to call this deautomization a regression to the perceptual and cognitive state of the child or infant. However, such a concept rests on assumptions as to the child's experience of the world that cannot yet be verified. In an oft-quoted passage, Wordsworth writes:

There was a time when meadow, grove and stream,

The earth, and every common sight,
To me did seem
Apparelled in celestial light,
The glory and the freshness of a dream.[35]

However, he may be confusing childhood with what is actually a reconstruction based on an interaction of adult associative capacities with the memory of the more direct sensory contact of the child. "Glory" is probably an adult product. Rather than speaking of a return to childhood, it is more accurate to say that the undoing of automatic perceptual and cognitive structures permits a gain in sensory intensity and richness at the expense of abstract categorization and differentiation. One might call the direction regressive in a developmental sense, but the actual experience is probably not within the psychological scope of any child. It is a deautomization occurring in an adult mind, and the experience gains its richness from adult memories and functions now subject to a different mode of consciousness.

Renunciation

The deautomization produced by contemplative meditation is enhanced and aided by the adoption of renunciation as a goal and a lifestyle, a renunciation not confined to the brief meditative period alone. Poverty, chastity, isolation, and silence are traditional techniques prescribed for pursuing the mystic path: To experience God, keep your thoughts turned to God and away from the world and the body that binds one to the world. The meditative strategy is carried over into all segments of the subject's life. The mystic strives to banish from awareness the objects of the world and the desires directed toward them. To the extent that perceptual and cognitive structures require the "nutriment" of their accustomed stimuli for adequate functioning, renunciation would be expected to weaken and even disrupt these structures, thus tending to produce an unusual experience.[36] Such an isolation from nutritive stimuli probably occurs internally as well. The subjects of the meditation experiment quoted earlier reported that a decrease in responsiveness to distracting stimuli took place as they became more practiced. They became more effective, with less effort, in barring unwanted stimuli from awareness. These reports suggest that psychological barrier structures were established as the subjects became more adept.[37] EEG studies of Zen monks yielded similar results. The effect of a distracting stimulus, as measured by the disappearance of alpha rhythm, was most prominent in the novices, less prominent in those of intermediate training, and almost absent in the master.[38] It may be that the intensive, long-term practice of meditation creates temporary stimulus barriers producing a functional state of sensory isolation.[39] On the basis of sensory isolation experiments it would be expected that long-term deprivation (or decreased variability) of a particular class of stimulus "nutriment" would cause an alteration in those functions previously established to deal with that class of stimuli.[40] These alterations seem to be a type of deautomization, as defined earlier — for example, the reported increased brightness of colors and the impairment of perceptual skills such as color discrimination.[41] Thus, renunciation alone can be viewed as producing deautomization. When combined with contemplative meditation, it produces a very powerful effect.

Finally, the more renunciation is achieved, the more the mystic is committed to his goal of Union or Enlightenment. His motivation necessarily increases, for having abandoned the world, he has no other hope of sustenance.

Principal Features of the Mystic Experience

Granted that deautomization takes place, it is necessary to explain five principal features of the mystic experience: 1) intense realness, (2) unusual sensations, (3) unity, (4) ineffability, and (5) transsensate phenomena.

Realness

It is assumed by those who have had a mystic experience, whether induced by years of meditation or by a single dose of LSD, that the truthfulness of the experience is attested to by its sense of realness. The criticism of skeptics is often met with the statement, "You have to experience it yourself and then you will understand." This means that if one has the actual experience he will be convinced by its intense feeling of reality, "I know it was real because it was more real than my talking to you now." But "realness" is not evidence. Indeed, there are many clinical examples of variability in the intensity of the feeling of realness that is not correlated with corresponding variability in the reality. A dream may be so "real" as to carry conviction into the waking state, although its content may be bizarre beyond correspondence to this world or to any other. Psychosis is often preceded or accompanied by a sense that the world is less real than normally, sometimes that it is more real, or has a different reality. The phenomenon of depersonalization demonstrates the potential for an alteration in the sense of the realness of one's own person, although one's evidential self undergoes no change whatsoever. However, in the case of depersonalization, or of de-realization, the distinction between what is external and what is internal is still clear. What changes is the quality of realness attached to those object representations. Thus it appears that (1) the feeling of realness represents a function distinct from that of reality judgment, although they usually operate in synchrony; (2) the feeling of realness is not inherent in sensations, *per se*; and (3) realness can be considered a quantity function capable of displacement and, therefore, of intensification, reduction, and transfer affecting all varieties of ideational and sensorial contents.[42]

From a developmental point of view, it is clear that biological survival depends on a clear sense of what is palpable and what is not. The sense of reality necessarily becomes fused with the object world. When one considers that meditation combined with renunciation brings about a profound disruption of the subject's normal psychological relationship to the world, it becomes plausible that the practice of such mystic techniques would be associated with a significant alteration of the feeling of reality. The quality of reality formerly attached to objects becomes attached to the particular sensations and ideas that enter awareness during periods of perceptual and cognitive deautomization. Stimuli of the inner world become invested with the feeling of reality ordinarily bestowed on objects. Through what might be termed "reality transfer," thoughts and images become real.[43]

Unusual Percepts

The sensations and ideation occurring during mystic deautomization are often very unusual; they do not seem part of the continuum of everyday consciousness.

"All at once, without warning of any kind, he found himself wrapped around as it were by a flame colored cloud."[44] Perceptions of encompassing light, infinite energy, ineffable visions, and incommunicable knowledge are remarkable in their seeming distinction from perceptions of the phenomena of the "natural world." According to mystics, these experiences are different because they pertain to a higher transcendent reality. What is perceived is said to come from another world, or at least another dimension. Although such a possibility cannot be ruled out, many of the phenomena can be understood as representing an unusual mode of perception, rather than an unusual external stimulus.

In the studies of experimental meditation already mentioned, two long-term subjects reported vivid experiences of light and force. For example:

> ...shortly I began to sense motion and shifting of light and dark as this became stronger and stronger. Now when this happens it's happening not only in my vision but it's happening or it feels like a physical kind of thing. It's connected with feelings of attraction, expansion, absorption and suddenly my vision pinpointed on a particular place and... I was in the grip of a very powerful sensation and this became the center.[45]

This report suggests that the perception of motion and shifting light and darkness may have been the perception of the movement of attention among various psychic contents (whatever such "movement" might actually be). "Attraction," "expansion," "absorption," would thus reflect the dynamics of the effort to focus attention — successful focusing is experienced as being "in the grip of" a powerful force. Another example: "...when the vase changes shape... I feel this in my body and particularly in my eyes... there is an actual kind of physical sensation as though something is moving there which recreates the shape of the vase."[46] In this instance, the subject might have experienced the perception of a resynthesis taking place following deautomization of the normal percept; that is, the percept of the vase was being reconstructed outside of normal awareness and the process of reconstruction was perceived as a physical sensation. I have termed this hypothetical perceptual mode *"sensory translation,"* defining it as the perception of psychic *action* (conflict, repression, problem-solving, attentiveness, and so forth) via the relatively unstructured sensation of light, color, movement, force, sound, smell, or taste.[47] This concept is related to Silberer's concept of hypnagogic phenomena but differs in its referents and genesis.[48] In the hypnagogic state and in dreaming, a symbolic translation of psychic activity and ideas occurs. Although light, force, and movement may play a part in hypnagogic and dream constructions, the predominant percepts are complex visual, verbal, conceptual, and activity images. "Sensory translation" refers to the experience of nonverbal, simple, concrete perceptual equivalents of psychic action.[49]

The concept of sensory translation offers an intriguing explanation for the ubiquitous use of light as a metaphor for mystic experience. It may not be just a metaphor. "Illumination" may be derived from an actual sensory experience occurring when in the cognitive act of unification, a liberation of energy takes place, or when a resolution of unconscious conflict occurs, permitting the experience of "peace," "presence," and the like. Liberated energy experienced as light may be the core sensory experience of mysticism. If the hypothesis of sensory translation is correct, it presents the problem of why sensory translation comes into operation in any particular instance.

In general, it appears that sensory translation may occur when
(1) heightened attention is directed to the sensory pathways, (2) controlled analytic thought is absent, and (3) the subject's attitude is
one of receptivity to stimuli (openness instead of defensiveness or
suspiciousness). Training in contemplative meditation is specifically
directed toward attaining a state with those characteristics. Laski
reports that spontaneous mystic experiences may occur during such
diverse activities as childbirth, viewing landscapes, listening to music,
or having sexual intercourse.[50] Although her subjects gave little
description of their thought processes preceding the ecstasies, they
were all involved at the time in intense sensory activities in which the
three conditions listed above would tend to prevail. Those conditions
seem also to apply to the mystical experiences associated with LSD.
The state of mind induced by hallucinogenic drugs is reported to be
one of increased sensory attention accompanied by an impairment or
loss of different intellectual functions.[51] With regard to the criterion
of receptivity, if paranoid reactions occur during the drug state they
are inimical to an ecstatic experience. On the other hand, when
drug subjects lose their defensiveness and suspiciousness so that
they "accept" rather than fight their situation, the "transcendent"
experience often ensues.[52] Thus, the general psychological context
may be described as *perceptual concentration*. In this special state of
consciousness the subject becomes aware of certain intrapsychic processes ordinarily excluded from or beyond the scope of awareness.
The vehicle for this perception appears to be amorphous sensation,
made real by a displacement of reality feeling ("reality transfer") and
thus misinterpreted as being of external origin.

Unity

Experiencing one's self as one with the universe or with God is
the hallmark of the mystic experience, regardless of its cultural context. As James puts it,

> *This overcoming of all the usual barriers between the Indi-
> vidual and the Absolute is the great mystic achievement. In mystic*

states we both become one with the Absolute and we become aware of our oneness. This is the everlasting and triumphant mystical tradition, hardly altered by differences of clime or creed. In Hinduism, in Neoplatonism, in Sufism, in Christian mysticism, in Whitmanism, we find the same recurring note, so that there is about mystical utterance an eternal unanimity which ought to make a critic stop and think, and which brings it about that the mystical classics have, as has been said, neither birthday nor native land. Perpetually telling of the unity of man with God, their speech antedates languages, and they do not grow old.[53]

I have already referred to explanations of this phenomenon in terms of regression. Two additional hypotheses should be considered: On the one hand, the perception of unity may be the perception of one's own psychic structure; on the other hand, the experience may be a perception of the real structure of the world.

It is a commonplace that we do not experience the world directly. Instead, we have an experience of sensation and associated memories from which we infer the nature of the stimulating object. As far as anyone can tell, the actual substance of the perception is the electrochemical activity that constitutes perception and thinking. From this point of view, the contents of awareness are homogeneous. They are variations of the same substance. If awareness were turned back upon itself, as postulated for sensory translation, this fundamental homogeneity (unity) of perceived reality — the electrochemical activity — might itself be experienced as a truth about the outer world, rather than the inner one. Unity, the idea and the experience that we are one with the world and with God, would thus constitute a valid perception insofar as it pertained to the nature of the thought process, but need not in itself be a correct perception of the external world.

Logically, there is also the possibility that the perception of unity does correctly evaluate the external world. As described earlier, deautomization is an undoing of a psychic structure permitting the experience of increased detail and sensation at the price of requiring does correctly evaluate the external world. As described earlier, de-automization is an undoing of a psychic structure permitting the experience of increased detail and sensation at the price of requiring more attention. With such attention, it is possible that deautomization may permit the awareness of new dimensions of the total stimulus array — a process of *"perceptual expansion."* The studies of Werner, Von Senden, and Shapiro suggest that development from infancy to adulthood is accompanied by an organization of the perceptual and cognitive world that has as its price the selection of some stimuli and stimulus qualities to the exclusion of others.[54] If the automatization underlying that organization is reversed, or temporarily suspended, aspects of reality that were formerly unavailable might then enter awareness. Unity may in fact be a property of the real world that becomes perceptible via the techniques of meditation and renunciation, or under the special conditions, as yet unknown, that create the spontaneous, brief mystic experience of untrained persons.

Ineffability

Mystic experiences are ineffable, incapable of being expressed to another person. Although mystics sometimes write long accounts, they maintain that the experience cannot be communicated by words or by reference to similar experiences from ordinary life. They feel at a loss for appropriate words to communicate the intense realness, the unusual sensations, and the unity cognition already mentioned. However, a careful examination of mystic phenomena indicates that there are at least several types of experiences, all of which are "indescribable" but each of which differs substantially in content and formal characteristics. Error and confusion result when these several states of consciousness are lumped together as "the mystic experience" on the basis of their common characteristic of ineffability.

To begin with, one type of mystic experience cannot be communicated in words because it is probably based on primitive memories and related to fantasies of a preverbal (infantile) or nonverbal sensory experience.[55] Certain mystical reports that speak of being blissfully enfolded, comforted and bathed in the love of God are very suggestive of the prototypical "undifferentiated state," the union of infant and breast, emphasized by psychoanalytic explanations of mystical phenomena. Indeed, it seems highly plausible that such early memories and fantasies might be re-experienced as a consequence of (1) the regression in thought processes brought about by renunciation and contemplative meditation, and (2) the activation of infantile longings by the guiding religious promise that s, "that a benign deity would reward childlike surrender with permanent euphoria."[56] In addition, the conditions of functional sensory isolation associated with mystic training may contribute to an increase in recall and vividness of such memories.[57]

A second type of mystical experience is equally ineffable but strikingly different — namely, a revelation too complex to be verbalized. Such experiences are reported frequently by those who have drug-induced mystical experiences. In such states the subject has a revelation of the significance and interrelationships of many dimensions of life; he becomes aware of many levels of meaning simultaneously and "understands" the totality of existence. The question of whether such knowledge is actual or an illusion remains unanswered; however, if such a multileveled comprehension were to occur, it would be difficult — perhaps impossible — to express verbally. Ordinary language is structured to follow the logical development of one idea at a time and it might be quite inadequate to express an experience encompassing a large number of concepts simultaneously. William James suggested that "states of mystical intuition may be only very sudden and great extensions of the ordinary 'field of consciousness.'" He used the image of the vast reaches of a tidal flat exposed by the lowering of the water level.[58] However, mystic revelation may be ineffable, not only because of the sudden broadening of consciousness that James suggests, but also because of a new "vertical" organization of concepts.[59]

For example, for a while while after reading *The Decline and Fall of the Roman Empire* one may be aware of the immense vista of a civilization's history as Gibbon recreated it. That experience can hardly be conveyed except through the medium of the book itself, and to that extent it is ineffable, and a minor version of James's widened consciousness. Suppose one then read *War and Peace* and acquired Tolstoy's perspective of historical events and their determination by chance factors. Again, this is an experience hard to express without returning to the novel. Now suppose one could 'see' not only each of these world views individually but also their parallel relationships to each other, and the cross connections between the individual conceptual structures. And then suppose one added to these conceptual strata the biochemical perspective expressed by *The Fitness of the Environment, a* work which deals, among other things, with the unique and vital properties of the water molecule.[60] Then the vertical interrelationships of all these extensive schemata might, indeed, be beyond verbal expression, beyond ordinary conceptual capacities — in other words, they would approach the ineffable.

Trans-sensate Phenomena

A third type of ineffable experience is that which I have described earlier as the "trained-transcendent" mystical experience. The author of "The Cloud of Unknowing," St. John of the Cross, Walter Hilton, and others are very specific in describing a new perceptual experience that does not include feelings of warmth, sweetness, visions, or any other elements of familiar sensory or intellectual experience. They emphasize that the experience goes beyond the customary sensory pathways, ideas, and memories. As I have shown, they describe the state as definitely blank or empty but as filled with intense, profound, vivid perception which they regard as the ultimate goal of the mystic path.[61] If one accepts their descriptions as phenomenologically accurate, one is presented with the problem of explaining the nature of such a state and the process by which it occurs. Following the hypotheses presented earlier in this paper, I would like to suggest that such experiences are the result of the operation of a new perceptual capacity responsive to dimensions of the stimulus array previously ignored or blocked from awareness. For such mystics, renunciation has weakened and temporarily removed the ordinary objects of consciousness as a focus of awareness. Contemplative meditation has undone the logical organization of consciousness. At the same time, the mystic is intensely motivated to perceive something. If undeveloped or unutilized perceptual capacities do exist, it seems likely that they would be mobilized and come into operation under such conditions. The perceptual experience that would then take place would be one outside of customary verbal or sensory reference. It would be *unidentifiable,* hence indescribable. The high value, the meaningfulness, and the intensity reported of such experiences suggest that the perception has a different scope from that of normal consciousness. The loss of "self" characteristic of the trans-sensate experience indicates that the new perceptual mode is not associated with reflective awareness — the "I" of normal consciousness is in abeyance.

Conclusion

A mystic experience is the production of an unusual state of consciousness. This state is brought about by a deautomization of hierarchically ordered structures of perception and cognition, structures that ordinarily conserve attentional energy for maximum efficiency in achieving the basic goals of the individual: biological survival as an organism and psychological survival as a personality. Perceptual selection and cognitive patterning are in the service of these goals. Under special conditions of dysfunction, such as in acute psychosis or in LSD states, or under special goal conditions such as exist in religious mystics, the pragmatic systems of automatic selection are set aside or break down, in favor of alternate modes of consciousness whose stimulus processing may be less efficient from a biological point of view but whose very inefficiency may permit the experience of aspects of the real world formerly excluded or ignored. The extent to which such a shift takes place is a function of the motivation of the individual, his particular neurophysiological state, and the environmental conditions encouraging or discouraging such a change.

A final comment should be made. The content of the mystic experience reflects not only its unusual mode of consciousness but also the particular stimuli being processed through that mode. The mystic experience can be beatific, satanic, revelatory, or psychotic, depending on the stimuli predominant in each case. Such an explanation says nothing conclusive about the source of "transcendent" stimuli. God or the Unconscious share equal possibilities here and one's interpretation will reflect one's presuppositions and beliefs. The mystic vision is one of unity, and modern physics lends some support to this perception when it asserts that the world and its living forms are variations of the same elements. However, there is no evidence that separateness and differences are illusions (as affirmed by Vedanta) or that God or a transcendent reality exists (as affirmed by Western religions). The available scientific evidence tends to support the view that the mystic experience is one of internal perception, an experience that can be ecstatic, profound, or therapeutic for purely internal reasons. Yet for psychological science, the problem of understanding such internal processes is hardly less complex than the theological problem of understanding God.

Indeed, regardless of one's direction in the search to know what reality is, a feeling of awe, beauty, reverence, and humility seems to be the product of one's efforts. Since these emotions are characteristic of the mystic experience, itself, the question of the epistemological validity of that experience may have less importance than was initially supposed.

Comments On The GAP Report On Mysticism

Mysticism: Spiritual Quest or Psychic Disorder?
GROUP FOR THE ADVANCEMENT OF PSYCHIATRY, New York, 1976.
120 pp. Paperback $4.00.

THE REPORT by the Group for the Advancement of Psychiatry entitled *Mysticism: Spiritual Quest or Psychic Disorder?* is intended to supply the psychiatric profession with needed information on the phenomena of mysticism, of which most psychiatrists have only a sketchy knowledge. Certain of the sections, especially those on Christian and Hindu mysticism, show an objectivity and scholarship that are quite commendable. As a whole, however, the report displays extreme parochialism, a lack of discrimination, and naïve arrogance in its approach to the subject.

From the point of view of scholarship, the basic error lies in the committee's ignoring the importance of the distinction made by both Western and Eastern mystics between lower level sensory-emotional experiences and those experiences that go beyond concepts, feelings, and sensations. Repeatedly, the mystical literature stresses that sensate experiences are not the goal of mysticism; rather, it is only when these are transcended that one attains the aim of a *direct* (intuitive) knowledge of fundamental reality. For example, Walter Hilton, an English mystic from the 14th century, is quite explicit about this distinction:

"...visions of revelations by spirits,... do not constitute true contemplation. This applies equally to any other sensible experiences of seemingly spiritual origin, whether of sound, taste, smell or of warmth felt like a glowing fire in the breast... anything, indeed, that can be experienced by the physical senses."[7]

St. John of the Cross, 16th century, states:

"That inward wisdom is so simple, so general and so spiritual that it has not entered into the understanding enwrapped or clad in any form or image subject to sense, it follows that sense and imagination (as it has not entered through them nor has taken their form and color) cannot account for it or imagine, so as to say anything concerning it, although the soul be clearly aware that it is experiencing and partaking of that rare and delectable wisdom."[3]

A similar distinction between lower (sensate) and higher (transcendent) contemplative states may be found in Yoga texts:

"When all lesser things and ideas are transcended and forgotten, and there remains only a perfect state of imagelessness where Tathagata and Tathata are merged into perfect Oneness..."[5]

Western mysticism, from which the authors derived most of their examples, constitutes only a minor segment of the literature in the field of mysticism, and its basic contemplative tradition actually derives from Eastern sources, as acknowledged in the report. Yet the goal of Eastern (Buddhist, Hindu, Taoist, Sufic) mysticism — "enlightenment" — is not visions of angels or Buddhas but the awakening of an inherent capacity to perceive the true nature of the self and the world. Over and over again, these texts warn that the type of mystical experience on which the GAP report focuses is not the goal of the mystical path. Such visionary experiences are regarded as illusions and, at worst, snares for the poorly prepared or the ill guided. An example from the Zen literature follows:

"Other religions and sects place great store by the experiences which involve visions of God or hearing heavenly voices, performing miracles, receiving divine messages, or becoming purified through various rites... yet from the Zen point of view all are morbid states devoid of true religious significance and hence only makyo (disturbing illusions)." [8]

In the Sufi literature, we find many explicit statements that Sufism is a science of knowing and is not a religion in the way that term is ordinarily understood.

"The Sufis often start from a nonreligious viewpoint. The answer, they say, is within the mind of mankind. It has to be liberated, so that by self-knowledge the intuition becomes the guide to human fulfillment." [11]

The Sufis regard most mystical experience as being essentially emotional with little practical importance — except for the harmful effect of causing people to believe they are being "spiritual" when they are not:

Sahl Abdullah once went into a state of violent agitation with physical manifestations, during a religious meeting.

Ibn Salim said, "What is this state?"

Sahl said: "This was not, as you imagine, power entering me. It was, on the contrary, due to my own weakness."

Others present remarked: "If that was weakness, what is power?"

"Power," said Sahl, "is when something like this enters and the mind and body manifests nothing at all." [12]

Despite these clear warnings in the mystical literature, the GAP publication emphasizes lurid, visionary phenomena which lend themselves readily to standard psychiatric interpretations. Because of this, the authors have failed to come to grips with the fundamental claim of mystics: that they acquire direct knowledge of reality. Furthermore, the authors follow Freud's lead in defining the mystic perception of unity as a regression, an escape, a projection upon the world of a primitive, infantile state. The fact is, we know practically nothing about the actual experience of the infant, except that whatever it is, it is not that of a small adult. No one who has read carefully the accounts of "enlightenment" can accept this glib equation of *mystical = infantile*. An infant mind could hardly have had the experience that conveyed the following:

> *"The least act, such as eating or scratching an arm, is not at all simple. It is merely a visible moment in a network of causes and effects reaching forward into Unknowingness and back into an infinity of Silence, where individual consciousness cannot even enter. There is truly nothing to know, nothing that can be known.*
>
> *"The physical world is an infinity of movement, of Time-Existence. But simultaneously it is an infinity of Silence and Voidness. Each object is thus transparent. Everything has its own special inner character, its own karma or 'life in time,' but at the same time there is no place where there is emptiness, where one object does not flow into another."* [8]

To confuse lower level sensory-emotional experiences with the transcendent "Knowledge" that is the goal of mysticism seriously limits the usefulness of the report and tends to perpetuate in the reader the ignorant parochial position that was standard in most psychiatric writings before the GAP publication and now, unfortunately, is likely to be reinforced.

This naive reductionism is all the more striking in the context of the numerous reports from physicists indicating that the world is actually more like the one that the mystics describe than the one on which psychology and psychoanalysis are based. Contemporary scientists have ample evidence that the world of discrete objects is an illusion, a function of the particular scale of our perception and time sense. For them, it is commonplace that the phenomena of biology and physics point to a continuous world of gradients, not a collection of objects. Percy Bridgman, Nobel Laureate in physics, comments:

"It has always been a bewilderment to me to understand how anyone can experience such a commonplace event as an automobile going up the street and seriously maintain that there is identity of structure of this continually flowing, dissolving and reforming thing and the language that attempts to reproduce it with discrete units, tied together by remembered conventions."[1]

What is missing from the GAP report is any acknowledgment that the mystic who has completed his or her development may have access to an intuitive, immediate knowledge of reality. The authors assume that the known sensate pathways are the only means to acquire knowledge of what is real. In fact, studies of how scientific discoveries were actually made show in almost every instance that this is not the case at all. Another Nobel prize-winning physicist, Eugene Wigner, has remarked:

"The discovery of the laws of nature requires first and foremost intuition, conceiving of pictures and a great many subconscious processes. The use and also the confirmation of these laws is another matter... logic comes after intuition." [6]

"Intuition" can be considered a lower-order example of the latent capacity to which mystics refer.

The eclectic ignorance of the authors has led them at one point to lump together Einstein, Jesus, Abraham Lincoln, biofeedback, Vincent Van Gogh, and St. John of the Cross. Interestingly enough, if the authors had pursued the case of Einstein alone, they might have come to the epistemological issue that is the core of mysticism — and paid proper attention to it; for Einstein's modern discoveries, as well as the discoveries of natural philosophers thousands of years earlier, were based on an intuitive perception of the way things are. Such perceptions are the source of our greatest advances in science. Michael Polanyi, at one time Professor of Physical Chemistry at the University of Manchester, made an extensive and thorough study of the actual process of scientific discovery and found that the revolutionary ideas of geniuses such as Einstein had "come to them" by some form of direct intuition, often presented as imagery.[10] Polanyi was led by his data to propose a theory of knowledge and human consciousness that is clearly "mystical." Furthermore, at least two books have been published recently documenting the strikingly close correspondence between the scientific conceptions of physicists and the insights of mystics.[2,9]

Thus, it is truly remarkable to have a group of psychiatrists issue a report in 1976, in which the only comment they make on the mystic perception of unity is that it represents a "reunion with parents." Nowhere in the report do we find a discussion of the possibility that the perception of unity occurring in the higher forms of mysticism may be correct and that the ordinary perception of separateness and meaninglessness may be an illusion, as mystics claim. Clearly, mystic perception could be true whether or not a particular mystic might wish, in fantasy, to be reunited with his or her mother.

The GAP report states:

"The psychiatrist will find mystical phenomena of interest because they can demonstrate forms of behavior intermediate between normality and frank psychosis; a form of ego regression in the service of defense against internal or external stress; and a paradox of the return of repressed regression in unconventional expressions of love" (p. 731).

How totally provincial our profession has become if this is a summary statement from a group that claims to be devoted to "advancing" psychiatry!

It is interesting that the only place in which the authors are able to allow themselves to think in positive terms of mysticism is when they discuss the concept of "creativity." Apparently, creativity is OK. In this section of the report, the authors venture to speculate:

"At the same time, intense or external perceptions may be heightened, and this sensitivity may open a path to hidden aspects of reality" (p. 795).

Unfortunately, that one sentence, like a lonely ray of sunshine, is soon swallowed up by a return of the monotonous clouds of reductionism. The very next chapter, entitled "Case Report," concerns a woman in psychotherapy who reported having had the sort of low-level, sensate mystical experience on which the authors focus. The report provides the following conclusion:

> "Her interests were reinvested in the fantasy universe, representing God, in which such problems do not exist, and she felt herself united with this God-Universe, a substitute for an unavailable or rejecting parent. The mystical union made up for the rejection she feared from her father, now represented by the therapist in another man ... so, while a psychiatric diagnosis cannot be dismissed, **her experience was certainly akin to those described by great religious mystics** (!) (emphasis mine) who have found a new life through them" (p. 806).

In the last paragraph it becomes even more presumptuous and confused:

> "The mystical state itself provided the illusion of knowledge. But unlike many mystical states in which the search ends with illusion, it stimulated her to seek further knowledge and led directly to the disappearance of her inhibition to serious reading (!) This continued search is characteristic of those in whom mystical states contribute towards creative activity" (p. 807).

The authors of this report are intelligent, educated, sincere men. It is hard to believe that they would display such provincialism, carelessness, and bias if they were discussing schizophrenia. Judging by this and other, similar psychiatric discussions, our profession, when it comes to mysticism, does not feel the need to ask serious questions about its own assumptions, nor to take the devil's advocate's position toward its too-easy conclusions. Ironically, the authors are capable of pointing out the problem in others. In discussing "the naive Western observers of the Indian scene" they say:

> "Confronted by such common symbols as that of the representation of the divine activity in sexual form, and bewildered by the profusion of deities in the Hindu pantheon, they could

impute to Hinduism a 'decadence' following from its essence, and they fail to apply to that religion the discrimination between enlightened and superstitious observance which they would be sure to demand for their own" (p. 747).

Exactly.

In trying to understand the phenomenon of the GAP report itself, I am led to two principal considerations. First, in order to understand and have some appreciation of "mysticism," it is necessary that psychiatrists participate to some extent in the experience. When it comes to its own discipline, the psychiatric profession is unwavering in its requirement that one must "know" through experience, not just description. Who can really understand "transference" without experiencing it? Actual experience is necessary because the position of the outside observer has its limits, particularly in areas not well adapted to language. I can give an example of the necessity for participation from my own research on meditation and mysticism. In surveying the literature, I had noticed that contemplation and renunciation were the two basic processes specified for mystical development by almost all mystical authors, East and West. I proceeded to study the effects of meditation in the laboratory and, naively, assigned that renunciation meant giving up the things of the world — in a literal sense. It was only later, when I both studied and participated in Soto Zen training, that I came to understand that renunciation refers to an attitude, not to asceticism, *per se*. That understanding enabled me to formulate the hypothesis of "bimodal consciousness," based on motivational considerations.[4] The hypothesis, in turn, enabled me to understand a wide variety of unusual states of consciousness.

Perhaps by stating that I have, myself, practiced meditation, I will automatically disqualify myself in the eyes of some readers as having any credibility in these matters. I refer those readers to the paper by Charles Tart, wherein he presents a compelling case for the development of "state-specific sciences" — sciences whose mode of investigation is specifically adapted to the area it is investigating.[13] Indeed, participation by scientists in these areas of mysticism would result in an understanding that is less exotic and less religious — and would help rid ourselves of the claptrap associated with mysticism that constitutes a burden to scientist and mystic alike.

Unfortunately, such participation is not likely to occur because of the other basic problem confronting psychiatrists when they approach this field: arrogance — reflecting the arrogance of Western civilization. In this connection, it is interesting that the fundamental requirement for participating in any of the mystical traditions has been, and still is, humility. This is so, not because humility is a virtue, something that earns one credit in a heavenly bank account, but because humility is instrumental — it is the attitude required for learning. Humility is the acceptance of the possibility that someone else or something else has something to teach you which you do not already know. In crucial sections of the GAP report, there is no sign of humility. It seems to me that in our profession we display the arrogance of the legendary British Colonial who lived for 30 years in India without bothering to learn the language of the inhabitants, because he considered them to be inferior. Perhaps medicine's long battle to free itself from religious control, from demonology and "divine authority," has left us with an automatic and costly reaction against anything that bears the outward signs of religion. In point of fact, mystics outside the Western tradition tend to share our suspicion and describe their disciplines as a science of development — not a religion, as ordinarily understood.

The authors of the GAP report have selectively ignored the central issues of mysticism and have made traditional interpretations of the secondary phenomena. If our profession is to advance, we must recognize our defenses against ideas that would change our assumptions. Mysticism, studied seriously, challenges basic Western tenets: a) the primacy of reason and intellect; b) the separate, individual nature of man; c) the linear organization of time. Great mystics, like our own great scientists, envision the world as being larger than those tenets, as transcending our traditional views. By not recognizing our defensiveness and by permitting our vision to be narrowed so as to exclude the unfamiliar, we betray our integrity as psychiatrists, showing no more capacity for freedom from prejudice than persons totally ignorant of psychodynamics — perhaps less.

Psychiatry's aversion to things ecclesiastical should not blind the profession to the possibility that "real gold exists, even though false coin abounds." It is unfortunate that the GAP report carries us little further toward gaining for ourselves that wider base for human fulfillment that we need. The attitude reflected in the report is myopic and unnecessarily fearful of an avenue of human endeavor, aspiration, and discovery thousands of years old — one productive of outstanding achievements in science and literature that we are only now beginning to recognize. Yet, if we learn nothing more from mystics than the need for humility, they will have contributed greatly to Western culture in general and to the profession of psychiatry in particular.

References

1. Bridgman, P. W. *The Nature of Physical Theory*. John Wiley & Sons, New York, 1964.
2. Capra, F. *The Tao of Physics*. Shambala, Berkeley, 1975.
3. *The Complete Works of St. John of the Cross*, Vol. 1. Newman Press, Westminister, 1953.
4. Deikman, A. Bimodal consciousness. ARCH. GEN. PSYCHIATRY, 25: 481-489, 1971.
5. Goddard, D., Ed. *A Buddhist Bible*. Dwight Goddard, Thetford, Vermont, 1938.
6. Greene, M., Ed. *Toward a Unity of Knowledge.* (Psychol. Issues, 22: 45, 1969.) International Universities Press, New York, 1969.
7. Hilton, W. *The Scale of Perfection*. Burns & Oates, London, 1953.
8. Kapleau, P. *The Three Pillars of Zen*. Beacon Press, Boston, 1967.
9. LeShan, L. *The Medium, the Mystic and the Physicist*. Viking Press, New York, 1974.
10. Polanyi, M. *Personal Knowledge*. University of Chicago Press, Chicago, 1958.

11. Shah, I. *The Sufis.* Anchor Books (Doubleday & Co., Inc.), Garden City, N. Y., 1971.
12. Shah, I. *The Way of the Sufi.* E. P. Dutton & Co., New York, 1970.
13. Tart, C. *States of consciousness and state-specific sciences.* SCIENCE, 176: 1203-1218, 1972.

Originally published in THE JOURNAL OF
NERVOUS AND MENTAL DISEASE, 1971

Evaluating Spiritual and Utopian Groups

S PIRITUAL AND utopian groups will always exist because they answer fundamental human needs. However, not all of those needs are spiritual or utopian, and that is the problem. Some groups may fulfill their announced goals, benefiting their members and society, others may turn into a nightmare of exploitation, fear and violence. So it becomes necessary to have a way of evaluating groups, avoiding those that are, at best, ineffective and, at worst, injurious.

In order to do this one must recognize that the experience of the truly spiritual is not a fantasy, a delusion or an emotional binge but a valid aspect of human life known to almost everyone to some degree. Even today, in a culture that has embraced the scientific worldview, most people have intimations of a larger, more perfect reality that transcends the material world. This intangible perception has been shared by some of the principal physicists who established modern science, such as Newton and Einstein. The intuition of the spiritual does not require esoteric, dramatic ecstasies; in its most convincing form it is part of everyday consciousness. There it is reflected in our awareness of "the good."

Tolstoy describes this perception in his novel *Anna Karenina*. At the end of the story, Levin, who has been struggling unsuccessfully to find meaning in life and is close to suicide, is talking to Theodore, a peasant worker, about two other peasants, Mityuka and Plato. Theodore comments:

"Oh well, you see, people differ! One man lives only for his own needs: take Mityuka, who only stuffs his own belly, but Plato is an upright old man. He lives for his soul and remembers God."

Theodore's words spark a transformation in Levin's understanding of his life. He sees that the value of his life has been linked to an inherent knowledge of goodness, a knowledge that lies outside reason:

"I looked for an answer to my question. But reason could not give me an answer — reason is incommensurable with the question. Life itself has given me the answer, in my knowledge of what is good and what is bad. And that knowledge I did not acquire in any way; it was given to me as to everybody, given because I could not take it from anywhere.

"Where did I get it from? Was it by reason that I attained to the knowledge that I must love my neighbor and not throttle him? They told me so when I was a child, and I gladly believed it, because they told me what was already in my soul. But who discovered it? Not reason! Reason discovered the struggle for existence and the law that I must throttle all those who hinder the satisfaction of my desires. That is the deduction reason makes. But the law of loving others could not be discovered by reason, because it is unreasonable."[1]

Unscientific as it may be, the spiritual shines ahead of us through the darkness and we seek its source. Even in dealing with material existence, the sense of a potential for unlimited love, beauty, and unity gives rise to utopian visions and repeated attempts to create a society in which suffering will be absent and people will lead joyous, satisfying lives. This wish has led many to join groups that promise such fulfillment. Spiritual groups have union with God as their goal, utopian paradise on earth. They both share a fervor, idealism and sense of mission that indicates their kindred origin although their stated aims may be at different levels. Both reflect a similar impulse, a similar hope of realizing a higher state. These hopes should be respected.

History records waves of such activity. The most recent was in the sixties when the United States experienced a proliferation of New Age spiritual and utopian groups. Although that wave began to decline in the late seventies, Christian fundamentalist and charismatic organizations then went through a similar phase of rapid increase. But throughout these recent decades there have been many casualties. The most notorious incident occurred when the members of one group committed mass suicide at the direction of their leader. In other less publicized groups members have been harmed by being sexually and financially exploited, and quite a few leaders, spiritual as well as utopian, have turned out to be other than they seemed, falling far short of delivering what they had promised.

The mystical tradition insists that despite the overabundance of such misguided, ineffective and damaging enterprises, effective spiritual groups have been in operation in all eras, including this one.[2] The fact that spurious groups also exist is not surprising, "Counterfeit coins are accepted because real coins exist." So we are left with the pressing questions, "How can one separate the genuine from the counterfeit?" and "How can one judge a spiritual or utopian group and its leader?"

The first step in answering the questions is to realize that confused with intimations of the spiritual are longings and impulses derived from childhood. Thus, although a person may wish to find meaning and certainty, to serve God and humanity, he or she may also want to be taken care of, to find a home, to be praised and admired, protected and loved. These latter yearnings are seldom acknowledged because adults are not supposed to be motivated by them. Nevertheless, in seeking to gratify those wishes we are drawn to join groups that seem to be new families and to accept leaders as surrogate parents. Covertly, the "bliss" that is sought and frequently experienced is that of children who have been rescued from uncertainty and responsibilities, who have found a home.

Furthermore, we are social beings and derive benefits from joining with others. Groups can provide a gratifying sense of belonging, support and purpose while leaders can teach and inspire. As I will show, these aims may be important and valuable but they are not spiritual, no matter how pious their outward presentation. Correspondingly, our motivations for joining a spiritual or utopian group may be other than we realize or wish to know. Detecting such covert purposes enables us to evaluate a group's legitimacy.

Judging a spiritual group is complicated by the fact that spiritual leaders often present a unique problem. The outsider as well as the member may be intimidated by the claim that the leader has special knowledge, is "enlightened," able to perceive and know what the ordinary person cannot and, therefore, immune from ordinary criteria of behavior. Such leaders say that what they might do in their wisdom may make no sense to the unenlightened. Indeed, the mystical tradition in the various forms it has taken throughout history has been quite consistent in defining its teachers as people whose spiritual development had progressed to the point that they could "see" what others could not. If we grant that such people do exist, how can it be possible for the ordinary person to judge them?

Actually, the problem is not as difficult as has been thought, for the spiritual traditions are quite consistent about their goal and the requirements for reaching it. It is this fact that permits us to make a functional assessment of spiritual groups and thereby avoid cultural bias. We can make a judgment based on how well the activities of a group and its leader are suited to its stated aims.

A careful study of the literature of the mystical traditions — Vedantic, Taoist, Zen and Tibetan Buddhist, Sufic, Hasidic and that of the English and Spanish Catholic mystics, as well as the writings of such people as Jacob Boehme and Meister Eckhart — shows that they share the same basic goal. Their diverse procedures represent different ways of reaching that goal, according to the type of people being taught and the culture in which the teaching is taking place. The aim of the mystical traditions is the development of the ability to perceive directly (intuitively) the reality that underlies the world of appearances, whatever that reality may be called. All the traditions

agree that the primary requirement for the development of this capacity is that a person shift from a self-centered orientation to one of
serving the Truth. This service must be without concern for personal
gain. As one saint put it:

O Lord!

If I worship you from fear of hell, cast me into hell.

If I worship you from desire for paradise, deny me paradise. [3]

The shift away from self-centeredness is not a matter of being vir-
tuous but is a functional necessity. The type of consciousness we employ is that which is appropriate for our intention. Thus, self-preservation and acquisitive activity call for the "object mode" of consciousness featuring distinct boundaries, focal attention and logical thought,
enabling one to act on the environment. In contrast, to receive, to take
in, requires a shift to a different mode, one featuring diffuse attention,
the dominance of the sensual over the formal and a blurring or
merging of boundaries.[4] The two modes of consciousness are different
because they address different tasks. Thus, our consciousness is a
function of our underlying intention, it adapts to our motivations, to
our purpose. You can grasp a stone but to scoop water from a stream
you need to cup your hand. Similarly, if you wish to perceive a world
of connectedness, of unity, you cannot rely on the same mode of
consciousness you use to attack or defend. For unitive perception, for
that access to the spiritual domain, a selfless orientation is required
in which the Truth is served for its own sake.

This selfless orientation is referred to in a variety of ways, depending on the tradition in question. For example, in the Upanishads
it is referred to as "the purified heart"; in the Buddhist literature it is
the attitude of "non-attachment." We might call it serving the task,
rather than the self. To serve the task a carpenter might finish the
underside of a chair out of a sense that it was called for, whether or not
the carpenter gained anything from doing what was correct. Developing
that selfless orientation requires years of the right kind of effort —
there are no shortcuts. Although brief glimpses of the larger reality are

possible to almost anyone without such development (as in the case of spontaneous mystical experiences), it is a different matter to establish such perception as the ongoing basis of one's actions in the world. To do so necessitates a long period of skillful work.

This fact, that enlightenment requires an enduring change in a person's motivations, has a number of interesting consequences. The most important is that "the secret protects itself." No matter what you may say or do, if your underlying intention is selfish, and even if you are unaware that this is the case, no perception of the Truth is possible. It follows that a teacher cannot bestow the Truth on someone else. The capacity for the perception of the Truth must be developed — there is no short cut. Teachers who imply that enlightenment is in their gift are frauds.

These requirements provide a basis for assessing both new religious movements and traditional ones as well. A genuine spiritual organization is run in such a way as to assist the student in making the shift from a self-centered life to one that is centered in service. Almost all groups advocate service and their members will work long hours for a bare subsistence. However, at the same time self-centered emotions and desires may be stimulated.

An organization whose methods of operation enhance self-centered intentions can be judged dysfunctional, no matter how much overt self-sacrifice is demanded of its members. For example, the members of one quasi-Christian group were told that if they left the Church they would be damned. In another group, members were told that terrible things had happened to people who had defected in the past. Fear for one's safety or fear of being damned is not the sort of motivation that promotes spiritual development.

Some groups make little use of fear but appeal directly to the members' greed. They maintain that only group members will receive the divine bliss that the leader can convey. Indeed, extensive use may be made of procedures that bring about dramatic alterations in consciousness and these unusual experiences are then interpreted as proof that "paradise" awaits faithful followers. Initiation into one Indian guru's group featured a procedure causing members to experience a bright white light in the center of the head. Other sensory experiences are induced, as well. These experiences are called "knowledge" and are interpreted as validating the claims and promises of the guru.

Sometimes it is not bliss that is promised but power. A well-known group advertised a series of meditation sessions that would enable participants to levitate! Such a group might do a good job of meeting other needs, but it is not actually engaged in spiritual development. Consequently there is no basis for its leader to claim the special status and authority of the enlightened spiritual teacher.

These examples are relatively crude, although very prevalent. There are more subtle behaviors indicating that a group is not really spiritual. Often one can see that considerable use is being made of flattery, of appeals to the members' vanity. It was common practice of recruiters for one organization to direct "love bombs" (lavishly bestowed attention and praise) toward potential converts. Lonely young people found them hard to resist. Most groups convey the message that the new member has shown marvelous spiritual discernment by joining them. The leader may be a potent dispenser of flattery, calling attention to converts' good qualities and promising great things to come. Indeed, attention alone may be enough to accomplish seduction, whether it is delivered in the form of praise or as a severe rebuke. Such appeals to egotistical concerns indicate the corrupt character of a group and its leader.

The manipulation of guilt is another sign that a group is spurious. Lifton has documented its central role in "thought reform" or "brainwashing."[5] Basically, it establishes a dependent, regressive relationship to the leader and group; the member tends to feel like a bad child.

Many groups rely heavily on indoctrination. We can understand the general problem of indoctrination procedures by remembering that real mystical schools are aiming at a type of development. Indoctrination is not development, it is substituting one belief system for another. If a group makes use of the components of indoctrination it is a sure sign that its purposes are mundane. It is not hard to determine if this is the case because the principles of indoctrination are well known. They include: the arousal of guilt; group rejection alternating with group approval; repetition of accusations and dogma; restricted access to information; restricted privacy; and attacks on a person's previous affiliations and way of life.

When one surveys new religious movements as well as traditional religions, it is very striking how few are free from the components of indoctrination. This is in contrast to the mystical literature's emphasis on the need to acquire freedom from fixed assumptions and culturally derived beliefs about the self, God, causality, good and evil. Furthermore, indoctrination is antithetical to the expression of individuality and the mystical literature makes clear that individuality is crucial to the developmental process and must eventually manifest itself. A Hasidic anecdote relates that Rabbi Zeya on his deathbed told his assembled disciples: *"When I get to the world to come they will not ask me 'Why were you not Moses?,' they will ask me, 'Why were you not Zusya?'"* [6]

Spiritual development requires the opposite of indoctrination: learning to discern how the perception of the world is influenced by egocentric thought and motivations. To the extent that groups employ indoctrination components they are not legitimate spiritual groups, no matter what other valuable functions they may perform. Accordingly, their leaders are not entitled to the authority claimed by genuine spiritual teachers, an authority that would otherwise render them immune from conventional criticism. This is an extremely important point because bogus leaders fall back on the argument of spiritual authority as justification for the most exploitive and destructive acts. Without relating a leader's behavior to the requirements of spiritual development, there is no adequate reply to the argument.

It is because the leader's role is functional rather than magical that genuine spiritual teachers can be seen to obey implicit rules.

Despite the general impression that great teachers indulge in any and all behavior, careful attention to traditional teaching stories and anecdotes reveals that there are certain principles that are never violated. For example, I can recall no anecdote depicting a teacher ordering one student to harm another or condoning such an action. Nor are there examples of students being encouraged to compete for the teacher's attention. There are no examples of teachers entering into sexual relations with their students or enriching themselves with their money. All these examples have been common among current and past "spiritual" groups.

The reason why such examples are absent in authentic spiritual groups is that real teachers do not use their students to advance their own personal interests. In this matter the mystical literature is quite consistent and clear: a spiritual teacher does not have license to exploit students in any way or for any cause — the only legitimate basis for the teacher's actions is the advancement of the student along the spiritual path. This is not to say that larger purposes may not be served at the same time; indeed, such synchronous activity is said to be the norm but it is never at the expense of the student's development. The fact is, far from having unlimited license, a genuine spiritual teacher obeys functional requirements that far exceed the restraints most people are accustomed to impose on themselves in the name of religion or common decency. The behavior of many spiritual leaders is a travesty of the authentic situation.

Utopian Aims

Some groups that do not have explicit spiritual goals speak in terms of rehabilitative and therapeutic aims (e.g. teaching convicts to be responsible and law-abiding, or curing emotional problems) or the more general idea of self-development, of actualizing one's potential. These groups may promote themselves as an ideal society that provides its members with all they need to live and develop in a wholesome, satisfying and creative way. Here, too, we have the means for evaluating the authenticity and genuineness of such an organization and its leader by the use of functional criteria.

A good place to start is with Freud's definition of a healthy individual as someone who is reasonably able to work and to love. The simplicity of the definition is deceptive. For example, to be able to work a person must have sufficient impulse control to persevere until a given task is completed. It is also necessary that he or she be able to detach from emotions and fantasies to the extent necessary to perceive the task requirements accurately and carry them out. Furthermore, for the work to be satisfying it must in some way be expressive of individuality, even if that expression is in terms of the quality of the work rather than in some unique design or process. The ability to be individual, creative or innovative is not an automatic capacity of human beings. For some, it is achieved only after years of effort; for others, it never takes place.

The ability to love is also complex. We can understand that phrase to mean the capacity both for intimacy and for unselfish concern for another person. Intimacy is measured by the extent to which two people can be unguarded with each other, expressing their most personal feelings, thoughts, fantasies and wishes. To do this requires three things: 1) the capacity for trust; 2) a basically positive evaluation of oneself; and 3) sufficient acceptance of one's own thoughts, feelings and desires to be able to accept those of another without rejecting the other person or engaging in dis-identification: "How could you possibly have such (childish, cruel, sexist, filthy, selfish, etc.) thoughts!" Unselfish concern requires the ability to set aside self-protective and acquisitive strategies — and that is not easy. Thus, to work and to love is an achievement often requiring considerable learning and effort.

Despite the wide ground that Freud's definition covers, it is helpful to supplement it by looking at health from another perspective, that of autonomy. Autonomy is measured by the capacity to stand alone; it is the mark of adulthood. To stand alone means to be able to decide for oneself what one should and will do. It does not mean amorality or lawlessness but, rather, "the experience of being the author of the law you obey."[7] To have that experience, one must be willing to give up the idea that there are Big People to whom one looks (up) for answers and to whom one assigns responsibility and power. Autonomy exists only in an eye-level world. In contrast to autonomy, dependency is the readiness to structure one's relationships, both real and fantasized, on the model of parents and children. Although the dependent person is assumed to be the one who takes the role of the child, a person who plays the role of the parent is also participating in the fantasy and has not reached a sufficient stage of autonomy to give up the fantasy.

With these three functions in mind — work, love and autonomy — we are in a position to assess the validity of organizations that aim at competency in any or all of these areas. Just as in the case of spiritual groups, it is important that a prospective member be able to discriminate between effective and ineffective organizations. The least ill effect of the latter is to waste time and resources; the worst effect is to retard and damage the psychological growth of those participating in them. This is especially true of groups that set themselves up as utopian communities within which their members are expected to live their entire lives.

Many groups are successful in achieving improvement in the basic work skills of their members. They offer support, behavioral contracts, attention rewards from the leader, and a ready-made work structure — all of which contribute to the ability to carry out tasks and be productive. Indeed, since the work performed by the members is in most cases the source of income for the group and its leader, it usually receives top priority and may, in fact, be the only priority — apart from recruitment — no matter what else may be said to the contrary. Unfortunately for individuality, its expression through a member's work is not really necessary for the economic success of the group. Since individuality is also perceived as a threat to group cohesiveness, it is seldom encouraged.

Individuality requires autonomy and when it comes to achieving autonomy the requirements are more difficult than in the case of basic work skills. This is due to the fact that the very thing that is often most attractive to potential members — a charismatic leader — tends to accentuate dependency. When leaders exploit this situation by making promises of what they will bestow through their power or largesse, it is clear that autonomy is not likely to be achieved. Pressure towards conformity to group standards and ideals, inhibition of critical thinking and reliance on the magic of the leader are also factors working in the wrong direction. One of the common signs that the development of autonomy is being impeded rather than assisted is the aping of the leader in dress or manner. The basic difficulty here is that the authority of the group and the leader tends to be challenged by autonomous individuals and such confrontations are seldom welcomed. Despite these problems, it is possible for a group to enhance autonomy. If it does not inhibit or punish challenge and criticism, if it refuses to play parent to its members and if it discourages their magical expectations, it can help reach that goal. Otherwise, it is likely to be a hindrance.

The goal of intimacy is also not easy to attain. Because issues of trust are strongly based on earlier life experience, therapeutic processes are often required to bring about improvement in that area. Furthermore, the group and the leader must sanction the development and maintenance of strong emotional ties between members, "pair bonds," if members are to have the opportunity to learn how to be close. It is a fact, however, that the power of the leader and the sense of security of the group is diminished by strong pair formation because it sets up conflicting loyalties. This has been illustrated by those who managed to leave powerful exploitive cults. In many cases it was the competing needs of children or the love for a spouse that finally brought about the break with the group. Arranged marriages; the breaking of relationships by order of the leader or the group; pressure towards promiscuity or chastity; sexual relationships with the leader; interference with bonds to children and to parents — all these are signs that individual intimacy is being sacrificed to increase the members' ties to the group and the leader. Since the group and the leader together constitute a parent-child structure, neither adult intimacy nor autonomy are fostered by such policies but are impeded. In fact, what often takes place is a regression of psychosexual development.

From one point of view, this is not surprising. After all, for many converts the last thing they want is the complex demands of adult sexuality and true intimacy, to say nothing of real autonomy. The organization may function as a haven and the restricted relationships within the quasi-sibling group may well be a relief after the difficulties the members had been encountering prior to joining. That this is often the case is suggested by research that found that the fewer social ties a convert had before joining, the more likely that he or she would remain in the organization.[8]

Of course, there is nothing wrong with a haven or a moratorium for people wishing to regroup their forces, heal their wounds or solve their personality problems before proceeding further with their lives. However, to be therapeutic a group must not only comfort, it must help resolve its members' difficulties and move them further along the development path. Fixation at the level of a sibling group is non-therapeutic. People leaving such ineffective or exploitive organizations are likely to be in the same developmental phase they were in at the time they joined — only worse off because they are older and more out of step with the life of their contemporaries.

There are two further reasons why progress in the ability to be intimate does not take place in most religious, spiritual or New Age utopian groups. The first is that it requires therapeutic skill and experience to be able to uncover and clarify the barriers to intimacy that may exist in any one individual. Few people in such organizations have the necessary skill and it is rare for time to be given to formal psychotherapeutic activities. Secondly, resolving the conflicts that interfere with intimacy requires that the person become aware of transference reactions; that is, inappropriate feelings and attitudes derived from childhood relationships. These feelings tend to be experienced towards parental and sibling surrogates without the person being aware that that is what is taking place. To clarify such misperceptions requires that group members examine their attitudes toward the leader and towards the quasi-sibling group. Such an examination is likely to diminish the emotional bonds that maintain and contribute to the power of the leader and the organization. For this reason, authoritarian organizations are not usually advocates of psychotherapy.

Any organization that purports to be a complete or ideal society must be capable of providing the means for its members to progress in the areas of work, love and autonomy. Otherwise, the organization is functioning as a haven, nursery, business, or summer camp, but not as a society that enables its members to mature and make their individual contribution in the world. The fact that a small society may be economically successful and have many members does not make it ideal, spiritual, therapeutic or even harmless.

It must be acknowledged that no organization can be pure. No matter how skilled the leader, no matter how sincere the group members, human imperfection will manifest itself to some extent. Any group will tend to be exclusive and dependent; leaders are not omniscient and they all have distinct personalities. The spiritual traditions have been well aware that organizations in the world partake of its imperfections. Here is a story from the Sufi tradition that deals with this reality:

The Celestial Apple

Ibn-Nasr was ill and, although apples were out of season, he craved one.

Hallaj suddenly produced one.

Someone said: "This apple has a maggot in it. How could a fruit of celestial origin be so infested?"

Hallaj explained:
"It is just because it is of celestial origin that this fruit has become affected. It was originally not so, but when it entered this abode of imperfection it naturally partook of the disease which is characteristic here."[9]

Human activity is always flawed. Nevertheless, there is a difference between an apple with a maggot in it and one that is rotten. A small area of imperfection can be isolated, it can be avoided and corrected. When corruption is pervasive the apple must be discarded. It is expected that whatever personality flaws a teacher may possess, they will not be allowed to interfere with the teaching activity; certainly not to determine it. Whenever inappropriate group behavior occurs it is to be noted and eliminated. The important and obvious point is that the behavior of the teacher and the group must contribute to achieving the stated goal.

These considerations make possible a preliminary judgment of a leader or of a group. Such a judgment need not be an esoteric matter but one that is possible to a sufficiently sophisticated observer. It is true that much of what a genuine spiritual teacher or a New Age leader/therapist might do could be quite incomprehensible or misunderstood by an outsider but the basic functional relationships I have outlined will hold and provide a basis for making a judgment:

Furthermore, there is no evading this assessment; indeed, we make judgments of groups all the time, whether we wish to or not. We decide whether to join or not to join, whether to support or to discourage, and it is necessary that we do so, both for ourselves and for others who look to us for guidance in these matters. As I discussed earlier, the unsatisfied hunger for spiritual fulfillment may take highly inappropriate forms and lead people to embrace organizations and leaders whose destructive activities can be extreme. In the case of less pernicious groups, precious time and resources are squandered and the person may be left with a barren and cynical outlook. For this reason alone it is necessary that we judge the legitimacy of a group and its leader.

Protection is not the only issue. If the mystics are correct, each of us has a need to develop our own capacity to perceive the fundamental nature of the reality in which we live and the self that is at the core of our being. Valid mystical schools exist to bring about that perceptual development. It is of considerable importance that we become able to detect the existence of genuine groups amid all the counterfeits so that progress in this area can be made.

The functional criteria I have presented permit at least a provisional assessment of spiritual and utopian organizations that is not heavily biased by the observer's social class, religion or political affiliation, because it makes use of criteria based on the spiritual literature itself, as well as on our psychodynamic understanding of individuals and groups. Since judge we must, we may as well judge skillfully, as befitting members of a culture in which our knowledge can provide a basis for our doing so.

References

1. Tolstoy, Leo. *Anna Karenina* (New York: W.W. Norton, 1970) p.170.
2. Shah, Idries. *The Sufis* (London: The Octagon Press, 1982).
3. Shah, Idries. *The Way of the Sufi* (New York: E.P. Dutton & Co, 1970 and London: The Octagon Press, 1980) p.219.
4. Deikman, Arthur. *The Observing Self* (Boston: Beacon Press, 1982) pp. 65-76.
5. Lifton, Robert. *Thought Reform and the Psychology of Totalism* (New York: Norton, 1963).
6. Buber, Martin. *Tales of the Hasidim, Early Masters* (New York: Schocken Books, 1947) p.151.
7. Knight, Robert P. 'Determinism, "freedom" and psychotherapy'. PSYCHIATRY, 1946, 9, 251-262.
8. Galanter, Marc. 'Psychological induction into the large group: Findings from a modern religious sect'. AMERICAN JOURNAL OF PSYCHIATRY, 1980, 137 (12).
9. Shah, Idries. *The Way of the Sufi*, p. 256.

The Overestimation of
the Mystical Experience

Editor's Note: Walter N. Pahnke was a graduate student at Harvard Divinity School when he conducted the 1962 "Good Friday Experiment," supervised by Timothy Leary. Graduate-degree divinity student volunteers from the Boston area were randomly divided into two groups. In a double-blind experiment, half of the students received psilocybin, while a control group received a large dose of niacin (which can produce temporary physiological effects but no psychoactive effects). Pahnke's experiment was intended to determine whether psilocybin would act as a reliable entheogen (a substance producing religious experience) in religiously predisposed subjects. This article apparently refers to a conference presentation of the experiment and some of Pahnke's subsequent research.

DR. PAHNKE's research helps us to define exactly what we are talking about when we speak of the mystical experience. The research shows a way in which the sacred can be scrutinized without negating or degrading it. Dr. Pahnke has thus made the sacred less exclusive. Furthermore, his research has shown the possible use of psychedelic drugs in producing a mystical experience in a properly controlled setting. Finally, by proceeding in a careful and systematic way, Dr. Pahnke has helped make the mystical experience a respectable field for scientific inquiry,

I believe that the relevance of psychedelic drugs for the religious experience lies precisely in their capacity to produce mystical experiences not only under the optimal conditions of Pahnke's experiment but even among persons with no particular expectations of that sort and in quite non-theological settings. For this reason, I would like to discuss what I feel to be a problem found in Pahnke's presentation and in that of preceding speakers; namely, an overestimation of the value of the mystical experience such that the mystical experience is pursued as a *goal.*

Prior to my taking up this issue directly, I would like to add to the testimonials already presented at this meeting some reminiscences of my own as background to my current view of the mystical experience. Quite some time ago, I spent two months in the Adirondacks camping alone, with the intent of resolving certain personal conflicts and of getting in closer contact with the essence of reality. Without knowing it, I engaged in what I later found out was contemplative meditation, and over the course of the first month of my stay developed the signs of at least a low-order mystical experience: heightening of colors and intensification of the detail of surrounding landscape; feelings of buoyant joy; relief of anxiety; decrease in concern about death and a perception of an unseeable radiance emanating from everything I regarded, an emanation that seemed palpably real, and seemed to be the source of value for the arts as well as religion. This experience lasted for a full month but then, with the change of environment from the Adirondacks to medical school, it suffered a gradual attrition and was finally gone — except for a memory that continued to intrigue me for some time to come.

Consequently, when I completed my psychiatric training I chose to do research on the nature of the state of consciousness I had induced. To this end, I corralled normal volunteers, sat them down opposite a blue vase and read them meditation instructions based on the Vedantic literature. I then sat back to observe the results as these subjects repeated the procedure for 40, 50, 70 and 90 sessions. Many dramatic phenomena were produced that compared in some respects to clinical mystical experiences and to the phenomena of LSD and psilocybin, substances which I later studied, sampled, and with which I performed a few experiments. Further research on meditation effects, combined with a clarification of my own mystical motivations through a personal psychoanalysis, resulted in my present perspective with these concepts for its foundation:

• Enhanced respect for the human mind as it operates normally (and very effectively) in our behalf.

• Enhanced respect for our capacities for self-deception since this same mind that protects us from unpleasant experiences is capable of prodigious feats of creative synthesis in the interest of self-deception.

Mystical experience achieved through meditation and psychedelic drugs is basically a process I call "de-automatization" — the undoing of autonomic processes of perception and cognition resulting in, temporarily, a capacity for perception and cognition that is less efficient but potentially of wider range.

Under the conditions of de-automatization, several processes may take place: a) "reality-transfer" — the transfer of the feeling of realness from objects to thought and feelings normally devoid of that quality; b) "sensory translation" — the perception of thought *activity* in our minds via basic amorphous percepts of light, force and motion; and c) "perceptual expansion" — access to stimuli and modes of perception normally in abeyance, or not perceived.

These concepts are elaborated in papers I have published and I cannot take more time now to discuss them. I mention them to indicate other ways of interpreting mystical phenomena as a preliminary to my taking up the question "Do psychedelic drugs have any usefulness for religions?" To answer that question, I will discuss four possible religious uses of psychedelic drugs:

1. Psychedelic drugs could be used to establish, increase, or maintain faith in a particular religion. The ethics of such a use depend very much on the validity one ascribes to the experiences obtained under the drugs. Since this validity is certainly questionable, the use of drugs for such a purpose would also be questionable at the present time. (Apart from that, the image of a church administering drugs that drastically alter the state of consciousness in order to promote its own perpetuity is one that makes me quite uneasy and smacks too much of "1984." Pahnke's experiment, if expanded in scope, would be uncomfortably close to such a picture.)

2. Psychedelic drugs could give people a taste of the mystical so that they would seek more of it through conventional means. One might ask "more of what?," for the validity of the mystical experience as knowledge is not established. However, there are additional reasons for being unenthusiastic about this possibility. For one thing, the use of drugs to achieve a mystical experience encourages people in the hope that they can bypass establishing the basis for "enlightenment" in their own personality. The use of a drug will certainly raise expectations that are likely to result in disappointment when hopes for an enduring, blissful state are not realized. However, assuming that the mystical experience derived from the drugs gives one an experience of valuable truths and possibilities for behavior, it can be argued that such a use is good. We will come back to that in considering the next possible basis.

3. Obtaining an intuitive knowledge of God. Some religious persons may consider this an end in itself that needs no further justification. Accepting this premise, the question still arises as to what the knowledge of the mystical experience pertains to. It seems to me that we should exercise great caution before accepting the feelings of reality, the knowledge obtained, and the mystical feeling itself, as literal indices of contact with God for the following reasons:

• the *feeling* of realness or profundity is not evidence in itself;

• a feeling of union resulting from the loss of the distinction between self and object is likewise not evidence for it being union with God, since both the feeling of intense realness and the loss of the self-object distinctions occur under distinctly non-sacred conditions ranging from vivid dreams to psychosis;

• LSD enables us to create a super dream in which wishes and conflicts are given disguised expression in a way that is marvelous and overwhelming, but not to be taken literally;

• The lovingness reported to follow the ingestion of LSD does not appear well based: a) It does not feel particular real to those towards whom it is beamed; b) there is experimental evidence that the perception of real hostility in others and in one's self may be blocked in such conditions; c) the feeling of loving everyone wears off and leaves a person with actions he has committed himself to, but without the affective base needed to carry them out; d) there is no necessary correlation with the *expression* of loving feelings and with the *actual behavior* which one would expect to arise from such love.

4. Improve behavior towards one's fellow men. One would assume that an intuitive knowledge of God would have considerable good effect. However, in this respect, the success story of psychedelic drugs is not very rousing. Too common are the examples of the "holy man" syndrome in which a person announces to you that he loves all things and all men — the birds, the cats and dogs, the policemen, Khrushchev, your girl and you — and the smile on his face is indeed beatific. However, as the recipient of such love one feels strangely unwarmed, for the holy man's eyes seem to be looking straight through you and one wonders, indeed, what it is he is seeing. Psychotherapeutic programs have been conducted with psychedelic drugs in the hope of producing behavior change and we shall hear more about that this afternoon. As far as I am aware, however, the hopes that one large dose of LSD producing a mystical experience would in and of itself produce behavior change has not been borne out except in a very few cases. Most therapeutic programs now use LSD as part of an ongoing treatment program requiring psychotherapeutic preparation and considerable psychotherapeutic follow-up so a person can make use of insights he may have received. Although the mystical experience is thought to be an important part of the therapeutic effects of LSD, the mystical experience in itself has not proved to be very effective beyond a few months.

Classically, the mystical experience has been reported to transform persons undergoing it, but years of work under a guru are actually involved there. The guru checks the aspirant's progress against his behavior. The individual's past history returns directly or in disguised form and is worked over repeatedly. A one-shot "trip," for which no such preparation has been made, is not the same.

Finally, it is my impression that personal resynthesis achieved through psychoanalysis, but without a mystical experience, often results in personal behavior closer to religious precepts than the actual behavior of those who have had mystical states.

These views that I have presented are personal views but they are derived from a wide range of experience with mystical states, I feel that mystical experiences are valuable. They are wonderful to experience, are beneficial at the particular moment in which they occur, and these experiences *may* reveal new dimensions of our existence. However, I do not think they are something to *seek*, either by taking drugs or by meditation. The forging of human love and human work is the labor of life. In the forging of that life, in its human passion and fallibility, mystical experiences will be found. They will appear — mysterious, joyous, and sweet — unsought for and unexpected.

Originally published in *Do Psychedelics Have Religious Implications?*,
ed. D.H. Salman and R.H. Prince. R.M. Bucke Memorial Society
for the Study of Religious Experience

Treating Former Members of a Cult

FROM TIME to time, a psychotherapist receives a request for help from someone who has recently left a cult.[1] These patients may present symptoms of anxiety and depression, as do many others, but they constitute a group with special problems that require special knowledge on the part of the therapist.

The story these patients recount is remarkably similar from one to the next, regardless of differing educational, social, or financial backgrounds. They usually tell of joining the cult when they were at a transition point in their lives. Dissatisfied with their ordinary pursuits and relationships and hungry for a meaningful life that would satisfy their spiritual longings, they encountered an attractive, smiling young man or woman who enthusiastically described the happiness to be found in his or her dedicated, loving group and its wonderful, enlightened leader. They were invited to visit the group and did so. At that first meeting, they were impressed, if not overwhelmed, by the warm attention they received. In addition, they may have been emotionally stirred by singing, meditation, or other activities and may even have entered an altered state of consciousness under the influence of the group's leader. Such impressive experiences were interpreted as proof of both the leader's advanced spiritual state and the newcomer's readiness to receive initiation. After one or two more meetings, they decided to join.

Having joined, the new convert's life was immediately filled with work meetings, and exercises that left little time or energy for the life he or she left behind. Even if the convert was married and had a family, the partner and the children were regarded as less important than the avowed mission of the group to benefit all of humanity to save the world. The conflict between group demands amid outside commitments grew steadily sharper until the convert relinquished all relationships with those outside the group or the family broke up as the spouse reached the limit of tolerance. The ally was now totally dependent on the group and the leader for emotional and financial support.

The group that initially was warm and loving revealed its cold, punitive side whenever a convert questioned the group's beliefs or criticized the behavior of the leader. Such dissent was labeled "selfish" or "evil," and group approval was withdrawn and the dissenter isolated. Members were taught, therefore, that what the group had given, the group could take away. Out of fear of such punishment by the group and of humiliation and censure by the leader, converts found themselves engaging in the intimidation and coercion of fellow converts, the deception and seduction of new recruits, and other behaviors that violated ethical standards held before joining the cult. Such actions were rationalized by reference to the overriding importance of the group's purpose and to the leader's superior wisdom.

Eventually, the strain of conforming to the demands of the group became too much, especially if children were involved. The convert protester refused to comply with the latest demands and was dealt with severely. Finally, in desperation, he (or she) left the cult. Immediately, the leader branded him as damned, possessed by Satan, and having lost his soul. At the very least, he had failed the test and lost his chance at enlightenment. Just as painful, people with whom he had shared his most intimate secrets and felt the greatest acceptance and love now turned their backs and refused to communicate. Feeling totally alone, the ex-cult member experienced a turmoil of feelings: rage at the betrayal, fear of retaliation, horror at the possibility of perpetual damnation, grief at the loss of group support and affection, and shame at having been duped. At this point, he may turn to a therapist for help.

The anxiety and depression such patients feel usually is secondary to a bigger problem: a loss of trust in others and, especially loss of trust in their own judgment and spiritual perceptions. Additionally, they may feel guilt over unethical actions they engaged in to please the group and despair at the loss of time, money, and relationships. To recover from the trauma of their cult experience, these patients need to understand what happened and why, and so does the psychotherapist who treats them.

Motivations for Joining

People who join cults do so for two principal reasons: (1) They want to lead a meaningful, spiritual life and (2) they want to feel protected, cared for, and guided by someone who knows what to do in a confusing world. The first motive is conscious and laudable; the second is unconscious or not recognized for what it is. Therein lies the problem: The wish to have a perfect parent and a loving; supportive group lies concealed in the psyche of even the most outwardly independent person. When the opportunity arises to gratify that wish, it powerfully influences judgment and perception and paves the way for exploitation by a cult.

There is good reason for cults to be associated primarily with religious-spiritual organizations. Religions are based on the belief in a transcendent, supreme power usually characterized along parental lines: God is all-powerful and all-knowing, meting out rewards and punishments according to how well a person has carried out the commandments He has issued. The doctrines vary, but even in non-monotheistic Eastern traditions Heaven and Hell in some form are designated as the consequences of good and bad behavior.

Although mystics are unanimous in defining God as incomprehensible and not of this world, human dependency needs require something more approachable and personal: Even in Buddhism, therefore, whose founder declared that concepts of gods and heaven were an illusion, many followers bow to a Buddha idol to invoke Buddha's protection and blessing. But even more satisfying to the wish for a superparent is an actual human with divine, enlightened, or messianic status. The powerful wish to be guided and protected by a superior being can propel a seeker into the arms of a leader who is given that status by his or her followers. Such a surrender to the fantasy of the perfect parent may be accompanied by a feeling of great joy at "coming home."

This analysis does not imply that the intimations of a larger reality and a larger purpose, sensed by human beings for thousands of years, are only a fantasy: The problem is that the spiritual dimension and dependency wishes can get badly confused. The patient needs to disentangle the perception of a spiritual dimension from less-than-divine longings that have infiltrated, taken over, and distorted what is valid. It is important that the psychiatrist treating an ex-cult member keep this distinction in mind.

One way to clarify the confusion is to help the patient see clearly the problems that she had hoped "enlightenment" and membership in the group would solve: These problems may include loneliness, low self-esteem, the wish for the admiration of others, fear of intimacy, fear of death, and the wish for invulnerability. Indeed, membership in the group may assuage loneliness and provide the support and closeness that the patient had not experienced previously; memories of such good experiences may occasion acute feelings of loss in the ex-cult member and give rise to doubts concerning whether or not leaving was the best thing to do.

To look objectively and critically at the cult experience, the ex-member needs to gain freedom from the "superior leader trap." As indicated earlier, this trap is sprung if there is criticism or questioning of the leader's actions and directives. Basically, it takes the following form: The Leader operates on a higher plane than you or I. Because of that, we are not able to judge the rightness or wrongness of his or her actions. Ordinary, conventional standards do not apply here.

Although this conclusion may sound reasonable, the leader in fact can be judged by criteria established in the mystical literature. There is a striking consensus in these writings concerning the nature of the spiritual path and the duties of a genuine teacher. The consensus permits one to make judgments of whether the teacher's actions advance spiritual development or hinder it.

It is important to realize that the basic activity of the spiritual traditions is to assist spiritual students to "forget the self." The self referred to is what is usually termed the ego but is better understood as being the psychological processes dedicated to biological survival. That primitive aim is expressed in greed, fear, lust, hatred, and jealousy: the traditional vices. These vices are functional for the intention of survival. The mode of consciousness one expresses is functional also, and it is adapted to one's intentions. For example, building a bookcase calls forth a particular form of consciousness — the instrumental — featuring an emphasis on the object characteristics of the world, a reliance on abstract concepts, and a focus on past and future and on differences and boundaries. This mode of consciousness is needed to fulfill the intention of making a useful object. When one wants to receive something from one's surroundings, however, as in relaxing in a tub of steaming hot water or having a massage, one needs a different mode of consciousness — the receptive — featuring an emphasis on sensual experience, a blurring of boundaries, a focus on now, and a sense of connectedness with the environment.

Ordinary survival aims, therefore, call forth instrumental consciousness: But if it is desired to experience the world in its wholeness, unity, and interconnection — the essence of spiritual consciousness — a different intention must be operative, along with a lessening of control by the survival self. [2]

Keeping in mind this functional relationship of motivation and self to consciousness, one can see that the spiritual traditions use a variety of means to transform the seeker's initial motivations, which are heavily weighted toward greed, dependency, and power; into motivations of service and contemplation. Meditation, teaching stories, service, and the example set by the teacher can be understood as tools for accomplishing a deep shift in basic intention, permitting access to spiritual consciousness.

This framework provides a means for making a preliminary judgment about people who declare themselves to be spiritual teachers. All one needs to do is observe their behavior and notice the intentions and type of self that is being reinforced. If there is considerable emphasis on what the convert will gain from following the teacher, such as "bliss," psychic abilities, or the joy of enlightenment, these promises will arouse greed and acquisitive strategies. After all, the desire for bliss is not fundamentally different from the desire for money. If the teacher warns that rejecting the teaching will result in damnation, loss of one's soul, and loss of all hopes of spiritual advancement, fear is aroused and the survival self is activated. Likewise, if the leader makes use of flattery by bestowing attention or praise, this can arouse vanity in the convert and competition in the group members. In all these instances, the teacher is intensifying the operation of the survival self and the form of consciousness it generates. These activities are antispiritual, and leaders that employ them are not genuine spiritual teachers; they are not entitled to any special deference or trust.[3]

Of course, exploitation of followers for sexual pleasure or financial gain cannot be justified in any manner and testifies to the unenlightened, self-centered state of the teacher. Such exploitation is not to be found in the lives of the great mystics. They operated by even more rigorous standards than those that are imposed by conventional society. This is not to say that mystics are examples of perfect human beings. Perfection is not part of earthly existence for anyone or anything. But financial or sexual exploitation represents a drastic failure of responsibility that disqualifies a teacher from any special consideration. Psychotherapists are well aware of how harmful such violations of trust can be.

The behavior of most cult leaders departs widely from the path laid down in the mystical literature and can be seen to be harmful to spiritual development. By employing this functional framework, cult members can judge for themselves the presumed sanctity of the leader and the appropriateness of the leader's behavior.

Cult Behavior in Normal Society

Just as it is important to have a means of judging a spiritual teacher, it also is important for the ex-cult member and the therapist to be able to answer the more general question: "Is this group a cult?" Patients need to be able to answer that question to avoid making the same mistake again, and therapists are likely to be asked that question by a worried parent or spouse. Usually, the group in question has obvious cult trappings, but society abounds with groups and organizations that appear normal but have the potential for cultlike behavior: large corporations, political groups, professional organizations, government bodies, and established religions. These sectors of normal society seldom are thought to share characteristics with The People's Temple or the less dramatic groups such as the Moonies and the Krishna devotees collecting money in airports, however, careful study of cults reveals four basic cult behaviors that occur to varying degrees in almost all groups, including those that do not have a strange appearance or engage in bizarre behavior.[4] Identifying these basic behaviors permits one to replace the question, "Is this group a cult?" with the more practical one, "To what extent is cult behavior present?" The latter question is more useful because in the field of the transpersonal, as elsewhere, there is a continuum of groups ranging from the most benign and least cultlike to the most malignant and destructive.

The Four Basic Cult Behaviors

Compliance With the Group

Everybody is concerned with how he or she is viewed by the people whose opinions matter to us, our "reference group." No matter how outwardly independent and nonconformist we may be, there is usually a group of people who share our values and whose approval we want.

Membership in this group is signaled by conformity in dress, behavior, and speech. People outside of cults may suppress deviant thoughts also, although less obviously, if they believe that their expression could result in loss of status with the people important to them.

The power of groups has been noted by psychologists beginning with Gustav Le Bon and Sigmund Freud, and analyzed in detail by Wilfred Bion, who proposed that members of groups tend to adopt one of three primitive emotional states: dependency, pairing, or fight-flight. His description of the dependency state is an apt description of cults, but he saw the process taking place in varying degrees in all groups:

The essential aim ... is to attain security through and have its members protected by one individual. It assumes that this is why the group has met. The members act as if they know nothing, as if they are inadequate and immature creatures. Their behavior implies that the leader, by contrast, is omnipotent and omniscient.[5]

It is plausible that natural selection favored individuals who were good at discerning what the group wanted because preservation of their membership in the group gave them the best chance of survival. As a consequence, it is likely that human beings have evolved to be exquisitely sensitive to what the group wants. "Political correctness" probably has a long history.

Dependence on a Leader

Leaders draw a power from their followers' wish for an ideal parent, a wish that is latent in all adults no matter what kind of parent they had. Although cult leaders may be charismatic, they need need not be as long as they are believed by the group members to possess superior powers and secrets. Cult leaders are authoritarian, encouraging dependence and discouraging autonomy. Obedience and loyalty are rewarded, and critical thinking is punished. Furthermore, to enhance dependency on the leader, pair bonding is discouraged. The leader must come first; family and lovers come last.

The disruption of intimate relationships is accomplished by a variety of means: enforced chastity, separation of parents from children, arranged marriages, long separations, promiscuity, or sexual relations with the leader. All these aspects are counter to healthy leadership, which fosters growth, independence, and mature relationships and has as its aim that the followers will eventually achieve an eye-level relationship with the leader.

Dissent

Dissent threatens the group fantasy that the members are being protected and rewarded by a perfect, enlightened leader who can do no wrong. The security provided by that fantasy is the basic attraction that keeps members in the cult despite highly questionable actions by the leader. Questioning the fantasy threatens that security, and for this reason, active dissent is seldom encouraged. To the contrary, dissenters are often declared to be in the grip of Satan. Sometimes they are scapegoated, and hidden, unconscious anger toward the leader is released against the dissenter. Almost all groups derive security from their shared beliefs and readily regard dissenters as irritations, to be gotten rid of. Nevertheless, the mark of a healthy group is a tolerance for dissent and a recognition of its vital role in keeping the group sane. Paranoia develops and grandiosity flourishes when dissent is eliminated and a group isolates itself from outside influence. As recent cult disasters have shown us, grandiose and paranoid cult leaders often self-destruct, taking their group with them.

Devaluing the Outsider

What good is being in a group if membership does not convey some special advantage? In spiritual groups, the members are likely to believe that they have the inside track to enlightenment, to being "saved," or to finding God because of the special sanctity and spiritual power of the leader. It follows that they must be superior to people outside the group: It is they, the converts, who have the leader's blessing and approval. Devaluation can be detected in the pity or "compassion" they may feel for those outside. This devaluation becomes most marked in the case of someone who elects to leave the group and is thereby considered "lost," if not damned. The more such devaluation takes place, and the more the group separates itself from the outside world, the greater the danger of cult pathology.

Devaluing of the outsider is part and parcel of everyday life. Depending on which group we designate as the outsider, our scorn may be directed at "liberals," "Republicans," "blacks," "Jews," "yuppies," or "welfare bums": however the outsider is designated. Such disidentification can authorize unethical, mean, and destructive behavior against the outsider, behavior that otherwise would cause guilt for violating ethical norms. Devaluation of the outsider is tribal behavior and so universal as to suggest a "basic law of groups:" Be one of us and we will love you; leave us and we will kill you.

Devaluing the outsider reassures the insider that he or she is good, special, and deserving, unlike the outsider. Such a belief is a distortion of reality; if one considers the different circumstances of each person's development and life context, one is hard put to judge another person to be intrinsically inferior to oneself. Certainly, actions can be judged, but human beings are one species, at eye level with each other.

Cult Behavior in the Psychotherapist

The psychotherapist treating an ex-cult member may be tempted to devalue the patient for being duped and exploited and for believing weird doctrines. Especially in the role of expert in human psychology, we therapists wish to be reassured that nothing like that would happen to us because we are too discerning, mature, and sophisticated. As a matter of fact, we are not immune by virtue of our profession; psychotherapists with the best credentials have participated directly in cults. There have even been psychotherapeutic cults led by fully trained and accredited psychoanalysts,[6] and noted psychoanalysts have commented on the cult aspects of psychoanalytic training institutes.[7,8]

Furthermore, cult behavior is evident within the psychiatric profession as a whole. Perusal of the psychiatric literature indicates a remarkable absence of dissent from the current enthusiasm for biological psychiatry, an enthusiasm not different from the overcommitment to environmental influences that characterized the 1950s, 1960s, and 1970s. Indeed, research that challenges the biological perspective is ignored.[4] The biological-medical consensus is reinforced by economic factors; those working in academic environments experience pressure to shape their research focus and strategy so that they will be funded. Being awarded a research grant usually depends on the approval of the "leading experts" in the field, the very persons who have established, and are committed to, the prevailing theoretical perspective. Furthermore, the same authorities are asked to judge articles submitted for publication to psychiatric journals. Avoidance of dissent and devaluation of the outsider can take the place unnoticed, therefore, through rejection of submitted papers and denial of research funds. To this may be added informal devaluation through unsupported derogatory comments made at professional gatherings.

The Value of Awareness

It is important that both the therapist and the ex-cult member be able to see that cult behaviors are endemic in our society. Such awareness can protect the therapist from the influence of such behaviors and allow ex-cult members to realize that they are not freaks, weak and dependent persons, or fools. Rather, they were led astray by unconscious wishes that they share with all human beings. These wishes were stimulated at a time when they were especially vulnerable and under circumstances that any person might have found difficult to combat.

Conclusion

Cult behavior reflects the wish for a loving, accepting sibling group that is protected and cherished by a powerful, omnipotent parent. The problem with such a wish and its accompanying fantasy is that no human being can fill the role of the superparent, and adults can never again be children. To preserve the fantasy, reality must be distorted, because of this distortion, cult behavior results in a loss of realism. In the more extreme cases, the consequences can be drastic. Diminished realism is a problem in any situation, however, and for this reason, cult behavior is costly no matter where it takes place: affecting business decisions, governmental deliberations, day-to-day relationships in the community, or the practice of psychotherapy. Fortunately, awareness of these cult behaviors offers protection from their influence. Psychotherapists can foster that awareness, benefiting patients, themselves, and society.

Originally published in *Textbook of Transpersonal Psychiatry
and Psychology* (New York: Basic Books), 1966

I = Awareness

Abstract

Introspection reveals that the core of subjectivity — the 'I' — is identical to awareness. This 'I' should be differentiated from the various aspects of the physical person and its mental contents which form the 'self.' Most discussions of consciousness confuse the 'I' and the 'self.' In fact, our experience is fundamentally dualistic — not the dualism of mind and matter — but that of the 'I' and that which is observed. The identity of awareness and the 'I' means that we know awareness by being it, thus solving the problem of the infinite regress of observers. It follows that whatever our ontology of awareness may be, it must also be the same for 'I'

'I'

We seem to have numerous 'I's. There is the I of 'I want,' the I of 'I wrote a letter,' the I of 'I am a psychiatrist' or 'I am thinking'. But there is another I that is basic, that underlies desires, activities, and physical characteristics. This I is the subjective sense of our existence. It is different from self-image, the body, passions, fears, social category — these are aspects of our person that we usually refer to when we speak of the self, but they do not refer to the core of our conscious being, they are not the origin of our sense of personal existence.

EXPERIMENT 1: *Stop for a moment and look inside. Try to sense the very origin of your most basic, most personal 'I' — your core subjective experience. What is that root of the 'I' feeling? Try to find it.*

When you introspect you will find that no matter what the contents of your mind, the most basic 'I' is something different. Every time you try to observe the 'I' it takes a jump back with you, remaining out of sight. At first you may say, 'When I look inside as you suggest, all I find is content of one sort or the other.' I reply, 'Who is looking? Is it not you? If that I is a content can you describe it? Can you observe it?' The core 'I' of subjectivity is different from any content because it turns out to be that which witnesses — not that which is observed. The 'I' can be experienced, but it cannot be 'seen.' 'I' is the observer, the experiencer, prior to all conscious content.

In contemporary psychology and philosophy, the 'I' usually is not differentiated from the physical person and its mental contents. The self is seen as a construct and the crucial duality is overlooked. As Susan Blackmore puts it,

> Our sense of self came about through the body image we must construct in order to control behavior, the vantage point given by our senses, and our knowledge of our own abilities, that is, the abilities of the body-brain-mind. Then along came language. Language turns the self into a thing and gives it attributes and powers. (Blackmore, 1994)

Dennett comments similarly that what he calls the 'Center of Narrative Gravity' gives us a spurious sense of a unitary self:

> A self, according to my theory, is not any old mathematical point, but an abstraction defined by the myriads of attributions and interpretations (including self-attributions and self-interpretations) that have composed the biography of the living body whose Center of Narrative Gravity it is (Dennett, 1991).

However, when we use introspection to search for the origin of our subjectivity, we find that the search for 'I' leaves the customary aspects of personhood behind and takes us closer and closer to awareness, *per se*. If this process of introspective observation is carried to its conclusion, even the background sense of core subjective self disappears into awareness. Thus, if we proceed phenomenologically, we find that the 'I' is identical to awareness: 'I' = awareness.

Awareness

Awareness is something apart from, and different from, all that of which we are aware: thoughts, emotions, images, sensations, desires, and memory. Awareness is the ground in which the mind's contents manifest themselves; they appear in it and disappear once again.

I use the word 'awareness' to mean this ground of all experience. Any attempt to describe it ends in a description of what we are aware of. On this basis some argue that awareness *per se* doesn't exist. But careful introspection reveals that the objects of awareness — sensations, thoughts, memories, images and emotions — are constantly changing and superseding each other. In contrast, awareness continues independent of any specific mental contents.

EXPERIMENT 2: *Look straight ahead. Now shut your eyes. The rich visual world has disappeared to be replaced by an amorphous field of blackness, perhaps with red and yellow tinges. But awareness hasn't changed. You will notice that awareness continues as your thoughts come and go, as memories arise and replace each other, as desires emerge and fantasies develop, change, and vanish. Now try and observe awareness. You cannot. Awareness cannot be made an object of observation because it is the very means whereby you can observe.*

Awareness may vary in intensity as our total state changes, but it is usually a constant. Awareness cannot itself be observed, it is not an object, not a thing. Indeed, it is featureless, lacking form, texture, color, spatial dimensions. These characteristics indicate that awareness is of a different nature than the contents of the mind; it goes beyond sensation, emotions, ideation, memory. Awareness is at a different level, it is prior to contents, more fundamental. Awareness has no intrinsic content, no form, no surface characteristics — it is unlike everything else we experience, unlike objects, sensations, emotions, thoughts, or memories.

Thus, experience is dualistic, not the dualism of mind and matter but the dualism of awareness and the contents of awareness. To put it another way, experience consists of the observer and the observed. Our sensations, our images, our thoughts — the mental activity by which we engage and define the physical world — are all part of the observed. In contrast, the observer — the 'I' — is prior to everything else; without it there is no experience of existence. If awareness did not exist in its own right there would be no 'I'. There would be 'me', my personhood, my social and emotional identity — but no 'I', no transparent center of being.

Confusion of Awareness and Contents

In the very center of the finite world is the "I." It doesn't belong in that world, it is radically different. In saying this, I am not suggesting a solipsistic ontology. The physical world exists for someone else even when I am sleeping. But any ontology that relegates awareness to a secondary or even an emergent status ignores the basic duality of experience. Currently, there are many voices denying the dualistic ontology of awareness and contents. For example, Searle attacks mind-body dualism, regarding consciousness (awareness) as an emergent property of material reality. He likens it to liquidity, a property that emerges from the behavior of water molecules composed of hydrogen and oxygen — atoms that do not themselves exhibit liquidity. "Consciousness is not a 'stuff', it is a feature or property of the brain in the sense, for example, that liquidity is a feature of water" (Searle, 1992).[1] But liquidity, understandable as it may be from considerations of molecular attraction, is part of the observed world, similar to it from that ontological perspective. To state that the subjective 'emerges' from the objective is quite a different proposition, about which the physical sciences have nothing to say.

Colin McGinn also insists that there is no duality of mind and matter — all can ultimately be explained in physical terms — but he asserts that the critical process by which a transition occurs from one to the other will never be understood because of our limited intellectual capacity (McGinn, 1991). McGinn believes that the observer/observed duality is apparent rather than real; there is a physical transition from the observed to the observer. But the ontological gap between a thought and a neuron is less than that between the observer and the observed; there is nothing to be compared to the 'I,' while thoughts and neurons are linked by their being objects of observation, contents of 'I' sharing some characteristics such as time and locality.[2] Granted that a blow on my head may banish 'I,' its relationship to the observed is fundamentally different from anything else we can consider. The best that can be said for the materialist interpretation is that the brain is a necessary condition for 'I'.

Confusion about 'I'

One can read numerous psychology texts and not find any that treat awareness as a phenomenon in its own right, something distinct from the contents of consciousness. Nor do their authors recognize the identity of 'I' and awareness. To the contrary, the phenomenon of awareness is usually confused with one type of content or another. William James made this mistake in his classic, Principles of Psychology. When he introspects on the core 'self of all other selves' he ends up equating the core self with 'a feeling of bodily activities...' concluding that our experience of the 'I,' the subjective self, is really our experience of the body:

> ...the body, and the central adjustments which accompany the act of thinking in the head. These are the real nucleus of our personal identity, and it is their actual existence, realized as a solid, present fact, which makes us say 'as sure as I exist' (James, 1950).

To the contrary, I would say that I am sure I exist because my core 'I' is awareness itself, my ground of being. It is that awareness that is the "self of all other selves." Bodily feelings are *observed*: 'I' is the observer, not the observed.

Beginning with behavioral psychology and continuing through our preoccupation with artificial intelligence, parallel distributed processing, and neural networks, the topic of awareness *per se* has received relatively little attention. When the topic does come up, consciousness in the sense of pure awareness is invariably confused with one type of content or the other.

A few contemporary psychiatrists such as Gordon Globus (1980) have been more ready to recognize the special character of the self of awareness, the observing self, but almost all end up mixing awareness with contents. For example, Heinz Kohut developed his Self Psychology based on considering the self to be a superordinate concept, not just a function of the ego. Yet he does not notice that awareness is the primary source of self-experience and concludes: 'The self then, quite analogous to the representations of objects, is a content of the mental apparatus' (Kohut, 1971).

We see the same problem arising in philosophy. After Husserl, nearly all modern Western philosophical approaches to the nature of mind and its relation to the body fail to recognize that introspection reveals 'I' to be identical to awareness.[3] Furthermore, most philosophers do not recognize awareness as existing in its own right, different from contents. Owen Flanagan, a philosopher who has written extensively on consciousness, sides with James and speaks of "the illusion of the mind's 'I'" (Flanagan, 1992). C.O. Evans starts out recognizing the importance of the distinction between the observer and the observed, 'the subjective self,' but then retreats to the position that awareness is 'unprojected consciousness,' the amorphous experience of background content (Evans, 1970). However, the background is composed of elements to which we can shift attention. It is what Freud called the preconscious. 'I' awareness has no elements, no features. It is not a matter of a searchlight illuminating one element while the rest is dark — it has to do with the nature of light itself.

In contrast, certain Eastern philosophies based on introspective meditation emphasize the distinction between awareness and contents.[4]

Thus, Hindu Samkhya philosophy differentiates purusa, the witness self, from everything else, from all the experience constituting the world, whether they be thoughts, images, sensations, emotions or dreams. A classic expression of this view is given by Pantanjali:

> Of the one who has the pure discernment between **sattva**
> (the most subtle aspect of the world of emergence)
> and purusa (the non-emergent pure seer)
> there is sovereignty over all and
> knowledge of all. (Chapple, 1990)

Awareness is considered to exist independent of contents and this 'pure consciousness' is accessible — potentially — to everyone. A more contemporary statement of this position is given by Sri Krishna Menon, a twentieth century Yogi:

> He who says that consciousness is never experienced without its object speaks from a superficial level. If he is asked the question "Are you a conscious being?" he will spontaneously give the answer "Yes." This answer springs from the deepmost level. Here he doesn't even silently refer to anything as the object of that consciousness. (Menon, 1952)

In the classical Buddhist literature we find:

> When all lesser things and ideas are transcended and forgotten, and there remains only a perfect state of imagelessness where Tathagata and Tathata are merged into perfect Oneness...
> (Goddard, 1966). [5]

Western mystics also speak of experiencing consciousness without objects. Meister Eckhart declares:

> There is the silent "middle," for no creature ever entered there and no image, nor has the soul there either activity or understanding, therefore she is not aware there of any image, whether of herself or of any other creature (Forman, 1990).

Similarly, Saint John of the Cross:

> That inward wisdom is so simple, so general and so spiritual that it has not entered into the understanding enwrapped or clad

in any form or image subject to sense (1953).

The failure of Western psychology to discriminate awareness from contents, and the resulting confusion of 'I' with mental contents, may be due to a cultural limitation: the lack of experience of most Western scientists with Eastern meditation disciplines.[6]

Eastern mystical traditions use meditation practice to experience the difference between mental activities and the self that observes. For example, the celebrated Yogi, Ramana Maharshi, prescribed the exercise of "Who am I?" to demonstrate that the self that observes is not an object; it does not belong to the domains of thinking, feeling, or action (Osborne, 1954). "If I lost my arm, I would still exist. Therefore, I am not my arm. If I could not hear, I would still exist. Therefore, I am not my hearing." And so on, discarding all other aspects of the person until finally, "I am not this thought," which could lead to a radically different experience of the 'I.' Similarly, in Buddhist vipassana meditation the meditator is instructed to simply note whatever arises, letting it come and go. This heightens the distinction between the flow of thoughts and feelings and that which observes.[7]

Attempts to integrate Eastern and Western psychologies can fall prey to the same confusion of 'I' and contents, even by those who have practiced Eastern meditation disciplines. Consider the following passage from *The Embodied Mind*, a text based on experience with mindfulness meditation and correlating Western psychological science with Buddhist psychology .

> ... *in our search for a self... we found all the various forms in which we can be aware — awareness of seeing and hearing, smelling, tasting, touching, even awareness of our own thought processes. So the only thing we didn't find was a truly existing self or ego. But notice that we did find experience. Indeed, we entered the very eye of the storm of experience, we just simply could discern there no self, no 'I'* (Varela et al., 1991).

But when they say, "...we just simply could discern there no self, no 'I,'" to what does 'we' refer? Who is looking? Who is discerning?

Is it not the 'I' of the authors? A classic story adapted from the Vedantic tradition is relevant here:

> *A group of travellers forded a river. Afterwards, to make sure everyone had crossed safely, the leader counted the group but omitted himself from the count. Each member did the same and they arrived at the conclusion that one of them was missing. The group then spent many unhappy hours searching the river until, finally, a passerby suggested that each person count their own self, as well. The travellers were overjoyed to find that no one was missing and all proceeded on their way.*

Like the travellers, Western psychology often neglects to notice the one that counts. Until it does, its progress will be delayed.

Similarly, discussions of consciousness (awareness) as 'point of view' (Nagel, 1986) or 'perspective' do not go far enough in exploring what the 'first person perspective' really is. In my own case, it is not myself as Arthur Deikman, psychiatrist, six feet tall, brown hair. That particular person has specific opinions, beliefs, and skills, all of which are part of his nominal identity, but all of which are observed by his 'I,' which stands apart from them. If awareness is a fundamental in the universe — as proposed most recently by Herbert (1994), Goswami (1993) and Chalmers (1995) — then it is 'I' that is fundamental, as well, with all its ontological implications. Arthur Deikman is localized and mortal. But what about his 'I,' that light illuminating his world, that essence of his existence? Those studying consciousness, who can see the necessity for according consciousness a different ontological status than the physical, tend not to extend their conclusions to 'I.' Yet, it is the identity 'I' = awareness that makes the study of consciousness so difficult. Güven Güzeldere asks:

> *Why are there such glaring polarities? Why is consciousness characterized as a phenomenon too familiar to require further explanation, as well as one that remains typically recalcitrant to systematic investigation, by investigators who work largely within the same paradigm?* (Güzeldere, 1995)

The difficulty to which Güzeldere refers is epitomized by the problem: Who observes the observer? Every time we step back to observe who or what is there doing the observing, we find that the 'I' has jumped back with us. This is the infinite regress of the observer, noted by Gilbert Ryle, often presented as an argument against the observing self being real, an existent. But identifying 'I' with awareness solves the problem of the infinite regress: we know the internal observer not by observing it but by being it. At the core, we are awareness and therefore do not need to imagine, observe, or perceive it.

Knowing by being that which is known is ontologically different from perceptual knowledge. That is why someone might introspect and not see awareness or the 'I,' concluding — like the travellers — that it doesn't exist. But thought experiments and introspective meditation techniques are able to extract the one who is looking from what is seen, restoring the missing center.

Once we grant the identity of 'I' and awareness we are compelled to extend to the core subjective self whatever ontological propositions seem appropriate for awareness. If awareness is non-local, so is the essential self. If awareness transcends material reality so does the 'I.' If awareness is declared to be non-existent then that same conclusion must apply to the 'I.' No matter what one's ontological bias, recognition that 'I' = awareness has profound implications for our theoretical and personal perspective.

References

1. Liquidity may not be the best example of emergence; both hydrogen and oxygen exhibit liquidity at very low temperatures.
2. For an interesting discussion of this point, see William James's essay, "Does consciousness exist?" (James, 1922)
3. Robert Forman is an exception. See Forman (1993).
4. For discussion of this point and its relationship to philosophical problems see Forman (1990) and Shear (1990).
5. For a detailed account see Daniel Goleman, "The Buddha on meditation and states of consciousness," in Shapiro and Walsh (1984).

6. The key activity of modern Western psychotherapy is to enhance the experience of the observing self, discriminating it from the contents of the mind. Indeed, Freud's basic instructions on free association bear a striking resemblance to the instructions for *vipassana* meditation.
7. In Buddhism, the meditation experience may be given different interpretations. Walpole Rahula is emphatic in saying that Buddha denied that consciousness exists apart from matter and therefore rejected the idea of a permanent or enduring Self or Atman (Rahula, 1959). In contrast, D.T. Suzuki identifies the Self with absolute subjectivity (Suzuki, *et. al.*, 1960). However, both Vedantic and Buddhist commentators agree on the illusory nature of the self-as-thing.

Blackmore, Susan (1994), *Demolishing the self,* JOURNAL OF CONSCIOUSNESS STUDIES, 1 (2), pp. 280-2.
Chalmers, David J. (1995), *The puzzle of conscious experience,* SCIENTIFIC AMERICAN, December, pp. 80-6.
Chapple, Christopher (1990), *The unseen seer and the field: consciousness in Samkhya and Yoga,* in Forman (1990a).
Deikman, Arthur (1982), *The Observing Self: Mysticism and Psychotherapy* (Boston, MA: Beacon Press).
Dennett, Daniel (1991), *Consciousness Explained* (Boston, MA: Little, Brown & Co.).
Evans, C.O. (1970), *The Subject of Consciousness* (London: George Allen & Unwin Ltd.).
Flanagan, Owen (1992), *Consciousness Reconsidered* (Cambridge, MA and London: MIT Press).
Forman, Robert K.C. (ed. 1990a), *The Problem of Pure Consciousness — Mysticism and Philosophy* (New York: Oxford University Press).
Forman, Robert (1990b), *Eckhart, Gezuken, and the ground of the soul,* in Forman (1990a).
Forman, Robert (1993), *Mystical knowledge: knowledge by identity,* JOURNAL OF THE AMERICAN ACADEMY OF RELIGION, 61(4), pp. 705 38.
Globus, Gordon (1980), *On "I": the conceptual foundations of responsibility,* AMERICAN JOURNAL OF PSYCHIATRY, 137, pp. 41722 .
Goddard, Dwight (ed. 1966), *A Buddhist Bible* (Boston, MA: Beacon Press).
Goswami, Amit (1993), *The Self-Aware Universe: How Consciousness Creates the Material World* (New York: Putnam).
Güzeldere, Güven (1995), *Problems of consciousness: a perspective on contemporary issues, current debates,* JOURNAL OF CONSCIOUSNESS STUDIES, 2 (2), pp. 112-43.

Herbert, Nick (1994), *Elemental Mind—Human Consciousness and the New Physics* (New York: Plume Penguin).

James, William (1922), *Essays in Radical Empiricism* (New York: Longmans, Green and Co.).

James, William (1950), *The Principles of Psychology*: Volume One (New York: Dover).

John of the Cross, St. (1953), *The Complete Works of St. John of the Cross,* Vol. I (Westminister: Newman Press).

Kohut, Heinz (1971), *The Analysis of the Self* (New York: International Universities Press).

McGinn, Colin (1991), T*he Problem of Consciousness: Essays Towards a Resolution* (Oxford: Blackwell).

Menon, Sri Krishna (1952), *Atma-Nirvrid* (Trivandrum, S. India: Vedanta Publishers).

Nagel, Thomas (1986), *The View from Nowhere* (Oxford: Oxford University Press).

Osborne, Arthur (1954), *Ramana Maharshi and the Path of Self Knowledge* (London: Rider).

Rahula, Walpola (1959), *What the Buddha Taught* (New York: Grove Press).

Searle, John (1992), *The Rediscovery of the Mind* (Cambridge, MA: MIT Press).

Shapiro, Deane H. and Walsh, Roger N. (ed. 1984), *Meditation: Classical and Contemporary Perspectives* (New York: Aldine).

Shear, Jonathan (1990), *The Inner Dimension: Philosophy and the Experience of Consciousness* (New York: Peter Lang).

Suzuki, D.T., Fromm, Erich and De Martino, Richard (1960), *Zen Buddhism and Psychoanalysis* (New York: Grove Press).

Varela, Francisco J., Thompson, Evan and Rosch, Eleanor (1991), *The Embodied Mind: Cognitive Science and Human Experience* (Cambridge, MA: MIT Press).

Originally published in
JOURNAL OF CONSCIOUSNESS STUDIES 3,
No. 4, 1996

The Meaning of Everything

W HEN I once told a friend it was my intention to explain consciousness, he exclaimed, "But consciousness is everything!"
After thinking about it, I agreed with him. Thus, my title, for I will
present a model of consciousness that explains what pure awareness
is, what the self is, and the "I" feeling, and the mystical experience,
and meditation, and other phenomena as well. It is a serious attempt
because this is what truly interests me. By its nature, it is also grandiose, for it is hard to see how one man can accomplish it all. However,
I can make the attempt, and other people can complete the job.

Awareness

Upon reflection you will find that thoughts can cease for a brief
while, that there can be silence and darkness and the temporary absence of images or memory patterns — any one component of our mental life can disappear, but awareness, itself, remains. Awareness is the
ground of our conscious life, the background or field in which these
elements exist. It is not the same thing as thoughts, sensations, or
images. To experience this, try an experiment now. Look straight
ahead and be aware of your conscious experience — then close your
eyes. Awareness remains. "Behind" your thoughts and images is
awareness. The distinction between awareness and the contents of
awareness is crucial to the discussion that follows.

The Biosystem

All around us is a world of structure. Brilliant, various, complex, the forms of our life surround us, and through them and in them we live. Most of these forms appear to be abiding structures or objects, like our bones, that are formed or are born, and disintegrate or die. We ourselves seem to be objects, and we think using a language that defines and creates relationships between objects. However, as we examine ourselves and other "objects" more closely, we begin to see them differently. Gardner Murphy (1956) has pointed out that our concept of biological boundaries is a function of the particular time and size scale employed. Apparent boundaries are sensory phenomena in terms of those scales; they are not absolutes. For example, we are in constant exchange with the surrounding environment through respiration, eating, and elimination. Radioisotope studies have established the fact that our bodies are in a state of continual turnover of materials; we are not the same collection of atoms that we were a year ago. Bertalanffy (1952) summarizes, "As a result of its metabolism, which is characteristic of every living organism, its components are not the same from one moment to the next. Living forms are not in being, they are happening" (p. 124). Bones and muscles are reinterpreted: "What are called structures are slow processes of long duration, functions are quick processes of short duration. If we say that a function, such as the contraction of a muscle, is performed by a structure, it means that a quick and short process wave is superimposed on a long-lasting and slowly running wave" (p. 134). Activity, change, process — these are the "substance" of our bodies, of our world, of the universe. Gradients, not boundaries, determine form.

Furthermore, our individual organisms exist within a meshwork of higher levels of organization that ultimately includes all individual life forms and our planet itself. A swarm of bees furnishes an example of two levels of organization — each bee is an individual, but the swarm functions together as an organism in its own right. Its individual members cooperate in fulfilling a function possible only for the swarm, but at the same time necessary to the members. That swarm is part of a larger biosystem unity that includes the flowering plants that the bees pollinate. As you begin to picture the dazzling spectrum of organizational hierarchies that make up our biosystem and the cosmic system of which it is a part, it is not hard to perceive that we are part of one system that extends throughout the universe. In this view the biosystem is a whole, and the distinction between what is usually called biological (organic) and the inorganic is neither necessary nor basic. In what follows I shall use the term biosystem to refer to the entire range of world components that we apprehend through our sensory apparatus.

Awareness and Organization

As I noted earlier, a major problem in thinking about consciousness has been the mixing together of awareness with mind functions, such as calculating, sensations, memory, perception, and symbol formation. It is plausible to assume that mind functions are performed in the brain, which is the thinking organ. On the other hand, I would like to suggest that awareness, as distinct from the contents of awareness, is not a special form of sensation, with a particular receptor organ or some other neurological system responsible, nor is it any kind of neural response at all. Rather than being the product of a particular neural circuit, awareness is the organization of the biosystem; that is, awareness is the "complementary" aspect of that organization, its psychological equivalent.

Complementarity

Niels Bohr (1958) introduced the term "complementarity" to account for the fact that two different conditions of observation yielded conclusions that were conceptually incompatible, i.e., light behaved like a particle on one occasion and like a wave on another. He suggested that there is no intrinsic incompatibility because the two aspects were functions of different conditions of observation, and no experiment could be devised that could demonstrate both aspects in a single observational condition. Similarly, the special characteristic of mental life, e.g., freedom from space considerations, is in apparent contradiction with the space characteristics of physical objects. The two realms of the mental and the biological are separate spheres of observation, and thus represent complementary aspects of the biological system that constitutes an individual. The conditions of observation of the physical world are those of the sensory apparatus (vision, hearing, touch, smell, taste), whereas the mental is "observed" by the non-sensory (memory, thought, imagery, and "intuitive" processes).

Organization

Questions that arise immediately are: "What is meant by organization?" and "If awareness or consciousness is the complementary aspect of organization, what is it that is organized?" Let us say that an organism is "any thing or structure composed of distinct parts and so constituted that the functioning of the parts and their relation to one another is governed by their relation to the whole" (Webster's 2nd, unabridged, 1961, p. 1719). Relation is "any aspect or quality that can be predicted only if two or more things are taken together" {ibid., p. 2102). Thus, we are talking about elements that are mutually interdependent. In this connection, Bertalanffy (1952) has specifically defined the characteristics of the biological organism:

(1) the organism is a complex of elements in mutual interaction;

(2) the behavior of an individual element is influenced by the state of the whole organism;

(3) the whole exhibits properties absent from its isolated parts; and

(4) a biological organism is a basically active system — it has an autonomous activity, and is not basically reflexive or basically reactive.

Are the elements that are organized mental or physical? This question is dualistic and assumes a separation of mind and matter. In terms of the hypothesis I am presenting, the answer would be that the elements organized are both mental and physical, because the mental and the physical are hypothesized as being "complementary" aspects of the biological system.

On the biological side, the elements of the person system range from such low-level elements as chemical entities to the higher-order, more strictly biological elements of muscles, nerves, bones, and skin, and to the still higher-level components of respiratory, digestive, vascular, and motor systems. On the psychological side, ideas, affects, and sensations are at one level, and memories, thinking, and self-concepts are at a higher level. On the biological side, the organization of these elements is life; on the psychological side, the organization is awareness.

Thus, when I state that awareness is organization, I do not mean that consciousness is the "experience" of organization. The latter phrase implies a separate system that senses consciousness, the way we see light and smell odors. Rather, I mean to say that awareness is the complementary aspect of organization — it is organization, itself, in its mental dimension.

Localization

The biosystem is a totality embracing our entire planet and the solar system. Awareness is the organization of that continuous system. It follows that awareness is not localized. The awareness that each individual believes to be his own is, in fact, an awareness that extends throughout existence, for it is the organization of reality. Since our thought contents are localized by the particular groups of perceptual and cognitive systems that constitute individual persons, we have taken for granted that the awareness that underlies our mental processes is localized as well. For example, our visual activity is usually experienced as being identical with awareness. However, if you close your eyes, you will recognize that your awareness and your visual field are not the same. Try it now. Once again, close your eyes and ask yourself what constitutes your awareness. With your eyes closed, you will tend to identify awareness with sounds and body sensations. If next you imagine these sounds and sensations to be absent, you will appreciate the fact that awareness is something other than sensations or thoughts. The sense that my awareness is my own is due to mixing the sensations and thoughts, which are indeed personal, with awareness itself, which is universal. Expressed in the more abstract terms I used earlier, the conclusion is that our individual centers of organizing activity are located within the general field of organization that is awareness.

Active Energy

Let us now go a step further and consider a departure from traditional assumptions concerning matter and energy. It is a basic axiom of contemporary physics that energy has no direction nor structural tendency of its own. Toulmin (1967) has discussed the historical development of this concept of inert or passive matter, and has shown it to be an assumption. Continuing from his discussion, I propose that matter is intrinsically active in the direction of increasing organization. By this I mean that progressive organization is a basic characteristic of matter, like mass. As a corollary, increasing organization is the intrinsic aim of energy.

Such a concept is not compatible with our ordinary assumption that matter is purposeless, inert, and passive. Since the seventeenth century, we have looked at the elements of reality and expected to find that events are the product of pre-existing vectoral forces, acting on inert entities. Only man seems to have prefigured goals toward which his actions tend. We regard it as erroneous and primitive to give to inanimate or lower animate forms the characteristics of our own mental life. However, we have not really been able to avoid doing so, because our analysis of the physical world is based on the psychological. For example, the concept of force is derived from our experience of our own willed action. At the same time, because we associate aim and direction with our own will and desires, the notion that energy might have an intrinsic aim (as postulated by Freud for mental energy) appears very strange, for that would make energy "human."

Likewise, our belief in the passivity of matter and the directionless nature of energy resides in our experience with inanimate objects: a stone does not move unless we push it. This assumption of inertness works well for analyzing problems within a particular spatial class and a particular time span. Because of these temporal and spatial limits, we may not be in a position to observe the "activities" of inanimate objects. However, if we increase our time scale and widen our spatial scale, it might appear that inanimate matter moves towards a goal similar to the animate. For example, from a long-term time scale we are aware of what appears to be a direction of change that produces life forms. Increasing diversity and increasingly complex organization appear to be a trend that is discernible biologically, sociologically, and psychologically. We have given the name "evolution" to the phenomenon. That this phenomenon has been apparent to man for a long time is witnessed by the ancient Vedanta and Buddhist texts, as well as by the more recent conceptual efforts of Darwin, Erickson (1950), Bertalanffy (1952), Piaget (1954), Polanyi (1958), Chardin (1959), and Spitz (1959).

Variable Awareness

If awareness is organization and thus extends throughout the universe, present in varying degrees everywhere, why is it that sometimes awareness is vivid and total (as in phases of meditation), but at other times is absent, for example, when we are intent on an intellectual calculation or absorbed in a conversation or a movie? Traditionally, psychologists have tended to handle such problems by falling back on the searchlight model. The field of our attention is likened to the field of a searchlight that illuminates one area after the other. But if awareness is the searchlight and we can be aware of being aware, what illuminates the searchlight?

The problem can be solved if we define mind functions as organizing activities. Thus, perceptual processes organize stimulus inputs into series of gestalts, and thinking activity organizes events in terms of meanings of different kinds — philosophical, arithmetic, and symbolic. Let us now compare the biosystem to a pond of water. When the system is quiet, not occupied with the organizing activities of various mental functions, the surface of the pond is smooth, still, and reflective. At such times we exist in pure awareness, in a state of relationships, of organization. When the organizing activity of thought functions takes place, the surface of the pond becomes transformed into patterns of ripples, as if a stone had been thrown into the quiet water. When the activity ceases, the surface of the pond is smooth and reflecting once again. We do not have to postulate a super-observer of both awareness and thoughts if we recognize that awareness depends on the state of the pond, or biosystem; thought functions are the organization's activity. There is no experiencing agency; the "experience" is the state or the activity, as the case may be.

One may ask, "If awareness is coextensive with everything, why is it that we can lose consciousness?" The answer is that when we lose consciousness, the individual receptor-organizing region ceases to function. Awareness, itself, does not cease, but the thought organization, including memory, of the individual person ceases to operate. When that happens, there can be no local (individual) articulation or memory of awareness. At such times, awareness cannot be known in that location. To put it in slightly different terms, the individual person is the means whereby reality articulates itself.

Mystics have stated that through mankind, God is able to know himself. Perhaps what basically has blocked our understanding of such pronouncements has been our automatic assumption that the feeling of awareness is as localized as our personal perceptual system. However, once we discriminate between the general awareness and local mental contents, the puzzling concepts of mystics become more clear.

It should be noted that, in terms of this model, the awareness of a tree is not different from our own, but continuous with it, because awareness is the organization of the entire system. Awareness probably cannot be known or articulated in the system of the tree, but the awareness of the tree is not less intense or less rich than our own. We are not more aware because we are more complex; awareness is not a quantitative function, not a mind-stuff that accumulates as forms become more complex. Rather, awareness is the mental aspect of the organization of the entire biosystem. It is "known" only in those locales whose systems of organization permit "knowledge" of awareness.

Ordinarily, we do not recognize "our" awareness for what it is. The awakening to the true nature of this awareness constitutes the Enlightenment of a host of mystic disciplines. As illustrated by the Zen monastery, these disciplines all feature techniques, attitudes, and living conditions designed to bring about a subsidence of the thinking activities that take the place of awareness (Deikman, 1971). These thinking activities are individual, in that they are the activity of the individual center of organization of each individual person. Insofar as the person is activated to individual goals, thought activity persists and is dominant. However, the cultivation of selflessness can decrease the goal activity of the individual. Individual activity then subsides relative to the general field of organization — awareness itself.

The classical meditation disciplines were developed as a means of heightening awareness by subduing thought activity. Meditation, properly done, facilitates a shift from individual-centered activity to the general field of organization. Here, too, giving up individual striving (e.g., for spiritual advancement) can be a special problem. Furthermore, although it is not too hard to fill one's mind completely with a particular percept, such as breathing sensations, it is hard to have that perception and not work at it, not apply the mind to it, not be exercising the mind muscle, as it were, on that percept. When this active attention or concentrating can cease, then the sense of personal boundary that is associated with the individual's organizing activity fades away, and limitless awareness grows clear, vivid, and dominant. It is this limitless awareness that constitutes the unity experience of the higher mystical states.

The "I" Feeling and The Self

The self is that collection of attributes that identifies me as a particular human being, "Myself" is my body, my memories, my personality, my fears, my assets — all the things that constitute who I am in the eyes of others and of myself. We can understand the self as being a particular field of organization for the individual. The limits of the self are the experienced limits of the individual; those based on sensory perception, language, and the space-time of the object world. The self is all those things that I consciously include in the zone of my personal organization.

But what shall we make of the "I" feeling? Is it just another sensation, some spurious illusion based on a synthesis of sensory impressions? Try and locate the feeling or sensation inside yourself that corresponds to the word "I." For example, if you say such phrases to yourself as "I am going to go on reading this paper" or "I want a new car," the referent to the word "I" is the feeling of intention, of will, of urge, or of desire. This "I" of "I want" is a tension along a particular axis, a force impelling in a particular direction, the intensity of which varies, but the basic quality of which remains the same. The "I want" feeling is the organizing force, itself, acting in the specific locus or node of an individual organism. Each of us is a circumscribed area of organizing activity, expressing the same organizing tendency or force that I have hypothesized to be a basic attribute of mass/energy. Awareness is the organization of the system but the organizing force, itself, specifically active in our own local region, is what we experience as the "I" or "I want."

However, there is another type of "I" that we can notice. This "I" emerges in periods when our urges do not dominate our awareness. Then "I" feels like an abiding, resting awareness, featureless and unchanging, a central something that is witness to all events, exterior and interior. It is the "I" of "I am." This "I" is identical with awareness. In most cases it is awareness circumscribed by the beliefs and assumptions that form actual barriers separating local awareness (local organization) from universal awareness (universal organization).

Beliefs and assumptions act as barriers because they are mental activities, action currents transforming the still water of awareness into waves and eddies. To extend the metaphor even further, it would seem that some type of spatial correspondence exists such that the belief that one is part of all mankind locates the delimiting barrier at a "wider" periphery than the belief that one is totally separate from other persons. This effect of a belief occurs because the psychological event is an event in the biosystem, not an event isolated in a "mental" world. Thus, a belief has a substantial existence, although that existence is not to be defined as physical. The physical and the mental are both aspects of the biosystem; they are a translation or manifestation of an entity that is basic to both. Reality is neither one nor the other.

Overview

Organizing activity takes place continuously and throughout the universe because it is a basic characteristic of mass/energy. Each person is a manifestation of that same activity, as if he were an eddy in a river. The organization of the entire system is awareness. We confuse our local mind-functions with the general awareness and believe we are separate selves. To the extent that we separate ourselves conceptually from other people, we perform an action that actually delimits our awareness by forming a biosystem barrier that interferes with the experience of oneness. Caught in the illusion of separateness, we engage in actions that bring suffering to ourselves and others.

In those cases in which, by means of an arduous discipline, a powerful drug, or an extreme life crisis, the delimiting barriers are temporarily dissolved, the individual awareness becomes the general awareness.

These events of barrier dissolution constitute the phenomena of mystical experiences, provide the basis for religious metaphysics, and introduce into our lives the reality of the transpersonal.

Mental Health, Aging, and the Role of Service

Freud defined mental health as being able to work and love, but that definition is insufficient because mental health depends also on the sense that one's life is meaningful, that it counts for something. Otherwise, we are terribly vulnerable to the transience of existence, the fact that everything passes. Transience cannot be changed, and this fact is a universal source of anxiety and despair. How an individual confronts this existential dilemma is an important measure of mental health.

Traditionally people have turned to religion to answer existential questions, and, in response, religions have developed stories to make the vicissitudes of life more bearable and controllable. But the biblical Job still speaks for many of us in modern times. Unable to respond to the reasoning of his comforters, he was satisfied only when he could say, "I have seen you." Seeing was the experience that answered his questioning. We can call his experience spiritual, but we must then ask how a modern, scientifically educated person can be similarly satisfied.

The spiritual is not easy to define, but almost all accounts include the feeling of being connected to something larger than oneself, something universal, intrinsically valuable, and good. This appears to be true no matter what individual features are reported. The experience of connectedness provides meaning and combats the view of oneself as an isolated part of a random universe.

The consensus of mystics across many cultures and times is that the perception of the self as an object, limited to our bodies and isolated within our own consciousness, is an illusion, a misconception that is the source of human suffering. People not ordinarily described as mystics also report experiences consistent with the mystical literature, and although they vary greatly in their depth and content, they constitute moments when a feeling of connection is vivid and boundaries dissolve. C. P. Snow, the English author and physicist, described a mystical experience that took place when, after a series of failures, he verified a scientific prediction:

"It was as though I'd looked for a truth outside myself and finding it had become for a moment part of the truth I sought; as though the world, the atoms and the stars were wonderfully clear and close to me, and I to them, so that we were part of a lucidity more tremendous than any mystery. I had never known that such a moment could exist... Since then I have never quite regained it. But one effect will stay with me as long as I live; once, when I was young, I used to sneer at the mystics who have described the experience of being at one with God and part of the unity of things. After that afternoon, I did not want to laugh again; for though I should have interpreted the experience differently, I thought I knew what they meant."

Keeping such testimony in mind, we can turn to developmental psychology for a way to understand barriers to our experiencing connectedness and thereby understand how service can help deal with aging and death.

From the time we enter the world, success in discriminating and manipulating objects is imperative for survival. Our early experience is used to develop that capacity. Indeed, even at birth we are equipped with special capacities for processing information about objects. We rapidly become adept at discriminating boundaries, recognizing faces, and registering differences of shape, size, texture, and color provided by the sensory system. Thus we develop a form of consciousness that facilitates acting in the world by responding to its object characteristics. This instrumental mode of consciousness features sharp boundaries, focal attention, and logical (object-based) thought. It serves the aims of the self; it is literally self-centered.

Although primitive survival is not usually an issue for adults in industrial societies, we do employ self-centered consciousness for a purpose, such as planning a business meeting or maneuvering strategically at a social event, that is outwardly more sophisticated but fundamentally no different from that of a child seeking to get its needs met. Instrumental consciousness serves the acquisitive and protective interests of the self, but it results in selective perception: we perceive the world as a collection of objects, of which we are one.

For most of us, instrumental consciousness dominates, but we do not realize it because our culture is strongly materialistic and competitive. Useful and necessary as this mode of consciousness may be (e.g., for scientific investigation), its boundaries and distinctions are a barrier to experiencing the connectedness that mystics say interpenetrates reality, not registered by the sensory apparatus. The instrumental state of mind is hard to transcend because it is present from the beginning of our lives and, in the absence of mystical experience, utterly convincing.

To meet our need for the experience of connection and meaning, a shift in the mode of consciousness is required. If you came to a stream and wanted to drink, but grabbed at the water, you would obtain nothing. Instead you must cup your hands. This requirement has nothing to do with piety; it is based on the nature of water. Similarly, to experience connection, an appropriate mode of consciousness is needed, one that is receptive rather than instrumental, other-centered rather than self-centered.

We need not rely only on mystical traditions to achieve an experience of connectedness. The experience of service can provide access to the connectedness of reality. However, the concept of "service" is filled with moral and religious associations. To some it means sacrifice, the handing over of time and money for the reward of being a "good" person entitled to a place in heaven. If one is oriented toward the acquisitiveness that mobilizes and reinforces instrumental consciousness, it is very hard to find a way of being active that is not ultimately self-centered. Indeed, the cynic argues: "Doing good gives you pleasure, makes you feel good, so it is just another pleasure-seeking activity and, therefore, basically selfish."

The argument can be hard to refute. One response is to introduce the notion of "serving the task." A carpenter who "serves the task" may finish the underside of a chair even though he will receive no more money for the work and his customers do not care. He does it because it feels called for. His motive is not to serve the survival self but to create a sense of wholeness. This is true service, the kind that opens the doors of perception. Persons performing service in this way are quite aware of the difference between self-consciously "doing good" and doing what is called for. The former can lead to burnout or self-inflation, whereas the latter energizes and connects. The difference was summarized for me by a physician who established a medical clinic in Tibet:

"There's three kinds of people — I don't know if I can say it right — there's the one who's walking on the beach, and he sees a beer can on the beach, and he looks around and makes sure everybody's watching and picks up the beer can and throws it away. The second kind of person is walking on the beach, sees the beer can thrown on the beach, but there's nobody around. He still picks it up and throws it in the garbage can because he knows God is watching. Then there's the third kind of person who's walking along the beach, sees the beer can, throws it in the garbage and doesn't care who is watching just because that's what needs to be done. I guess it's that third kind of motivation that's not ego-directed that one seeks. It's hard to get there."

Of course, each of these motives can help keep the beach clean, but the third type expands perception. People who serve the task for the benefit of others experience a sense of connection to something larger than themselves. Their reports are very consistent. Here is a representative statement from a man who founded an organization to provide care for people with AIDS:

"… a self-conscious, highly moralized 'doing-good' is very far from the place that I recognize as valuable. When I'm more self-consciously helping, it's usually because I'm in a survival mode. What's going through my mind is fundamentally different. [In true service] I'm not serving myself. There is not that aspect to it. [I'm not trying] to get brownie points for Heaven. 'Doing what needs to be done' is the way I used to say it to the Shanti volunteers. You're serving something greater and deeper than the person in front of you. [You know] that person will benefit as a consequence if you can get to this place."

Almost the same words are used by a physician who founded an organization to provide support for cancer patients. She said she knows when something is really service:

"It's a sense of connection…to something beyond the moment when you do [it]. It's like seeing both of you as part of a much larger process that has no beginning and no end."

Descriptions of the experience of connection by people who "serve the task" are striking and compelling. From their point of view, the importance attributed to service in the mystical traditions makes perfect sense. When those who serve reduce the dominance of their self-centered needs, they can experience a different organization of consciousness, one that is responsive to connectedness.

This alternative organization of consciousness is beneficial when we face aging and death. When a patient's depression, anxiety, or lone-liness reflect disillusionment with material goals, it helps to expand the therapeutic inquiry beyond their distress over an irreversible loss of function or the ultimate loss that is death. Therapists should explore with patients their degree of connection to others, the presence or absence of service activities, and the influences that may be depriving them of the experience of being part of a larger process — contributing to something that will extend beyond their deaths and continue the beneficial effect of their transient lives.

Originally published in *The Nature of Human Consciousness: a book of readings* ed. Robert Ornstein, W.H. Freeman, 1973

Mindfulness, Spiritual Seeking
and Psychotherapy

A DIALOGUE WITH CHARLES T. TART, PH.D.

*C*HARLES *T. TART:* A topic of great interest to both of us, as well as to many colleagues, is the Eastern and Western traditions promoting *mindfulness* and personal growth. These disciplines are based on the recognition that people are often not clear about the actual state of affairs they find themselves in, what they are doing and why we are all too *mindless.* Such mindlessness causes immense amounts of human suffering, suffering which is stupid and unnecessary, because if you knew what you were doing and why you were doing it, you would have the possibility of acting more adaptively.

Eastern spiritual traditions have specific techniques for developing mindfulness, usually formal meditation practices of some sort, such as *Vipassana* mindfulness meditation. These Eastern practices consider the development of mindfulness as an ultimate goal, leading to enlightenment.

In the West we have many kinds of psychotherapy which is our kind of recognition that people's experience and behavior are often determined by unconscious reasons. That is, people often do not fully know what they are doing, why they are doing it, or have a really accurate grasp of the situation they are in. Consequently there is a lot of unnecessary suffering. There are many techniques whereby you can train people in psychotherapy to become more mindful and insightful, and as a consequence, lead a happier and more effective life.

Now the question I am particularly interested in and that I would like us to discuss is this: Consider our Western mindfulness traditions — our psychological, psychiatric, and humanistic growth traditions, to give them a very broad name — what can they accomplish that is either not done at all or not done efficiently in the traditional Eastern mindfulness approaches? What do you do as a psychotherapist to help your clients become mindful, which would probably not happen if they sat on their cushions by themselves practicing Vipassana or other traditional Eastern forms of meditation?

Does The Mind That Looks Inside Really Want To Know?

ARTHUR J. DEIKMAN: One of the basic ideas behind Western psychotherapy is that our minds have endeavored to protect us by shielding us from things that would make us too unhappy or frightened. Thus, if a person consciously decides to look inside and see what may be motivating certain actions, the same mind that is looking is also trying to make sure that he or she does not see something that his or her mind has classified as too stressful to bear in the past. This factor sets certain limits on what the person himself can see.

On the other hand, an outside observer, the therapist, does not usually have the same blocks on seeing certain things that the client may have. So by virtue of the fact that the therapist is on the outside looking at the client's behavior, he or she is in a position to say, "Hey, this area here is pretty covered up; what is going on there?" The therapist can put pressure on the client's psychological systems in a way that the client would find hard or impossible to do. Thus the client, the person seeking greater mindfulness, has a blind spot; they do not see certain areas of mental and emotional functioning, especially if they are problematic areas. Much of the training of a therapist in Western psychotherapy has to do with learning to detect those places of restricted functioning and begin to open them up, so the underlying problems they conceal can be dealt with. Psychotherapy training is fairly systematic; it is directed specifically to that.

CTT: I would like you to elaborate on the training. Any intelligent person, for instance, can see that somebody else is behaving stupidly and give them advice on how to behave in a way that would be generally accepted as a more sensible (given cultural norms) way to behave. What is different about the therapist?

AJD: A therapist might say, "You must have received lots of advice by now on what you obviously should be doing, but you are not doing it. So clearly there is something else going on. What are your own thoughts upon the fact that this comes up? How do you react inside when someone tells you that you should do such and such?" You direct the client's attention to the fact that he or she is making choices. The client may not know why he or she is making those particular choices, but there is an emotionally important basis for it. Instead of mistakenly seeing the maladaptive behavior as a lack of will power, you help the client see that the symptoms represent strategic choices, ways of apparently solving a problem. Then you can try to help the client become more mindful, to discover the unconscious assumption(s) on which the presenting problems and solutions are based.

Isn't Mindfulness Enough?

CTT: Let me push this deeper. Suppose I am viewing this same situation of a client's maladaptive behavior from the perspective of an Eastern mindfulness tradition. I would agree that your analysis is right: if the person keeps doing something stupid, there must be a reason. But in terms of what to do, I would instruct the client that he or she should take up mindfulness meditation, "You must look inside and understand your mind by systematically focusing attention on it. Then you will understand what causes your problems and resolve them."

AJD: Well, I would say that is naive because the same mind that is looking inside is, as I said before. also determined to protect the person by not getting into any areas that are dangerous. So some kind of outside assistance is needed, directed specifically to the problem areas, the areas that the client's mind does not want to look at.

CTT: How does the therapist get around this problem of resistance?

AJD: Basically the therapist has to be aware of what aspect the client is resisting and the nature of the resistance, and to skillfully point it out to the client. The symptom serves a function. The therapist needs to clarify that function. This skillful pointing out must be based on an attitude that combines a certain firmness and intent to break through the resistance, with a genuine respect for the client's nature and symptoms.

It may not be easy to see the defenses or the resistances and not be caught yourself by them. But an easy thing, one you learn relatively early in your training, is to begin to notice places in which there is a tiny gap, a gap in logic or a gap in emotional affect. The client may be talking about something, for example, but the affect, the emotional tone, does not quite match. You may find it profitable to direct the client's attention to such gaps: "I notice you were saying such and such, but you did not seem very happy while you were talking about it." You pick up one of these places where the defenses are imperfect.

It is as if the mind tried to put everything under the rug, but it cannot get everything under the rug at the same time.

The free association technique, for example, is often used as a way of bypassing that controlled, hiding self. The more a person just allows their thoughts and emotions to flow, the more the underlying issue will manifest itself in the content. Then the client may begin to see connections where there was isolation before, as well as the therapist seeing connections that may be helpful in guiding therapy. Working with these gaps is a major dimension of Western psychotherapy. Freud was important in pointing out the usefulness of working with inconsistencies, although he certainly was not the only contributor in this area.

The Importance of the Therapeutic Relationship

Freud also highlighted another important dimension of psychotherapy. This is based on the observation that the client's strategic solutions will manifest in therapy in the relationship with the therapist

— the transference — as well as in relationships with other important people. So in psychotherapy you can make use of that relationship manifestation, be aware of it, be alert for it, point it out, and explore it. This analysis or focus on the transference is very useful and important because it is a here and now situation.

If you look at the literature on the Eastern traditions, indeed on the mystical traditions in general, you can see in the anecdotes examples of where a master, if he is skilled, is using some daily interaction to reflect information back to the person about what he or she is actually doing, regardless of what he or she says or believes they are doing. They make use of everyday behavior to show students what they are actually doing.

Sometimes such teaching by reflection can involve transference responses, too. But apparently the use of transference is sporadic and we have to infer it from anecdotes. In the psychotherapeutic tradition you can do much more focused work with it, particularly in dealing with dependency and idealization of the therapist.

In the Eastern traditions veneration of the Master, the Teacher, the guru, the lama, or someone else like that, is usually built into the system as a central feature. The teacher is represented as vastly superior to the student or even as fully enlightened. While there is a sense in which this superiority is true, there is another sense in which it is not. Unfortunately the student may use that belief in the great superiority of the teacher as an excuse to avoid necessary self-confrontation, "Of course the Master can do that apparently unspiritual or negative action because he is enlightened and special, etc., and I am just down here, an ordinary sinner, so I cannot expect to understand what is happening, much less criticize it... especially since I need the Master's blessing and guidance if I am to have any chance of spiritual progress." There are all kinds of evasions of growth that can take place in that framework of veneration of the teacher. The knowledge of human psychology gained from Western psychotherapy has shown us that analysis of dependency fantasies is extremely helpful for maturation.

Active Focus on Relationships

CTT: Let me play devil's advocate here. A master might respond by agreeing that students have projections about the master, but since the students are supposed to be mindful of what they are doing, you can see this simply as an opportunity for them to observe what they are doing. What is different in the psychotherapeutic approach to bringing about mindfulness of projections?

AJD: Our Western psychotherapeutic approach might say not only is there an opportunity, but we are going to be active in making sure that opportunity is realized. The fact that the opportunity is there does not mean the person is going see it or use it. Western psychotherapy has to do with attempting to make sure the person sees it by using the technical approach of the psychotherapy situation.

CTT: Could you give me examples of the sort of techniques that would be used in an active way to make the person use the opportunity?

AJD: For instance, suppose a client might be rather embarrassed to talk about something or is afraid of bringing in some area of his or her life. When this area is touched on, you notice this embarrassment or fear. You might then inquire as to what they were expecting from you, and it might turn out they were expecting a very critical, denigrating kind of response. So you might inquire further, "Why does that seem plausible to you?"

We assume, of course, that you are not the type of person the client expects to be dealing with, that you have not actually been behaving that way in the therapy sessions. Then, as you explore in depth the details of the fantasy the client has towards you, the underlying bias becomes more clear. You and your client can become aware of the specific images and tendencies that are distorting perception.

What I have described is an example of transference, responses to the therapist that are out of proportion. Usually these responses are revealed only over time in certain behaviors. For example it might come out in the form that the client never presents his or her critical thoughts of the therapist, or the client is always presenting himself or herself as weak. Suppose your client is a therapist herself, for example. At some point you might say, "We have worked together for two years, you are a therapist. You are very bright, but apparently, I do everything right. Isn't it a little odd that you have never commented on a single mistake of mine or a single failing?"

CTT: So we have an interesting note here. The therapist admits weakness, admits his or her humanity, instead of being perfect. This is very different from working with a Teacher who claims to be or is seen as perfect.

AJD: I would not use the word "admit." The position would be: "Of course I make errors and mistakes, of course you have some aware-ness of this. So the fact that it is never voiced does not reflect either that I am perfect or that you are oblivious to it. It means you have certain concerns about what would happen if you were to voice them. It would be valuable — and would increase your mindfulness — to find out what those concerns are."

CTT: Let us go back a little more to the issue of directing the activity of therapy. Insofar as I understand them correctly, the Eastern traditions would generally argue that a person cannot observe himself or herself very well when they first begin to practice meditative mindfulness. This is because there are "obscurations," blocks to clear perception, in the mind. But the really important thing people need to develop is the power of observation *per se.* In classical vipassana mindfulness meditation you are supposed to watch what is happening. You get distracted, but the instruction is to come back to the focus of attention as soon as you know that you have become distracted. Quite aside from specific insights you may have while doing this, what you train is the ability to observe *per se.* You build up general purpose "observation muscles" by keeping up the practice, always bringing your mind back to the task.

I have no doubt that with this kind of practice many people do de-velop a greatly increased capacity to observe internal events in general. Why do you feel this is not enough from the therapeutic point of view?

Elaborate on why active assistance from the therapist is an improvement over pure mindfulness cultivation.

Why Isn't Pure Mindfulness Enough?

AJD: It does not seem to be enough, judging by my own scattered
observations of people who practice only meditative disciplines. From
a theoretical point of view, it comes back to what I said earlier, that
such training of the mind may be to observe more clearly what it sees,
but there can be a dynamic there, an activity in the person to make
sure that certain things are *not* seen. That dynamic is not necessarily
taken care of by meditation exercises *per se.* (I will add, though, as I
discussed in *The Observing Self* [Deikman, 1982), that I think this
heightening and focus on the observing self is an important activity in
both meditation and psychotherapy, and an important link between
them.) So developing skill in self-observation is helpful, but Western
psychotherapy is a more dynamic process. An important component
of the Western view of the mind is that we are continually trying to
resolve conflicting wishes, needs, hopes, and aspirations. The importance and subtlety of resolving conflicts is not dealt with sufficiently
in the Eastern traditions, insofar as I understand them.

To elaborate on this, conflicts arise not so much because reality is
so inherently conflictual, although it is complex enough, but because
each of us grows up in a world comprised primarily of one or two
vitally important people, our parents, and they represented the world
to us in a particular way. So we took in their distortions, produced by
their own conflicts and adapted to their bias as if they were an accurate
representation of the world. These early, distorted adaptations then
become forgotten or are repressed or otherwise shut off from conscious
awareness. In our present life we react to the general world on the
basis of what we learned earlier, that is we systematically bias our perceptions of the world and our relationships with other people through
this early, distorted learning and its subsequent projection onto current reality. The projection of this early learning onto one's spiritual

teacher can be quite an obstacle.

CTT: So you would agree with the position I have advanced (Tart, 1986) that it is possible that someone might practice some kind of insight meditation and in general get very good at observing more and more precisely what is happening, get relatively enlightened, but still have certain areas of personal functioning that they never looked at because of defenses that deflect attention?

AJD: Absolutely.

Meditative Insightfulness and Psychotherapy

CTT: Now there is something implicit in what we have discussed earlier, and I would like to see if you will agree with this. A person who became skilled at insight meditation or other forms of self-observation, such as Gurdjieffian self-observation, will probably have an advantage at being able to pick up things quickly if they go into psychotherapy. Yes?

AJD: What does "skilled" at insight meditation mean?

CTT: Suppose we start with a model of a person who is relatively insensitive to their inner feelings and the subtleties of their experience. Psychologically sophisticated outside observers might independently agree, for instance. that this person is fairly agitated in a given situation. but the person honestly reports that he feels calm. Or outside observers might independently agree that the person's behavior suggests a mixture of fear and jealousy, but the person reports, to the best of his or her ability to sense their experience, only that they are feeling jealous. After successful training in traditional insight meditation or other self-observation techniques, the person is now able to sense agitation in a similar situation where he could not sense it before. If he now can report a mixture of feelings of both fear and jealousy, I would say that person is becoming better at self-observation, "skilled" at it. As Shinzen Young expressed it, gross experiences become more articulated into subtler components of experience (Young. in Tart, 1989).

AJD: I generally find that people's styles do not change all that much. There are people who are very well tuned in on inner processes and they sensitively pick up cues about situations, and there are people for whom that sensitivity is almost like a foreign process. These latter kind of people can make some progress in the direction of more sensitivity, but a therapist might have to work differently with them than with the other clients. So I do not know if you can take various personality styles, have them do insight meditation and get the result that someone who was relatively obtuse in that respect becomes sensitive. If that happened, I would think that would be an advantage for someone undergoing psychotherapy, but I do not know enough about the empirical data of what happens to those who practice meditation to say much about it.

CTT: So you are saying people might maintain their habits of sensitivity or lack thereof.

AJD: It might be a cognitive habit, a personality style or a genetic predisposition.

CTT: To recognize anger, an insensitive person might simply have to learn to observe that their fists are clenched and infer anger, even if they have not internally "felt" it yet. Another person might get a subtle little tight feeling in their chest long before anything manifests in their observable behavior, and immediately know they are feeling angry.

AJD: There are some people who, when you ask them to free associate, or to "tune in" on their feelings, just go right to it. There are others who just do not seem to get it, and you have to work differently.

Using Psychotherapy To Aid Meditative Development

CTT: Suppose a person sincerely seeking personal and spiritual growth was planning to spend a considerable amount of time doing insight meditation in one of the classical Eastern modes. Let us assume you were hired as a consultant, with the idea of adding some aspects of psychotherapy to the meditation practice or retreat to make it more "efficient." What would you do? What would you suggest? Assume for the moment that you have great resources available for this project, rather than worrying about practicalities.

AJD: Let us think about the kind of concentrated practice you would have in a retreat. What length of time are we considering?

CTT: Let us assume one to three months.

AJD: It would go something like this. Each person would have the opportunity, two or three times a week, to meet individually with a therapist to explore whatever issues were coming up in the context of their meditative practice. It should be the same therapist for each session for a given person. Ideally psychotherapy should be long term, as this allows the rhythms of a client's life to bring up a variety of important material. On the other hand, here the therapeutic work would take advantage of the time frame of the retreat. If you have, say, a month, and you know that you are going to meet with someone eight to twelve times, you might work in a more focused way than if you felt it was a more open-ended situation.

CTT: In practical terms, you are calling for about one full-time therapist for every ten people or so. Suppose we have less ideal conditions, where, for example, you only had one therapist for every hundred people or so. How could a therapist delegate some of the work of therapy so that people could do various things themselves or in groups that do not require the presence of a therapist?

AJD: You can do a lot in group therapies, but then that addresses a different level of phenomenon, how people behave in groups. This can be quite useful for people, but it would take a fairly long time for the group process to begin to reveal the individual's psychological processes, unless it was one of these quasi-groups in which the therapist worked individually with a person in the group while the other people just watched, or something similar.

But I do not think there is a substitute for the one-to-one relationship with the therapist. Therapy does not really consist of a bunch of separate techniques that you can farm out. There is a lot of art and a lot of mystery to the process. Books can tell you what to do, but not when to do it. This issue of timing and finding a way of working that meets the client's personality takes a while to develop. The answer to your question could be that one therapist cannot do it.

Using Meditation To Aid Traditional Psychotherapy

CTT: Let us look at this issue from the opposite approach. Suppose you had a number of clients who were scheduled for psychotherapy, and I said, "What could you ask them to learn from a meditative tradition that you think could facilitate their psychotherapy?" You could have meditation teachers as consultants if you want or teach aspects of meditation, but what would you ask people to learn, to practice?

AJD: I am not sure. I have had a little experience with clients who were practicing meditation, and also with clients who, in the course of therapy, raised a question about taking up meditation.

In the latter case, I referred them to meditation teachers. I did not find that meditating was a significant help for my clients' psychotherapeutic issues. My own feeling is that the main power of meditation is in terms of spiritual development; however the knowledge of how to use such meditation and for which people and under what circumstances is not really within my ken. So I would not want to fool around in an area for which I am not really trained and for which I do not have the specific knowledge. I might even jeopardize or interfere with the potential use of the meditation for its intended spiritual purpose. If a client thought it might be useful, if they wanted to try it, I would refer them to a meditation teacher, but generally I would not "prescribe" meditation.

Goals of Psychotherapy and Spiritual Development

CTT: How are you distinguishing growth in psychotherapy from spiritual development here?

AJD: I could characterize them both as having the goal of increased *realism,* but the realism with which psychotherapy is concerned is at a different level than the realism which the mystical techniques address.

I think it is important that therapists have an appreciation of the reality that the spiritual disciplines reflect because that will inform what the therapist does in an overall sense. It will affect how he or she views a human being and what outcomes the therapist can see as possible.

In psychotherapy, you are basically working to help the client clarify the motivations that underlie behavior that is frustrating and restricting him or her at the level of interpersonal relationships and also with regards to their work efficiency and creativity. Such limiting behaviors and experiences might include anxiety and depression, restrictions on intimacy, self-defeating behavior, and the like. Now all kinds of behaviors might be improved in the course of spiritual development, but only as a secondary byproduct of something that really has a different focus. Indeed, spiritual development may require a certain degree of health to have things go well. Thus I could see psychotherapy as providing a very important foundation from which someone might gain access to larger dimensions of reality. But psychotherapy is not a spiritual discipline *per se.*

CTT: One of the ways I have compared Eastern and Western approaches to growth is that both agree that increasing mindfulness is good, but they have a different set of beliefs of what human beings ultimately are and what their possibilities are. In this sense, Western psychotherapy has a very limited view of what a person can be, compared to the mystical traditions (both Eastern and Western).

AJD: Yes, absolutely. I think that limited view is a largely unrecognized problem in Western psychotherapy.

CTT: I recall that Freud said something to the effect that the best we can hope for as a result of growth is ordinary suffering, without added neurotic suffering, or something cheerful like that!

AJD: In my experience, most people can deal with ordinary suffering. It is the added neurotic suffering that breaks our back. Maybe that is what Freud meant.

Faith and Skepticism

CTT: You mentioned skepticism. Let us follow this up. Obviously science is, in a sense, institutionalized doubt, and it has gotten us a long way...

AJD: Institutionalized doubt? I do not know what you mean.

CTT: In my understanding of the basic process of science (Tart, 1972; Tart, 1975, pp. 11-58) you do not simply accept things as they are, you ask why they are that way; you want to look behind the obvious. Someone may give you a plausible-sounding explanation, but it is your job as a scientist to doubt it, because we know that just because something sounds plausible and rational does not guarantee that it really explains the state of affairs. The plausible explanations you create as a scientist — the theories — are always subject to test, as we can always rationalize any pattern of events in front of us. Your theory has to make verifiable predictions to be a good scientific theory and you have to test those predictions to see if they actually work out.

AJD: You really think that is what science is about?

CTT: That is an important aspect.

AJD: An aspect of it, yes.

CTT: A very important aspect of it. Now most spiritual traditions, in contrast, talk continuously about *faith,* not doubt; they advocate respecting and venerating the tradition and the teacher. Do you see a place for doubt in spiritual growth?

AJD: Yes. I think you frequently get distortions of the mystical tradition in which this veneration and faith are misunderstood. If you believe that sincerity is extremely important in the spiritual quest, then for a person to pretend to a faith, to pretend that he or she has complete faith when actually they have real questions or doubts, is a forced position of the mind that is not very sound. In Sufism and in Zen Buddhism, as well, if you look carefully at the talks or teaching materials *per se,* you will see that they take a dim view of someone who never has any doubts. Faith in the mystical sense probably has a much more profound meaning than we are accustomed to assign to it, so I do not know that doubt is at all incompatible with deep faith.

CTT: Let me press you a little on this. Take for instance, the Sufi teaching story (Shah, 1970b; pp. 84-85) about the learned Dervish who heard these hermits out on an island mispronouncing their sacred chant. He corrected them and told them the right way, then sailed away. As his ship drew away, he could hear them saying it correctly, but then they fumbled and went back to their old, incorrect way. But soon one of the hermits came out to him on his ship, walking on the water, to ask him how to pronounce correctly, as they could not remember! One reading of that is obviously that faith is what really matters, not technical skill *per se*. There are many teaching stories in many traditions with this theme.

AJD: I do not think that story illustrates faith so much as it does sincerity.

CTT: How can we distinguish faith and sincerity?

AJD: Sincerity is honesty of intention. Faith has to do with belief, especially a belief that may be challenged by ordinary experience. So really I think they are two different concepts. Someone's sincerity could be expressed in the fact that he or she does not believe. The seeker wants the truth, but he does not believe or does not trust the teacher or the teachings. Being honest and sincere enough to express those doubts would be more important than someone saying, "Oh, the teacher is just wonderful, and I have no doubts about him or his teaching."

Spiritual Development as Psychotherapy

CTT: Let us consider an earlier point in more depth. You made clear separation between what psychotherapy can do and what spiritual development is about. You agreed that psychotherapy might be a basis for more effective spiritual development, but it is not the same thing.

In many mystical traditions you can find a theory or description of the ordinary human condition that one can read as essentially calling for psychotherapy. These traditions basically claim that we all started out as pure, wonderful beings, but somehow we got distracted and lost touch with our real nature, and experienced a Fall. This idea is expressed in different ways, such as the hypothesis that our perception of our original purity became clouded over, or got attached, greedy, fearful, and consequently became stupid by being identified with our surface perceptions. We became *mindless* instead of *mindful.*

Thus spiritual development can be presented analogously to psychotherapy, emphasizing removing the obscurations to clear consciousness (defenses), as curing a basic kind of neuroticism that distorts our perception of the reality of who we really are. I am sure you are familiar with some of these approaches.

Many other spiritual paths, indeed all to some extent, focus on the positive goals, like developing love and compassion or having mystical visions. But many focus on the idea that if you were to remove the obscurations, there is nothing else fundamental to do. Our pure nature will then shine through. *A Course in Miracles* (Anonymous, 1975; Volume 2, pp. 347). for example, says that "Those who seek the light are merely covering their eyes. The light is in them now. Enlightenment is but a recognition, not a change at all." From this kind of perspective how strongly do you want to make that division between psychotherapy and spiritual development?

AJD: My response to your description of the possibility of "spiritual psychotherapy" is "Yes. but can they do it?" It is fine to say that true spiritual training can remove the obscurations and solve all these problems. Terrific, but does that actually happen?

CTT: Don't we need to have some faith that it can happen? That otherwise the lack of faith means you do not really try, so it does not succeed, and we're caught in an endless regression?

AJD: I do not want to take this on faith; I want to have some basis in experience to decide this.

CTT: Are you questioning the goal and the practicality of attaining some sort of spiritual enlightenment, or simply questioning psychotherapy as a suitable analogy or training style for getting there?

AJD: No, I am questioning spiritual training achieving what psychotherapy can do. You speak of spiritual practice removing the obscurations that give rise to neurosis and, therefore, liberating people from their neuroses. That is a theory, and there may be a very small number of people for whom that was true. But as a general rule, for a person who has the kind of conflicts I am talking about, I do not see the evidence that spiritual training will substitute for psychotherapy.

CTT: I did not mean that ordinary neuroses necessarily go away as a result of spiritual training. I meant that if the spiritually "fallen" human condition can be thought of as a kind of neurotic state, then in a sense removing these obscurations is what happens in spiritual development.

AJD: That is why I talk about *realism* rather than illness. I think the goal of psychotherapy is increased realism, as is the goal of spiritual development. The Fall that is talked about, whatever that symbol actually represents, would have to do with a constriction in our ability to perceive reality, a constriction in ourselves and others. Certainly the goal of spiritual development is to increase perception so that you see what is really going on, who we are, why we are, and so forth.

In psychotherapy, the increased realism pertains mainly to things having to do with your childhood inheritance, to your development. Each of us learned about ourselves and the world in terms of the imperfections of this world. Thus there are misconceptions and distortions that are bedeviling us within this range of ordinary life, let alone a larger sphere. Psychotherapy tries to give us more freedom within this ordinary range of relating to the world and people, to give us the breathing space to accomplish something in it. You cannot be drowning and study Sufi poetry too well.

So psychotherapy would have to say, "Let us see if you can learn to float, and then maybe you can learn to swim across the bay." Psychotherapy and spiritual development are two different levels of the same continuum, but they do not substitute for each other, as far I can tell. They work synergistically with each other.

For instance, in both the spiritual disciplines and psychotherapy, one of the important things that happens is that the student or the client takes in, incorporates, or identifies with the point of view of the teacher or therapist. This is an important kind of learning that can be very helpful. The student or client sees alternative ways of viewing things, ways that, hopefully, are more spiritually or psychologically mature.

An accomplished and mature therapist may express, in his or her behavior, attitudes and behaviors very much like those a spiritual master would show. They may be at a different level or they may overlap. However, the focus of the two areas, spiritual learning and psychotherapy, continues to be different.

Whereas some people can jump right into psychotherapeutic exploration, others require a lot of preliminary work before they really can participate fully. They are not ready to go right to the deeper material. When these people come into a psychotherapy office, they are likely to be more focused on the therapist than on their problems. They are hoping the therapist will cure them as a surgeon might, or will supply the missing love they feel is the problem. I am sure the same thing is true for spiritual teachers. Some people come in and they want to crawl up into the teacher's lap; they want some magical power to be conveyed to them that will solve their problem. It is not that the wish is bad; it is just not realistic. It does not work that way.

Other people come in but are really troubled with existential questions and they may have a more realistic sense of what is needed. It is like the difference between saying, 'Give me some money!" and "Teach me how to be rich." This kind of attitude problem comes up in both psychotherapy and spiritual disciplines. As a therapist I sometimes read statements by spiritual teachers about their students and say to myself, "Boy, I know what this guy is talking about."

Differing Strategies in the Spiritual Path

CTT: Given the difference in focus, what are some things a spiritual teacher might do that a psychotherapist would not, and vice versa?

AJD: Well, I think the sincerity that a teacher might require of someone for the spiritual path might be quite different from the sincerity you would require for someone to begin psychotherapy. I think the demands would be much less.

CTT: For psychotherapy?

AJD: Yes, because you are operating at a more basic level. So you might accept all kinds of attitudes that the spiritual teacher might feel made a person unsuitable for serious spiritual work. A teacher might tell an aspiring student to go to work in the garden for several years before offering formal teachings, for example, but we would not do that in psychotherapy.

CTT: Why is that effective with a spiritual teacher but not for psychotherapy?

AJD: A spiritual seeker is, in a sense, presumably functioning decently in their ongoing life, so the spiritual goals he or she has require a challenge of a different order than a psychotherapy client needs. If three years go by, for example, and the aspiring student realizes that he is not actually interested in the truth after all, that is an important thing for him to have learned. If a person is severely depressed or behaving in a violently aggressive way, on the other hand, seeking spiritual truth is not useful or appropriate. He has more basic problems and needs that must be addressed immediately. So I would think the kind of development that the spiritual teacher is involved in has a different kind of time scale than the psychotherapeutic ones.

CTT: Can you create another example of the differences in focus?

AJD: Well, a spiritual teacher might prescribe certain exercises to induce particular altered states of consciousness. In the psycho-therapeutic situation that might not be good at all. Some people can-not tolerate altered states; their psychological boundaries are too shaky.

Starting Level of the Spiritual Path

CTT: You are setting up a distinction or "admissions criterion" here which is interesting. Ideally, when a person wants to become a stu-dent of a real spiritual discipline, she should have handled all her nor-mal developmental tasks for getting along well in the ordinary world. Practically, though, I think we would say, that is never completely true.

AJD: Of course not.

CTT: All sorts of people who are doing reasonably well coping in the ordinary world would still have some significant neurotic kinds of problems, yet are sincerely interested in spiritual growth. How should a spiritual teacher deal with them? To what extent can a spiritual teacher concentrate on a totally different kind of development versus how much does she or he need to be aware of unresolved psychological issues in otherwise healthy people?

AJD: The more aware a teacher is of these issues, the better he or she can deal with them as they come up. There is not an expectation that people be perfect or fully analyzed. There is no such perfection for anyone in this world, including spiritual teachers, because this is a world of imperfection. But a teacher would want a person to have enough unrestricted attention to be able to proceed, to not have conflicts seriously interfere with the other training that is going on.

You might want the student to be meeting his or her work and social obligations reasonably well, so he or she was not attempting to use the spiritual discipline to bypass achieving maturity in ordinary functioning. You want them to have enough inner security, in the sense of psychological stability, that they can let go a little. You do not want someone to be overwhelmed by various states and experiences. Also, you would not necessarily provide dramatic experiences to someone who just loves dramatic experiences.

The whole spiritual field is so confusing because of the expectations we have from our training in formal religions. There is an ingrained habit of approaching spiritual development in terms of religious fantasies of super-parents and the super family. We easily fall into that mode because of unresolved developmental issues. A good spiritual teacher must be aware of this psychological issue and not play into it. We all know of people who thought of themselves as spiritual teachers who were betrayed by their own psychological limitations in this area.

The Imperfect Teacher

CTT: We have discussed the unresolved issues and flaws in the client and student, but let us shift the focus to similar flaws in the spiritual teacher.

A person goes through some developmental experiences, and ends up as a spiritual teacher. I do not mean teacher in the sense of receiving a high-sounding title in an organized religion, which may have lost much of its originating spiritual knowledge, but spiritual teacher in the sense of someone who has some genuine spiritual attainment. This does not mean that she is necessarily perfect, but she has at least some ability to teach some of this knowledge and attainment to other students.

Chances are that even if this person qualifies as a spiritual teacher, though, she is also an ordinary human being like the rest of us; she has some unresolved psychological flaws. The spiritual quest can take them into many unusual areas of consciousness and functioning which, while the most important thing in the world for some people, are psychologically dangerous for others.

Now, there are two broad paths that people of this sort go on. One is that they work as "independents," outside an organized tradition. Each teacher tends to work in isolation with just his or her students. I and many others have observed that the risk an independent runs is of his or her unresolved psychological flaws being incredibly inflated by the projections of students and other factors, so the teacher may end up doing more harm than good.

The other path that the human, imperfect teacher may travel on is working within an institutional structure. There we have a historical tradition and official colleagues who put some dampers on the manifestation of the teacher's unresolved psychological issues. This may range from collegial advice to censure from the hierarchical power structure, including the threat of being thrown out of the institution.

Can Western Knowledge Help Spiritual Teachers?

CTT: What kind of advice can Western psychotherapy give to either of these two broad categories of spiritual teachers about seeing what their own character flaws are, so they might resolve them or at least control them sufficiently so the teacher does not inflict them on his or her students erroneously thinking they are a spiritual manifestation? How do we help a spiritual teacher maintain basic human sanity? 1 think this issue is very important, because we all know of cases where certain teachers who probably started out teaching from a basis of real spiritual insight and accomplishment ended up in states we would describe as neurotic or just plain crazy, hurting themselves and a lot of their followers in the process. What can Western psychotherapists do to help people like that?

AJD: I think there is a difference between the teacher whose character problems are flaws that can hinder his or her own spiritual development and the teacher who ends up exploiting students. I would question the spiritual development of anyone who exploits others. I would not necessarily accept the premise that they initially had real insight, that they were enlightened or something like that and then these unfortunate events happened ...

CTT: Yes, that is certainly a category of people among those called "teachers." They did not have genuine spiritual development; they were deluded about that. But do you accept that there is this category of people who have genuine spiritual development but still have character flaws?

AJD: Oh sure!

CTT: It is these people I am concerned about now.

AJD: Such people do not have to be perfect in order to function as spiritual teachers, provided they maintain what Freud would have called a condition of abstinence, that is, that you do things for the benefit of the student, not at the expense of the student for the benefit of yourself. You do not have to be perfect to do that.

CTT: How about cases where the teacher's distorted psychological function blinds them? They do not realize they are not acting for the benefit of the student.

AJD: I think they know it but push the knowledge away.

Ethical Standards for Teachers

AJD: As you know from some material I have written (Deikman, 1983), I think the mystical traditions set up certain functional requirements for teachers that are at odds with exploitation. Likewise in psychotherapy. There is a lot of training devoted to countertransference in psychotherapy training, and there are also certain rules and barriers that are not supposed to be violated. Some people do violate them. I think the fact that they are violating them does not indicate that they do not understand something about psychodynamics, but that his or her training, his or her personality has significant flaws. That probably means that his or her ability to do psychotherapy is quite constricted, also.

I think that if someone's spiritual development has gone to the point where his or her intuitive perception has been developed, it should preclude gross violations of ethics and trust.

As to the kind of people you are thinking of, who have manipulated and abused students, I see no reason to assume that these people actually reached a high state of development and then for some reason degenerated. Apart from the possibility of brain tumors or something like that, I think it is safer to assume that these people developed certain mind powers, not enlightenment. Once you have such mind powers, it is no trick at all to collect a thousand people around you and play such games. So I think there is a certain incompatibility between exploitation and development, and I think that is true at every level. Maturity does not include this kind of behavior.

CTT: I want to address a less extreme model. Suppose a person of genuine good will has an important spiritual experience and has some ability to teach about at least some aspects of what he or she has learned from the experience. The person is certainly not perfectly enlightened, if there is such a thing as "perfect" enlightenment, but he or she has something worthwhile to teach people and has some skill in teaching. Then it is not so much that he or she becomes exploitative of people but that some unresolved psychological flaws make him or her a less effective teacher. The person might, for instance, set up teaching techniques which do work for some people but set unnecessary barriers for some other people.

This could be manifested as the common problem in adapting a spiritual tradition to another culture, where the teacher brings along a lot of what we think of as "cultural baggage." The teacher may see these truly irrelevant cultural customs as an essential part of the training technique because it was in that context that he or she had their own realizations.

Being heavily conditioned by a particular culture can also lead to more extreme problems when a teacher comes to another culture, as their (partial) enlightenment was and is supported by specific and limited culture-specific behaviors. We can think of some teachers who came from India, for instance. They seemed to have reached relatively high spiritual levels in that culture where celibacy is part of that particular spiritual tradition. They come here to our relatively uninhibited sexual culture and ended up involved in scandalous sexual exploitation. You could argue that there was no need for them to work on that part of their personality structures in Indian culture as there was little temptation. These unresolved flaws that did not manifest in the other culture are important here and become important barriers.

AJD: I do not agree.

CTT: What do you think happens instead?

AJD: I do not think they had that much development in India, or that exploitation is excused by cultural background differences *per se.* You could be trained in lots of things, know the Vedas, know the Upanishads upside-down, have all that material, meditate, have visions, be pious and have powers, but in terms of real maturity, in terms of the surrender of the ego self to the larger Self, there has not necessarily been that development.

CTT: If I understand you correctly, you operate from a model here that there are certain basic standards of human decency that are universal, cross-cultural. I share that model too. I guess I am allowing for the cases where psychological problems can obscure your perception of what is exploitation and what is teaching. I am also thinking in terms of a Buddhist model here that allows that one can become one-sidedly accomplished in a genuine spiritual sense. You can become fantastically skilled at concentrative meditation, experiencing various bliss states, but without developing insight and compassion. You are very enlightened in a way, but it is built on a lopsided foundation that does not involve full understanding of your real spiritual identity, namely our Oneness with all life.

AJD: I think we are unduly respectful of people who speak some other language than ourselves, wear strange clothing, and say mysterious-sounding things.

CTT: And charge us heavily to hear them!

AJD: Right! If you stop and think about it, why should that mean a damn thing? There are technologies that we have and technologies that can be developed through mind power, but in terms of maturation, in terms of that development in which a person experiences a larger identity through serving a larger task or role, those physical or mental technologies are irrelevant, and possibly misleading. A person does not need to do any of that stuff.

We have too much misplaced respect. The fact that something is written in Sanskrit makes people think that this must be really profound spiritual stuff, but perhaps it is just academic speculation in Sanskrit. There is one scale of profundity of meditation, for example, where it says something like, "And then you lose awareness of this and then you lose awareness of that, on and on," and finally there is no "awareness of awareness." All I could think of when I read that was how did they know the experience happened in that case? Is this an example of some compulsive academic needing to finish the logical series?

CTT: There has always been a place for obsessive compulsive thinkers!

AJD: It is the same problem for us. It comes up over and over again, the problem of discriminating the container and the content. Outer appearance does not mean very much. We pick friends on a different basis than that. But it is hard to remember the difference and discriminate when we deal with exotic spiritual traditions.

It may be a mistake for Westerners, at least Americans, to be involved in spiritual disciplines where they have to wear clothing other than what they would normally wear. Anytime someone puts on a robe, they are apt to feel like Snoopy in a Peanuts cartoon: "Here's the World War I flying ace...." In this case it is something like "Here's the Zen monk walking in the garden." It can be a terrible burden.

CTT: Let us cap this discussion by coming back to the central theme. We Westerners have a lot of knowledge about mindfulness and the lack of it, particularly in the form of mindlessness we call psychopathology. What is our unique contribution to the general, transcultural development of mindfulness? What have we got to contribute that is not coming out of the traditional approaches to training mindfulness? Can you give me a summary statement on that?

AJD: Suppose you showed up at a traditional Eastern monastery seeking spiritual instruction and were told to sit outside the gate for a week, but you were not willing to do that. Your refusal could be good or bad, but let us say that you were not able to pass this entrance test for reason of neurotic conflict with authority, or fears of passivity, or feeling of rejection, or whatnot. Western psychotherapy has some means for dealing with these kinds of problems other than dismissing a person as the Eastern traditions would do. That is one definite contribution: psychotherapy says there is a basis for these feelings and shortcomings and it is possible to free oneself from them by uncovering their origin in the person's earlier life experience. This is different from most spiritual disciplines. It also is different from meditation, but is likely to prove much more effective in dealing with problems stemming from an individual's personal history. In this respect, Western psychotherapy can help set the stage for a much broader advance in spiritual development than has been possible in the past.

References

Anonymous (1975). *A Course in Miracles.* Tiburon, CA: Foundation for Inner Peace.

Deikman, A. J. (1963). *Experimental meditation.* JOURNAL OF NERVOUS AND MENTAL DISEASES, *136,* 329-73. Reprinted in C. Tart (Ed.), *Altered States of Consciousness.* San Francisco: Harper & Row, 1990, pp. 241-64.

Deikman, A. J. (1966). *Deautomization and the mystic experience.* PSYCHIATRY, *29,* 324-38. Reprinted in C. Tart (Ed.), *Altered States of Consciousness.* San Francisco: Harper Collins, 1990, pp. 34-57.

Deikman, A. (1976). *Personal Freedom: On finding your way to the real world.* New York: Grossman Publishers.

Deikman, A. (1982). *The Observing Self: Mysticism and Psychotherapy.* Boston: Beacon.

Deikman, A. (1983). *Evaluating spiritual and utopian groups.* JOURNAL OF HUMANISTIC PSYCHOLOGY, *23,* 8-19.

Deikman, A. (1990). *The Wrong Way Home: Uncovering the patterns of cult behavior in American society.* Boston: Beacon.

Shah, I. (1970). *Tales of the Dervishes: Teaching stories of the Sufi masters over the past thousand years.* New York: E. P. Dutton .

Tart, C. (1972). *States of consciousness and state-specific sciences.* SCIENCE, I 76, 1203-10.

Tart, C. (Ed.) (1975). *Transpersonal Psychologies.* New York: Harper &Row.

Tart, C. (1986). *Waking Up: Overcoming the obstacles to human potential.* Boston: New Science Library.

Tart, C. (1989). *Open mind, discriminating mind: Reflections on human possibilities.* San Francisco: Harper & Row.

Originally appeared *in* THE JOURNAL OF TRANSPERSONAL PSYCHOLOGY, **1991, Vol. 23, No. 1**

A Guide to Implementing
the Receptive Mode

Written as a guide for rangers in the National Park System

M ost visitors are looking for something in the parks but do not really know what that is. It is likely that they want and need more balance in their lives; they have spent too much time in the action mode as an exclusive way of living. But because they do not understand the problem, they will try to obtain satisfaction in the parks using the way they have always used, even though that way — the action mode — excludes them from the very experience they need. For this reason, they need to be shown how to do things differently.

At the same time, the visitor will need some explanation so that the receptive mode "makes sense" and does not seem foreign. The background material, developmental psychology, and research that I have included in the seminar and in this supplement is something that you can use for this purpose. Draw upon it as needed for a given situation and also to clarify the concept for yourself.

The receptive mode is a straightforward psychological phenomenon and need not be mysterious or beyond the capacity of the normal person. If you understand this yourself, it will not be difficult for you to give that same perspective to the visitor. Remember, there are two objectives to be fulfilled:

1) for the visitor to have the unique, satisfying, restorative experience that the parks can provide, and

2) for the visitor to learn how to have a similar experience in his or her everyday life at home, in the natural urban settings where he

or she lives, and where the possibility for receptive mode enrichment is always present.

It is important to remember that because each individual has somewhat different backgrounds, expectations, fears, strengths, and capacities, there will never be a uniformly positive (or negative) response to your presentation of this material. What you do is not going to benefit everyone, and the receptive mode experience will not please or be meaningful for everyone. That is something you may find useful to say to those who are disappointed or feel left out when others tell of positive and exciting experiences. People differ and those differences are important. Therefore, you should not expect that you will be able to "reach" everyone in the group you are addressing. It is more a matter of creating an opportunity for those who are ready to take advantage of it — opportunities they are not likely to encounter anywhere else.

The Psychology of the Visitor

The psychological situation of each visitor will be somewhat different, depending on their age, the context of their visit to the parks (whether with family, friends, or alone), the atmosphere of the park site, and other conditions. However, certain basic tendencies are likely to be present. To begin with, if the visitor comes to an interpretive talk, a nature walk, or some other activity, they are likely to be in what is termed a "dependency" situation. They look to you, the interpreter, for parental functions: providing guidance, protection, entertainment, giving something to them. There is nothing bad about that — we all need the chance to shift roles periodically, and have the experience of being cared for, of placing responsibility in someone else's hands. Such a dependency situation permits a kind of relaxation that is otherwise not possible. With that orientation, the visitor will unconsciously invest you with more power, authority, and wisdom than you are likely to feel you have yourself.

In this way, you may experience each visitor's characteristic attitude towards authority figures. Some might expect you to be sternly judging; others might look to you for praise or reward; others might be very wary, expecting some intrusion on their freedom. Still others may give you the feeling that they want to crawl into your lap and stay there forever. Truculence, flirtatiousness, deference, childishness — you've undoubtedly encountered all these attitudes, or you will before long. Basically, however, the visitor's attitudes towards you will tend to be positive and they will be quite ready to follow your suggestions. They will appreciate your being an authority figure who, at the same time, allows personal interaction, rather than someone who is distant and forbidding. It is possible to be warm and friendly without relinquishing your responsibility or your role as a guide.

A second important facet of the visitors' psychological situation is that they are in unfamiliar surroundings without the structure of their work role and customary routines. The novelty of being away from home, the nonordinary characteristics of the situation, encourages the desire to experiment, to try new things and at the same time is a potential source of anxiety. The old patterns that are temporarily set aside may have been a burden and a constriction, but they were familiar and reliable. However, with the interpreter available to provide a feeling of protection, visitors will find it possible to experiment in ways that they could not do alone.

Introducing the Visitor to the Receptive Mode

How then do you go about introducing the visitor to the receptive mode? Basically, this question will be answered through your own experience of the receptive mode. By drawing on your own experience, you will find the words that are natural and meaningful for you. It is the communication of your experience and discoveries to the visitor that will make the exchange alive. For example, you may have experienced a feeling of relief when you "quit."

That sense of relief was your experience and your discovery; it can be the basis of your talking to the visitor. Or, the receptive mode might have given you a different experience of a pine tree, a feeling that you were not looking at it — it was looking at you. Such an experience might lead you to tell a visitor that the park has something to say to him or her without their making any effort to receive it. On the other hand, you may have found that the most difficult thing for you to overcome has been the nagging feeling that it is wasteful to spend time not doing anything. Or you might have been bothered by the concern that once you really "stopped," you would not want to start again. However, having "quit" several times, you realize that these fears and concerns are groundless. Accordingly, when you speak from your own experience about such problems or phenomena, the visitor will feel your sincerity and your communication will be natural.

This applies to myself, as well. My scientific research papers are all based on personal experience and that permits me to speak in a way that has the best chance of being understood. The same will be true for you. Thus, there is no prescribed presentation to memorize — or to worry about forgetting. Each time you talk to the visitor about the receptive mode, you'll be talking from where you are at that moment in your life, in that day, in that place. You don't have to worry about anything in particular that you need to say — just talk to the visitor about what you would like to be able to share with him or her.

I'll give you an example of how I might talk to a visitor or a group to introduce them to the receptive mode. This would be my way. Some of it might fit naturally with your style, too; but, inevitably, the way that is right for you would have its own form, would be in your own words and with your own personal flavor. That way, you will feel at ease and the visitor will, too. So, read what follows as an example, only. Then see what comes from you in the actual situation. Remember, there is no way to fail because there is no way to do this perfectly.

Let's assume that I am addressing a group of visitors who are travel-ing by car and sightseeing in a national park — one with forests. Ini-tially, I might have given them a talk supplying information about the particular park and terrain in which they find themselves. Then, in conjunction with the talk, I would walk with them; moving them away from the meeting area, away from cars into some area that offers more privacy — an undisturbed setting, if possible. Then I might say, "There is a lot to learn about the park, but we've found that there are two kinds of learning. One is the kind you've been taught in school: listening to the facts that someone gives you and understanding them — such as the facts I've just given you about this park. But there is another way, too, equally important that we often don't have a chance to do. It's what you learn when you stop being so active with your mind and relax so that your surroundings, the place that you are in, can communicate to you.

"I don't know about you, but I usually come to work all wound up with what I have to do, worrying about getting someplace on time, thinking of a hundred details. I notice a lot of visitors come to the parks the same way and I think it's a gyp for all of us. Suppose we say that for the next 10 or 15 minutes we are all going to quit. After all, no matter what our problems might actually be, we really don't have to do anything about them in the next 10 or 15 minutes. We could take that time just for ourselves and stop making any effort, any straining of any kind — just receive. Wouldn't that be nice? I sure like it when I get the chance to do that.

"One of the reasons I like giving these talks is that it gives me a chance to stop, also. So, in a few moments, what I'm going to suggest that you do is just find some comfortable place to sit down and see if you can take a real vacation.

"You know, the very thoughts that we have are trying to get us to do some kind of work. When I examine my thoughts, I find that I usually am trying to solve some problem — either something that occurred a while back, or something that is going to happen in the future. Even if I'm not thinking, my body may be trying to get me to work by telling me to move or scratch or some other thing and I'm always obeying those kinds of orders. But, this

*time, let's refuse to obey any of those orders. If a thought comes
up, we'll just ignore it and let it go its way. If there's a funny
feeling in your leg — to heck with it. Let's be real selfish; let's just
sit there and see what the world is like for us when we don't do
anything.*

*"Let's really quit from working but let's not go to sleep. It al-
most seems as if we've been taught that if we aren't busy — busy
inside our heads — we should go to sleep. That's a gyp.*

*"Let's quit for a little while, but not go to sleep, and let's have
the experience of just being for ourselves, whatever it is. You don't
have to close your eyes, you don't have to look solemn — there's
nothing solemn about it. Take a vacation for 10 to 15 minutes
and don't even worry about remembering it.*

*"Just take the next 10 or 15 minutes for yourself and see what
that experience of the trees, or the flowers, or anything is like when
you're not doing anything at all. In fact, you don't even have to
enjoy it because sometimes we put that burden on ourselves, too.
Let's just be wide open and quit, quit all our activity and see
what the park, in this spot and in this time, is saying to us. If you
want to look at one thing, such as a tree, that's OK. If you want
to look at nothing in particular, just letting your eyes go out of
focus — that's OK, too. It's for you. Find out what it's like to quit
and stay awake."*

Suppose, instead, I was addressing a group of campers. I might adopt
the same talk with a somewhat different introduction, such as this:

*"Well, I see you've been camping here. How long has that
been? How many people have been here one day? Three days?
Five days? In all that time, have you ever quit? I mean stopped
working inside your head, as well as outside. Do you know what I
mean? A lot of people look at me and say, 'Wouldn't it be great to
be a park interpreter, just wander around enjoying the scenery!'
But, you know, a lot of the time I'm as much in my head as you*

might be, back in your job. I find it's really hard to stop all that busyness, even in the midst of these parks and, unless I do, I miss out on something.

"I think what we might try and do today is to see if we can get in touch with a way of being in the parks that's different from what we usually do. I mean, let's try and be lazy, really lazy. So lazy that we don't move even if our toe itches, so lazy that we don't move even if our back feels stiff, so lazy that we don't obey all those thoughts that want to get us to worry about what we are going to have for lunch, or how many days of vacation are left, or where the kids are, or your friends — or anything like that, 'cause each of those thoughts is trying to get us concerned about something, trying to make us figure something out, do some kind of work inside our head. Let's see if we can get so lazy that we just let all that stuff go by — no matter what comes up. So lazy, in fact, that we don't even go to sleep 'cause we're going to be lazy and selfish and we want to know what it's like, how we experience the world when we don't do anything but stay awake to enjoy it. In fact, if enjoying it feels like another burden, don't even try to enjoy it. Just see what it's like. What is it like for us when we sit here in the park, with the trees around us and the sky and the earth? What can they give to us, if we stop doing things, if we just quit for 10 or 15 minutes?

"I don't know about you but I rarely have a chance to do it, except during talks like this and it's really something special, something really different — at least it is for me. Whatever it is, it will be your experience. Let's try it. I'll keep track of the time — so you don't even have to worry about that, and I promise I won't leave you sitting out here forever. Let's just sit here and see if we can take the next 10 or 15 minutes for ourselves, for us. Let's see what it is like to be here when we really quit wide awake — but not doing anything."

To put people at ease and to involve them in what you are doing, you may find it helpful to pause during your description of the receptive mode, or after giving instructions, and ask them if they understand what you mean. You might ask whether they have had any experiences of their own that relate to it; whether they can recognize what you are talking about from their own experience — such as the trouble you yourself have in stopping thoughts from going through your head, or the sense of frustration in not being able to really relax, or the wish for something you can't quite name.

Usually, the first time someone tries, it's such a new experience that they can only get into it in a limited way. Therefore, if possible, it would be a good idea with any group to do it a second time, perhaps after an interval of answering questions or some discussion. The second time around people will usually get into it much more. You could try it, at that time, for something like 20 minutes. If they are on a walk, you might encourage them not to talk to each other after they finish the second quitting exercise — but to just get up and follow silently with you as you walk along. In this way, the succeeding walking period may be one in which they are able to continue the receptive mode — and you might explicitly suggest that. That would help get across the idea that one doesn't necessarily have to be sitting in order to have the benefits of that mode of experiencing.

The Time-Limited Approach

Sometimes the interpretive situation, or limitations of time, make it inappropriate for the sort of approach described above. In such cases, you need not make any explanation or introduction but could suggest that the visitors take a moment or two to sense, feel, or listen to their surroundings. For example, suppose you are showing a small group a room in a historical building. After giving the facts about the room and whatever background information might be appropriate, you could say,

"Now let's stop for a moment and see if we can get a feeling for what the room conveys to us. Just relax. Don't do anything but just stay open and see what your senses can tell you about this place. What does it say to us if we relax and listen?

"So let's quiet down for a moment so that we can take in the room through all our senses."

Another approach might be:

"Now, instead of thinking about this room or looking at it, let's imagine that the room has its own life and it has something to convey to you, a message for you, as it were. It may be different for each person, but a message is there. So let's relax and just be very still for a few moments and see what you can sense of what the life of this room is and what it has to say."

You might then encourage the visitors to try that same procedure with other aspects of the area that they are visiting. Similarly, in a natural setting, the same format can be used.

Because you understand the process and the nature of the visitor's problem, you will be able to come up with ways of introducing the visitor to the experience in terms that are comfortable to you and appropriate to the situation — whether it be a two-hour walk or five minutes; a seashore, a mountain, or an historic mansion.

Helpful Techniques

Campfires

It is interesting to consider a longtime favorite activity in the national parks: the campfire gathering. At its best, the campfire brings together the visitor with the nighttime and the open fire. These are basic and deep-rooted elements that evoke feelings and perceptions often ignored during the course of our lives. The campfire at night is attractive to almost everyone, particularly if it offers something beyond listening to a park ranger lecture. The campfire can be a wonderful setting for letting go of striving, for just being alert and relaxed, without effort, taking in the night, the fire, and the presence of the quiet, surrounding group.

Unfortunately, many campfire scenes in the parks are filled with talking from start to finish, fulfilling only a social/educational function so that there is actually very little space for the night to enter — except in brief pauses between songs, stories, a formal interpretive talk, and the like. Stories and songs are fine, but cessation of speech and human noise, letting go of effort of any kind can create conditions for a different sort of experience, one that for many people will be a totally new one. It requires its own time. Perhaps 20 minutes, twice in one evening, could be set aside for just stopping and being.

The last session could be done just before the campfire ends; the group could be encouraged to leave silently when the 20 minutes is over, enjoying and savoring their receptivity as they go slowly and quietly back to their camp. If this is presented as a positive and potentially rich experience, the visitor may appreciate the walk from campfire to camp as something other than a hurried transition from one place to another.

Physical Fatigue

Physical fatigue is a powerful ally in establishing the receptive mode. On long hikes, there is often much chatter at the beginning, but after awhile, as people begin to tire, talking ceases. Over the course of a hike, the natural world seeps in. During periods of rest, the hiker is often more open and in the present than at other times. At such moments, the receptive mode instructions will appear both natural and meaningful; the hike will have cleansed the usual tension and preoccupations from the visitor's mind.

Other Senses

Because we tend to orient ourselves almost exclusively through the use of our eyes, having a visitor experience a particular setting with his eyes closed can often be a valuable way to acquaint them with the world of immediate sensation. To walk slowly through a meadow or forest, guiding yourself only with touch, sound, and smell, can be a revelation for many people. This is because suspending the visual sense tends to enhance all the others. Such an exercise could be a useful prelude to "quitting," as it makes perfectly clear how much of the world is accessible by routes other than that of sharp, focused vision. Also, the information entering through touch, smell, and natural sounds tends to be less conditioned to thoughts than that of vision. Thus, when those avenues become central, there is a good chance that the visitor will have an experience of the world which seems new, fresh, and vivid.

Breathing

Sometimes it can be useful, for a brief period, to have the visitors become aware of their breathing. You might suggest that they see if they can allow their breathing to become free and easy — and to relax at the same time. Tension tends to restrict our breathing. We tighten our stomach muscles and our chests, or we may accelerate our breathing to make it rapid and shallow. But deep, slow respirations are associated with relaxation, with the taking-in function of the receptive mode. Having people focus on the sensations set up by deep and slow breathing can quiet them in cases where the group may seem to be nervous or hyperactive. Even with a fairly relaxed group, you may find such a procedure to be a useful preparation for the receptive mode.

Your Own Experience

Remember that the basic technique for teaching the receptive mode to visitors is the use of the interpreter's own "receptivity." That is, your own experience of the receptive mode will serve to guide you and will provide an example for the visitor. Your own confidence in and enjoyment of the receptive mode will be indirectly communicated to the visitor and he or she will grasp that it is both possible and desirable. By expressing your understanding and appreciation of receptivity in your own terms, informed by your own experience, you will be most effective in aiding the visitor in having his or her own enriching experience of the parks.

Understanding the Visitor's Resistance

Not only is there a lack of information or instruction about the receptive mode but most people, despite themselves, will consciously or unconsciously tend to resist "not doing" at least to some extent. For some, the resistance may be very strong and they will not get into the receptive mode at all.

Anyone who has practiced "quitting" can understand most of those resistances, fears, or concerns. Some of the principal ones are as follows:

1) "Not doing" seems bad (lazy, idle, sinful). Even if the person is on vacation, to actually stop doing things may make them uneasy or guilty. This reaction can be diminished by conveying the idea that not-doing is important and can be viewed as a biologic need, something that has a useful function in itself.

2) Fear that once a person stops, he or she might never be able (or want) to become active again. In part, this is due to the way we drive ourselves, compulsively making ourselves do what we "should." Something inside of us rebels against this pressure and gives rise to the suspicion that if you didn't "have to" do anything you would just lie around all day and rot. Thus, giving oneself permission to stop may feel like giving in to the inner rebelliousness that we assume is what we really want. This reaction reflects a cultural assumption that our natural tendencies, instincts, or drives are to be distrusted, part of our bad animal nature which requires taming, control, direction, and coercion. For some people, the receptive mode may feel like opening the door of the cage in which they have kept and keep controlled all their various inner impulses of which they are afraid.

3) "Not doing" is associated in our minds with helplessness, and helplessness has links to basic anxiety going back to days of infancy and childhood. Pain or traumas associated with being helpless may be stirred up to some extent by something that feels like a giving up of control. This reaction is lessened by the presence of the interpreter who implicitly signifies safety and parental protection. At still deeper levels, letting go and letting whatever happens happen — the basic

attitude of the receptive mode — is the equivalent of letting time flow by, allowing change. Change has connotations of loss and death. One of the ways in which we fight our fear of death is by using our minds to control our experience. Not only does the receptive mode put the experience back in charge, but in the receptive mode the consciousness of self diminishes.

Indeed, the "forgetting" of the self is the key to the benefits that the receptive mode provides. We want that experience and yet may be afraid that it could go too far or last too long.

For most people, it is unlikely that these factors will be that important or will emerge so strongly as to prevent them from getting a taste of the receptive mode experience, particularly when they participate in an exercise such as I have demonstrated. However, those for whom such concerns are quite strong will tend to be conscious of why they are having trouble getting into the receptive mode or why they can't seem to stop thinking. The best way to deal with such situations is to reassure them that not everyone experiences things in the same way, that the process does take time and whatever anyone experiences is fine. Actual explanations of why people may find it difficult should be phrased simply and with discretion. If you can empathize with a person's difficulties from your own experience, you will be able to say the right thing when it is needed. In most cases, no explanation is called for, just reassurance and a relaxed attitude.

Most of the resistance to going into the receptive mode originates from the customary orientation in the action mode. Once a person has shifted to the receptive mode, the frame of reference is changed and the experience is positive and relatively free from anxiety. If the interpreter personally practices the "quitting" exercise, he or she will become familiar with those internal things that tend to resist the process. Such personal resistances can provide insight into the way we have conducted our lives, the assumptions behind those rules of conduct, and the way towards increased personal freedom.

Because we have a tendency to think in terms of either-or

choices, it may be important to emphasize more than once that what we're talking about is a balance, a restoring to the individual of a function that does not replace the action mode, but supplements it or is complementary to it.

The principle of "complementarity" originated in physics. Scientists have found that, depending upon the conditions of an experiment, the results may indicate two different and logically incompatible views of reality. For example, some experiments showed that light behaved as if it were a wave, others indicated that light must be a particle. Rather than treat the two views as a contradiction and try to disprove one or the other, Niels Bohr, a physicist, realized that both aspects were legitimate expressions of reality, depending on the conditions of observation. Similarly, the action mode and the receptive mode are complementary to each other; they do not coexist simultaneously but one can be selected according to what is needed. One does not invalidate the other. Our culture has taught us to actively and consciously master our world and ourselves. This is a most important and necessary function.

The receptive mode feels like a loss of that control, but it is really an activity of a different kind, for a different purpose, to meet different needs.

Typical Questions and Problems

The composition of groups will vary but certain questions are likely to come over and over again. Problems may also be presented. The following is a series of hypothetical questions and problems and some examples of ways to respond to them.

PROBLEM: "My eyes go out of focus."

REPLY: "That's OK, either way, just stay aware of whatever your experience is and enjoy not doing anything. Seeing things out of focus is probably interesting in itself, so just let it happen and see what that's like. On the other hand, if you want to keep things in focus, you can do that, too. Suit yourself, just don't strain or work — but let things come to you."

PROBLEM: "I couldn't seem to stop thinking."

REPLY: "It certainly is hard, isn't it? It just goes to show how much we've been trained to go on thinking even when we don't have to. I have found that it helps to remind myself that thinking is a kind of work; I then see if I can relax further and quit that kind of effort. I just sort of sag inside. So be patient and you'll have the chance to do it again. I think you'll find that the second time you try it, you'll be able to do it a little better."

QUESTION: "I feel strange — is that OK?"

REPLY: "Sure, this can't hurt you. It's really just a matter of resting while staying alert. Sometimes, something feels 'strange' when it's just very unfamiliar. For example, when we let a part of our body relax that we usually keep tense, it can feel 'strange.' However, remember that you're free to stop any time you want. So, if you get uncomfortable in some way that bothers you, just stop. The whole thing is really under your control and it's for you. Don't be afraid to stop or to start again, depending on how you feel."

PROBLEM: "I don't want to do it."

REPLY: "That's OK, you don't have to. This is just an experiment to try a new way of experiencing things and most people find it interesting to try. There is nothing you have to do or accomplish. Whatever happens is fine — but if you still don't want to try it, that's OK. You can just sit and think about anything that you want to, if that's what seems best to you."

QUESTION: "I hear a high-pitched sound — did you hear it? Is it OK?"

REPLY: "No, I didn't. But everyone has their own experience — that's the really nice thing about this. It's a question of each person finding out what his own experience really is and enjoying it. Just let it happen, and see what that's like — as if you're just curious to see what the world is like when you don't make any effort, when you're just there experiencing it. Most people find the experience tends to change, and that's interesting, too. So don't worry about it — just see what kind of show the world puts on for you."

PROBLEM: "I fell asleep."

REPLY: "That can happen, can't it? As I said, we've been conditioned to either be hard at work or to go to sleep and at any time we
stop working, our eyes start to close automatically. But that's a gyp,
you don't have to go to sleep just because you're not doing anything,
because you quit. So stay awake. Be curious. Be a little bit selfish, like
'Hey, this time it's for me. I don't want to go to sleep, I want to enjoy it.'"

PROBLEM: "I go off into daydreams without realizing it."

REPLY: "Yeah, me too. Almost everyone does that — but as soon as
you become aware that that's what happened, just relax a little further
and come back to your experience. Don't get upset about it, you didn't
do anything wrong — it's just the way our minds typically work. When
you find you've been daydreaming, just come back to your experience
and enjoy it."

PROBLEM: "I feel so tense, edgy — I can't get with it."

REPLY: "Yeah, I know what you mean. Next time we (you) do it,
why don't you see if there are places in your body where you can relax
further, where you can just let go and sag some more. But if you can't,
that's OK, we all have periods when we get too tight. But try it anyway.
You may be able to do it for short periods and it will feel good."

QUESTION: "Is this the same as meditation?"

REPLY: "Well, the term meditation covers such a wide variety of
things that almost anything could be considered a kind of meditation.
But this isn't meditation in any formal sense, such as yoga, TM, or
anything like that. This is a basic way of just relaxing or quieting
down and letting things come to you. Most meditations do try to
encourage that kind of attitude. However, what we're talking about is
so simple and basic that it probably shouldn't be called meditation in
the way people usually use that term."   - OR -

QUESTION: "Is it the same as TM? Yoga? Zen?"

REPLY: "For all those things you use the basic attitude of letting
go and letting whatever happens happen, instead of trying to control

everything and straining. So it sort of shares that attitude with TM and Yoga and Zen, but it isn't the same as those things. It isn't that complicated or formal. You're not saying a mantra for example, and you don't have to sit with your legs crossed — nothing like that. So, it isn't the same as TM or Zen but it has things in common with them."

QUESTION: "Should the Park Service be teaching us Eastern religions like this?"

REPLY: "I think the problem is that you probably associate this to what you've read about meditation, and you associate meditation to Eastern religions. But don't worry, this is not a religion, or even part of a religion, or anything like that at all. What we're doing isn't a religion of any kind — it's practicing a basic capacity that we all have that we tend to forget about and not use. Babies and children probably do it pretty well.

"It's just that most of us adults have been working so hard in one particular way that we've lost the ability that we originally had, and that we need. For example, if you want to remember a name that you've forgotten, you stop straining to remember, right? You say, 'It will come to me in a minute.' You're doing it then, you're 'quitting' to allow your mind to do something that's only possible when you relax. Another example: when you get into a hot tub, you need to be able to relax to really enjoy it. Relaxing isn't a religion. Maybe it should be a religion, but it isn't. So it's the same thing here. It makes a lot of sense for the Park Service to teach people what they need to do in order to enjoy the parks — instead of just wandering around with your mind buzzing the way it usually does. Don't you agree? It's like being taught swimming. It isn't all that hard to do, the ability is there in everyone and, once you learn, you can really enjoy the water."

QUESTION: "Can I do this at home? Where? How long? How often?"

REPLY: "I hope you do it at home; that's the great thing about it. It isn't just a matter of enjoying the parks while you're here; it's learning how to enjoy your world wherever you are — especially at home. Whether it's the backyard, an art museum, the city at night, or a flower in a vase — this is a way to really enjoy it and be nourished by it, restored by it. Twenty minutes is often a good length of time, but you could do it for ten minutes or half an hour, or whatever.

"Usually, it takes ten minutes or so to get into it — so something like 20 minutes gives you some time to really enjoy it. Do it as often as you like, or is practical. Most of the time you may need to be in the action mode, doing and striving — but the time when you feel like receiving something, being given to — well, that's a good time to try it."

QUESTION: "Is it OK for the kids to do it?"

REPLY: "Sure, in fact they may be able to do it better than you and, in fact, they may be doing it on their own — just naturally."

Approaching Different Park Situations
Example: Historical Sites

Not every park situation will be optimum for teaching this approach. But the receptive mode can have applicability anywhere. It's a matter of helping people to tune in to the intrinsic character of a special park area or site, its presence. For example, in a historical home, after the necessary information has been given to the visitors, you might have people direct their attention to a particular article of furniture, or a particular room — and make use of the receptive mode to have that piece of furniture or room "speak," allowing the flavor, the style and feeling of that particular time to manifest itself. (See "Time-Limited Approach.") In the case of a battlefield, the receptive mode may not yield the experience of the battle, for the actual field or meadow is now something else. But whatever is there, it will be helpful for the visitors to *experience* it — perhaps after they have been given a talk or had a chance to read about what that site was some years ago. The receptive mode does not require any particular setting — it's a way of *receiving*, a way of having a non-conceptual experience of the environment. Use of the receptive mode will give the visitor a personal experience of the quality of his or her environment, its intrinsic uniqueness as the visitor encounters it, at that moment.

Mode Cues

1) In general, human speech tends to reinstitute the action mode. You may have noticed that after the quitting exercise, if you and others around you remained silent, the mode tended to persist, whereas as soon as you began talking and chatting, it disappeared. It is important to keep this in mind when visitors are given the experience of the receptive mode.

2) Machine noise of different kinds is associated so strongly with the world of the action mode that it serves as a conditioning cue. Likewise, radio and TV tend to disturb or block the establishment of the receptive mode. Those persons who bring a radio or TV with them into the wilderness probably do so as a way of bringing their usual orientation there, too. Such stimuli fill time and are a distraction, preventing the person from experiencing the world in the receptive mode. As mentioned earlier, this is a matter both of habit and fear of the unfamiliar.

3) Information or other signs tend to reinforce the action mode when they a) urge consumption, b) emphasize time, c) stress danger, or d) urge action. These are goals and functions for which the action mode was developed and it is to be expected that they would call forth a matching psychological and physiological response.

4) Manmade garbage, plastic wrappers, tin cans, and bottles are similarly associated with the action mode-world and are like intrusive visual noise.

5) Buildings made out of aluminum steel and plastic with sharp, straight lines and angles, and with reflective surfaces have a similarly disturbing effect. This is due not only to the use of synthetic, "unnatural" materials, but to the special character of manmade objects. In nature, nothing develops, grows or exists that is independent of its surroundings — straight lines are rare. A tree grows in accordance with the pattern in its cells and according to the environmental conditions that exist during different phases of its growth. Thus, trees growing during a period of drought will grow differently than if they were having abundant rainfall. However, when man puts up a building,

the blueprints determine the form and it doesn't matter what takes place in the environment during the process of the building. Straight lines stay straight. The lack of interaction creates a definite effect so that we perceive the usual building as not blending in, not "fitting." In addition, plastics and metals do not exist as such in the natural world and they stand in our minds for the world of the action mode. However, it is possible to use materials and to design forms in such a way as to encourage the shift to the receptive mode. This is the special challenge for architects and designers in the National Park Service.

6) On the positive side, the national parks are extremely valuable because they contain an abundance of cues and opportunities for instituting and enhancing the receptive mode. For example, in the parks it is possible to experience the night. Whereas in cities, smog, street lights, and neon signs obscure the stars, in the national parks the nighttime sky blazes down with stars that most visitors have never seen in that quantity and intensity. Also, in the cities, the fear of violence leads people to shun the out-of-doors at night. Although the nighttime world of forests or deserts may still hold some anxiety, after sitting quietly for a period of time, the visitor begins to experience the nighttime as a special kingdom containing riches and beauty.

7) In the national parks there is the opportunity for that increasingly rare experience: silence. Silence from the noise of automobiles, radios, TV, machines can be a strange and incredibly delicious experience. To sit and listen as intensely as one can and hear only the music of the natural sounds — wind, birds, running water — that can be a peak experience to the visitor to the parks. Such sounds convey no concepts; they convey quality, a feeling, a presence — communication channels suitable for the receptive mode.

8) Along with silence is the possibility of solitude, of being by oneself in the midst of a living powerful world. It is one thing to be alone in an urban environment alien to our biologic selves; it is another thing to be alone amidst a living forest, a desert, or on an ocean shore. Aloneness under natural and positive conditions enhances the receptive

mode. In contrast, when engaged in social interaction with others, a thousand psychological reflexes are touched off, dealing with protection, survival, acquisition, and security. When we are alone in the natural world, it can speak to us of our biologic home and the possibility for a new and positive experience of aloneness arises.

9) The odors of the natural world are seldom appreciated. Odors are powerfully evocative and communicate in their own way. When we experience odors, it is like experiencing music; a type of a perception that is timeless and spaceless enters our consciousness through the oldest part of our brain. The smog-free air of the national park permits the experience of the realm of aromas; subtle, rich, provocative, and unfamiliar. They represent an unconditioned world and can be an exciting discovery for a visitor in the receptive mode.

10) Perhaps most important, experiencing the natural parks is to experience the *presence* of the mountains, streams, deserts, oceans — those entities that speak to us powerfully and directly given the least chance to do so. The effect of that presence further enhances the process of receptivity. Having absorbed a small amount of what emanates from the natural world, the visitor is better able to return to that mode again.

Benefits to the Visitor,
the National Park Service and the Nation
The Visitor

The visitor can be restored by the parks. He or she can be rested and reconnected to the real world instead of scurrying endlessly in the abstract realm of thinking and planning, of anxiety and depression, of too much concern with the past and with the future. The dissatisfaction and restlessness that can be noticed in many visitors can be markedly reduced, if not eliminated, for a time. This becomes possible if the visitors know how to do it, learn to go about getting what they really want and need. Not only can the visitors learn to get what they need in the national parks, they can learn a way of getting what they need from their home environment also. This is the most important goal of all.

Having experienced the natural and cultural world as something that gives to you, preservation and ecological concepts become matters of self-interest, rather than issues of virtue or morality. Thus, the visitor becomes motivated to enhance a resource that actually meets his or her needs. Therefore, it is important to emphasize to the visitor: 1) the receptive mode is a natural, inherent function which has been forgotten in our education and fallen into disuse; 2) it is rewarding and necessary to our wellbeing; 3) the receptive mode needs to be practiced until it becomes familiar as part of the person's daily experience; 4) the receptive mode helps us to enjoy our normal world wherever we may be living. It can make us independent of elaborate satisfactions because it permits us to be satisfied and restored by the everyday world.

The National Park Service

The need for elaborate programs to "satisfy" the visitor can be lessened by facilitating the receptive mode experience of the parks. The park setting — the mountains, the deserts, beaches, ruins, memorials — can do the job. The National Park Service provides the opportunity but the power is in the park itself, not in lectures or talks no matter how well-conducted. Perhaps the old term "guide" is closer to this function of the Park Service than the term "interpreter." When the visitor *experiences* the park environment *directly*, no interpretation is needed or called for. Most trails are well-marked now, but the psychological path to being receptive to the mountains or deserts needs a guide more than ever.

If this function is fulfilled, the visitor to the park will leave knowing the importance to him or her of our natural unspoiled resources and will be an energetic ally in preserving, extending, and enhancing the parks.

The Nation

We are in a crisis, looking for firm ground under our feet. Words seem to have lost their meaning, their usefulness as a guide. It appears that a sense of connection and purpose needs to be experienced to have real meaning. Having had such experience in the parks, a person has a new option, a way that he or she can use to help find satisfaction and harmony on "space ship earth." We came from the ocean and the land; our biological survival and growth requires reestablishing our connection to our source so that we can have the strength and wisdom to establish the future that should be ours. The national parks can be schools for refinding our place in the world.

A Caution

The interpreter is not a guru and the quitting exercise is not a path to salvation. Rather, you will be encouraging visitors to rediscover a skill that can be very useful to them for certain purposes, at certain times. The value of the receptive mode does not at the same time mean that the normal way of functioning of the visitor is without value or is of less importance.

Enthusiasm and conviction is important in any teaching situation and is important for interacting with park visitors. However, missionary zeal is neither necessary nor helpful. A relaxed, positive, permissive attitude is best suited to allowing people to set aside their usual concerns and allow the parks to affect them. Too much zeal can turn recreation into another task. The parks are there to provide true enjoyment; what you can do is to show the visitor a way to make that possible. Make no promises beyond that, but help the visitor to create the opportunity he or she may need.

Need for the Interpreter to Practice the Receptive Mode

"Quitting" is good for the visitor; it is good for the interpreter, also. After all, you probably are working for the Park Service because you instinctively turn to the world of the parks for the same reasons that many of the visitors come there. You, too, need to be restored, to continually re-establish your direct connection with trees and streams and sand dunes. Be selfish; give yourself time each day to have your own experience of the park, to let it speak to you, to give to you what you also need. It needn't be a task for you any more than for the visitor. Rather, it should be a vacation, a period of recreation and satisfaction. You can't do it perfectly; your thoughts will continue and distractions will occur — but it doesn't matter. There will be spaces of time when the connection occurs and that's quite enough. I would suggest you take 15 to 20 minutes in the morning right after getting up.

Take a walk out somewhere and quit for a while. You don't even have to sit down, although that may make it easier; it is the attitude that is important. Do the same thing whenever you are feeling harried, "uptight," or notice that you are hungry for distractions of any kind — food, reading, radios — whatever. That kind of hunger is often a sign that you're disconnected.

Enjoy it all; don't wait for the summer season to be over. If you can receive what the parks offer, there will be no problem about helping the visitor to do the same.

Appendix
Research Findings Supporting the Bimodal Hypothesis

Apart from its application to the issue of the visitor's experience of the national parks, the bimodal model offers a way of understanding a number of interesting research findings.[1] Its usefulness in organizing and clarifying poorly understood phenomena offers indirect support for its validity. Some examples follow.

Otto Poetzl, in 1917, observed a difference in what happens to visual stimuli that are perceived in the margin of awareness as compared with those perceived in the center.[2] He found that a stimulus that is incidental, on the periphery, is "processed" differently than one that is central. In the first case a dreamlike style is used; whereas in the second case, rational logic is employed. These phenomena can be understood as functions of the action and receptive modes. Sharp focused vision is needed and used for object manipulation where a softer more diffused vision (such as represented at the periphery of awareness) is employed for maximum intake. Thus, stimuli in the center of awareness are subject to a mode of organization associated with the manipulation of objects — the action mode. The thinking is based on object logic. Stimuli at the edge of awareness are processed according to a sensually oriented, intake goal of the receptive mode, which uses paralogical strategies.

Julian Silverman and his colleagues have noted changes in the style of thought and attention of schizophrenic patients who have lengthy hospitalizations.[3] When patients stay for three years or more in confinement, they distinguish objects less sharply and there is diminished "scanning" of the field.

Similar results were found in prison inmates, so these findings are not likely to be due to chemical deficits or "deterioration." The bimodal model does suggest, however, a way of understanding the change. A decrease in the articulation or definition of the visual field means that an object is less sharply differentiated from the background field and diminished scanning means that fewer objects have awareness centered on them — perception is spread out and diffuse (receptive mode). In contrast, where field articulation is sharp and scanning is wide, a person is prepared to detect and manipulate objects, to actively engage the environment. However, the action mode is specifically defeated by the usual hospital environment. If the patient must stay in such an environment several years, the frustration of active striving would be expected to result in a shift away from the action mode towards the receptive.

Mercedes Gaffron studied the differences in a person's experience when he or she focused on the near or the far side of an object.[4] Specifically, when attention was focused on the near side of an object ("grasping"), the object was perceived "exteriorally" — the dominant qualities of the experience were form, surface, distance and separateness from the observer. However, when attention was focused on the far side of an object ("mere looking") the experience featured "proprioceptive" qualities of volume, weight and "interior" feelings of tension and movement. In that situation, the object seemed to expand or intrude into the boundaries of the observer. (You can check this out for yourself by stopping for a moment and looking at a nearby object in these two ways).

These different experiences can be understood if we consider the process of eating a pear. In reaching for the pear, we focus on the near side, in preparation for grasping it. As the pear is brought towards the mouth, our focus shifts to the far side and beyond. In the act of eating, the pear is located within the zone of sharp visual focus, too close to be sharply defined, and is being literally taken into our organism. The grasping of the pear is associated with the receptive. The linking of visual focus and body activity that took place during our development persists even though the objects involved may on other occasions not be ones that can be eaten. The shifts in vision which accompany this process are integral parts of the change in mode so that a shift of visual activity may also be accompanied by a shift in other dimensions of that mode, for example, muscle relaxation and stimulation of the parasympathetic (digestive) system.

David Shapiro has studied the way in which an individual pays attention to stimuli — his attentive style.[5] He found that the style has important effects on his conscious experience.

Shapiro distinguished between two principal styles: sharply-focused attention (obsessive compulsive and paranoid styles) and diffuseness of attention, with absence of sharp focus (hysterical styles). He concluded, "The most conspicuous characteristic of the obsessive compulsive's attention is its intense sharp focus. These people are not vague in their attention, they concentrate and particularly do they concentrate on detail... (they) seem unable to allow their attention simply to wander or passively permit it to be captured. Thus, they rarely seem to get hunches, they are rarely struck or surprised by anything." The consequence of such a pervasive style of attention is that: "He will often miss those aspects of a situation that give it its flavor or impact: thus, these people often seem quite insensitive to the 'tone' of social situations." "Certain kinds of subjective experiences, affect experiences, particularly require, by their nature, an abandonment or at least a relaxation of the attitude of deliberateness and where such relaxation is impossible, as in the obsessive compulsive style, those areas of psychological life tend to shrink."

Shapiro's conclusions support the hypothesis of two modes of organizing experience. In the case of the obsessive compulsive person, his thought and style is in the service of object manipulation, an activity at which he is usually quite successful. However, hunches or moments of inspiration that come about involuntarily in a creative state, or moments of a mystical revelation, are quite absent from the experience of persons rigidly committed to the object mode of cognition and experience. Likewise, rich emotional experience is not found with that mode because "abandonment" and "relaxation of the attitude of deliberateness" is not compatible with the action mode. However, in what Shapiro terms "the diffuse hysterical style," we see the counterpart to the receptive, sensory mode. Such persons are less efficient in manipulating objects and tasks of that order, while sensory details, inspiration, and emotion figure prominently.

The increasing use of biofeedback techniques to produce muscle relaxation as well as the more traditional European treatment technique of autogenic training (self-suggestive relaxation) has shown that deep levels of muscle relaxation are often associated with changes in the person's experience of their body boundaries.[6,7] Similar changes in body boundaries have been noted under conditions of sensory isolation and in the induction phase of hypnosis. These findings can be understood if we identify fluid boundaries (diminished self-object differentiation) and muscle relaxation as components of the receptive mode, and if we consider that the components tend to vary as an organized group when a shift in mode takes place. Autogenic training, sensory isolation and hypnosis all tend towards the taking-in of the environment rather than acting on it. Thus, they all favor the receptive mode. Although they are also attempting to influence muscle tension and sensory input directly, the shift in mode may be due just as much to the accompanying shift in the functional orientation of the subject.

This reasoning also suggests an explanation for those situations where anxiety is reduced as a consequence of muscle relaxation; for example, biofeedback training or massage. Insofar as anxiety is an affect linked to future action (e.g., "If I perform this destructive or forbidden act, I will be destroyed"), the shift to the receptive mode could be expected to decrease anxiety because the state of receptivity is not organized for action. As far as the time dimension is concerned, the action mode is the Future while the receptive mode is the Now.

Finally, recent studies of differences in functioning of the two halves of the brain have shown functional differences that in some respects parallel the action and receptive modes. According to David Galin, the left hemisphere, that which usually controls the right hand, appears specialized for a particular cognitive style — an analytic logical mode employing words as the basic tool.[8] The right hemisphere, which ordinarily controls the left hand, functions with a holistic, gestalt mode that is particularly suited for spatial relations. While the left hemisphere's analytic style employs a linear processing system, the right hemisphere appears to integrate many inputs simultaneously, rather than dealing with them one at a time, in sequence. Both modes have important functions and, ideally, both modes are used by an individual depending on the situation in which he finds himself. Studies employing EEG measures have shown that lawyers and artists have differences in left and right side functioning, as predicted from the functional studies.

Although the brain model does not perfectly fit the action and receptive modes, the parallels are striking. In both cases, it can be said that the individual will function optimally if he or she has the capacity for employing whichever mode is most appropriate to the situation.

References

1. Deikman, A: *Bimodal Consciousness*. ARCH, GEN. PSYCHIAT. 25, 481-489, 1971. Also in, *The Nature of Human Consciousness*, Ornstein, R. (Ed.), W. H. Freeman and Co., San Francisco, 1973.
2. Poetzl, 0, et al: *Preconscious stimulation in dreams, associations, and images.* PSYCHOL ISSUES 2:1-18, 1960.
3. Silverman, J: *Variations in cognitive control and psychophysiological defense in the schizophrenias.* PSYCHOSOM MED 29:225-251, 1967.
4. Gaffron, M: *Some new dimensions in the phenomenal analysis of visual experience.* J PERSONALITY 24:285-307, 1956.
5. Shapiro, D: *Neurotic Styles*. New York, Basic Books, Inc. Publishers, 1965.
6. Schultz, J, Luthe W: *Autogenic Training: A Psychophysiologic Approach in Psychotherapy*. New York, Grune & Stratton Inc., 1959.
7. Kleinsorge, H, Klumbies G: *Technique of Relaxation*. Bristol, England, John Wright & Sons Ltd., 1964.
8. Galin, D: *Two modes of consciousness and the two halves of the brain*, in *Symposium on Consciousness*, Lee, et al, New York, The Viking Press, 1976.

Originally published by Division of Interpretation,
National Park Service, U.S. Department of the Interior, 1976

Service as a Way of Knowing

S ERVICE IS usually seen as a moral issue, a matter of doing, of being "spiritual" in an instrumental way. I suggest, however, that service is best understood as a matter of epistemology; it is itself a way of knowing and is one that goes beyond conventional empirical epistemologies. Service is a way of knowing in our connection — at a deeper level — with a reality much larger than our object selves.

What we call "the spiritual" pertains to the connected aspects of reality; service enables us to experience that kind of connectedness. The function of this connectedness or knowing is seldom appreciated; nevertheless, service is one of the most direct routes to the spiritual — a route often obstructed and confused by moral preaching, religious mythology, and everyday assumptions about the motivations and possibilities of human beings. To understand how this is so we need to consider instrumental and receptive functional modes of consciousness and also the way in which our intentionality determines the forms our consciousness takes. In this chapter, I discuss these two basic modes of consciousness, the role of intentionality, the survival self, the spiritual self, and the special function of service in allowing a shift from the exclusive experience of a separate self to a more balanced and connected self.

Instrumental Consciousness

Most of our lives are spent with a form of consciousness that enables us to act on the environment so that we will survive as biological organisms. This form or mode of consciousness develops to obtain food and defend against attack. In order to do so successfully, we need to learn to deal with the world in its object aspects, evoking a specific type of consciousness I call the instrumental mode.

The instrumental mode is the result of a developmental process. As the work of Gesell (1940), Erikson (1951), Piaget (1952) and Spitz (1965) demonstrated, the infant objectifies his or her world and uses the body as a template for learning. In one of Piaget's examples, a child is unable to solve the problem of opening a box with a lid, until he suddenly opens his own mouth, and then, immediately afterward, opens the box. In such ways the body becomes the means to organize and understand the world. Similarly, our early experiences with objects establish the structure of our thoughts. The most abstract and fundamental concepts ultimately are derived from the equation: object = body = self. The space, time, and causality with which we are familiar are the space, time, and causality that pertain to objects. That there are logics of reality beyond the instrumental or objective modes is indicated by the discoveries of modern physics, particularity the particle/wave duality of light, the evidence for nonlocality, and other paradoxes that have been proved true but that we cannot understand. The late physicist Richard Feynman, commented:

> *I think it is safe that no one understands quantum mechanics. Do not keep saying to yourself, if you can possibly avoid it, "But how can it be like that?" because you will "go down the drain" into a blind alley from which nobody has yet escaped. Nobody knows how it can be like that."* (cited in Pagels, 1982, p.113)

The limitations of instrumental, object-based consciousness can be experienced without the benefit of a degree in physics. Just try to imagine the universe coming to an end, spatially. I think you will find you cannot do so. Every object has a border and there is always space beyond any border you can visualize. Now try to imagine the universe not coming to an end. You can't do that either. Objects are never infinite. We cannot encompass the universe because it is not an object, and our thought processes, our very perceptual systems, have evolved to deal effectively with objects. Thus, we automatically perceive boundaries, discriminate between ourselves and others, and are wedded to linear time.

Other aspects of experience are affected also. Shapiro demonstrated that as children age, their responses to the Rorschach test change: The youngest groups responded primarily to the color and texture of the pictures, but those in the older groups paid progressively more attention to the shape and meaning of the figures (Shapiro,1960). Above all, we perceive the self as an object, separate, competing with others, dependent on others. That self — the survival self — is the one with which we are most familiar. Depending on what literature you are reading, it is called the ego, the Commanding Self, the drunken monkey, Small Mind, and so on. It is the organization of all the psychological structures that employ instrumental consciousness for its own benefit. This is the self that is busy acquiring, defending, controlling. All these functions are necessary, but they have their price: They set the agenda for the form of consciousness with which we experience the world and limit the information open to us.

We spend most of our lives in instrumental consciousness, serving the survival self. A summary of that mode's characteristic follows:

Example: Driving in heavy traffic
Intent: To act on the environment
Self: Object-like, localized, separate from others; sharp boundaries; self-centered awareness
World: Emphasis on objects, distinctions, and linear causality
Consciousness: Focal attention; sharp perceptual boundaries; logical thought, reasoning; formal dominates sensual; past/future
Communication: Language

This is the mode of consciousness we typically employ when driving a car in heavy traffic, or planning a business strategy, or maneuvering strategically at a social event. It's the one you are probably involved in as you read this chapter, checking for errors in logic, endeavoring to grasp my meaning, perhaps (if you are an author) waiting to see if I will reference something you've written. It's a good mode for that purpose.

Useful and necessary as this self may be, when it dominates consciousness it creates problems. It underlies the exploitation of others, it supports violence and war, all of which depend on separateness, on disconnection. Disregard for the natural environment is another consequence. From the point of view of instrumental consciousness, "When you see one redwood, you've seen them all." Furthermore, because it forms a barrier to experiencing the connectedness of reality, instrumental dominance leads to meaninglessness, "the mid-life crisis," alienation, fear of aging and death.

Thus, as infants and children we acquire concepts that later, as adults, we assume constitute the structure of reality. In the absence of alternative experience, these concepts are utterly convincing. But they are limited. The instrumental mode can raise the Big Questions: "Who am I? What am I? Why am I?," but it cannot hear the answers. A different mode of consciousness is needed, one responsive to reality in its connected aspects.

Receptive consciousness

Suppose you've driven your car to the airport, have flown to another city and checked in to your hotel. You want to relax, to unwind, to be comforted. So, you fill the bathtub with steaming hot water, ease your body into it, and relax your muscles... *Ahhhhh!* How good that feels! Chances are you were able to shift out of the instrumental mode and into the receptive, that mode whose function is to receive the environment. In that mode, awareness of separateness diminishes, there is a sense of merging with heat, the water, the surrounding environment. Boundaries relax; past and future drop away; the sensual takes over from verbal meanings and formal properties. Thinking becomes tangential, scattered, and slows down; boundaries blur. As boundaries soften, the sense of self becomes less distinct and less dominant, the object self subsides, relinquishing control. NOW, merging, and allowing are the dominant aspects of receptive experience. A summary of receptive mode characteristics follow:

Example: Soaking in a hot tub

Intent: To receive the environment

Self: Undifferentiated, nonlocalized, not distinct from environment; blurring or merging of boundaries; world-centered awareness

World: Emphasis on process, merging, and simultaneity

Consciousness: Diffuse attention; blurred boundaries; alogical thought, intuition, fantasy; sensual dominates formal; Now

Communication: Music/art/poetry/dance

Intention

The critical dynamic that determines the form of consciousness is intention. The intention to act on the environment necessarily features control. In contrast, to take in the environment, to be nourished, requires allowing and a kind of merging. Just as the instrumental mode is associated with the understanding of objects, separation, and borders, the receptive mode gains access to knowledge of a different sort. In order to appreciate this, try an experiment. (A human partner is best, but a flower or a tree will do.) Look into your partner's face with the specific intent of making a model of it, a sculpture. Analyze the planes of the head, the spacing of the eyes, the balance of the shapes. Spend a few moments doing that. Then shift your intention to one of receiving, allowing. Relax your gaze, surrender to the experience, allow your partner's face to be whatever it may be. Stay open and receptive to what comes to you. The shift in intention is from controlling to allowing.

Most people notice a distinct difference in their perception of the other when they shift their intention in this manner. The instrumental experience is easier to describe, it lends itself to measurement, comparisons, analysis. The receptive experience is more difficult to talk about. Receptive perception evokes words like "mysterious," "deeper," "richer," "soul." Whether face or flower, the Other emerges as a presence, filling consciousness, saying, "Here I am!" Each mode reveals different aspects of your partner's reality.

Self

There is an additional dynamic shaping consciousness that is as important as intention: the degree of activation of the survival self. To get a taste of this, try the same experiment again. First look at your partner (or flower or tree) while maintaining a strong sense of yourself. Then allow that sense of self to diminish, subside, and disappear. Notice the change in your experience of your partner. Again, I think you will find that as the sense of self diminishes and drops out, the experience becomes deeper, richer — your partner acquires the dimension of presence.

I had a vivid demonstration of this phenomenon while attending a seven-day Zen retreat. Part of the day was spent chanting. We held up stiff white sheets of paper covered with Japanese words printed starkly black. As the retreat progressed the words seemed to become more intense, more vivid. About the fourth day, I began to think that the letters didn't need me to be there, the chanting would continue and the words would go on marching across the page by themselves. The thought grew that the world did not need me to be here. In an internal dialog I urged myself, "Go on, disappear! Let yourself vanish from the world without "me." In some psychological sense that I cannot specify further, I gave up my existence in the world and let it exist without me. At that precise instant in which I allowed myself to disappear, the room and the others sitting there were suddenly transformed, becoming transfigured, archetypal, super real. Each student was a Buddha, awesome. At one point, a bell was rung and the sound rolled toward me like shimmering silver. I don't know how long the state lasted; I returned to my usual consciousness as we walked from the meditation hall. But afterward, I tried to understand what had happened, why my state changed so dramatically when my self "vanished." I now believe it was because the unusually profound deactivation of the survival self — its abdication of dominance — permitted a deeper experience of reality in its fundamental, holistic aspects.

The survival self of instrumental consciousness has distinct characteristics related to that mode. The emphasis is on boundaries, differences, form, and distinctions. Consequently, the self is experienced as a discrete object, more isolated than not. And we suffer the consequences. After all, the goals of the survival self — acquisition, pleasure, and permanence — are doomed. Acquisition is defeated by death; sensual pleasure is defeated both by aging and by the invidious design of our central nervous system that adapts to most sensory stimuli — except that of pain. This adaptation is an everyday experience. The initial ice cream cone may be thrilling, but if you want a repeat of the experience you will have to double the scoops and add sprinkles. The next serving had better be a banana split. And so on, until boredom or indigestion sets in. In contrast, a toothache never gets boring. Our response to money also demonstrates the problem. Lewis Lapham (1988) did an informal survey of his friends and acquaintances, asking them if they made enough money. All said no. When asked how much would be enough, they all named a figure double what they were currently earning, whatever that might be.

What is required for a healthy life is flexibility of consciousness. Most activities involve both modes to some degree and this ability to make use of the appropriate balance is essential to a healthy life. Flexibility is key. When flexibility is absent we see pathological manifestations of the modes: obsessive-compulsive character disorder in the case of a rigid adherence to instrumental consciousness and hysterical character disorder in the case of over-commitment to the receptive, a fixation on impressionistic, diffuse consciousness (Shapiro,1960).

Both modes are needed. Problems arise when one mode excludes or crowds out the other. In most of our spiritual experiences we are still conscious of the world's object qualities, but our perceptions take on additional qualities such that the experience is "deeper," "transcendent," "profound" by virtue of an increase in connectedness to and in the world. We feel gratitude for that widening, that larger sense of ourselves as part of a beautiful and awesome reality.

Especially in creative work, a balance of modes is critical. I think Yeats (1951) conveys the flavor of this when he writes of Michelangelo, "Like a spider upon the water, his mind moves upon silence" (p. 327). Most of us are limited by excessive instrumental dominance, but we do not realize this since our culture is strongly materialistic and our science is based totally on instrumental consciousness. To the extent that instrumental consciousness rules experience, life can easily seem meaningless. Meaning arises from connection but instrumental consciousness features separation. This effects our experience of self. The self of instrumental consciousness is now described:

The Survival Self

Characteristics: Aim of self-preservation; self-focused;
    self as object distinct from environment
Positive Effects: Able to defend, acquire; able to achieve material
    goals
Negative Effects: Basis for traditional vices; dissatisfaction; access to
    conceptual meaning only; fear of death
Importance: Needed for individual survival

In contrast, experience of self when receptivity is high and the survival self subdues can be quite different. This other-centered consciousness produces a qualitative change in the experience of self. I will call that other-centered self the spiritual self since it exists in connection. Its characteristics and effects are now summarized:

The Spiritual Self

Characteristics: Aim of service, attunement; other-centered; self
    identified with larger life process, resonant with environment

Positive Effects: Satisfaction; basis for traditional virtues;
   experiences meaning; equanimity
Negative Effects: Tendency toward passivity; ineffective in
   defending, acquiring
Importance: May be needed for survival of the human species

Our scientific, materialistic society continuously reinforces the survival self, the object-like self of the instrumental mode. Once formed, the survival self activates the instrumental mode in its own behalf. Because of this, if we wish to experience the connectedness of reality it is necessary not only to shift our intention in the direction of allowing and taking in, we need also to lower the level of activation of the survival self. The overall situation can be expressed in an equation: $C = f[I + S]$. *Consciousness is a function of intention and self.*

It is particularly hard to lower one's invisible survival self aims, those that operate unconsciously and are reflected in our characteristic attitudes and assumptions. To do this generally requires help. For this we can turn initially to psychotherapy to decrease the intensity of intrapsychic threats (Deikman, 1982) and then to the spiritual traditions to deal with survival self aims that are hidden from our sight. The spiritual traditions assist in developing an ongoing attitude, an outlook, that facilitates the emergence of the spiritual self.

The Spiritual Traditions

The bimodal model of consciousness provides a way of understanding the spiritual traditions because the spiritual path is often described as learning to "forget the self." The self to be forgotten is the survival self that evokes a mode of consciousness featuring separation. To shift to an experience of reality in its connected aspects, receptivity must be combined with a decrease in control by the survival self. This is a straightforward, functional matter. It has to do with an internal attitude, the guiding intent. I think that is what Thomas Merton (1968) was referring to in his book, *Zen and the Birds of*

Appetite when he described meat-eating birds (the survival self) looking for carrion:

> *Zen enriches no one. There is no body to be found. The birds may come and circle for a while in the place where it is thought to be. But they soon go elsewhere. When they are gone, the "nothing," the "no-body" that was there, suddenly appears. That is Zen. It was there all the time but the scavengers missed it, because it was not their kind of prey.* (p. ix)

Outer behavior may be misleading. For example, acquisitiveness need not be directed at money alone. Imagine a very successful businessman who decides he is no longer interested in amassing wealth, because from what he has read the only true satisfaction comes from Enlightenment. So he joins a spiritual group. His new intention is faxed down to the computer center in his brain. There, an underling picks up the fax and runs to the boss, "He says he no longer wants money. Now he wants enlightenment. Shall we change the program?"

"No" says the boss, "it's the same program: Acquisition."

In his case, and most others, the survival self is still running the show. After all, to use Abraham Maslow's wonderful phrase, "If all you know how to use is a hammer, you tend to treat everything you meet as if it were a nail." Being spiritual is no exception. What is needed for the perception of connectedness is for the survival self to become the servant, not the maser. That is what "forget the self" means. The survival self is still needed to function in the world, but it must not be the boss if a different experience of reality is to be made possible. There is no cheating on this one. Sitting cross-legged, inhaling incense, wearing a saffron robe, and going vegetarian won't necessarily change the guiding intention. So what can be done to find freedom from self-centered motivations. How does the spiritual teacher help the student to "forget the self?" If we turn to the mystical literature we find that most traditions make use of meditation, teaching stories, and service.

Meditation can be viewed as enabling a person to identify with the observing self, the "I," and to separate that core self from the concerns and mental activity of the survival self (Deikman, 1982). This increases freedom from concepts and lessens the dominance of instrumental consciousness, especially as meditation is based on allowing rather than making something happen. Teaching stories can be viewed in the same way; they enable the student to recognize patterns of thought and behavior that would otherwise remain hidden, influencing the form of consciousness. The functional approach to consciousness also can enable us to understand the emphasis on renunciation that can be found in most spiritual traditions. Renunciation is often misunderstood as giving up sensual pleasure, wealth, and power. When I first began doing research in the mystical experience I noted that the literature stressed both meditation and renunciation. Meditation was a lot more appealing than renunciation; I wasn't about to be an ascetic. So I began investigating meditation. Much later, Shunryu Suzuki-roshi, a Zen master, clarified the issue by explaining that renunciation was not giving up the things of this world but accepting that they go away (Suzuki, 1970). Such acceptance means an open hand, whereas the hand of the survival self is grasping, controlling.

We are now in a position to understand the vital function of service in providing access to the spiritual. You have undoubtedly heard the cynical argument that everything we do is selfish because even doing a good deed gives us pleasure. One expression of that idea was provided by Forbes magazine in which the view of economists concerning charity was summarized: "People gain satisfaction from charitable giving. It makes them feel good, and they tend to consume more of this feeling as their incomes rise" (Seligman, 1998, p.94).

There is some truth in that. Furthermore, a fantasy of a heavenly account book is often in operation, making good deeds a commercial operation — pay now, collect in Heaven. Perhaps that is why the Sufi saint, Rabia, prayed:

Oh Lord:
If I worship you from fear of Hell,
cast me into Hell,

If I worship you from desire for Paradise,
deny me Paradise

What she is countering in dramatic fashion is spiritual activity for gain, or from fear. Prayer, helping others, following a discipline, may all be performed on the basis of hidden vanity, greed, and fear, with the result that the survival self is enhanced, not diminished. Spiritual experience calls for a marked decrease in self-concern. For this, service is ideal, permitting a "forgetting" of the self that markedly reduces survival self concerns.

However, the call to service usually arouses conflicted feelings, for helping others may feel like being good on command, showing that you are a good person because service is what good people do. People who spend their lives doing service are categorized as saints and saints are the most good of the good. So service is widely believed to be something you should do to show your spiritual side, your concern for other human beings.

This idea of service gets mixed with basic teachings learned by the child in the family setting: Do good and you will be rewarded; do bad and you will be punished. These childhood beliefs persist and suggest an omnipresent parent who is watching, keeping score (Deikman, 1990). Most of us do not admit to such notions, but I have found that almost everyone, including myself, has a background fantasy of some celestial entity that is watching, keeping track of what we do, keeping accounts for a final settling up after we die. The idea of service seen in that context can easily result in a sense of obligation and nagging guilt, it can lead to resentment at the burden and resistance to action. For those who do act on the basis of reward and punishment — no matter how hidden the fantasy may be — there is the danger of self-inflation and self-righteousness on the one hand, disappointment and "burn-out" on the other. Perhaps most important of all, such expectations and reactions interfere with appropriate, creative action and render service useless for spiritual development. Fortunately, there is a way of acting that allows us to "forget the self." I call it serving-the-task.

Serving-the-Task

This type of service is not for any personal wish of our own, but to satisfy the needs of the task, to do what is called for. A carpenter may finish the underside of a chair because it feels right, is called for, even though the selling price will remain the same and the customer may not notice or care. I am aware that in writing this chapter, I have a mixture of personal motivations, concerns, and hopes, but I can also feel a sense of what is needed to accomplish the task. That guiding sense of what is needed is impersonal and may be resisted by my survival self, but it is there. It is not a compulsion but a recognition that tugs at me. When I surrender to it I get in touch with another dimension that is hard to describe and elusive to the grasp. This place, where I meet the task and merge with it, feels more important, more meaningful than personal desires. The surrender to the task can occur in any setting. Psychotherapists may recognize this as the "good hour" where everything flows and the therapist feels part of a subtle dance, one that carries as much as leads. Self-interest and self-concern subside and disappear as what-is-called-for takes over.

People who are truly serving the task experience something they cannot name, something that can answer the Big Questions. They do not ask, "What is the meaning of life?" because the question no longer arises. The answer is implicit in the experience of connection that service makes possible, the experience of a self —enlarged by connection and freed from its object goals. This "enlightenment" is not a guru's gift; it arises as a consequence of the forgetting of the self that service makes possible. That is why it is said that if a person is ready for enlightenment it cannot be withheld; if they are not, it cannot be given.

You may wonder if an evil task can be served — such as following the orders of an Adolph Hitler — and still further spiritual development. The answer is no. Not only do motives of hatred and fear reinforce identity with the survival self, the task of harming another human being cannot be done in a state of psychological connection. Barriers must be raised, the Other must be established as different from oneself, inferior, bad — connection must be abolished. If you doubt this, experiment once again with a partner. Be receptive to his or her face, allow your experience of self to subside so that the other's presence extends to you. Now imagine you are going to stab your partner. Visualize it happening and notice the change in your experience as you carry it out. You will find that in order to do so, even in your imagination, you have to "step back" psychologically and separate yourself, breaking connection. Service must necessarily be generous, beneficial in intent, in order to open the gates of perception. The more the survival self can subside, can cease to dominate consciousness, the wider the gates can open.

Knowing by Being What is Known

Imagine that our awareness is a pond connected by a narrow outlet to the ocean. At the mouth of the outlet there is a standing wave — the survival self — that blocks the ocean currents from entering the pond. As the survival self subsides, more and more of the ocean currents can gain access to the pond that then begins to resonate with the ocean. The pond then "knows" the ocean by resonating with it, in part becoming it. Probably, it is this experience that underlies the statements of mystics such as the tenth-century Sufi, Hallaj, who declared, "I am God" and was executed for apostasy. He did not mean "I, Hallaj, am the object God of your imagination," but "I am at one with the Reality that transcends understanding." The perception of the ocean's currents may lead to the experience of serving the Truth or "serving the Will of God," a phrase often misused by those still serving the survival self.

Service is a way of knowing our connection. The experience of the ocean's currents provides a sense of purpose and a guide to action that can use the survival self to fulfill a larger task. This alignment with the currents is referred to by mystics as "choiceless choice." In this way, we best can balance the instrumental and receptive modes so as to preserve connection and yet be effective in the world. The knowing that takes place is not easily communicated. You may be acquainted with someone who is very active helping others. If you praise such a person for what they are contributing they will likely reply, "I've received more than I've given." If you ask what it is they have received, they have difficulty saying. What they are experiencing is a kind of knowledge different from that to which they ordinarily have access. Rather than it being something they perceive, like a movie, or concepts, like a book, it is knowledge by being that which is known. Through service they are able to connect with the larger field and, the varying degrees, become it (see also "knowledge by Identity" in Forman, 1999, pp.109-127).

Here is the experience of a person who established an organization that cares for people suffering from AIDS. His life is focused on service. He was responding to my question "Why do you feel that you have received more than you have given?" He said he could only answer by referring to those times when he felt truly connected to the person he was serving:

In the caregiving work itself, in the service work, itself, when I truly connected with the other person, what happened was something about healing the separation I felt in my own life and the separation I believe we are all born into. The connection with that person felt like a tremendous gift, a kind of union that I wanted more of in my life, not only in service encounters but in relationships outside the normal connection of personalities, outside of social norms, personal expectations. Something deeper was happening that I craved considerably; only aware of it when the need started to get filled, like a hungry person being weak but unaware of the source of the hunger and then food shows up —"This is it!"

It all takes the form of my being the best person I could be, of my deepest humanity being expressed this way, "This is why I am here." Here is the answer to the question, "What am I here for? What is the purpose of my life?" Nothing else I do elicits the feeling of "Yeah, this is it!" more than service does — not creative work, not any other action in the world, not the completion of a project that I'm proud of. All that makes me feel good but nothing meets as deep a need in as profound a way as service work does. (C. Garfield, personal communication, 1998)

There is nothing exotic here, nothing hidden, nothing arcane. But the knowledge does have its own requirements. It is as if you came to a steam and wanted to drink. If you persisted in trying to grab the water — your usual approach — you would obtain nothing. If you want to drink you would have to cup your hands. It has nothing to do with piety; it has to do with the nature of water.

Advantages of the Functional Model

From a clinical point of view we can begin to understand the phenomena of mid-life crisis, meaninglessness, burn-out, and preoccupation with death as reflecting a weakness of connection to something larger than oneself. While these problems can reflect intrapersonal problems with intimacy and self-worth, we also need to evaluate the extent to which they may reflect self-absorption and isolation in that person's daily life, the extent to which he or she lacks activities that could connect and expand his or her identity. We may ask ourselves to what extent and how often does this person shift to other-centered consciousness?

This model featuring intention and self offers a means of evaluauation of spiritual groups and their leaders. Seekers can be tricked by the assertion, "The Teacher is enlightened and perceives things on a different plane. What he/she does has a spiritual significance that is beyond your comprehension. Therefore, you are not capable of judging the Teacher's actions." Whether or not the Teacher actually is fostering spiritual development can be assessed by listening carefully to what he or she says, noting whether or not the survival self is being stimulated or being subdued. If the Teacher emphasizes the promise of bliss or enlightenment, greed is being stimulated; if the seeker is defined as being special, vanity is encouraged; an emphasis on the harm seekers will suffer if they leave the group stimulates fear. Greed, vanity, and fear reinforce the operations of the survival self and the teacher who employs them is impeding — not helping — spiritual development. No matter what powers the Teacher might manifest, he or she is not a spiritual teacher, is not above criticism, and is not entitled to special prerogatives.

In addition to the considerations just described, it is important that we achieve an integration of the scientific worldview with our intuition of the spiritual. For myself, that has been a problem ever since I entered medical school. The reductionistic, materialistic ethos was totally incompatible with my own experience of the spiritual dimension. So, in the closet of my mind, I kept the spiritual domain in a shoebox on the top shelf. I would take it down for periodic inspection but couldn't help feeling that what it contained was not really real, not real the way my cadaver's brain was real. And yet, the shoebox contained the experiences most important to my life. When I was quiet, open, and receptive and looked into my wife's eyes the experience was mysterious and profound, different from our ordinary contact. I perceived something that carried beyond our location in time and space and conveyed the sense of a much larger, more important reality. What my scientific and psychoanalytic teachers offered as explanation for this I never found convincing. According to them such perceptions should be regarded as a projection of unconscious wishes, memories, and primitive feeling states. In other words, it was something I imagined, something of internal origin that I misidentified. True, people do imagine and project, but these explanations seemed shallow, they did not fit the experience. I could not integrate this materialistic, positivistic world of science with the transcendent world labeled "spiritual."

Looking back over my research I can see that it has been a persistent effort to find a framework that could unite these domains in a nonmysterious manner. With the concept of different ways of knowing depending on intention and self, I think the integration can be accomplished in a straightforward way that is consonant with discoveries in developmental and motivational psychology, and with the world sketched for us by quantum physics, and with the spiritual traditions. Finally, the functional model of consciousness can help us understand service without interference from the myths of childhood and from religious dogma. With serving-the-task as our motivational guide, we can spot the emergence of hidden self-interest and reestablish the task-oriented attitude that we need. This monitoring protects us from the distorted perspective introduced by self-centered consciousness, enabling our service to be more creative and effective and expanding our view of the world and of ourselves.

References

Deikman, A.J.(1982). *The Observing Self: Mysticism and psychotherapy.* Boston: Beacon Press.

Deikman, A.J.(1990). *The Wrong Way Home: Uncovering the patterns of cult behavior in American society.* Boston: Beacon Press.

Erikson, E.(1951). *Childhood and Society.* New York: Norton.

Forman, R.(1999). *Mysticism, Mind, Consciousness.* Albany: State University of New York Press.

Gesell, A.(1940). *The first year of life: A guide to the study of the pre-school child.* New York: Harper & Row.

Lapham, L.(1988). *Money and Class in America: Notes and observations on our civil religion.* New York: Widenfeld & Nicolson.

Merton, T.(1968). *Zen and the Birds of Appetite.* New York: New Directions.

Pagels, H.(1982). *The Cosmic Code: Quantum physics as the language of nature.* New York: Simon & Schuster.

Piaget, J.(1952). *The Origins of Intelligence in children.* New York: International Universities Press.

Seligman, D.(1988, June 1). *Is philanthropy irrational?* FORBES, 161(11). 94-103.

Shapiro, D.(1960). *A perceptual understanding of color response.* In M. Richers-Ovisiankina (Ed.), *Rorschach Psychology.* New York: Wiley.

Spitz, R.(1970). *Zen Mind, Beginner's Mind.* New York: Walker/Weatherhill.

Yeats, W.B.(1951). *The Long Legged Fly. The collected poems of W.B. Yeats* (pp. 327-328). New York: The Macmillan Company.

Originally published in *Transpersonal Knowing: Exploring the Horizon of Consciousness,* State University of New York Press, 2000

The State-Of-The-Art Of Meditation

I N RECENT YEARS meditation has become acceptable to Western culture and a subject of increasing interest to scientists. It has been studied in university laboratories, adapted to statistical analysis, and translated into various physiological dimensions, all of which has yielded data of increasing refinement. Through these procedures, meditation has been demonstrated to have "real" effects. However, there is a problem in the way it is being put to use. As meditation has become approved, it has been employed for personal benefit, for better health or increased power. That is not surprising, for the power of meditation makes such benefits appear likely. In fact, increased calmness, creativity, concentration, and endurance are reported to accompany meditation practice and it has been suggested as a remedy for stress-related illnesses such as hypertension and for problems of chronic anxiety. In more esoteric circles, psychic abilities, healing powers, and "enlightenment" are promised.

What could be the problem with all that? The problem is the acquisitive, self-centered attitude that lies behind such usage, for that attitude affects the outcome of meditation. This issue has been overlooked, perhaps because dealing with it is quite difficult and its implications are ones that we do not wish to face. Whatever the reason may be, it is hard to find a single research paper m this field that mentions: (1) the importance of the context within which classical meditation was developed and practiced, and (2) the instructions in the classical meditation literature that specify the need for humility, service, and sincerity. Ironically, although the power of meditation to affect physiological and psychological functions has been substantiated in many different laboratories, we have paid little attention to what the originators of meditation have said about its intended purpose and the requirements for its appropriate use.

Meditation was developed as part of a teaching system whose purpose was spiritual growth. "Spiritual growth" is an awkward goal for the scientific community to embrace — it sounds religious. It would appear, however, that mystics have had as little interest in formal religion as Western science does now. What mystics meant by "spiritual growth" was the development of an inherent intuitive capacity to perceive the reality that underlies the world of appearances. That goal was said to be the supreme task and the greatest benefit of human life.

The sages who invented the powerful techniques of meditation apparently knew what they were doing. Shouldn't we give careful consideration to what they said and respect the instructions that accompany their technical inventions? Those instructions are rather specific. They deal, first, with the necessity for "purifying the *heart*" — developing a *selfless* orientation — before acquiring special powers. "Purifying the heart" was evidently a difficult process in every spiritual tradition, requiring years of effort and the right attitude. It would be fair to say that such correctly-attuned effort is practically nonexistent among most Westerners who practice meditation. Second, they emphasize that meditation function as only one component of an integrated, individualized teaching system requiring the supervision of a Teacher, someone whose own perceptual capacity has been developed and thus knows how to prescribe meditation according to the specific needs of the student.

Focusing primarily on the experiences and bodily effects of meditation is like collecting oyster shells and discarding the pearls. Such "spiritual materialism" inevitably interferes with the real potential of meditation. The remedy is take *motivational* dimensions as seriously as those we measure with the EEG, the EMG. and the GSR. Unless we do we will continue to select only what attracts us from the technology of mysticism and discard the rest.

What is the state of the art of meditation? It is about what it has been for over 3000 years except in the Western world, where there appears to be a real danger that it is deteriorating. If we wish to practice meditation and contribute to the art, perhaps we should first master its fundamental requirements, whether they appeal to us or not.

Originally published *in Meditation: Classic and Contemporary Perspectives,*
Deane H. Shapiro, Jr. and Roger N. Walsh, Eds.
New York: Aldine Publishing Company

The Missing Center

T HE CENTRAL problem of understanding states of consciousness is understanding who or what experiences the state. Our theories evolve with the center missing; namely, the "I" of consciousness, the Witnesser. We need a science of the self with which to explore that center. With our present procedures and methods we cannot touch it and so we turn away to pay attention to everything else, the things that we can grasp. We are fascinated by unusual forms of consciousness. Yet the question remains: Considering the thousands of states of consciousness that we may have, what makes them "ours"? Perhaps the first step toward understanding is to examine the basic assumption that we are separate selves, objects in an object world.

Learning the Idea of Self

Imagine the infant's world: shifting fields of sensations within shifting levels of sleep and waking; swirling mists of warm sleep giving way to bright colors and simple patterns, mixed with gnawing feelings, persistent and demanding; then muscle tensing and crying sounds; then the warmth and pleasure and the smell of mother, liquid warmth and mouth tensions; then dissolution into darkness — and then the light and color — discomforts — relief, and on and on. Memoryless, the flow holds all attention. Gradually the patterns form: mother's smell and comfort, eyes and mouth, muscle grasping, mother's sounds.

Sensations separate: those that disappear and those that persist, becoming "inside" and "outside" much later on. Now, they come and go. Pain, hunger, touch, and smell are the teachers. Pain draws a line around

the edges of fingers, and vision tidies up the clutter. Together they
teach the body as the baby's will begins to command. Grab the bottle
— grab the nose — pat fire — grab the food — stuff the mouth — drop
the glass — move the fingers for the eyes to see. Pain, loss, and intention
separate the world. Mother leaves, but pain remains; the arm can be
moved, but the crib stays still (Freud, 1957, p. 232).

Yet the separation is not so clear. Crying can summon others' presence, and the baby may not be able to move from the holding arms.
What is cause and what effect comes later. For the moment, patterns
rule the day and may continue, if the culture wills it, without an
automatic road of Time (Lee, 1950). At first, related only in the total
moment, the world just happens.

The Human Object

We objectify our world and others in it. "Others," indeed!

*[They] mostly treat contemporaries as physical objects or
disregard them completely. Five in one room may each disregard
one of the others. If two were together near an object, one may just
push the other out of the way impersonally, as though he were an
object... one as [he] climbs, pushes a second, who falls on a third.
All ignore this. Or two may try to climb up in exactly the same
place. Both struggle with each other, but merely for the space, not
aggressively, as later. Child wanting to sit on chair filled by other
child may either sit on other child or may spill him out. May
walk around or just bump into other child.* (Ames, 1952, p. 199)

So much skill has been acquired, so many lessons learned. Yet,
still no Other. No Self like you in all your world because you know
no Self — you, the person, are not there — although your memory,
thoughts, sensations make up all the world.

At first your will is in the service of acquiring. It is possessive and
slow to emerge. At twelve months of life, about to talk, with words to
say and understand, "even the sense of personal possession is practically
absent, and [the child] makes very meager distinctions between himself

and others" (Gesell, 1940, p. 32). Possession comes late and precedes Self; possessive pronouns are used first, "Child grabbed from may hang onto object; and may let it go and cry; may just let it go; may shout 'mine'" (Ames, 19 52, p. 199). At twenty-four months of age, "pronouns, *mine, me, you, and I* are coming into use approximately in the order just given" (Gesell, 1940, p. 3 7),"Mine" leads to "me" (the object) and "you" {the object) and finally to "I" — an "1" whose shape and meaning are ruled by the possessive mode.

Growth of the Action Mode

When we see and when we think and walk and eat and breathe we serve ourselves, our purpose. The purpose guides the rest. In the beginning, floating in the maternal ocean, we allow the environment in and are nourished. Indeed, I should not say "allow." Allowing is an adult decision. In the womb we just exist in a state of permeation, perfused with the blood and vibrations of our world. Then, during the cataclysm of birth, we struggle for the first time. What had been only comfort is now pain, and we contract to shut it out, to gain control, to act and so to change the turbulence back into peace. With the first breath, and the first breast, peace does return. And then the infant body loosens, relaxing as the warmth flows in, allowing what is needed to enter once again, receptive to the world. In the early weeks all is intake, relaxation, sleep, and food. Briefly, however, between feeding and sleep, eyes focus on the world; they are active, following, reaching out in interest rather than in pain (Wolff, 1960). Now the motive differs, but the function is the same — to act upon the world. A mode of living has begun: life as doing — doing to all the objects of the object world, bringing about possession and relief from pain.

The lessons: bottle, ball, mother, nose — are lessons in possession, in reaching for what is shiny, bright, warm, and safe. Name what's good and squeeze it with fingers, draw it to the mouth and take it in. The baby reaches for the bottle, eyes focused, brain intent, arms extended and waving with excitement. Into the mouth pops the nipple

— and what a change! The body softens, eyes cross, lids droop, arms relax. And then — sleep. All functions are eased — immersed back into a resting world. Action mode, receptive mode, phasing back and forth. Reception is the beginning and dominates the infant life.

School continues. More and more the action mode rules the day. With practice and reward it grows in scope until, with symbols, it creates thought. Abstraction is born. Words seem real. Memory and imagery establish Time. Mine, me, you, I: in that order we learn. Possession shapes the Self and the world.

As our bodies teach our minds, so our minds instruct our bodies. The desire for the ball will focus eyes. The broad, impressionistic world narrows to a central stage whose sharp details and clear edges separate the ball from all the rest, which now recedes, vanishing into background. Muscles tense and capillaries shunt the blood from gut to muscles; adrenalin executes the change. Breathing hastens; chest expands. Eyes and neck and body synchronize, directed to the target. Watching the ball roll, learning what it does, teaches object logic: A is not B. Object thought is born with the rolling ball. The ball, an object; the ball, a thought. They are linked together, welded tight, until our thought blankets our perception.

Thinking is for action, for acquisition and control. Thinking guides effort until thought itself is effortful. The knitted brow, the intent look, the tensing of the eyes — all partners to a single purpose, a mode of being in the world. "Me" and "you" and "I" are sharpened, suitable for object games. "Mine" is the favorite, and clear boundaries are the rule. Day by day, body and mind coordinate, learning control, learning to manipulate the world. The action mode becomes the norm. Reception, where we started, is set aside for sleep and food and comforting.

As conscious doing is the essence of the action mode, allowing is the key to the receptive. With the action mode we divide and conquer our environment. With the receptive, we take in, receive and unify. It is the difference between breathing out and breathing in. Try it now. Take a full breath; breathe in and then breathe out. Notice the difference in your state of mind during those two phases. On inhaling, the world flows in, mental contents become diffuse, thinking tends to stop. On exhaling, energy flows out, the vision sharpens, boundaries are more clear, and thinking comes to life.

When manifesting in the action mode, when striving in the world, the electrical currents on the surface of the brain are fast and short. In the receptive mode, alpha waves appear: slow, irregular, and higher waves, they indicate a change in attitude, something subtle, beyond words (Deikman, 1975).

And words themselves, where do they belong? Our words are from the object world — the world we made by separation. Words are the tools of that mode: With them we discriminate and divide reality into pieces — objects and things — that we can grab with our minds or bodies. The Eskimo has many words for snow, the skier several, the average man just one — according to snow's importance in the action mode.

Objects have many names, sensations very few. We can discriminate a thousand hues of color but not name them. How many forms of love have we to match against the one word? The action mode has forms, boundaries, words, logic, and the Road of Time. The receptive mode is sensory, diffuse, and unifies; its Time is instantaneous and synchronous. The self merges into Now. What do you call relationships where A is B? I-Thou, Buber (1958) named it; relating in receptivity. I-It, the Other as object, occurs in the action mode.

The function, the goal we set, controls the mode. What's the goal? Is it combat, control, capture; or receive, synthesize, allow? It is not activity versus passivity. "Allowing" is an action but of a different kind. We say "I-It" and fire the bullet so that it intersects the racing deer. We say "I-Thou" and receive our love's embrace. We need both modes; each has its place and function. Merge with the infinite and you lose the deer. Calculate your "making love" and it becomes another task, depriving you of re-creation. Yet they can blend together. You can work in your garden, uprooting the weeds one by one, but still be receptive to the breeze and the soft earth.

Infants and children must perform their biologic task: survival in a biologic world. That primary need begins in the womb and pervades the childhood years; it has trained us all too well in the action mode. The receptive comes occasionally, hardly at command, as if it were an alien being. That which should be familiar we come to perceive as strange. Years later, as adults, we may go to special schools to learn receiving, to regain the mode with which our life began. Until then, the receptive mode lies dormant, receding from the repertoire but not forgotten.

There was a time when meadow, grove and stream
The earth, and every common sight,
To me did seem
Apparelled in celestial light,
The glory and the freshness of a dream.
(Wordsworth, 1904, p. 353)

Glory? Not likely in the child. But when adults recover their receptive mode and grow to a new wholeness, recruiting to the soft, wide span of childhood vision the complex meanings of creative thought — then glory, then a dream transcending the dreams of one-eyed man.

Self, Time, and Anxiety

The action mode creates a world. The world has dimensions of its own, distinctive features, normally unquestioned in their status as elemental facts. Who does not assume a separate Self and the flow of Time? They are the pillars that uphold the world, but they were not given, they were grown.

The self grew, for the organism has its plan. Our starting self was pure happening; we were what was occurring in the womb. With the birth process, intention formed; fear and desire took their roots in that elemental chaos, then grew in strength like other parts. With intention, the body-self takes form. The body is the agent of intention and executes the biologic plan: possession. (Mine, me, you, I — in that order.) The body is the source of pain and pleasure, qualities that dominate our sensory world. Qualities so powerful that they define what is "personal." Memory and symbol engage sensation: Objects and their laws emerge. Others see your body as an object, helping you to do so, too (Mead, 1934). "What a pretty smile you have! Come here!" "Wave your hand!" "Here is your bottle." "Give me the ball. Want the doll?" The body possesses and possession is the game. What the body hugs belongs to Self; what it does not touch may disappear.

First the ball, then the reaching arm, then the body of the arm, and then the reaching wish — "me" — all objectified into the landscape of the object world, seen from a window. The window frames the world, and in the space behind the window an invisible object forms — "I." Gradually, the solitary self is born.

Memory creates time and orders objects in the Past. Images and words create a Future, ordering the objects yet to come. Between the past and future, laws are found, connecting both in a smooth path on which walks the form of Self. Like a cage of tigers, the trained objects stiffen to the whip of logic and take their places in an even line, arrayed in a demonstration of predictive power. Wild applause greets success, but when the noise subsides, another character appears — anxiety. What if the tigers all jump down and in disordered rage make a bloody meal of the maestro? These shadows of the future, cast by the past, can overwhelm the bright display. The scene of gaiety and pride may give way to troubled dreams.

The action mode has welded past and future into an arrow. As it flies there can be no rest, for Now has disappeared. Xeno's paradox is lived by us. By the action mode we acquire Self, gain power, and survive. But Past and Future, joined by anxiety, has no room for Now. Scurrying in memory, images, and thought, there is no time to stop and be nourished by the world.

The Receptive Mode

Now change the goal, shift to Being. Receive the world. The gaze will soften, vision diffuse, maximizing entry of the sensate world (Allison, 1963). Time dissolves and Now emerges, accompanied by satisfaction. The Self subsides and the world enters. Muscle tension eases; breathing slows; judgments fall away. Beyond fear, beyond pleasure, Now is. All questions are answered — or the questions have disappeared; they are the product of another mode, another world. The mode of Being, the receptive mode, serves a different function — our nourishment, perhaps. It is not "higher," not more "spiritual," just breathing in instead of breathing out. Half a breath cycle is not enough. We need both halves to live. We need both modes.

But the action mode prevails — it has the school — and a hunger grows: dissatisfaction. Forgetting how to eat, we have begun to starve at the banquet. Believing what we're taught, we cannot fit the world.

More school, defining Self: boy, girl, good, bad, fast, slow, happy, sad, strong, weak, pretty, ugly, smart, dumb. The Self stands like a naked armature, and the others fire away, heaving globs of clay to spatter, stick, and lump together as the self-shape grows. "Tommy is a good boy with blonde hair, a nice smile, smart and fast. Jennie is a pretty girl, delicate and sweet, with brown hair, a merry laugh, and very understanding. Jim is a roughneck, not too bright. Helen has black hair and big feet, homely but kind." Animated sculptures taking shape, sitting in rows in school. Eyes peering out of the hardening clay.

Adolescence, we are told, is the time of identity. Teenagers intimately converse, "Who are you and who am I?" No wonder the question is asked. Awkwardly, the clay figures stagger around the room, trying to walk after a very different birth.

"You tell me and I'll tell you." (Maybe we'll find out that way.) "You are really very sensitive!" (Not much help, just more clay.)

Rough places smoothed and a hole or two filled in. Adult statues serve as guides, and they so stiff they have forgotten what the young ones still can feel that something doesn't fit. "It looks just fine!" (But it doesn't feel right.) The clay binds and cramps in all the wrong places. Still, a memory of freedom haunts the room.

When you reach adulthood, you look around and find that the strangest part of this strange world is yourself. There are so many varieties of you, moment by moment, state by state, that only a very selective memory allows the illusion of a constant, continuous self to be maintained.

Think about all the various conditions that constitute your moment-by-moment life. Sometimes you are in a state of remembering and 90 percent of you is — at that moment — memories. Sometimes you are emotional, sometimes angry or ecstatic or sad, and 90 percent of what is you is then emotion. At other times you may be what you see, or what you fantasize. Sometimes it's a mixture, 50-50 or 20-20-60; it really doesn't matter.

Through all these variations, all these changes, you assume you are there. Indeed, sometimes "I am" may be your only feeling, very powerful, very "spacy." Most of the time you're busy, so it's 90 percent something else.

There are so many selves: the thought-self, the body-self, the I am-self, the I want-self, the emotion-self; and now the left-brain self, the right-brain self, the limbic-self, the midbrain-self. So many, so changing, not continuous at all. Each self appears and disappears, fades from view while another takes its place. So where in all this is you? If you are your experience and that experience always changes, what makes you think you have a self at all?

And what of the times when the "I" is zero: engrossed in a movie or performing some action too quickly to permit thought? Yet you assume, nevertheless, that you have been there all along. Your "I" is discontinuous, but your memory fills in the gaps, just as your eyes, creating an optical illusion, fill in the "correct" line.

"What's the difference?" you may ask. "Other people are witness that I don't disappear." You are right. But the "I" they see and the "I" you mean may not be the same.

When you began, age zero, you did not assume that "you" were there or that anyone else was there when they had passed from sight. "Out of sight, out of mind" and out of thought, as well. Maturation meant you could find the pea under the shell of memory. Once you remembered you could predict, and soon existence needed no proof — because existence itself had changed. Where once it had been all sensation, now thought and memory had become real, most real of all.

"Mine, me, you, and I" in that order. In that order we create ourselves. Emotions become "mine." Thoughts are "mine" — whose else could they be? Desires are mine — what is more me than my wants? And fear is "mine," for who else will die? "Mine" becomes "me," the social object, collector of labels, possessor of things. "Me" encounters "you," the object, the Other, who tells us we are objects, too, and tricks us into categories that enclose us like snug beds: man, woman, Indian chief.

What do you color the object-you? Color it with thinking, with emotion, with desires, and with fear. Use all the "inside" colors to make it bright and clear.

There is no end to object making. Go to India, climb the highest mountain, and sit cross-legged observing all the other objects, all the inside colors, until you become, finally, the Witness — the finest object of them all. Most of us are content with the usual "I's": old, handsome, dumb, and on and on. What a collection! Look at all we think we are: joy, anger, calculations, desires, objects, labels, fear, and "soul." Look at that merry-go-round, the way it spins, and then, watching it go round, perhaps suddenly you'll ask, "How do I know it's me?"

The question seems absurd and never does get asked aloud. The "I" of awareness is the last to join, but join it does — and so we enter Objectland. We become a Thing and reap a rich reward: identity with all the Others, the reassurance of our kind, something made necessary by Objecthood!

Possessing gives life to the Thing. "I want" almost everything (the energy of possession); "I have," the locus of possession, of substance and mortality; "I will," the energy of intention, put to work collecting; and, then, there is "me," the social object, staggering forward with all my attributes in a huge bundle on my back, like a peddler.

Possession creates suffering. Pain hurts because it's "mine." Pain, old buddy, what happens when I step a pace away, look you squarely in the eye, inspect you head to toe like a new recruit? "What's your shape, mister? What color are you? Hot or cold? Thick or thin?" Pain, old buddy, you seem to change, learn manners, drop your eyes, turn in your badge of power.

Behind pain, in a line, stand all the others: vision, hearing, joy, and grief — a whole company of pseudo-selves presented for inspection, more obedient, now, to my command.

Unlearning the Self

Eastern science takes a different route to knowledge, by-passing the intellect, to learn by being. Where we have journeyed outward, Eastern disciplines have gone within, hunting the true self among the decoys. Academies of Eastern science, called spiritual schools, teach the unlearning of the decoy self as preparation for discovery. All the selves you thought you were must go. The self of thought, the self of emotion, the self of desire, the self of sensation — all must be unlearned. These conditioned selves cling to you as shells and vegetation cling to a tide-washed rock. But the schools know what to do; they have many ways to clean the rock. Meditation is a velvet crowbar that pries thought-mussels loose, leaving the bare surface to be bathed again by the sea. The crowbar slides beneath emotions, too, those clumps of feeling, those subtle forms of memory, that open and close like the carnivorous flowers they are, all mouth and color — now separate from the rock, afloat in the wash of the tide. In school, in meditation, sitting like a rock, just sitting, sensations spatter like the spray and drip away, polishing the rock until it reflects the sun.

Desires are the last to loosen. They are lodged in the heart of the rock and must dissolve. Many things are tried: the ascetic life, koan

dynamite, the hypnotic energy of dance, and the deep chant, resonating in the center, the teaching story, holding a mirror to the form of
desire, and — finally — the Teacher, whose radiant vibration shakes
the atoms of the rock into harmony and peace and praise in the
rhythm of the sea.

The mirror of the school shows you many selves, shifting, changing: the I of intention, the I of I Am, the I of emotions, the I of possession, the I of the body, and the I made by Others. The selves come and
go, and the mirror-school reflects them all. But it cannot show them
all until they all are there. Our Western culture, like an obsessive
tailor, has spent so much time on the intellectual jacket that it has yet
to get around to the emotion-shirt and the body-pants. No wonder we
are spectacles, displaying our new clothes, annoyed and yet haughty
in the face of the laughter of children. Not long ago, some other
tailors set up shops in California, where East meets West. There are
so many tailors now they don't know whose needle they are using.
Back then, the Esalen shop opened a new frontier, featuring the shirt
and pants. The emotion-self and the body-self were taught in class.
Encounter by the sea, nude bodies, massage and sex, here-and-now
orgasms for "intimate strangers." How ridiculous! The New York
tailors almost died of laughter but were saved by their indignation
at the sight of so many customers discarding jackets in California.
The colors of the shirts were often weird and the pants let it all hang
out, but at least it was a suit of clothes for the whole person, giving
warmth to the heart and covering all that land below the neck. Although Wilhelm Reich, a tailor of the body-self, died in prison (he
opened up his shop too soon), times have changed; the body has
returned, although it still is seen as an appendage of the head.

Esalen is more than laughs — how strange to find one's state of
mind sparkle like a fresh-rinsed glass when it receives a body bath. The
emotion-self emerging from a weekend smiles with delight to see the
sky again. Strange how the wrinkles disappear and the face is young
— how the thinking slows and senses sharpen when the rediscovery

is made. Catharsis and the body — old-fashioned clothes indeed, to be selling so briskly — but that's the frontier West, you know, unsophisticated, no culture, no tradition.

Yes, the body has returned, bringing with it sensual life and feeling. Just in time. The spiritual schools teach letting go of self — but not to babies or retarded children or psychic cripples, deformed beyond belief. The Western student knocking at the door presents a gigantic inflated head, spindly legs, and a sunken chest, announcing with intellectual fervor. "I surrender!" What a prize! How can there be a harvest before the crop is grown? Before the self is ripe, what can you give away?

No wonder the schools have strange routines, depending on the students who stumble to the door. Weird diets, heavy work, incense, singing, meditation, dancing, breathing, postures, flowers, swords, or sex may be prescribed. Five or seven centers, say the texts, form the path and source of energy that needs to flow without constriction. You learn to open all the chakras. Until you are fully there, in all your strength, you do not have the power to surrender.

The many routines work, but for whom are they correct? The druggist lines his shelves with little bottles; a doctor must prescribe. Which meditation is right for you? Maybe none. Go to a doctor, if you can find one. The diagnosis should be made before the treatment starts, and you've been ill a long time. Leave the drugstore, you don't know what the labels mean, and it isn't candy on the shelves, despite the bright colors. Go find a doctor. Now.

"Where?"

"Try the Yellow Pages: If you are really sincere, you will find a doctor. The door is always open. You are already in the doctor's hands."

Not much help to a Western mind. The Yellow Pages show only religious listings. Perhaps it is time we broke that "spiritual" monopoly, remembering that our mandate to understand has no restrictive clauses — we gave no franchise to the monks.

Conclusion

"Who — or what — am I?" seems to concern every inquiring mind in its own way. It is the question I most want answered and am least equipped by training to understand; the science I have learned has been of objects, and no object is the self. The Eastern schools, employing traditional means, may not meet contemporary needs. New tools and a new curriculum would seem to be required, a form that suits a television world.

What must we do and how should we proceed? Perhaps we can construct a calculus of the subjective. Should we even try? Do language and logic have a place or will they interfere?

What do you suggest?

References

1. By cult, I mean a group headed by a charismatic leader who has spiritual, messianic, or therapeutic pretensions and indoctrinates the followers into an idiosyncratic belief system.
2. Deikman, A. (1982). *The observing self: Mysticism and psychotherapy*. Boston: Beacon Press.
3. Deikman, A. (1983). The evaluation of spiritual and utopian groups. *Journal of Humanistic Psychology*, 23(3), 8-19.
4. Deikman, A. (1990). *The wrong way home: Uncovering the patterns of cult behavior in American society*. Boston: Beacon Press.
5. Rioch, M. (1975). The work of Wilfred Bion on groups. In A. D. Colman & H. D. Bexton (Eds.), *Group relations reader*. Sausalito, CA: GREX. Quotation on p. 24.
6. Temerlin, M., & Temerlin, J. (1982). Psychotherapy cults: An iatrogenic perversion. *Psychotherapy: Theory, Research and Practice,* 19(2), 131-141.
7. Arlow, J. (1972). Some dilemmas in psychoanalytic education. *Journal of the American Psychoanalytic Association*, 20, 556-566.
8. Kernberg, O. (1986). Institutional problems of psychoanalytic education. *Journal of the American Psychoanalytic Association*, 34, 799-834

Originally published in *Altered States of Consciousness, A Book of Readings,* ed. Charles T. Tart. New York: John Wiley & Sons, 1969.

ACKNOWLEDGMENTS

Etta Deikman wishes to acknowledge the contributions of the following people in collating, organizing, and presenting the papers comprising this book:

The Staff of San Francisco General Hospital
       Barnett-Briggs Medical Library
Gari Thompson
Norman Zukowsky PhD
Charles Tart PhD
Judy Tart RN
D. Patrick Miller of Fearless Books

Founded in 1997 by author and editor D. Patrick Miller, Fearless Books specializes in titles about spirituality and advanced capacities of human consciousness. Fearless has a limited publishing program under its own imprint, and produces exemplary book projects that may not be deemed sufficiently commercial for mainstream houses. Our aim is to provide an effective publishing program for both original and out-of-print properties of great intrinsic value, as well as commercial potential.

This work is supported through Fearless Literary Services, helping authors at all levels of experience develop, revise, and finish manuscripts for publication. In many cases, we assist the same authors to produce and publish their books independently through our Assisted Publishing Program.

For a complete list of print and electronic books published by Fearless, as well as our full range of editorial and publishing services, visit us online at *www.fearlessbooks.com*.

Made in the USA
Middletown, DE
19 August 2024

59391150R00239